Civil War Wests

*Published in cooperation with the William P. Clements
Center for Southwest Studies, Southern Methodist University*

Civil War Wests

TESTING THE LIMITS OF THE UNITED STATES

EDITED BY

Adam Arenson and Andrew R. Graybill

UNIVERSITY OF CALIFORNIA PRESS

University of California Press, one of the most distinguished university presses in the United States, enriches lives around the world by advancing scholarship in the humanities, social sciences, and natural sciences. Its activities are supported by the UC Press Foundation and by philanthropic contributions from individuals and institutions. For more information, visit www.ucpress.edu.

University of California Press
Oakland, California

© 2015 by The Regents of the University of California

Library of Congress Cataloging-in-Publication Data

Civil War wests : testing the limits of the United States / edited by Adam Arenson and Andrew R. Graybill.
    pages cm
    Includes bibliographical references and index.
    ISBN 978-0-520-28378-7 (cloth : alk. paper) — ISBN 0-520-28378-3 (cloth : alk. paper) — ISBN 978-0-520-28379-4 (pbk. : alk. paper) — ISBN 0-520-28379-1 (pbk. : alk. paper) — ISBN 978-0-520-95957-6 (ebook) — ISBN 0-520-95957-4 (ebook)
    1. Reconstruction (U.S. history, 1865–1877)—West (U.S.)
2. United States—History—Civil War, 1861–1865. 3. West (U.S.)—History—1860–1890. I. Arenson, Adam, 1978- editor. II. Graybill, Andrew R., 1971- editor.
E668.C57 2015
973.7—dc23   2014024850

Manufactured in the United States of America

24 23 22 21 20 19 18 17 16 15
10 9 8 7 6 5 4 3 2 1

In keeping with a commitment to support environmentally responsible and sustainable printing practices, UC Press has printed this book on Natures Natural, a fiber that contains 30% post-consumer waste and meets the minimum requirements of ANSI/NISO Z39.48–1992 (R 1997) (*Permanence of Paper*).

CONTENTS

Introduction 1
Adam Arenson

PART ONE
BORDERLANDS IN CONFLICT

1 · Thwarting Southern Schemes and British Bluster in the Pacific Northwest 15
James Robbins Jewell

2 · Death in the Distance: Confederate Manifest Destiny and the Campaign for New Mexico, 1861–1862 33
Megan Kate Nelson

3 · Kit Carson and the War for the Southwest: Separation and Survival along the Rio Grande, 1862–1868 53
Lance R. Blyth

4 · Scattered People: The Long History of Forced Eviction in the Kansas-Missouri Borderlands 71
Diane Mutti Burke

PART TWO
THE CIVIL WAR IS NOT OVER

5 · "The Future Empire of Our Freedmen": Republican Colonization Schemes in Texas and Mexico, 1861–1865 95
Nicholas Guyatt

6 · Three Faces of Sovereignty: Governing Confederate, Mexican, and Indian Texas in the Civil War Era 118
Gregory P. Downs

7 · Redemption Falls Short: Soldier and Surgeon in the Post–Civil War Far West 139
William Deverell

8 · Still Picture, Moving Stories: Reconstruction Comes to Indian Country 158
Martha A. Sandweiss

PART THREE
BORDERS OF CITIZENSHIP

9 · Race, Religion, and Naturalization: How the West Shaped Citizenship Debates in the Reconstruction Congress 181
Joshua Paddison

10 · Broadening the Battlefield: Conflict, Contingency, and the Mystery of Woman Suffrage in Wyoming, 1869 202
Virginia Scharff

11 · "Dis Land Which Jines Dat of Ole Master's": The Meaning of Citizenship for the Choctaw Freedpeople 224
Fay A. Yarbrough

12 · "Citizen's Clothing": Reconstruction, Ho-Chunk Persistence, and the Politics of Dress 242
Stephen Kantrowitz

Epilogue 265
Steven Hahn

Acknowledgments 275
Secondary Bibliography 279
Contributor Affiliations 307
Index 000

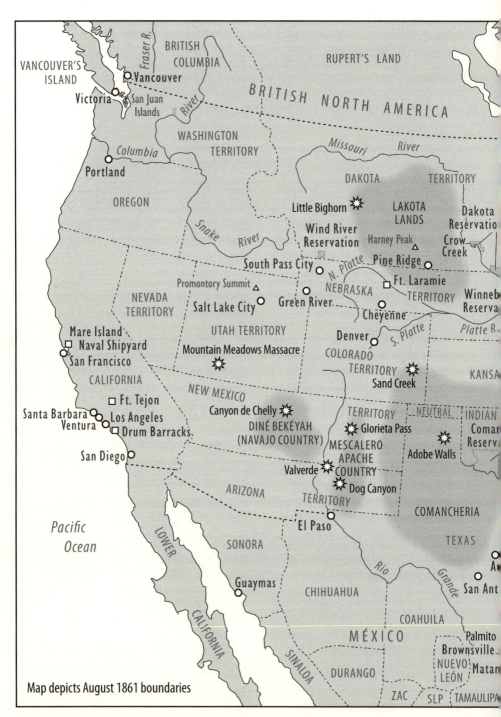

Key Locations and Sites of Conflict in Civil War–Era North America.

Introduction

Adam Arenson

THE CIVIL WAR AND THE AMERICAN WEST are some of the most familiar subjects in U.S. history. The journey of Lewis and Clark and the discovery of gold in California; the firing on Fort Sumter and the battle at Gettysburg; the assassination of President Lincoln and the driving of the Golden Spike to complete the transcontinental railroad—each has inspired hundreds of studies and preoccupied scholars and enthusiasts since the events themselves unfolded.

But little attention has been paid to the intersections of the Civil War, Reconstruction, and the wider history of the American West, and how these seemingly separate events compose a larger, unified history of conflict over land, labor, rights, citizenship, and the limits of governmental authority in the United States.

Traditionally, Civil War history has focused on the challenge of secession, the timing and reasoning behind the eradication of slavery, and the ways that large-scale military actions shaped the lives of soldiers and civilians on both sides. Histories of Reconstruction, meanwhile, have measured the promise of emancipation against the nation's failure to achieve so many of those new possibilities. By contrast, histories of the American West have begun with the so-called frontier spaces of encounter, and have told the history of how these new territories and new peoples were integrated into European and then U.S. realms.

In geographical terms, Civil War history has generally been rooted in the battlefields and plantation landscapes of the "South" (which may or may not include Missouri, Oklahoma, Texas, or other southern border states)—while the "West" of western history has most often meant the trans-Mississippi, and sometimes west of the 100th meridian. When Civil War historians talk about the war's "western theater," they usually mean the military engagements in Kentucky, Tennessee, and Mississippi. But the Department of the Trans-Mississippi included armed conflict in Missouri, Arkansas, and Texas, reaching as far as the crucial Sibley Campaign and the founding of Confederate Arizona. The extensive Civil War fortifications along the Pacific coast and their role in the war generally merit only a footnote.[1]

Historians have long fixed the endpoints of the Civil War and delineated the concerns of Reconstruction from vantage points along the eastern seaboard. On the battlefields between Washington and Richmond, there seems to be a clearly defined conflict between the United States and the Confederacy, with obvious geographical and temporal parameters. Much of the Civil War history concerning the West drifts toward the counterfactual: how much more significant it would have been if a Confederate raider attacked Seattle or San Francisco; if the Confederacy had held Arizona, conquered Southern California, captured St. Louis, or threatened Chicago; or if the Indian Territory representation in the Confederate Congress would have changed the course of the war. From the perspective of traditional Civil War scholarship, it can be hard to see these stories as much more than red herrings. Yet our contention that testing the limits of U.S. sovereignty is the central story of both the Civil War and the American West means that, even in failure, these pivot points provide a profound new understanding of the experience of the war years.

The importance of the West among the causes of the Civil War is well established, with the question of the extension of slavery into the lands conquered or annexed between 1845 and 1848 generally understood as the precipitating cause of the Civil War. Yet the West continued to matter to political and military leaders during the conflict itself, and the Civil War and Reconstruction transformed the region along with the North and South. The Mexican Cession and the Emancipation Proclamation both shaped the settling of the West and the meaning of the Civil War. Fighting in New Mexico affected fighting at Gettysburg, while the civil war in Mexico shaped the experience of the U.S. Civil War (and vice versa). The transcontinental railroad stitched the country closer together, but its regions were already deeply engaged in similar debates over citizenship, economic opportunity, and the legacy of conquest.

These facts were obvious and essential to nineteenth-century Americans. Presidents Abraham Lincoln and Jefferson Davis, Secretary of State William Henry Seward, and other U.S. and Confederate officials thought of the Civil War in continental and even global terms. Many of the men who led soldiers in the Civil War had spent the years just prior to the conflict in the West, engaged in "total war" conflagrations with Native peoples that some scholars have called U.S. attempts at genocide. For instance, Nathaniel Lyon, who would die a Union hero at the Battle of Wilson's Creek in Missouri, directed massacres against the Pomo Indians of California in 1850, at Clear Lake and in the Russian River Valley. Philip Sheridan led troops in the Yakima War that roiled Washington Territory in the late 1850s. Before George Pickett led the ill-fated Confederate charge at Gettysburg, he was posted at Fort Bellingham, Washington Territory to watch for British aggression; during this interlude he fathered a son with Morning Mist, his Haida wife. In 1860, future Confederate general J. E. B. Stuart participated in campaigns against the Kiowas and Comanches.

Service during the U.S. War with Mexico (1846–48) was the first battle experience for many eventual Civil War generals, and it influenced their expectations in combat. But these bloody encounters in the American West occupied and tested these men right up to the moment that U.S. troops were recalled from western postings to fight against the Confederacy.[2] And, after Appomattox, Army officials continued to move between posts in the West and the South, applying the techniques of one theater in another.

Despite these lived connections, historians have long fixed the endpoints of the Civil War and delineated the concerns of Reconstruction while standing along the eastern seaboard. Traditional Civil War and Reconstruction scholars have resisted the redefinitions and expansions that a wider history of all of the nineteenth-century United States would create, thus refusing to put the American West and the Civil War in one frame.[3]

Confederate secession created new and shifting borderlands, and stories of refugees and conflicts over allegiances have complicated our understanding of the path from slavery to freedom for white as well as non-white Americans. In the West, both Civil War battlefields and Civil War politics engaged a wider range of ethnic and racial distinctions, raising questions that would arise only later in places farther east.

This volume teases out the limits of this traditional perspective, this unnatural division between histories of the Civil War and the American West. By nearly any measure—lives lost, property destroyed, economic and emotional costs—the Civil War was the most momentous challenge to the existence of the United States ever mounted. But it was also only the largest conflict among many over the limits of U.S. authority. Since the Constitution was ratified, threats of disunion had emerged frequently in U.S. political discourse, but the pressure had clearly increased in the 1850s, and attacks came from Californios, from Mormon settlers in southern Utah, from filibusterers and Free Staters and jayhawkers, from raiders from Mexico and British troops in the Juan de Fuca Strait, and from American Indian nations pushed to the brink.[4]

To date, the histories of occupation, reincorporation, and expanded citizenship during Reconstruction in the South have ignored the connections to previous as well as subsequent efforts in the West.[5] The ways in which questions of race, religion, citizenship, and federal oversight during Reconstruction were sorted out at least as much in the West as in the states of the former Confederacy is a process that western historian Elliott West has called "Greater Reconstruction," an engagement with the nature and limits of federal power that can inform our study of U.S. expansionism from its origins.[6] This volume erases the artificial divides scholars have created between western and Civil War America.

Slavery or union; empire or freedom; North or South—none of these binaries sufficiently captures the participants' experience of the United States in these years, because the fundamental test of authority was wider and more profound. This becomes obvious in the West, through the category-expanding or category-defying histories presented in this volume: multiracial and multilateral conflicts of the Civil War, including battles among Native American nations; the multiple crises of sovereignty that roiled the entire continent, from Canada through the United States and into Mexico; the varied environmental realities that shaped the war and the nation; and the importance of a range of international and borderlands interactions in shaping the war. Indeed, the final national borders of the "lower forty-eight" states are a history of the Civil War as well as expansion into the West, just as the absence of change after 1853 is bound up in the relative strength of America's continental neighbors in defending their territory during and immediately after the Civil War.[7] It is only by considering events and tensions playing out in all three national regions that we can see new throughlines and turning points, and thus write a new, more inclusive narrative of nineteenth-century American history, attuned to the crises of authority and identity faced by the United States.

There are some precedents for bringing together these histories of the American West and the Civil War. Mabel Washbourne Anderson's *The Life of General Stand Watie, the Only Indian Brigadier General of the Confederate Army and the Last General to Surrender* (1915) and Annie Heloise Abel's *The American Indian as Participant in the Civil War* (1919) were foundational works in the field, marking these connections through the lives of American Indians from the West in the U.S. and Confederate militaries.[8] Aurora Hunt's *The Army of the Pacific, 1860–1866* (1951) and Ray Colton's *The Civil War in the Western Territories: Arizona, Colorado, New Mexico, and Utah* (1959) provided the first examination of the military and political history of the Civil War in those western places.[9] In 1978, David Nichols's *Lincoln and the Indians* provided a groundbreaking look at the failures of the "Indian System" during the Civil War, from the U.S. abandonment of forts and treaty obligations in order to fight the Confederacy, to the concentration of refugees on new reservations, to the escalation of threats and countermands that led to the mass execution of Dakota men in 1862 and the massacre of Arapahos and Cheyennes at Sand Creek in 1864, among other atrocities.[10]

More recently, Alvin Josephy's *The Civil War in the American West* (1991) narrated both the struggles between uniformed Union and Confederate forces and the concurrent engagements with American Indians in the region.[11] Laurence Hauptman's *Between Two Fires: American Indians in the Civil War* (1995) provided an overview that opened in the West before emphasizing Indian service in both the North and South.[12] Josephy's and Hauptman's analyses suggested that the Civil War years marked a turning point for many Indian nations, as some lost autonomy, some lost their lands, and some faced brutal massacres—and even renewed genocide—at the hands of Union soldiers or other Indians.[13] As in so many areas of U.S. history, greater attention to the history and historiography of American Indian nations reveals the defining threads of the U.S. national project, uniting western history, Civil War history, and the study of the United States as empire.[14]

Scholars of the American West have long emphasized the importance of borderlands and borders, the extent of federal power, and the incorporation of new peoples into the United States.[15] Howard Lamar's pair of territorial histories, *Dakota Territory, 1861–1889: A Study of Frontier Politics* (1956) and *The Far Southwest, 1846–1912: A Territorial History* (1966) are by rights the first works of western history to engage these questions through the experience of the Civil War, although not many historians have taken up these subjects in the years since.[16] Eugene Berwanger's *The West and Reconstruction* (1983) was an early call to focus on the region's role in the postwar nation, but it also has gone mostly unheeded.[17]

In 1991, Richard Maxwell Brown argued for conceptualizing U.S. history from 1850 to at least 1910 as a grand nationalizing struggle, turning to a great degree—along with the eastern conflict—upon a "Western Civil War for Incorporation."[18] That same year, Richard White emphasized how the American West "served as the kindergarten of the American state," the region where the military, the Corps of Engineers, land and water managers, and Indian agents learned their skills. Emphasizing the processes of empire west of the Mississippi River, White wrote that "in the West federal power took on modern forms," connecting U.S. military and bureaucratic action in the West before and after the Civil War, but again ignoring integral connections to the conflict in the East.[19] These formulations have influenced the most recent work expanding the subject, including Heather Cox Richardson's *West from Appomattox: The Reconstruction of America after the Civil War* (2007), and Elliott West's *The Last Indian War: The Nez Perce Story* (2009), which demonstrated how "the forces transforming America were at work in Idaho and Oregon as much as in South Carolina and Massachusetts," with results and consequences for all regions of the country.[20] My own work on St. Louis, alongside Richard Etulain's recent book on Lincoln and the Oregon Country and Susan Schulten's research on Colorado as a nexus of Civil War and western conflicts, has emphasized how these national and even continental conflicts were experienced in some of the key locations of the U.S. West.[21] This volume continues the work that these scholars began, making connections between rebellions against U.S. authority at different moments and in multiple places. The volume is divided into three parts:

In part 1, "Borderlands in Conflict," four historians focus on the West as a theater of political maneuvering and military conflict. James Robbins Jewell begins the volume in unfamiliar Civil War geography: the Union forts of Washington Territory, where the United States tracked spies and thwarted Confederate plots hatched on Vancouver Island and in British Columbia. Megan Kate Nelson considers the high hopes for a Confederate march to the Pacific and how the harsh realities of the New Mexico desert proved as formidable an enemy as any army. Lance R. Blyth ponders the complex and combustible interplay among a borderland political economy, U.S. Indian policy, and the increase in manpower created by the Civil War as he narrates the experience of three American Indian nations targeted by local forces under General Kit Carson. Diane Mutti Burke then describes how four western counties of Missouri—once claimed by waves of Indian nations, Mormon emigrants, free soilers and proslavery bushwhackers, and then Confederate sympathizers—were emptied out as a way to secure that borderland homefront for the Union.

The title of part 2, "The Civil War Is Not Over," announces the main insight of its chapters, as together they demonstrate how the military, political, and economic exigencies of the conflict continued beyond Appomattox. Nicholas Guyatt examines why Republican leaders sought to convince ex-slaves to settle in Mexico, Texas, or Latin America throughout the 1860s, while Gregory P. Downs discusses how Union commanders in Texas sustained a war footing in facing down challenges from ex-Confederate, Mexican, and Indian adversaries in 1866. William Deverell describes the psychic and physical repercussions of the battles at Gettysburg and elsewhere for veterans living in California but reliving their war experience continuously. And then Martha Sandweiss considers the paths into and out of the Civil War evident in a photograph taken to commemorate the signing in Wyoming Territory of the Fort Laramie Treaty in 1868.

The chapters of part 3, "Borders of Citizenship," consider how geography as well as race, ethnicity, religion, and gender shaped the possibilities of citizenship after the passage of the Reconstruction Amendments. Joshua Paddison describes the political contortions of Republican senators from western states as they sought to embrace the voting rights for African Americans while preventing Chinese or American Indian men from gaining suffrage. Virginia Scharff considers what racial factors informed the decision to grant woman suffrage (the first instance in U.S. history) in Wyoming Territory in 1869. Fay A. Yarbrough considers how the struggle between Choctaw leaders and their former slaves reflected the national debate over the expansion of citizenship. And Stephen Kantrowitz considers how and when members of the Ho-Chunk nation could use "citizen's clothing" to accentuate their claims to U.S. citizenship through land holdings, even in states from which they had been removed.

Steven Hahn's epilogue brings the volume to a close by considering how our narratives of nineteenth-century U.S. history could change dramatically if we take these connections between the American West and the Civil War to heart.

The geographic sweep from Missouri and Indian Territory (present-day Oklahoma) to the desert Southwest—where, one might say, West meets South—receives the greatest attention here. The combination of empires in the history of this demanding environment—Comanches, Spanish, Mexican, Texan, U.S., and Confederate—and the multiple and also incomplete attempts at incorporating this area into the United States highlight many of the volume's central concerns. As many locals know, if one considers the Southwest and tells the history of the Civil War or the American West, it looks very different than it does from Boston or Charleston, Los Angeles or San Francisco, even different from Dallas or St. Louis. That southwestern sensibility is essential to the story told here. But more stories, from antebellum California and Texas, from Montana and Utah, from Matamoros and Hawai'i, belong here, and we encourage students and scholars to bring these connections to their work.

In the American West and in the Civil War and Reconstruction, the United States was redefined. Scholars have much to gain by seeing these events as a sustained test of the limits of U.S. governmental authority and that government's ability to shape land, labor, and rights. What emerges from such a reconceptualization is a richer, truer, and more provocative vision of mid-nineteenth-century U.S. history, one that reaches beyond North and South.

NOTES

Thanks to Stephen Aron, Carolyn Brucken, Virginia Scharff, Andrew Graybill, Niels Hooper, and the contributors for their help with earlier drafts of this chapter.

1. In James M. McPherson's *Battle Cry of Freedom: The Civil War Era* (New York: Oxford University Press, 1988), coverage is even less: the states and territories of Arizona, California, New Mexico, Oregon, and Utah are referenced only in the prewar years; Colorado and Nevada each receive one passing mention (both on p. 818); Washington Territory receives no mention at all.

2. David A. Nichols, *Lincoln and the Indians: Civil War Policy and Politics* (Columbia: University of Missouri Press, 1978); Robert Wooster, *The American Military Frontiers: The United States Army in the West, 1783–1900* (Albuquerque: University of New Mexico Press, 2009), chap. 8.

3. Gary Gallagher, one of this generation's leading experts on the Civil War, has strenuously objected to the idea that government action in the West and the South during the Civil War and Reconstruction should be studied together. "When you don't think there's anything to say about what Reconstruction actually *was,* why don't you pretend it was really about the West! Some historians of the West do that," Gallagher told an interviewer from Civil War Trust in 2013. "That way you can bring Native Americans in, you can pretend that some of the things going on with

Native Americans and African Americans are sort of the same, but it's a real strain. Reconstruction is about reconstructing the former Confederate states. That's what the term means. It's really not about the West, it's not about California," Gallagher declared, though he concluded his answer by noting that "thousands of Union veterans ended up in California." Clayton Butler, "Understanding our Past: An Interview with Historian Gary Gallagher," Civil War Trust, 2013. www.civilwar.org/education/history/civil-war-history-and-scholarship/gary-gallagher-interview.html. Thanks to Steve Kantrowitz and Kevin Levin for the reference.

4. Elizabeth R. Varon, *Disunion!: The Coming of the American Civil War, 1789–1859* (Chapel Hill: University of North Carolina Press, 2008); Timothy J. Henderson, *A Glorious Defeat: Mexico and Its War with the United States* (New York: Hill and Wang, 2007); Ernesto Chávez, *The U.S. War with Mexico: A Brief History with Documents* (Boston: Bedford/St. Martin's, 2008); Amy S. Greenberg, *A Wicked War: Polk, Clay, Lincoln, and the 1846 U.S. Invasion of Mexico* (New York: Knopf, 2012); Richard D. Poll and Ralph W. Hansen, "'Buchanan's Blunder': The Utah War, 1857–1858," *Military Affairs* 25, no. 3 (1961): 121–31; Poll and William P. MacKinnon, "Causes of the Utah War Reconsidered," *Journal of Mormon History* 20, no. 2 (1994): 16–44; Matthew Pratt Guterl, *American Mediterranean: Southern Slaveholders in the Age of Emancipation* (Cambridge, MA: Harvard University Press, 2008); Amy S. Greenberg, "A Gray-Eyed Man: Character, Appearance, and Filibustering," *Journal of the Early Republic* 20, no. 4 (Winter 2000): 673–99; Charles Henry Brown, *Agents of Manifest Destiny: The Lives and Times of the Filibusters* (Chapel Hill: University of North Carolina Press, 1980); Jerry D. Thompson, *Cortina: Defending the Mexican Name in Texas* (College Station: Texas A&M University Press, 2007); E. A. Schwartz, *The Rogue River Indian War and Its Aftermath, 1850–1980* (Norman: University of Oklahoma Press, 1997); Stephen Dow Beckham, *Requiem for a People: The Rogue Indians and the Frontiersmen* (Norman: University of Oklahoma Press, 1971); Benjamin Logan Madley, "American Genocide: The California Indian Catastrophe, 1846–1873," PhD diss., Yale University, 2009. Thanks to Ben Madley and Gray Whaley for their help with the sources about American Indian nations and their conflicts between 1848 and 1860.

5. Yael A. Sternhell, *Routes of War: The World of Movement in the Confederate South* (Cambridge, MA: Harvard University Press, 2012); Drew Gilpin Faust, *The Creation of Confederate Nationalism: Ideology and Identity in the Civil War South* (Baton Rouge: Louisiana State University Press, 1988); James Downs, *Sick from Freedom: African-American Illness and Suffering during the Civil War and Reconstruction* (New York: Oxford University Press, 2012); Gary W. Gallagher, *The Confederate War* (Cambridge, MA: Harvard University Press, 1997); Gary W. Gallagher, *The Union War* (Cambridge, MA: Harvard University Press, 2011); LeeAnn Whites and Alecia P. Long, eds., *Occupied Women: Gender, Military Occupation, and the American Civil War* (Baton Rouge: Louisiana State University Press, 2009); David Goldfield, *America Aflame: How the Civil War Created a Nation* (New York: Bloomsbury, 2011); Patricia Nelson Limerick, *The Legacy of Conquest: The Unbroken Past of the American West* (New York: Norton, 1987); James Oakes,

Freedom National: The Destruction of Slavery in the United States, 1861–1865 (New York: Norton, 2013); Daniel E. Sutherland, *A Savage Conflict: The Decisive Role of Guerrillas in the American Civil War* (Chapel Hill: University of North Carolina Press, 2009).

6. Elliott West, "Reconstructing Race," *Western Historical Quarterly* 34, no. 1 (Spring 2003): 6–26; Heather Cox Richardson, *West from Appomattox: The Reconstruction of America after the Civil War* (New Haven: Yale University Press, 2007); Stacey L. Smith, *Freedom's Frontier: California and the Struggle over Unfree Labor, Emancipation, and Reconstruction* (Chapel Hill: University of North Carolina Press, 2013); Joshua Paddison, *American Heathens: Religion, Race, and Reconstruction in California* (Berkeley: University of California Press published for the Huntington-USC Institute on California and the West, 2012); Susan Lee Johnson, *Roaring Camp: The Social World of the California Gold Rush* (New York: Norton, 2000); D. Michael Bottoms, *An Aristocracy of Color: Race and Reconstruction in California and the West, 1850–1890* (Norman: University of Oklahoma Press, 2013); Downs, *Sick from Freedom*, epilogue.

7. See the chapters of Nicholas Guyatt and James Jewell in this volume for more on this point.

8. Mabel Washbourne Anderson, *Life of General Stand Watie: The Only Indian Brigadier General of the Confederate Army and the Last General to Surrender* (Pryor, OK: Mayes County Republican, 1915); Annie Heloise Abel, *The American Indian as Participant in the Civil War* (Cleveland: Arthur H. Clark, 1919); Wiley Britton, *The Union Indian Brigade in the Civil War* (Kansas City, MO: F. Hudson, 1922). For the most prominent American Indian in the Union Army, see Arthur Caswell Parker, *The Life of General Ely S. Parker, Last Grand Sachem of the Iroquois and General Grant's Military Secretary* (Buffalo, NY: Buffalo Historical Society, 1919); and William Howard Armstrong, *Warrior in Two Camps: Ely S. Parker, Union General and Seneca Chief* (Syracuse, NY: Syracuse University Press, 1978).

9. Aurora Hunt, *The Army of the Pacific: Its Operations in California, Texas, Arizona, New Mexico, Utah, Nevada, Oregon, Washington, Plains Region, Mexico, etc., 1860–1866* (Glendale, CA: Arthur H. Clark, 1951); Ray Charles Colton, *The Civil War in the Western Territories: Arizona, Colorado, New Mexico, and Utah* (Norman: University of Oklahoma Press, 1959).

10. Nichols, *Lincoln and the Indians*.

11. Alvin M. Josephy, *The Civil War in the American West* (New York: Knopf, 1991).

12. Laurence M. Hauptman, *Between Two Fires: American Indians in the Civil War* (New York: Free Press, 1995).

13. For an emphasis on the terror of the Civil War years experienced by Indian nations far from the traditional battlefields, see Madley, "American Genocide"; Ari Kelman, *A Misplaced Massacre: Struggling Over the Memory of Sand Creek* (Cambridge, MA: Harvard University Press, 2013); Ned Blackhawk, *Violence over the Land: Indians and Empires in the Early American West* (Cambridge, MA: Harvard University Press, 2006), especially chap. 6; and the work of

Madley and Walter L. Williams. See also David E. Stannard, *American Holocaust: Columbus and the Conquest of the New World* (New York: Oxford University Press, 1992).

14. For essays that engage this historiographic question directly, see the papers offered at "Why You Can't Teach U.S. History without American Indians," a symposium commemorating the fortieth year of the D'Arcy McNickle Center American Indian Studies Seminar Series at the Newberry Library in Chicago, May 3–4, 2013. www.newberry.org/why-you-cant-teach.

15. For a sense of this convergence, read especially the introductions of Samuel Truett and Elliott Young, eds., *Continental Crossroads: Remapping U.S.—Mexico Borderlands History* (Durham, NC: Duke University Press, 2004); Jeremy Adelman and Stephen Aron, "From Borderlands to Borders: Empires, Nation-States, and the Peoples in Between in North American History," *American Historical Review* 104, no. 3 (1999): 814–41; Benjamin H. Johnson and Andrew R. Graybill, eds., *Bridging National Borders in North America: Transnational and Comparative Histories* (Durham, NC: Duke University Press, 2010); Jay Gitlin, Barbara Berglund, and Adam Arenson, eds., *Frontier Cities: Encounters at the Crossroads of Empire* (Philadelphia: University of Pennsylvania Press, 2013); Pekka Hämäläinen and Benjamin H. Johnson, eds., *Major Problems in the History of North American Borderlands* (Boston: Wadsworth Cengage Learning, 2011); Brian DeLay, ed., *North American Borderlands* (New York: Routledge, 2013); Sterling Evans, ed., *The Borderlands of the American and Canadian Wests: Essays on Regional History of the Forty-Ninth Parallel* (Lincoln: University of Nebraska Press, 2006). See also Pekka Hämäläinen, *The Comanche Empire* (New Haven: Yale University Press, 2008); Brian DeLay, *War of a Thousand Deserts: Indian Raids and the U.S.-Mexican War* (New Haven: Yale University Press, 2008); Andrew R. Graybill, *Policing the Great Plains: Rangers, Mounties, and the North American Frontier, 1875–1910* (Lincoln: University of Nebraska Press, 2007); Samuel Truett, *Fugitive Landscapes: The Forgotten History of the U.S.– Mexico Borderlands* (New Haven: Yale University Press, 2006); Sheila McManus, *The Line Which Separates: Race, Gender, and the Making of the Alberta–Montana Borderlands* (Lincoln: University of Nebraska Press, 2005).

16. Colton, *The Civil War in the Western Territories;* Howard Roberts Lamar, *Dakota Territory, 1861–1889: A Study of Frontier Politics* (New Haven: Yale University Press, 1956) and *The Far Southwest, 1846–1912: A Territorial History* (New Haven: Yale University Press, 1966).

17. Eugene H. Berwanger, *The West and Reconstruction* (Urbana: University of Illinois Press, 1981).

18. Richard Maxwell Brown, *No Duty to Retreat: Violence and Values in American History and Society* (New York: Oxford University Press, 1991), 44 and 191 n19; the meaning and consequences of this conceptualization were explored in Richard Maxwell Brown, "Western Violence: Structure, Values, Myth," *Western Historical Quarterly* 24, no. 1 (February 1993): 4–20; and "Violence," in *The Oxford History of the American West,* Clyde A. Milner, Carol A. O'Connor, and Martha A. Sandweiss, eds. (New York: Oxford University Press, 1994), 393–425.

19. Richard White, *"It's Your Misfortune and None of My Own": A New History of the American West* (Norman: University of Oklahoma, 1991), 58.

20. Richardson, *West from Appomattox;* West, "Reconstructing Race"; Elliott West, *The Last Indian War: The Nez Perce Story* (New York: Oxford University Press, 2009). West lays out these challenges of seemingly divergent history in *The Last Indian War,* xviii–xxii; quote from xxii.

21. Arenson, *The Great Heart of the Republic;* Richard W. Etulain, *Lincoln and Oregon Country Politics in the Civil War Era* (Corvallis: Oregon State University Press, 2013); Susan Schulten, "The Civil War and the Origins of the Colorado Territory," *Western Historical Quarterly* 44, no. 1 (Spring 2013): 21–46.

PART ONE

―――

Borderlands in Conflict

ONE

Thwarting Southern Schemes and British Bluster in the Pacific Northwest

James Robbins Jewell

FOUR MONTHS BEFORE JOHN BROWN seized the armory at Harpers Ferry, Virginia, events in the far northwestern corner of the United States also brought the nation to the brink of war—not with itself, but with England. The blood spilled in June 1859 belonged to a pig, leading to one of the most bizarre episodes in U.S. diplomatic history. After Abraham Lincoln's election as president, the tensions from decades of mutual suspicions between the United States and its northern neighbor, compounded by the presence of a vocal group of southerners in the regional capital of Victoria, took on overtones of the Civil War.

As the Civil War began, the Pacific Northwest presented very real concerns for the Union government. Royal Governor James Douglas was openly belligerent toward the United States. Therefore, he might have ignored British neutrality and launched preemptive strikes into Washington Territory, or ignored attempts by southern sympathizers on Vancouver Island trying to outfit a raider with which to attack U.S. commerce in the Pacific.[1] Miners in the Fraser River region with Confederate sympathies might have launched paramilitary attacks into Washington Territory.

A new northern front of the Civil War opened in December 1863 when Confederate agents seized the S.S. *Chesapeake* off Cape Cod and sailed it to Nova Scotia.[2] A second cross-border operation occurred in September 1864 when twenty Confederate agents attempted to capture the U.S.S. *Michigan*, the sole Union warship patrolling the Great Lakes. The attempt was foiled when one of the conspirators was captured and revealed the plot.[3] Most famously, on October 19, 1864, a Confederate lieutenant and twenty men crossed from Québec into Vermont, robbing three banks in the small town of St. Albans, making off with $200,000 before fleeing back across the

MAP 1.1. The Pacific Northwest in the Civil War Era.

border.[4] That no military (or paramilitary) operations emerged in the Pacific Northwest during the Civil War demonstrates how effectively Union officials in the region controlled the situation and avoided another front of the war breaking out on the Pacific Slope.

Long before the outbreak of the Civil War, however, U.S. officials wrestled with the dilemmas posed by their uncertain northwestern border. Political maneuvering between the two countries had dominated the "Oregon question" ever since Lewis and Clark spent the winter of 1805 at Fort Clatsop, Oregon. In 1818, the United States and England agreed to the joint occupation of the disputed Oregon lands (essentially from 54°40' latitude south to the present-day California–Oregon border, and west of the Continental Divide). Failure to work out a satisfactory division of those lands in 1827 led to an extension of the joint occupancy agreement, a policy that was still in place in the 1840s. Growing U.S. expansionist sentiments in the Pacific Northwest rekindled British distrust and led to rising tension between the British and Americans, reaching a critical level during the 1844 presidential campaign. James K. Polk based his enthusiastic expansionist candidacy on American braggadocio, political rhetoric, and Manifest Destiny. Polk's campaign platform called for the "reannexation of Texas and the reoccupation of Oregon." The British took the hostile political language quite seriously, and prepared to defend the farthest western region of British North America from U.S. expansionism.

Despite the heated rhetoric, which served its purpose in helping to get Polk elected, the president-elect softened his demands.[5] Although in his inaugural address he spoke boldly about pursuing all of Oregon, Polk's initial offer to the British was more restrained.[6] Like his predecessors, Polk's first official proposal to settle the nagging Oregon question was to extend the 49th parallel as a boundary line all the way to the Pacific Ocean.[7] When British officials refused the offer, Polk asked Congress to terminate the 1827 joint occupation agreement.[8] The expansionist House quickly complied, but the measure was shot down in the Senate. In response to the rapidly deteriorating situation, one British official suggested sending naval vessels both to the Puget Sound region and to the mouth of the Columbia River. In March 1845 it appeared the two nations might go to war over the unsettled Oregon question.

By then, with the annexation of Texas underway and war with Mexico looming, the vigor of President Polk's expansionism was evident. Fortunately, the British ambassador returned with a new offer: England agreed to the 49th parallel line, excluding Vancouver Island, with the details regarding the San Juan Islands (between Vancouver Island and the mainland) to be worked out in arbitration. In April 1846, with General Zachary Taylor's forces already south of the Rio Nueces, provoking war with Mexico, Congress agreed to arbitration with Britain and averted war on two fronts.[9]

Relations between the two nations improved after 1846 but remained precarious, as the dispute over San Juan Island made obvious in 1859. Both U.S. and British citizens had settled the island, repeating the pattern of joint occupancy and uncertain ownership. Then came a military showdown that commenced with the death of a pig.

The British inhabitants, who outnumbered the Americans until May 1859, were employees of the Hudson's Bay Company (HBC), and they did not recognize U.S. claims to any part of San Juan Island. One interloping American named Lyman Cutler sparked the international conflict when he took matters into his own hands. After building a cabin he planted a garden, which he fenced as best he could. Unfortunately for Cutler, free-roaming HBC livestock easily trampled the garden and uprooted his potato patch. Following unsuccessful complaints to the local HBC official, Cutler shot and killed an offending hog, for which he attempted to pay the pig's owner. The seemingly justifiable killing of the wandering British pig very nearly ignited a war, bringing England and the United States closer to armed conflict than at any time since Andrew Jackson won the Battle of New Orleans in January 1815.[10]

Fortunately, the Pig War, as it is now known, did not lead to the shedding of human blood. However, the bluster and maneuvering revealed the complicated international relations that existed in the Pacific Northwest. Soon the bonds between the U.S. Army officers would be cut asunder by the Civil War. As summarized after the fact by Captain L. C. Hunt, an officer with the American contingent on San Juan Island: "I am confident that this whole imbroglio is a disgraceful plot involving General Harney, a dull animal, Mr. Commissioner Campbell, a weak, wordy sort of man; Captain [George E.] Pickett, to some extent, whose main fault perhaps has been bad judgment in allowing himself to be used as a tool by the main conspirators."[11]

Another officer, Major Granville Haller, contended that Harney and Pickett, both southern-born, had conspired to ignite a conflict with the British as part of a plot to help the South in its growing political disagreement with the North; indeed, their Civil War records gave credence to suspicions about their roles in bringing on the Pig War. Pickett, who had served in the Pacific Northwest since 1855 and had fathered a child during that time with a Haida woman named Morning Mist, resigned his commission in June 1861 and left to join the Confederacy. A major general's commission and infamous failure at Gettysburg awaited him. William S. Harney never joined the Confederacy, but while serving as the commander of the Department of the West in April 1861, he failed to prevent the pro-Confederate state militia, commanded by future Confederate general Sterling Price, from nearly taking control of the State of Missouri as part of the Price-Harney Truce. This action led Missouri's Unionist leaders to press for his removal. He was replaced by General Nathanial Lyon in late May and recalled to Washington, D.C.[12]

In an attempt to prevent the pig incident from causing a war, Haller advised proposing a joint occupation to the British authorities that might mollify both sides, at least temporarily.[13] However, the firebrand Pickett would have none of it. According to Haller, "He assured me that if they [the British] attempted to land he would fire on them. He believed they would land, and considered war inevitable."[14] The British authorities had heard that Pickett was encouraging Americans to settle on the island: Pickett "promised protection to any and every American Citizen who might think proper to squat on the Island of San Juan."[15] As Captain Hunt saw it, "Nothing has saved us from a bloody collision but the patient dignity and forbearance of the old admiral [British Rear Admiral Lambert Baynes], who had an overwhelming force at hand."[16]

The mistrust caused by the Pig War was still percolating two years later when civil war broke out in the United States. It was in this atmosphere that pro-Confederate elements in the provinces of British Columbia and Vancouver Island (then separate) schemed to initiate operations against U.S. targets, both on land and afloat, during the war years. In light of the history of periodic cleavages in the relations between Americans and Britons in British North America, made worse by the 1859 Pig War, Department of the Pacific leaders had to craft policies that addressed all the potential dangers that might lurk north of the border while treading lightly on issues of sovereignty.

After the firing on Fort Sumter, the order came for U.S. troops to leave Camp Pickett on San Juan Island and head east for combat service.[17] District commander General George Wright found a way to countermand the order to abandon the U.S. post. Wright's long service in the region enabled him to invoke the ghosts of ten years of white–Native American conflict in the Pacific Northwest (which included a Native attack on the tiny frontier town of Seattle in 1856) to change minds in Washington, D.C.[18] Using the threat of Native American raids as a pretext, Wright gave new orders, nullifying those issued just ten days earlier, thereby ensuring that an American presence remained on the island throughout the war. While at most of the other posts in the Department of the Pacific, where volunteers replaced the professional soldiers, Regular Army forces garrisoned Camp Pickett throughout the duration of the war.

While Americans may have believed in 1861 that the true conflict lay far to the east, Royal Governor James Douglas saw an opportunity to seize the old Oregon country. Authorities in London refused.[19] Undeterred, in December 1861 the pugnacious governor wrote to the British Secretary of State for the Colonies, the Duke of Newcastle, arguing there "was no reason why we should not push overland from Puget Sound and establish advanced posts on the Columbia River."²⁰ Knowing that U.S. troop dispositions were in flux and that some northern posts were likely to be abandoned, he informed the Colonial office that "there is little real difficulty in that operation, as the Coast is entirely unprovided with defensive works."²¹ Furthermore, there was no doubt that the British Navy could easily take control of Puget Sound and the Columbia River. The governor assured his superiors that "with Puget Sound, and the line of the Columbia River in our hands, we should hold the only navigable outlets of the country—command its trade, and soon compel it to submit to Her Majesty's Rule."²² It was just the sort of move Confederate sympathizers in the Pacific Northwest hoped the British would make.

Fortunately for the Union, officials in London did not share Douglas's enthusiasm for a conflict with the United States. Although England did send five thousand troops to British North America in the aftermath of the November 1861 *Trent* Affair, they were stationed in the more populated eastern region.²³ Left with few options, the royal governor authorized the raising of two volunteer rifle corps to complement the royal marines and engineers stationed in the region, but for defensive purposes only.²⁴

Douglas, however, was not the only threat to the United States north of the border. Ever since the 1858 Fraser River gold rush, thousands of Americans had been roaming the rivers and creeks of British Columbia in search of gold. Inevitably, few found the wealth they sought, and while most drifted back across the border, a sizeable contingent remained in British Columbia or tried their luck on Vancouver Island. By the outbreak of the Civil War, Victoria (on Vancouver Island) was home to a growing southern population. The editor of the Victoria *Chronicle* noted, "Shortly after the outbreak of the war many sympathizers with the Slave States came to reside in Victoria. Some leased residences, others took apartments at hotels, still others went into business while a fourth class proceeded to Cariboo and engaged in gold mining and trading."²⁵

British Columbia and Vancouver Island afforded southern sympathizers a perfect haven. "With few exceptions the English residents sympathized with the rebels," an investigation determined.²⁶ Union officials worried that Confederate partisans might use the two British colonies as bases from which to launch raids south across the border, or from which to attack Union shipping interests in the Pacific, including the crucial gold shipments (each one worth more than a million dollars) that were leaving from San Francisco.²⁷

The transitory population of expatriated Americans on Vancouver Island and in British Columbia worried Union officials; however, it was the royal governor who maintained the southern-sympathizing atmosphere in the region. Governor Douglas's tolerant attitude toward pro-Confederates is intriguing given his background: the governor, who was born in Guyana, was of one-eighth (or possibly one-fourth) African heritage, and his wife was half Cree. The fact that neither of them would have had any rights under Confederate law was, however, less important than the prevailing sense of British opportunism and disdain for the U.S. federal government.[28] During the time that Douglas served as governor of Vancouver Island, there was a small population of persons of African descent in the colonies, most of whom had come from the California gold fields, further adding to the puzzle.

The outbreak of the Civil War brought racial tensions to the fore on Vancouver Island, as demonstrated by an incident in September 1861. During a benefit concert for the Royal Hospital in Victoria, two white men attempted to bribe some of the night's performers to keep them from singing as long as African-descended patrons were in the audience. When the performers rejected the bribe, they were pelted by food, and flour was poured on two of the black audience members. A riot ensued and eventually arrests were made, although no one was convicted. Whatever the nationality of the men who started the riot, the incident illustrates that Victoria was not devoid of racial tension.[29] In such an unstable environment, made more so by a growing populace of expatriated southerners as well as a governor driven by the opportunity that an America at war with itself presented him (and by extension, Great Britain), Union concerns about the Pacific Northwestern border make perfect sense.

The level of concern among officials in Washington, D.C., is indicated by the fact that an American consulate post was established in Victoria in 1862. There had never been any such consulate on the Pacific Coast of British North America, nor had there been much reason for such a post. Once the Civil War was under way, however, and British and U.S. relations deteriorated, President Lincoln needed someone he knew and trusted to keep a vigilant eye on the British governor and southern sympathizers on Vancouver Island and in British Columbia. So he sent Allen Francis. Few people had known Abraham Lincoln as long or as well. Francis had moved to Springfield, Illinois, in 1834 to work for his brother Simeon at the Springfield *Sangamo Journal*. During their time in the Illinois capital, the Francis brothers became intimate friends with Lincoln and, according to legend, loaned him books on the legal profession and later helped him reconcile with Mary Todd, his future wife. The two brothers left Springfield in 1859—Simeon for Oregon and Allen for California. The presence of trusted friends in a remote region, vulnerable to both internal and external threats, was fortuitous for the new president.[30] When war broke out Simeon Francis was appointed paymaster for the military District of Oregon, and Allen Francis became the first U.S. consul at Vancouver Island Colony.[31]

Francis's activities far exceeded the normal responsibilities of such a political office. He maintained a network of spies in Victoria employed to keep him abreast of any pro-Confederate activity on either Vancouver Island or in British Columbia, with its transitory population of American miners from the now-divided states.[32] As he told District of Oregon commander Brigadier General Benjamin Alvord, "I have neither spared time, pains, nor expense in endeavoring to learn what our enemies were doing."[33]

Francis went about his task with a diligence that bordered on paranoia. He reported everything, no matter how implausible or insignificant, that came to his consulate post in Victoria.[34] As he quickly found out, little of what he was told had to do with odd or threatening British military activities. Instead, most of his reports focused on insults, schemes, or dangers posed by Victoria's openly pro-Confederate population, almost all of whom were U.S. expatriates. No matter how far removed they were from the Confederate states, this pro-Confederate element sought to pose a threat to the Union cause.

Just a few months after assuming his post, Francis informed Secretary of State William H. Seward that "congregated here and in towns of British Columbia, are some desperate men from the rebel States, talking of expeditions to California and Nevada Territory for revolutionary purposes."[35] Gold shipments sailing from San Francisco remained a tempting target, and Confederate sympathizers might also try to organize a raiding force of expatriated southerners to attack Union targets in Washington Territory. The South's need for gold to purchase supplies in Europe was desperate, and Confederate sympathizers in Victoria eventually attempted to acquire and outfit a raider. (There was no attempt to launch land-based raids across the northwestern border.)

The early Confederate successes at the battles of Bull Run (in Virginia) and Wilson's Creek (in Missouri), emboldened the city's southern enclave, a number of whom gathered in the rooms of two Alabama brothers, John and Oliver Jeffreys, at the St. Nicholas Hotel, where they "became noisily jubilant."³⁶ *Chronicle* editor David W. Higgins, whom the southerners considered a loyal friend, remembered celebrating one "great rebel victory, and the company excelled all previous efforts in singing Confederate airs, while their rebel hearts, bursting with enthusiasm, found frequent vent in loud cheering."³⁷ Not long after assuming his post, Consul Francis informed his superiors about the overtness of Confederate sympathy displayed in Victoria, assuring them that "I am watching their movements, and if any demonstration is made, or any of their schemes are developed, shall demand the interference of the authorities, and communicate the facts to [Department of Pacific commander] General Wright in San Francisco."³⁸

As the residents prepared to celebrate the Prince of Wales's birthday with a two-day extravaganza on November 10 and 11, 1862, southern sympathizers, including one J. S. Shapard, seized that very public opportunity to display their allegiances by raising a Confederate flag. Francis informed Secretary Seward that a number of northern residents urged him to protest the affront, which he did. Governor Douglas, however, chose not to respond to the U.S. official until after the celebration had ended, feigning ignorance of the incident when he did.³⁹ Governor Douglas's nonchalant response to Francis's protest led some to assume that such actions would be openly tolerated.⁴⁰ Soon Confederate flags flew over a number of homes throughout Victoria, remaining a troubling (and insulting) issue until near the end of the war. As the governor of Washington Territory informed Seward in July 1864, "The officers and crew of every American Vessel that enters the Harbor of Victoria is insulted, & indignant, at the sight of the Rebel Flags flying in Victoria." Of course, there was little Seward could do beyond putting political pressure on the British ambassador in Washington; officials with the Department of the Pacific could do even less.⁴¹

The population of unabashed Confederate sympathizers in Victoria was sufficiently large that in 1863 Shapard opened a new watering hole named the Confederate Saloon.⁴² Consul Francis reported how "the miners are now coming down from the upper country, generally in desperate circumstances, mostly secesh, and ready for anything."⁴³ This establishment soon became the meeting place of a group of roughly fifty southerners who called themselves the Southern Association.⁴⁴ This bar, and its churlish proprietor, quickly became a thorn in Consul Francis's side. The saloon stayed open throughout the war. Only when Robert E. Lee surrendered at Appomattox Courthouse did Shapard face a rebuke, at the hands of a Union-sympathizing ship captain who publicly thrashed him in April 1865.⁴⁵

It took time for Victoria's growing southern community to seize upon a specific idea of how best to aid the Confederate cause from so far away. As Confederate victories mounted in the East, southern sympathizers like the Jeffreys brothers decided that the best way to assist the southern cause was to disrupt Union commercial efforts along the Pacific coast. Of course, the gold shipments were the ultimate prize, but other Union targets plied the northern Pacific waters, too.

Before any attempts to attack Union commerce in the north Pacific could take place, however, local southern sympathizers needed a ship capable of serving as a raider. This proved to be a serious impediment to the privateers' visions of glory and plunder. Their first effort played out in the pages of Victoria's two rival newspapers, the *Chronicle* and the *Daily British Colonist*. The entire affair crystallized the difficulties facing Consul Francis and his operatives in Victoria. Despite the public nature of the incident, until the Confederate sympathizers actually violated England's official neutrality policy there was nothing he could do. Unless they crossed into U.S. territory on land or sea, Francis knew the local officials would not pay very close attention to the southerners' machinations.

On February 4, 1863, the Victoria *Chronicle* published an article declaring that a Confederate Navy officer had been in the city for a month, supposedly looking to purchase a ship with which to attack Union shipping. It was reported that he was trying to purchase an English ship, the *Thames,* which he intended to man with local sympathizers before setting out to capture San Francisco gold shipments.[46] Ultimately, as the *Chronicle* reported, the plan failed due to a lack of funds, which seems odd considering the presence of a number of southerners leading rather ostentatious lives in Victoria.[47] Allen Francis's reports demonstrate that he was intimately aware of the plot, to the point that he seemed to understand it had no chance to succeed. This failure forced the conspirators to come up with an alternate plan.

Simultaneous to the *Thames* affair Francis heard a rumor about an effort not to buy but to capture a ship already armed and ready to serve as a raider. The ship the conspirators hoped to seize was the U.S.S. *Shubrick,* which one old pioneer later recalled as "a handsome sidewheel steamer, far from slow for those days, perfectly seaworthy and safe for ocean navigation, [which] carried four or five brass cannon, and had a good supply of small arms, ammunition, etc."[48] However, designs to capture the *Shubrick* fell apart, "for the want of a leader in whom the banditti could confide," as Francis informed Captain Thomas Selfridge, the commander of the Navy yard on Mare Island in San

Francisco Bay.[49] Furthermore, Francis was confident in the ship's commander, noting that "Lieut. Selden is a true, reliable and efficient officer."[50] With the ship in trustworthy hands and the Confederate sympathizers disorganized and directionless, the second plot had no better chance to proceed than the first.

The failure of this second plot illuminates two points about Confederate sympathizers in western British North America. First, that no one was jailed, or even investigated, for their very public efforts to violate English neutrality laws made it clear they had little to fear from the British authorities in the colonies of Vancouver Island and British Columbia. Second, despite their self-confidence, disorganization and bad luck plagued the southern expatriates doing much of the work for Allen Francis and his agents.

Consul Francis took no public action but kept Secretary of State Seward apprised of developments. As Francis told the *Chronicle*'s editor, once that particular danger had passed, "I knew what was going on all the time. My detectives kept me well informed."[51] Whether or not there was much truth to those particular stories is difficult to ascertain, but it kept the competing papers busy postulating on the veracity of the story; the *Chronicle* believed it, while the *Daily British Colonist* did not.

On March 15, 1863, officials in San Francisco seized the S.S. *Chapman*, which had been outfitted as a privateer vessel and was poised to leave the harbor.[52] Two boats full of armed seamen from the U.S.S. *Cyane*, which protected San Francisco harbor at General Wright's request, captured the would-be raider and its crew of twenty-one without a fight. After boarding the vessel, San Francisco police, working with the customs collector, Ira Rankin, discovered "a number of guns, ammunition, and other military stores were found on board."[53]

The capture of the *Chapman* conspirators demonstrated the gravity of the threat to the Union along the Pacific Coast and led Secretary of State Seward to reevaluate Consul Francis's report about the *Thames* uproar in Victoria. Given the heightened concerns about the Confederate threat to Union shipping, Seward sent a letter on March 31 to the British ambassador to the United States, Lord Lyons, explaining: "I regret to inform you that reliable information has reached this department that an attempt was made in January last, at Victoria, Vancouver's island, to fit out the English steamer *Thames* as a privateer, under the flag of the insurgents, to cruise against the merchant shipping of the United States in the Pacific. Fortunately, however, the scheme was temporarily, at least, frustrated by its premature expose."[54]

In addition to drawing Lord Lyons's attention to the topic, Seward applied considerable diplomatic pressure to the British ambassador and asked "the attention of her Majesty's colonial authorities to the subject, in order that such violations of the act of Parliament and of her majesty's proclamation may not be committed."[55] In other words, Seward expected the British government to compel Governor Douglas to enforce the neutrality policy.

But diplomatic pressure alone was not enough to assuage Francis's fears or General Wright's concerns.[56] In an effort to take more aggressive steps to protect Union shipping, the U.S.S. *Saginaw* was ordered from San Francisco to Puget Sound "without any unnecessary delay . . . for the purpose of obtaining information from the authorities, and from other sources, in relation to the equipment of rebel privateers in those waters."[57] The combination of the capture of the *Chapman,* the presence of a Union military vessel patrolling Puget Sound, and a series of Confederate reverses in the second half of 1863 quieted pro-southern rumblings on Vancouver Island, but only briefly. The *Saginaw* could not remain in the area long, which meant the plotters would resume their efforts. However, as Francis assured the ship's captain, those "connected with the scheme . . . are being closely watched."[58]

Despite these setbacks, the Southern Association continued to meet and brew desperate schemes amid drinks at the Confederate Saloon. As Francis told the naval commander at Mare Island, "There is still in this city a rebel organization, which has had several meetings within the last few weeks. They are awaiting, it seems from rumors, the receipt of letters of marque from the President of the so-called Confederate States."[59] Once again, Francis's agents had done their task well. The association's president, Jules David, had indeed submitted a request to the Confederate government in Richmond for official recognition of their effort to begin operations of a privateer for the southern cause as early as April 1862, but Richmond did not respond.

Having heard nothing for more than a year, David again requested letters of marque in October 1863.[60] In this second note he attempted to convince Confederate officials—among them Confederate Secretary of State Judah Benjamin, who received the letter—of the association's earnestness and the possibilities for success by writing: "It is our most anxious wish to do something for our country, and we can not serve her better than in destroying the commerce and property of our enemies. If you will for a moment reflect upon the extensive commerce of the Federal States with South America, California, the islands, China, and Japan, you can well imagine what a rich field we have before us."[61] David further explained, "We have at our disposal a first-class steamer of over 400 tons, strongly built, and of an average speed of 14 miles. The money required to arm her and fit her out as a privateer will be raised without difficulty amongst our friends here."[62] The ploy worked, but in the wrong circles. With the war now going against the South, Confederate officials in Richmond did not consider the desperate scheme, and once again chose not to reply. However, the ever-vigilant American consul, Allen Francis, responded in his own way.

Once again proving just how well informed he was about the Confederate sympathizers' activities, Consul Francis described very accurately the Southern Association's plans in a letter to his brother, who was stationed at Fort Vancouver in Washington Territory (why he did not contact the proper military officials is a mystery).[63] He informed his brother that ever since a very fast 300-ton, all steel ship had arrived in Victoria the "rumors have been rife that the rebels have been trying to buy her for a privateer."[64] Simeon Francis understood the significance of the letter, but because he was not at his post when it arrived, a month passed before he turned the communiqué over to district commander Alvord on November 20.

General Alvord responded immediately to Consul Francis. After rebuking the diplomat for not directly informing the proper authorities, Alvord reassured Francis that he had requested naval reinforcements for Puget Sound months earlier. Alvord also informed the consul that he had passed the contents on to General Wright's headquarters, with the assumption the department commander would take action.[65] General Alvord acknowledged Francis's continued work, telling him he was "pleased to hear of your ceaseless vigilance, which should never be relaxed."[66]

Wright immediately took steps to strengthen the U.S. military presence in the waters of Puget Sound by requesting that Captain Thomas Selfridge, naval commander at the Mare Island Navy Yard, send a man-of-war to the region.[67] Unfortunately, the only possible naval vessel suited for the task was the U.S.S. *Narragansett*, which needed both repairs and additional men to fill out its crew to a serviceable contingent.[68] After being assigned men from the U.S.S. *Saginaw*, the *Narragansett* sailed for Puget Sound on December 11, 1863. Finding no privateer activity in the region, the ship returned to San Francisco by March 1864 and underwent more extensive repairs.[69]

The onset of winter seems to have sapped much of the Confederate sympathizers' eagerness to acquire a vessel for privateering and diminished their commitment to begin anew in the spring. Richmond's failure to acknowledge the request for letters of marque combined with the South's deteriorating military fortunes only exacerbated the erosion of the southern sympathizers' privateering dreams. In 1864 Governor Douglas was replaced, and the new governor, Arthur Kennedy, proved more cooperative when enforcing British neutrality and discouraging the clandestine schemes of Victoria's southern element. Within a few months of the change in governorship, Francis reported, "It is gratifying to notice the change in the sentiment of the English people here in regard to our Government and its effort to put down the rebellion."[70]

Although the Confederacy was in decline by late 1864, a few ardent members of the Southern Association continued to meet in Shapard's bar. There they talked about attacking U.S. commercial interests on the Pacific. However, in November the ubiquitous Consul Francis confidently informed the new Department of the Pacific commander, Major General Irvin McDowell, that "Governor Kennedy will do all in his power to prevent them from fitting out any vessel on this island."[71] In 1865 the Southern Association's continual scheming fell silent when even the most ardent southern sympathizers realized their larger cause was lost.

By 1865 diplomatic relations between the United States and Great Britain had improved since the early days of the war. For the Department of the Pacific and the Pacific Squadron, interactions with the British on Vancouver Island and on the waters off the Pacific Northwest coast were relaxed, and in some cases even cordial. With the new royal governor on Vancouver Island proving more amendable in allaying U.S. concerns about southern sympathizers, and not harboring any expansionist dreams like his predecessor, the only problems that remained were on San Juan Island, the site of the 1859 Pig War. Those minor frictions were caused by the confusion over police authority, a point that both U.S. and British military personnel took great pains to work out together.

In the end, British forces never crossed the far western American border, nor did Confederate forces or southern sympathizers successfully use Vancouver Island or British Columbia as a base of operations for attacks on the United States during the Civil War. The danger was genuine, and the potential damage to the Union effort significant—successful attacks on the gold shipments alone might have prolonged the war. The failure of these threats to the Union conveys the false impression that no danger ever existed for the Union cause from Vancouver Island or British Columbia. As the Pig War demonstrated, conflict could be just a hair's breadth away. That no threat succeeded is a testament to the multilayered efforts of the Department of the

Pacific on land and the vessels of the Pacific Squadron—skillfully aided by U.S. Consul Allen Francis on Vancouver Island, who seemingly knew all of the dangers before they materialized. These efforts kept Governor Douglas from causing a political row and prevented southern sympathizers from attacking Union interests in the Pacific Northwest. Only because of such machinations was the Pacific Northwest a quiet theater of the U.S. Civil War.

NOTES

1. Sir James Douglas was royal governor of both Vancouver Island and British Columbia colonies.
2. Bruce Hutchinson, *The Struggle for the Border* (Toronto, New York, London: Longmans, Green, and Co., 1955), 333. For the Chesapeake seizure, also see Greg Marquis, *In Armageddon's Shadow* (Montreal: McGill-Queen's University Press, 1998), chaps. 6 and 7.
3. *Official Records of the Union and Confederate Navies in the War of the Rebellion* (Washington, DC: Government Printing Office, 1896), series 1, 3: 352–54. All other references to the naval records of the war are for series 1, unless otherwise noted, and are cited as *ORN*.
4. For the St. Albans Raid see Stuart Lutz, "Terror in St. Albans," *Civil War Times Illustrated*, 40 (2001): 3.
5. James Polk had been a relative unknown prior to the 1844 presidential, therefore his aggressive expansionist stance played a key role in launching him out of obscurity.
6. Paul H. Bergeron, *The Presidency of James K. Polk* (Lawrence: University of Kansas Press, 1987), 117.
7. Frederick Merk, *The Monroe Doctrine and American Expansion* (New York: Vintage, 1966), 73. Merk points out that President Tyler and the lame duck House of Representatives pushed "All Oregon" legislation –meaning to the northern extreme of the Canadian portion of Oregon –but that it died, as expected, in the Senate.
8. Ibid., 78; Bergeron, *The Presidency of James K. Polk,* 119–20.
9. Treatment of the final phase of the Oregon crisis can be found in Bergeron, *The Presidency of James K. Polk,* 124–13, Merk, *The Monroe Doctrine and American Expansion*, 102–3, and William H. Goetzmann, *When the Eagle Screamed* (New York, London, Sydney: John Wiley and Sons, 1966), 47–48.
10. Information on the origins of the Pig War can be found in Keith A. Murray, *The Pig War* (Tacoma: Washington State Historical Society, 1968), 32–33.
11. Keith A. Murray, "Pig War Letters: A Romantic Lieutenant's Account of the San Juan Crisis," *Columbia* 1, no. 3 (Fall 1987): 17.
12. For Pickett see Leslie J. Gordon's *General George E. Pickett in Life and Legend* (Chapel Hill: University of North Carolina Press, 2001) and for Harney see

George Rollie Anderson's *General William S. Harney: Prince of Dragoons* (Lincoln: University of Nebraska Press, 2001).

13. Granville O. Haller, *San Juan and Secession* (Seattle, WA: Shorey Book Store, 1967; original publication date, 1896), 12.

14. Ibid.

15. Royal Governor James Douglas to Lord Lytton, British Colonial Secretary, August 1, 1859. The Colonial Despatches of Vancouver Island and British Columbia, 1846–71, digitized by the University of Victoria (bcgenesis.uvic.ca). Hereafter cited as Colonial Despatches.

16. Murray, "Pig War Letters," 17.

17. *War of the Rebellion: Official Records of the Union and Confederate Armies* (Washington, DC: Government Printing Office, 1897), 50: 1, 512. Hereafter cited as *OR*. The abandonment of the American post on San Juan island, as directed from the department headquarters, is given in District Special Order 9, dated June 11, 1861.

18. Beginning in 1848 the Pacific Northwest was the site of the following wars: Cayuse War (Oregon), Yakima War (Washington Territory), Rogue River War (Oregon), Puget Sound War (Washington Territory), and finally culminating with the Palouse War (Washington Territory).

19. Robin W. Winks, *Canada and the United States: The Civil War Years* (Baltimore: Johns Hopkins University Press, 1960), 158.

20. Benjamin F. Gilbert, "Rumors of Confederate Privateers Operating in Victoria, Vancouver Island," *British Columbia Historical Quarterly* 18 (1954) 3/4, 241. Douglas to Duke of Newcastle, Colonial Secretary, December 28, 1861. Colonial Despatches.

21. Douglas to Newcastle, December 28, 1861. Colonial Despatches.

22. Ibid.

23. On November 8, 1861, the U.S.S. *San Jacinto* stopped the British ship R.M.S. *Trent* in international waters and took two Confederate diplomats who were on their way to England and France into custody. The fact that the ship was both British and in international waters fueled anti-Union sentiment in England. To avoid any potential rupture in Anglo–Union relations, the Lincoln administration quickly disavowed the actions taken by the *San Jacinto's* captain, Charles Wilkes, and released the two Confederate diplomats. Dean B. Mahin, *One War at a Time* (Washington, DC: Brassey's, 2000), 58–82.

24. Winks, *Canada and the United States*, 162.

25. D. W. Higgins, *The Mystic Spring and Other Tales of Western Life* (Toronto: William Briggs, 1904), 107.

26. Allen Francis to William H. Seward, October 1, 1862. Dispatches from the United States Consuls in Victoria, 1862–1906 (microfilm, roll 1, 1862–1869). National Archives, Seattle branch. Hereafter cited as Dispatches US Consul.

27. According to congressional documents cited in Aurora Hunt, *Army of the Pacific* (1951; Mechanicsburg, PA: Stackpole, 2004), 329.

28. Douglas was born in 1803 in Demerara, then a Dutch Colony in South America (and now part of Guyana), to a Scottish father and a Barbadian mother.

His wife was the daughter of his former boss at the North West (fur) Company. Early Douglas biographies ignored his racial background, choosing not to mention it at all. For a contemporary biography see John Adams, *Old Square Toes and His Lady: The Life of James and Amelia Douglas* (Victoria, BC: Horsdal and Schubert, 2001).

29. Patricia M. Johnson, "McCreight and the Law," *British Columbia Historical Quarterly* 12, no. 2 (1948) 2: 138.

30. For the role played by Abraham Lincoln's close friends in Oregon country politics on the eve of the Civil War see, Richard Etulain, *Lincoln and Oregon Country Politics in the Civil War Era* (Corvalis: Oregon State University Press, 2013). Chapter 2 is especially useful for understanding the relationship between Lincoln and Edward Baker and Simeon Francis, however, there is no information on the younger (Allen) Francis.

31. Biographical information on Allen and Simeon Francis comes from Jacob Piatt Dunn and William Harris Kemper, *Indiana and Indians: A History of Aboriginal and Territorial Indiana and the Century of Statehood* (Chicago and New York: American Historical Society, 1919), 3: 1505–6.

32. Donald F. McLarney, "The American Civil War in Victoria, Vancouver Island Colony," unpublished paper, Highline (Washington) Community College, 7–9, and, *OR*, 50, 2: 678–79, 682.

33. *OR*, 50, 2: 682.

34. Although Francis never mentioned the names of any of his operatives, Victoria *Chronicle* editor D. W. Higgins wrote that Francis told him one of them was Dick Lovell, who helped thwart the plan to capture the *Schubrick*. Higgins, *The Mystic Spring*, 123–24. Writer Ken Mather asserted that Lovell was beaten by the southern conspirators for revealing their plans in time for them to be thwarted. Ken Mather, *Buckaroos and Mud Pups: The Early Days of Ranching in British Columbia* (Surrey, BC: Heritage House, 2006), 38.

35. Allen Francis to William H. Seward, October 10, 1862. Dispatches US Consul.

36. Ibid. The Jeffreys brothers began running cattle herds from Oregon to British Columbia in 1858 and appear to have taken up residence in Victoria after their 1862 herd was delivered. F. W. Laing, "Some Pioneers of the Cattle Industry," *British Columbia Historical Quarterly* 6, no. 4 (1942): 260.

37. Ibid., 111.

38. Allen Francis to William H. Seward, October 1, 1862, Dispatches US Consul.

39. McLarney, "The American Civil War in Victoria," 17–19. Governor Douglas letter to Francis enclosed in Francis to Seward, November 13, 1862. Dispatches US Consul.

40. McLarney, "The American Civil War in Victoria," 20–21.

41. Quoting Pickering to Seward, July 5, 1864, *Territorial Papers, Washington Series*, in Ibid., 43.

42. Ibid., 31.

43. *OR*, 50, 2: 678.
44. Ibid., 37 and 38.
45. Victoria *Daily British Colonist,* April 12, 1865.
46. Gilbert, "Rumors of Confederate Privateers Operating in Victoria," 241. For the *Colonist*'s reaction see their February 5, 1863, issue.
47. Ibid., 242–43.
48. Charles Prosch, *Reminisces of Washington Territory* (1904; Fairfield, WA: Ye Galleon Press, 1969), 52.
49. *ORN,* 2: 258.
50. Francis to Seward, February 14, 1863. Dispatches US Consul.
51. Higgins, *The Mystic Spring,* 124.
52. *OR*, 50, 2: 352.
53. *ORN,* 2: 122. For General Wright's version of events, see *OR,* 50, 2: 363–64.
54. Seward to Lyons, March 31, 1863. *House Executive Documents,* 1, 38th Congress, 1st Session: 1, 535.
55. Ibid.
56. In reality, Brigadier General Benjamin Alvord, District of Oregon commander, had been more vocal in his calls for a stronger naval presence in Puget Sound—and at the mouth of the Columbia River. He sent his first request for naval reinforcement to the Secretary of the Navy in September 1862. *OR,* 50, 2: 96.
57. *ORN,* 2: 165.
58. Ibid., 261.
59. Ibid., 260. The letters of marque were official documentation that proved that those privateers holding the letters were operating on behalf of a specified government—the Confederacy in this case—and were therefore not pirates, but sanctioned military forces. Essentially, it legalized piracy, as long as the captured ships went before an admiralty court in the country that issued the letters.
60. David was hoping the Confederate government would authorize him and his fellow plotters to launch raids on Union commerce in the Pacific Ocean.
61. *ORN,* 3: 1, 934.
62. Ibid.
63. The consul could have written to either General Alvord or Alvord's superior, department commander General Wright, or the senior naval officers—Pacific Squadron leader Admiral Charles Bell or Captain Thomas Selfridge at Mare Island.
64. *OR,* 50, 2: 678.
65. Ibid., 679–80.
66. Ibid., 714.
67. Ibid., 684.
68. Gilbert, *British Columbia Historical Review,* 252; *ORN,* 2: 574.
69. *OR,* 50: 2, 789.
70. Francis to Seward, March 4, 1865. Dispatches US Consul.
71. *OR,* 50: 2, 1061.

TWO

Death in the Distance

CONFEDERATE MANIFEST DESTINY AND THE
CAMPAIGN FOR NEW MEXICO, 1861–1862

Megan Kate Nelson

THE EDGES OF THE HARD-PACKED TRAIL were blurry with sand, lingering evidence of a howling storm that had swept through the Albuquerque Basin a few weeks before. James "Paddy" Graydon's horse kicked up clouds of dust as the Union scout scanned the landscape in front of him. Sand sage and blue grama pushed up out of the ground and mesas crouched low on the horizon. From here, the road climbed further southwest into the Magdalene Mountains, winding through forests of ponderosa pine and gambel oak. The next water hole was more than twenty miles away. Graydon knew this landscape well. He had enlisted in the First U.S. Dragoons in 1853 and with his company he had ranged across the deserts of the southwestern territories; he was in New Mexico when word came of the secession of Texas and, a few months later, the firing on Fort Sumter. Graydon had tracked the Texans when they first entered the territory in December 1861. Now, in late April 1862, he was scouting their retreat.[1]

Bulky shapes materialized on the road's periphery. Graydon pulled up and looked down. They were the bodies of three men, half-buried and starting to deteriorate in the late spring sun. It was unclear to which Texas regiment they belonged; the Confederates wore little but tattered pants and shirts and no insignia to speak of. It was likely that the sandstorm had covered them; the Texans had not stopped to inter their dead but used all of their energy to push themselves forward on the road.[2]

What Graydon saw on his scout—the strewn debris of an army desperate to shed itself of all but the necessary items for survival, the dead bodies of men and also mules and horses—tells us a great deal about the nature of the Civil War in the Southwest. Here the war's outcome depended less on fighting and killing the enemy and more on moving quickly through the desert

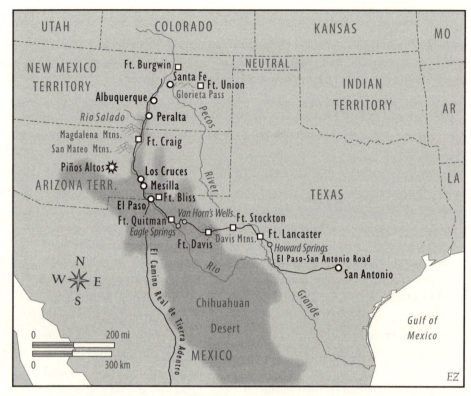

MAP 2.1. The Route of the Sibley Brigade during the Confederate Campaign for New Mexico, 1861–62.

landscape and successfully managing supplies of food and water. The desert Southwest was a uniquely difficult landscape of war; its natural features and resources were not conducive to traditional military strategies that amassed large armies to fight long-term campaigns. In the end, Union troops were able to adapt to environmental conditions more successfully than the Confederates, and this explains their ability to force the Texans back where they came from and to retain their somewhat tenuous control over the region and its many fractious inhabitants. The story of the Texans who marched into New Mexico in the fall of 1861 and dragged themselves home again nine months later also reveals how Confederate Manifest Destiny was made and unmade on the desert roads of the Southwest.

Between October 1861 and July 1862 more than twenty-seven hundred soldiers and thousands of animals moved across Texas and New Mexico in a series of long marches. The shortest stint was the mountain route, 109 miles of volcanic terrain giving way to the northeastern reaches of the Chihuahuan desert. The longest was the San Antonio—El Paso Road, a military thoroughfare traversing the state of Texas, established in 1849. Nearly seven hundred miles long, this set of wagon ruts wound through some of the most spectacularly beautiful and unforgiving landscapes in the state. As the Confederates marched westward on this road in the fall of 1861 they did so, as Fifth Texas private William (Bill) Davidson put it, "fully bent on doing all in their power to carry the Southern cross to victory, and to make the Confederate states a free and independent nation."[3]

The Anglos of Texas had long coveted the lands to their west. In the 1830s, they had claimed the Rio Grande in its entirety as their territorial border and included Santa Fe within their domain.[4] After securing independence from Mexico in 1836, the new Republic attempted to make this claim a reality in 1841, sending a military expedition into the Southwest.[5] This excursion and two subsequent filibusters failed, and during the 1850s this region became the center of sectionalist rancor as northerners and southerners argued about the establishment of slavery there. Southerners could not create plantation landscapes in New Mexico and Arizona; although Pueblo and Mexican farmers had successfully planted food crops, orchards, and vineyards along stretches of the Rio Grande, Pecos, and Gila River valleys for hundreds of years, beyond these valleys the region's low levels of annual rainfall and alkaline soils were not conducive to intensive monoculture.[6] Slaves could have labored in the copper, silver, and turquoise mines in the region, and most proslavery expansionists had designs on the mineral wealth of the desert Southwest.[7] But mostly southerners desired the Territories as a landscape of mobility, a vast region through which one could travel quickly and in all seasons, from stage and railway stations in eastern Texas to the Pacific coast of California, or southward to Sonora and the Gulf of California. New Mexico and Arizona were part of a "golden circle" of imagined slave societies in southern climes; what southerners pictured in the desert Southwest was a crossroads of empire.[8]

One of the loudest voices for this vision of Southern Manifest Destiny was Jefferson Davis. As William Cooper has argued, while Davis led the War Department during the Pierce Administration (1853–57), he "made his chief concern the great American West, for in it so many of his interests overlapped and intersected." In Davis's view, it was imperative that Americans cross its vast distances, high mountain ranges, and desert basins, for these topographical obstacles threatened the nation's possession of the Pacific states.⁹ He therefore championed a transcontinental railroad along the 32nd parallel (known as "the Southern Route"), which would take travelers through Texas, New Mexico, and Arizona on the way to California. His vision of the conquered West also led Davis to argue for a more adaptive strategy: the use of camels for military transportation and as mounts in the U.S. Army's campaigns against Comanches and Apaches. Camels were fleet of hoof, able to clamber over mountain passes with heavy loads on their backs, and they could eat cacti and other desert vegetation. They could also store and reabsorb water in the gelatinous fat of their humps, a distinct advantage over horses and mules. In March 1855 Davis convinced Congress to appropriate $30,000 for the purchase of camels in the Middle East and North Africa and their conveyance back to the United States. By 1859, there were more than eighty camels lodged at military forts in Texas and California.¹⁰

Most Americans were skeptical about the use of camels as transportation, but they believed that the intermountain West could be traversed and that its settlement and cultivation were vital to the nation's future. However, by 1861 many proslavery southerners had come to believe that they were the authentic inheritors not only of the Revolutionary right of rebellion but also of Manifest Destiny. They resented federal attempts to prevent slavery's expansion and "used the liberating mechanism of secession" to claim what they believed was rightfully their own. "Building a Confederate Empire from the rubble of the Union," historian Donald Frazier has argued, "was a basic goal of Southern independence, not an afterthought."¹¹

Southern imperialists believed that the geographic proximity of the southwestern territories and their cultural connections to the southern states ensured their fealty to the Confederacy. New Mexico's Anglo and Hispanic traders, ranchers, and farmers had close commercial ties along the Santa Fe Trail with the slave state of Missouri, as Diane Mutti Burke shows in her chapter in this volume. And most of the political appointees and military officials living in New Mexico were southerners. Under their leadership New Mexico passed a "black code" restricting the mobility of free blacks in 1857 and a harsh slave code in 1859, despite the fact that fewer than a hundred free blacks and slaves lived in the Territory at the time. Confederate general Henry H. Sibley voiced a common belief among Anglo southerners when he announced to the residents of New Mexico in December 1861 that "by geographical position, by similarity of institutions, by commercial interests, and by future destinies New Mexico pertains to the Confederacy."¹²

Sibley, who was born in Louisiana and graduated from West Point, spent the 1840s and 1850s serving in the U.S. Army, fighting Florida Seminoles and Mexicans before heading to the southwestern territories to wage war against the Mormons and Navajos. In mid-April 1861, he was in command at Fort Burgwin near Taos; when he heard about the Confederate success at Fort Sumter he resigned his U.S. Army commission and joined the next wagon train eastward. After his arrival in Montgomery, Alabama (then the capital of the Confederacy), Sibley met with Jefferson Davis, informing the Confederate president that he could recruit Texans, arm them with rifles and artillery from federal arsenals, and feed them with provisions taken from abandoned forts. Once the territories were theirs, the Confederates would vanquish California, using its ports to reestablish international trade and subvert the Union blockade.

The silver deposits buried deep in New Mexico's Piños Altos mines and the gold extracted from the mountains of Colorado and California's Sierras would fund the Confederate government and its war effort. Through the instruments of empire honed by American expansionist efforts in the previous decades—military presence, government structure, and extractive industry—southerners would prove that the Confederacy could act as a nation on the world stage and maintain its own independence. Given Davis's already strong emotional and political investments in the West, he was not difficult to convince. But it helped that Sibley was able to articulate the central tenets of Confederate Manifest Destiny, offering a military blueprint for fulfilling "long-cherished Southern dreams."[13]

Sibley was also able to persuade Davis that, given his recent service in New Mexico, he knew the country and its people well enough to wage a successful campaign.[14] The centerpiece of Sibley's strategy—that his army would sustain itself—depended on his knowledge of the landscape and the location of its military posts. The Confederate Army of New Mexico would march from fort to fort, defeat the Union troops stationed there, and gather fresh provisions for men and animals before moving on. This meant, Sibley argued, that there would be no need for supply lines.[15]

As Sibley and his men would soon discover, there were several problems with this plan, all of which contributed to the campaign's failure and exacerbated the suffering of the Texans who undertook it. These difficulties were rooted in the inability of Confederate officers to adapt successfully to the topography, hydrology, and climate of the Southwest, despite having prior experience with desert warfare in the region. In the 1840s and 1850s the U.S.

Army had battled Native American tribes using many of the same tactics that these tribes had honed over hundreds of years of desert warfare, which Lance Blyth describes in his chapter in this volume: small, mobile bands of mounted soldiers launched surprise attacks against enemy positions, raided their herds and supplies, and quickly withdrew. But as the Confederates moved against Union troops in the fall 1861, they amassed large numbers of men and supplies instead, attempting to fight a traditional, large-scale "hard" war across the vast distances of a desert landscape. As would soon become clear to Sibley's Texans, these tactics were uniquely unsuited to the environmental realities of the desert Southwest.

Sibley began recruiting soldiers for his New Mexico campaign in the summer of 1861. Most of the men who answered the call came from south central and eastern Texas, inland counties that tracked the arc of the Gulf coast. The lands here were rolling, the soil hard with clay and lush with prairie grass used mostly for pasture. The recruits from this area were farmers, stock raisers, or day laborers. Many volunteers—like Bill Davidson, Alfred Peticolas, and Theophilus Noel—were born elsewhere and had moved to Texas as boys, part of a larger emigration stream that fueled Anglo settlement of the West in the 1840s and 1850s. The majority were young men between eighteen and twenty-three years old, like most of the first recruits in the eastern theater.[16] When they arrived at the rendezvous in San Antonio, these Texans brought their own horses, saddles, harnesses and tack, and weapons.[17] Some were experienced in frontier warfare, having joined local militia groups to defend their ranches and towns against Native and Mexican raiders; they brought this experience—and a prodigious self-regard—with them to the rendezvous camps. Ultimately, they were mustered into the Fourth, Fifth, and Seventh Texas Mounted Rifles: the Confederate Army of New Mexico, more commonly known as the Sibley Brigade.

And then they waited. And waited. Still focused on launching a traditional military campaign, Sibley insisted on building a wagon train that could sustain the Army on the road to El Paso. It took several months for the general to purchase and commandeer enough wagons (more than three hundred) to satisfy him as well as the mules and oxen (more than three thousand) to pull and carry the loads. In addition to this supply train the brigade brought along its own beef herd. The Confederates gathered nearly four thousand animals, all of which waited along with the men, becoming "weak and thin from lack of pasture" in the hinterlands of San Antonio.[18]

Finally, they were ready. On October 23, 1861, the first companies of Sibley's brigade marched out of San Antonio and onto the road heading west. But they did not move all at once. Sibley's experience in the Southwest had taught him that desert springs and water holes were small and thus slow to replenish. Water had to be rationed in order to sustain thousands of men and animals. Thus, the regiments departed at intervals; the Fourth Texas led the way, followed by the Fifth and then the Seventh.[19] This adaptive strategy was Sibley's best plan for the campaign, but his insistence on conventional logistics—a large wagon train and herd of cattle—hampered the Texans as they marched toward New Mexico.

The road itself exacerbated these problems. As a fixed route, the San Antonio—El Paso Road restricted access to water and grass, both of which were needed to sustain the animals. Cattle, for example, need to consume anywhere from three to thirty gallons of water and 2 percent of their weight in dry feed on a daily basis to remain healthy. The first stage of the march—from San Antonio to the Pecos River—moved through rolling hills covered by juniper and mesquite-oak savanna and cut through by a network of perennial streams. The cattle, mules, oxen, and horses were initially able to eat their fill but they quickly dispatched with roadside grasses. The soldiers could not afford to let them wander very far, however. From the moment they began their march to New Mexico, the brigade had fallen victim to Apache and Comanche attacks; raiders ambushed their flanks, often at night, stampeding horses, draft animals, and beef cattle and driving them through the desert to their own camps. Any hungry animals that strayed from the road were animals lost.[20] And when the brigade did come to water holes, the men drank first. At the twelve-foot-deep Howard Springs near Fort Lancaster, for example, soldiers had to bring water up to the surface in buckets. This was a labor-intensive operation, so only the men and their horses drank; the draft animals and beef cattle went without.[21]

As the brigade crossed the Pecos River the landscape became more mountainous and arid, its higher elevations covered in oak, juniper, and piñon pine. John Shropshire of Company A, Fifth Texas, noted that within a few days of the long march through this region, "our mules and oxen are broken down, having been 36 hours without water. Our horses are all in as good a condition as could be expected—all poor and some very poor." The animals, a vital part of Sibley's subsistence strategy in the New Mexico campaign, deteriorated quickly. "We dragged our slow way onward," wrote Private Henry Wright of the Fourth Texas, "handicapped by the weakness of the cattle that we depended on for food, and the want of grass for our horses and mules."²²

The men suffered along with the animals. Many of them grumbled about provisions—"a half-ration of blue beef and a piece of flour dough without shortening of any sort," according to Bill Davidson—and the weather. Because of their delayed departure, the Texans walked right into a series of blue northers: quickly moving autumnal cold fronts bringing freezing rain and snow, and in their wake, clear blue skies and frigid temperatures. Davidson noted that these storms were "beginning to tell heavily on our horses and teams, although the men had walked half the time in order to keep warm while facing these northers."²³ Because they hailed from southeastern Texas, most soldiers in the Sibley Brigade had rarely experienced such weather and had never seen such rough land. "I candidly confess," John Shropshire wrote to his wife, "I would never have come this way had I imagined the country was so mean."²⁴

As the Texans slogged along, they exemplified the Civil War as a revolution in motion. As historian Yael Sternhell has argued, Confederate soldiers on the way to Virginia from points south and west became a "visible manifestation of the Confederacy's emerging war effort."²⁵ The Sibley Brigade marched in the other direction, but they too were a mass of armed men moving together and with purpose, representing the new nation and its expansionist aspirations. After Sibley arrived in New Mexico in early January 1862, he lauded the Texans' "patience, fortitude, and good conduct" on the road, commending their ability to make a "successful and rapid march of seven hundred miles in mid-winter and through a country entirely devoid of resources... in spite of great deficiencies in their supplies." When reports of this long march filtered eastward, the New Orleans *Daily Picayune* asked, "Is this not enough in itself to make veterans of men?"²⁶

Although many soldiers were frustrated with the pace of the march—as one member of the Fourth Texas promised himself, "When I go to another war, I'm goin' to it a way I can get to it quicker than I can this 'ere one"—most were impressed with their accomplishment.²⁷ Their ability to move through hundreds of miles of desolate terrain made them proud, creating a sense of regimental pride and cohesion. Although they wanted to believe that their suffering had made them better soldiers, the Texans did not emerge from this march a stronger fighting machine. The long march had taken an enormous toll on men and animals. And they had found very little to sustain them when they arrived at Fort Bliss, near El Paso; men serving in the Second Texas Mounted Rifles under

John Baylor had consumed everything in the months before the Sibley Brigade's arrival. As Theophilus Noel of the Fourth Texas remembered, "Forage there was none; commissary supplies were getting scarce; the cold season was coming on; clothing was being needed; all of which the country afforded none."[28] As they moved northward from El Paso into New Mexico in January 1862, the Texans' depleted cache of supplies and their physical exhaustion shaped the campaign to follow. Four months later this disastrous combination created the conditions for the Sibley Brigade's defeat and their retreat back the way they had come.

In the mid-afternoon on March 28, 1862, a detachment of Colorado soldiers crept through the thick growth of cedar and piñon at the top of Glorieta Mesa northeast of Santa Fe. They could see the Texan supply train more than a thousand feet below, filled with provisions and ammunition and under heavy guard. Union major John Chivington gave the order and the men leapt up and "descend[ed] the mountain steep, which was exceedingly precipitous, and difficult to do." They overran the Texan guards, spiked their guns and burned their wagon train. The Coloradans then turned to the mules and the oxen, bayoneting them "so that the greatest possible damage might come to the enemy."[29] Confederate lieutenant colonel William R. Scurry, in command of the Sibley Brigade during the Battle of Glorieta Pass, had no alternative but to order a retreat back to Santa Fe. Over the next several days, the Texans "rode, some walked, and some hobbled in" to the territorial capital, the *Santa Fe Weekly Gazette* reported. It was but a small taste of what was to come.[30]

The Texans were especially vulnerable to this kind of attack at precisely that moment because in February Sibley had bypassed Fort Craig in order to fight Union soldiers on more favorable ground; in doing so he abandoned his plan of securing that fort's supplies. After their victory in the Battle of Valverde the Texans advanced, but as they did the Federals abandoned Albuquerque and Santa Fe, burning their own supplies. "If it could have been possible for us to have hindered this," wrote Theophilus Noel, "the Confederate Army of New Mexico would never have experienced any inconvenience for the want of clothing or commissaries."[31] After the destruction of their wagons at Glorieta, the Texans were in dire straits. Within the week Sibley chose to abandon Santa Fe—so long the centerpiece of the dream of southern empire—and retreat to Albuquerque.

The Texans soon vacated that town as well, and marched southward to Peralta in the first weeks of April. Along the way, men "clung to the wagons and sat on the tongues to get a little rest," Bill Davidson reported, and the column slowed, "owing to the condition of the animals and the deep heavy sand we had to go through, and the men having to force the wagons along [by pushing and pulling on the wheels]."[32] The men and the animals were all badly in need of food, which was not to be found. As Union governor Henry Connelly reported to U.S. Secretary of State William H. Seward on April 13, 1862, "The Territory has been completely exhausted of grain on the route of the military movements, and nothing can be obtained of forage for animals." Any remaining subsistence stores were cached at Forts Union and Craig or were, as Union soldier George Pettis reported, "in the hands of the people" and "all of it ... hidden away." New Mexican residents needed to feed their families, and they refused to sell anything to Sibley, especially since all he had to offer them was Confederate scrip.[33]

The Texans stayed only briefly at Peralta, seizing Governor Connelly's house and celebrating their conquest with a fandango. A Union cannonade the next day came to nothing and the Confederates took advantage of a howling dust storm to cover their retreat that night.[34] The next morning the Texans marched down the west bank of the Rio Grande while Union troops shadowed them on the river's eastern side.[35] It was a novel sight, Bill Davidson remembered. "Two hostile armies marching down a river valley in plain view of each other with only a narrow river between them. Marching together, halting together, one imitating every move of the other." Davidson was astonished. "What did they mean? Their movements puzzled us greatly."[36]

Some Union soldiers were equally mystified and many were angry. Ovando Hollister, who had made a forced march from Denver City to Fort Union with the First Colorado in order to meet the Texans at Glorieta a few weeks before, could not believe that his regiment had quickstepped "sixty miles per day to catch the traitors and then to let them go."[37] There was a good reason for this strategy, however. Even though his soldiers wanted a fight, Union general Edward Canby knew that supplies were dwindling and his men and their animals were exhausted. Therefore, as Union soldier George Pettis wrote, Canby "considered it more expedient to allow [the Texans] to retreat out of the territory and through the wilderness to San Antonio, Texas, than to capture the entire party and be forced to subsist them."[38]

And so the shadow march continued until another sandstorm stopped both armies in their tracks on April 17. As grains of sand pelted their tents, the officers of the Sibley Brigade weighed their options. They could continue southward along the river, and then loot and destroy Fort Craig; but it was clear to all that a considerable force of Union troops would be waiting for them, and that in its crippled condition the Sibley Brigade would not win any general engagements.[39] The other option was to take a route westward through the mountains, and strike the Rio Grande below Fort Craig, with no Union troops between them and the Confederate stronghold of Mesilla. Captain Bethel Coopwood—Paddy Graydon's counterpart in the Sibley Brigade, a scout and horse raider from El Paso—knew the country well and he would, as Sibley reported, undertake "the difficult and responsible task of guiding the army through this mountainous, trackless waste."[40]

The decision was made and the orders were given. After emptying the remaining wagons and strapping packs filled with rations and handfuls of ammunition to their ragged horses and mules, the Texans moved out of camp after nightfall. For the Union soldiers who woke up to find only thirty-eight smoldering wagons across the river from them, this action seemed to foretell the "complete annihilation" of the Sibley Brigade. For the Texans, this signaled the end of the brigade's dreams of military victory in the Southwest.[41]

It was not long before the Texans realized that taking the mountain route had been a mistake. They made a dry camp at around 2 A.M. on the 18th, and later that morning their need for water become acute. The men trudged along the heavy sand road to Rio Salado, abandoning wagons and animals along the way, and when they finally arrived in camp at 5 o'clock that evening—having traveled eight miles in ten hours, less than half their usual pace—Davidson and his men were "almost exhausted for water." But when they reached the banks of the Rio Salado, they understood how it had earned its name. "It was so salty we could hardly drink it," several privates bemoaned, "or the coffee made from it."[42] The Texans were desperate, however, and so they gulped it down. They collapsed on the riverbanks and, as Alfred Peticolas noted, "no order was observed, no company staid together, the wearied sank down upon the grass, regardless of the cold, to rest and sleep."[43]

Over the next several days, the Confederates destroyed or buried still more equipment so it would not fall into Union hands. When they moved back out on the path they had only a few wagons, one caisson, and the six pieces of artillery: the "Valverde Guns," which the brigade had captured in their first military victory of the campaign. The guns were the only tangible reminders of their success in the field, and dragging them up and down mountains took the work of the entire company.[44] On this particular route, which climbed in elevation through the Magdalene and San Mateo Mountains on a trail that sometimes disappeared, with more than twenty miles between water sources, such gratuitous physical exertions took an immense toll on both animals and men.[45] The most grueling section wound its way through the San Mateos, which boast high summits (its tallest peak stands at more than ten thousand feet) and deep, cliff-sided canyons, before finally descending into the Chihuahuan basin, one of the most arid landscapes in New Mexico. On April 22, as they entered the basin, the Texans had another long march to water—thirty miles—and by the end of the day, as several men reported, "the strongest rushed frantically forward . . . before being consumed by thirst, while many of the weak laid down to die."[46]

Those who could trudged on. "Just substitute mules for camels and a dreary, barren, desolate, mountainous, and 'trackless waste,' for the Great Desert of Africa, and you have it," wrote Theophilus Noel. "A caravan indeed; not of adventurous and money seeking individuals, but a caravan of care worn, disappointed, feet sore soldiers."[47] On April 25, the remnants of the Sibley Brigade finally reached the banks of the Rio Grande. At this point, the men remembered, they had "no enemy between us and home, and no more suffering for water." Somewhat refreshed, the Texans continued their march southward and camped below Las Cruces near an aqueduct. In a turnabout that struck Noel as particularly cruel given the brigade's suffering in the mountains, in the dead of night a "thieving or knavish individual" destroyed one of the aqueduct's ramparts and flooded the Confederates' camp.[48]

It is unclear how many Texans died along the mountain route, and in what manner. "We left San Antonio eight months earlier with near three thousand men finely dressed, splendidly mounted and elegantly equipped," wrote Bill Davidson. "[There is] a list of four hundred and thirty-seven dead, but where are the other sixteen hundred men?" Davidson found few definitive answers. "Some died upon the mountains' highest peaks, some went to sleep in the rugged canyon's lowest valleys and some upon the arid plain." Some succumbed to battle wounds, while others died of starvation or thirst. Suffering and dying of thirst is a "horror," as one medical journal put it in 1906. It comes on slowly in five phases, each corresponding to increasing amounts of water depletion. "Desert rats" in the Southwest had colorful yet physiologically accurate names for each phase: "Clamorous, Cotton-mouth, Shriveled Tongue, Blood Sweat, and Living Death." The first three phases were survivable but in the final two phases "there is no alleviation but the end." A person exerting himself could progress through these phases in seven hours; the loss of water and sodium through sweating causes blood volume loss and brain cell swelling. Sufferers who have reached the "Shriveled Tongue" stage begin to stumble as they walk, tortured by intense headaches, hallucinations, and seizures.[49] It was true, Davidson admitted, that he and his stronger comrades had abandoned those who were stumbling along or too weak to continue. But he urged his readers to "blame us not. We know not where they are.... We did all for them we could and they did all that lay in mortal power for us."[50]

The Sibley Brigade left bodies behind. They also left a desert road strewn with debris. When Paddy Graydon followed their path, he found the charred remains of wagons and caissons, feather beds, harnesses, iron ovens, "in fact everything but small ammunition."[51] The long trail of debris may have been a novel sight for both Confederate and Union soldiers, but it was not unusual in the desert Southwest. The ruins of Sibley's New Mexico campaign joined abandoned Native pueblos, Spanish missions, and New Mexican towns; destroyed copper and silver mines; and the wreckage of migrants' wagons as symbols of what historian Sam Truett has called the "fugitive landscape" of the Southwest. Over time, many communities had tried to control and transform this region, but it was a space "characterized by mobility and flexibility, that survived by eluding the scrutiny of empire and resisting incorporation."[52] The ruins of war on the mountain route told a familiar story of failure, of dreams of conquest dashed in the harsh land and climate of the southwestern desert.

The Sibley Brigade encamped around Mesilla for three weeks. The men rested, recovering from illnesses and regaining their strength. And their supplies dwindled further. The Confederate-leaning citizens of Mesilla, who had welcomed them with open arms four months earlier, were less enthusiastic to see them now. The ravenous soldiers and animals were like a swarm of locusts in their fields, Governor Connelly reported. "They have consumed and destroyed everything, even the growing crops." When Sibley received word that Union general James Carleton's California column was advancing across the Sonoran Desert in Arizona to reinforce Canby, Sibley decided that the brigade would have to continue their retreat and return to San Antonio.[53] The orders went out in early June, and the Confederates prepared for another weary march through the desert wastes of west Texas.

The Confederate dream of building an empire in the far West was obliterated on their retreat eastward on the San Antonio–El Paso Road. They had a few wagons and almost no animals left; they carried only a little flour and some "miserably poor beef" along with six sacks of coffee. And they began to march through one of the hottest regions in the United States in the middle of summer. The high temperatures in the Trans-Pecos region in July average between 95 and 100 degrees, and because of its clear skies, elevation (more than five thousand feet), and latitude, the area has the highest mean annual solar radiation of anywhere in the United States.[54] People walking on foot cannot endure such temperatures and radiation for very long. For physiological reasons that remain unclear, the human body in such an environment cannot survive even the smallest increases in temperature. A soldier of the Sibley Brigade, trudging along the San Antonio—El Paso Road in July 1862 would have grown hotter by 2 degrees per hour. And when his body temperature reached 105 degrees he would have experienced convulsions and lapsed into unconsciousness. For those in advanced stages of heatstroke, drinking water would not have helped. However, dehydration would have made things much worse, weakening a body that was already suffering.[55]

Sibley staggered his troops on the retreat, just as he had during the march westward—the Second Texas left Fort Bliss first, followed by the Fourth, Fifth, and a month later, the Seventh. However, the water holes seemed impossibly far apart, often more than thirty miles. When Theophilus Noel and the men of the Fourth Texas finally reached Eagle Springs after a long march across the desert highlands from Fort Quitman, they found the forty-foot-deep water hole, sixty feet in diameter with a "live subterranean stream of pure water flow[ing] through a cavernous rock." Unfortunately, they also found a pile of dead sheep and "the carcasses of some of the oxen of the detachment ahead of us," at the bottom, bathed in its waters. They had no water kegs, so they had to move on to Van Horn's Wells, which was similarly contaminated, with dirt and the bodies of sheep and wolves. Noel figured that it was Edward Canby who had ordered these acts of biological warfare (to use the modern term for it) and his chief scout, Kit Carson—"the terror of the plains"—who had helped to carry it out.[56]

It is unlikely, though, that Canby was engaged in such plotting from his headquarters in Santa Fe, and Carson was no longer focused on the Texans. Instead, he was preparing for the Union's military campaigns against Native tribes, which Lance Blyth describes in his chapter in this volume. It is more likely that Comanches or Apaches had fouled these water holes as part of their own war efforts. As noted earlier, they had raided the Sibley Brigade's wagon trains during their march into New Mexico, capturing and driving huge herds of horses and mules across the desert to their own camps. Now, the Texans were again vulnerable to attack (although lacking in animals to steal). Water sources are "convening" locations, exposed sites at which the region's Native Americans asserted control over desert resources, and thus their enemies too.[57]

The Sibley Brigade had no choice but to keep going.[58] They marched through the night, and when the sun came up the temperatures soared. "Tired and weary we limped along," Davidson wrote, "the road lined with broken down wagons and carcasses of dead horses, and oxen that had starved for water." Theophilus Noel believed that as a result, some of his comrades were "more crazed than rational, they looked like frantic mad men." One man shot a steer that had been abandoned by a company on the road ahead; he then cut the animal's throat with his pocketknife and "drank of the animals [sic] blood to quench [his] thirst." The Texans walked into huge dust plumes kicked up by winds blowing from the southwest, and buzzing clouds of gnats. There seemed no relief from the heat that, as Noel put it, "once felt, can never be forgotten, but which can never be described."[59]

Those winds were a good omen, however, for soon a massive summer thunderstorm rolled in. Davidson and his comrades fell to the ground on their backs, opening their mouths to catch the "water, good, pure, soft, sparkling water" that "poured down upon us," letting it "run down and cool their parched and burning throats."[60] This summer storm saved the strongest of the men and they pushed on. Those who reached the uncontaminated Dead Man's Hole sent word back "to the next and to the next" but for many soldiers—including one of Noel's friends whose corpse he had to load into a wagon the next day—such happy news no longer mattered.[61] The Texans who made it to Fort Davis found supplies of food, water, and wood. They stayed for two days and then moved on, with just enough energy to put one foot in front of the other and stagger into Fort Stockton, and then into Fort Lancaster on the Pecos, and then southeast toward San Antonio. In the end, around eighteen hundred of the twenty-seven hundred recruits who had rendezvoused in July 1861 made it back to Texas the next summer. They were furloughed for sixty days to "go home and remount and re-outfit themselves," to recuperate from injuries and illnesses, and the effects of starvation and dehydration. As they did so, the Texans thought back over their trials and tribulations in the desert.

One year before, New Mexico Territory had lain before them, the centerpiece of their dreams of Confederate expansion. Now, in their memory, it had become a hellish wilderness, a landscape of doom. Most did not want go back under any circumstances. Captain Jerome B. McCown of the Fifth Texas could not imagine returning, "throwing our lives away" in a "country which is not worth the life of one good man, of the many who have breathed their last on its arid sands." One Sibley Brigade member told the Houston *Tri-Weekly Telegraph,* "The Territory of New Mexico is utterly worthless. It will never be the abode of civilized man. The naturalist is the only character that could be benefited by traveling" in such a desolate wilderness.[62]

For his part, General Sibley insisted he had done all he could in such a hostile environment. He wrote his final campaign report before leaving Fort Bliss for San Antonio, acknowledging that the New Mexico Territory was still desirable from a "political geographical position." However, he believed that the dream of Confederate empire in the desert Southwest was not achievable through military means. "As a field of military operations," he wrote, "it possesses not a single element, except in the multiplicity of its defensible positions. The indispensable element, food, cannot be relied on." It was simply impossible for an army of any considerable size to provision itself while marching more than a hundred miles between military targets, through a landscape largely devoid of agricultural fields and water sources. The Confederate States of America could try to conquer the Southwest diplomatically, Sibley suggested. But even then "the Territory of New Mexico is not worth a quarter of the blood and treasure expended in its conquest."[63] The man who had so clearly articulated the central goals of Confederate Manifest Destiny in the summer of 1861 had abandoned them only a year later, after losing a third of his men "chasing a shadow" in the deserts of the Southwest.[64]

The Sibley Brigade's New Mexico campaign began and ended on long roads. The Confederates thought they would be fighting the Union troops for control of the West, but it was not the battles in this theater that shaped the campaign. It was the road itself, in its different forms—the San Antonio—El Paso Road, the *el camino real* along the Rio Grande, the narrow and barely trodden path of the mountain route—that made Confederate designs manifest, and that doomed them in the end. So it is on these roads that we can best understand the nature of the Confederate New Mexico campaign and its place in a long history of failure in this region. Here, more than in any other theater of the war, landscape and climate brought the inadequacies of conventional military strategies into sharp focus. Here, men had to adapt to the environment or die. In the desert Southwest, the long roads between towns, stage stations, water holes, and forts articulated the vast distance between Confederate dreams and reality.

NOTES

The author thanks Adam Arenson, Andy Graybill, and Jim Jewell for their incisive comments on earlier versions of this essay.

1. James Graydon to Col. Paul from Polvadera, May 14, 1862, in United States War Department, *The War of Rebellion: A Compilation of the Official Records of the Union and Confederate Armies* (Washington, DC: Government Printing Office, 1880–1901) [hereafter *OR*], I: 9, 671; R. S. C. Lord to Colonel Canby from Canad a la Mosa, December 25, 1861, in John P. Wilson, *When the Texans Came: Missing Records for the Civil War in the Southwest* (Albuquerque: University of New Mexico Press, 2001), 140; Jerry D. Thompson, *Desert Tiger: Captain Paddy Graydon and the Civil War in the Far Southwest* (El Paso: Texas Western Press, 1992); G. E. Griffith, J. M. Omernik, M. M. McGraw, G. Z. Jacobi, C. M. Canavan, T. S. Schrader, D. Mercer, R. Hill, and B. C. Moran, *Ecoregions of New Mexico* (color poster with map, descriptive text, summary tables, and photographs) (Reston, VA: U.S. Geological Survey, 2006).

2. Graydon to Paul, *OR* I: 9, 671; Three Privates, "Account of the Sibley Brigade" (1887–1888), in *Civil War in the Southwest: Recollections of the Sibley Brigade,* ed. Jerry Thompson (College Station: Texas A&M University Press, 2001), 124; Alfred Peticolas, as quoted in Donald S. Frazier, *Blood and Treasure: Confederate Empire in the Southwest* (College Station: Texas A&M Press, 1995), 252.

3. William Lott Davidson, "History of the Sibley Brigade," in *Civil War in the Southwest,* ed. Thompson, 9.

4. Frazier, *Blood and Treasure,* 6, 7.

5. George W. Kendall, *Narrative of the Texan Santa Fé Expedition: Comprising a Tour through Texas and Capture of the Texans* (Office of the Great Western Advertiser and Chronicle, 1846), 3.

6. Patricia Nelson Limerick, *Desert Passages: Encounters with the American Deserts* (Albuquerque: University of New Mexico Press, 1985), 29.

7. Samuel Truett, *Fugitive Landscapes: The Forgotten History of the U.S.–Mexico Borderlands* (New Haven: Yale University Press, 2006), 38–43.

8. Martin Hardwick Hall, *Sibley's New Mexico Campaign* (1960; Albuquerque: University of New Mexico Press, 2000), 8; Frazier, *Blood and Treasure,* 13, 36, 75; Truett, *Fugitive Landscapes,* 25.

9. William J. Cooper Jr., *Jefferson Davis, American* (New York: Vintage, 2001), 274–75; Jefferson Davis (1859), as quoted in Thomas L. Connelly, "The American Camel Experiment: A Reappraisal," *Southwestern Historical Quarterly* 69, no. 4 (April 1966): 444.

10. Cooper, *Jefferson Davis, American,* 277; Los Angeles [*Times*], November 23, 1857, as reprinted in *Portland Oregonian,* December 26, 1857, as quoted in Fred S. Perrine, "Uncle Sam's Camel Corps," *New Mexico Historical Review* no. 4 (October 1926): 442; Henry C. Wayne to Jefferson Davis, April 10, 1856, in Jefferson Davis, *Report of the Secretary of War [. . . regarding] The Purchase of Camels for the Purposes of Military Transportation* (Washington, DC: A. O. P. Nicholson, 1857), 54, front matter.

11. Frazier, *Blood and Treasure*, 4, 5.

12. Judah P. Benjamin to Jefferson Davis, December 14, 1861, *OR* IV: 1, 791; Hall, *Sibley's New Mexico Campaign*, 5–6; Proclamation of Brigadier General H. H. Sibley, Army of the Confederate States, to the people of New Mexico, December 20, 1861, *OR* I: 4, 90.

13. Hall, *Sibley's New Mexico Campaign*, 21–22; Thompson, Introduction to *Civil War in the Southwest*, xiv; Frazier, *Blood and Treasure*, 75; Trevanion T. Teel, "Sibley's New Mexican Campaign—Its Objects and the Causes of Its Failure," in Robert Underwood Johnson and Clarence Clough Buel, eds., *Battles and Leaders of the Civil War* Vol. 2 (1887), 700.

14. Adjutant and Inspector General S. Cooper to Brigadier General H. H. Sibley, July 8, 1861, *OR* I: 4, 93.

15. Hall, *Sibley's New Mexico Campaign*, 23.

16. Thompson, Introduction to *Civil War in the Southwest*, xxi–xxii; Frazier, *Blood and Treasure*, 85–86, 88–89; G. E. Griffith, S. A. Bryce, J. M. Omernik, J. A. Comstock, A. C. Rogers, B. Harrison, S. L. Hatch, and D. Bezanson, *Ecoregions of Texas* (color poster with map, descriptive text, and photographs) (Reston, Virginia, U.S. Geological Survey, 2004).

17. Frazier, *Blood and Treasure*, 30; Hall, *Sibley's New Mexico Campaign*, 27; Davidson, "History of the Sibley Brigade," 9.

18. Frazier, *Blood and Treasure*, 96, 118, 119.

19. Thompson, Introduction to *Civil War in the Southwest*, xv; Frazier, *Blood and Treasure*, 118; Hall, *Sibley's New Mexico Campaign*, 30; Davidson, "History of the Sibley Brigade," in *Civil War in the Southwest*, 11; Theophilus Noel, *A Campaign from Santa Fe to the Mississippi, Being a History of the Old Sibley Brigade* (Shreveport, LA: Shreveport News Printing Est., 1865), 10.

20. See Megan Kate Nelson, "Indians Make the Best Guerrillas: Native Americans in the War for the Far West," in *The Civil War Guerrilla: Unfolding the Black Flag in History, Memory, and Myth*, ed. Matthew C. Hulbert and Joseph Beilein, Jr. (Lexington: University of Kentucky Press, 2015).

21. Connelly, "The American Camel Experiment," 446; "Alberta Agriculture and Rural Development," agric.gov.ab.ca; Rick Rasby, "Daily Water Intake," UNL Beef, http://beef.unl.edu; Griffith et al., *Ecoregions of Texas*; Hall, *Sibley's New Mexico Campaign*, 34.

22. Griffith et al., *Ecoregions of Texas*; Frazier, *Blood and Treasure*, 125; Shropshire, as quoted in Frazier, *Blood and Treasure*, 125; Wright, as quoted in Frazier, *Blood and Treasure*, 121.

23. Davidson, "History of the Sibley Brigade," 10, 12–13; Roy R. Barkley, "Blue Norther," *Handbook of Texas Online*, Texas State Historical Association, www.tshaonline.org/handbook.

24. Shropshire and Smith, as quoted in Frazier, *Blood and Treasure*, 128.

25. Yael Sternhell, *Routes of War: The World of Movement in the Confederate South* (Cambridge, MA: Harvard University Press, 2012), 15.

26. As quoted in Hall, *Sibley's New Mexico Campaign*, 34; Henry H. Sibley, General Order No. 2, January 1862 and New Orleans *Daily Picayune*, March 27, 1862, as quoted in Hall, *Sibley's New Mexico Campaign*, 36.

27. San Antonio *Herald*, December 14, 1861, as quoted in Hall, *Sibley's New Mexico Campaign*, 34.

28. Noel, *A Campaign from Santa Fe to the Mississippi*, 12.

29. Chivington, "The Pet Lambs" (1890), Folder 65, Box 2, MSS 141, Colorado Volunteers: Civil War Collection, Stephen H. Hart Library, History Colorado Center, Denver.

30. *Santa Fe Weekly Gazette* (April 26, 1862), as quoted in Thompson, introduction to *Civil War in the Southwest*, xix.

31. Noel, *A Campaign from Santa Fe to the Mississippi*, 22.

32. Peticolas, as quoted in Frazier, *Blood and Treasure*, 238; Davidson, "History of the Sibley Brigade," 102–3.

33. Henry Connelly to W. H. Seward, April 13, 1862, *OR* I: 9, 663; George H. Pettis, "The Confederate Invasion of New Mexico and Arizona," in Johnson and Buel, eds., *Battles and Leaders of the Civil War*, vol. 2 (1887), 110.

34. Henry Connelly to William H. Seward, April 20, 1862, *OR* I: 9, 665; Hall, *Sibley's New Mexico Campaign*, 130; Davidson, "History of the Sibley Brigade," 105; Frazier, *Blood and Treasure*, 247.

35. Hollister, as quoted in Flint Whitlock, *Distant Bugles, Distant Drums: The Union Response to the Confederate Invasion of New Mexico* (Boulder: University Press of Colorado, 2006), 232; Hall, *Sibley's New Mexico Campaign*, 130; Noel, *A Campaign from Santa Fe to the Mississippi*, 27.

36. Davidson, "History of the Sibley Brigade," 119; Noel, *A Campaign from Santa Fe to the Mississippi*, 27.

37. Hollister, as quoted in Hall, *Sibley's New Mexico Campaign*, 132.

38. Hall, *Sibley's New Mexico Campaign*, 131; B. S. Roberts to Brigadier General Lorenzo Thomas, April 23, 1862, *OR* I: 9, 666; Pettis, "The Confederate Invasion," 110.

39. Davidson, "History of the Sibley Brigade," 120.

40. Henry H. Sibley, Report from Fort Bliss, May 4, 1862, *OR* I: 9, 510–11; Davidson, "History of the Sibley Brigade," 120.

41. Henry H. Sibley, Report from Fort Bliss, May 4, 1862, *OR* I: 9, 511; Thompson, Introduction to *Civil War in the Southwest*, xx; B. S. Roberts to Lorenzo Thomas, April 23, 1862, *OR* I: 9, 666; Davidson, "History of the Sibley Brigade," 118.

42. "Three Privates," "Account of the Sibley Brigade," in *Civil War in the Southwest*, ed. Thompson, 122–23.

43. Peticolas, as quoted in Frazier, *Blood and Treasure*, 252.

44. Hall, *Sibley's New Mexico Campaign*, 137; Peticolas, quoted in Whitlock, *Distant Bugles, Distant Drums*, 234.

45. Norman R. Malm, "Climate Guide, Las Cruces, 1892–2000" (Las Cruces, 2003) [Table 1], 4.

46. Hall, *Sibley's New Mexico Campaign*, 137; Three Privates," "Account of the Sibley Brigade," 124; Griffith et al., *Ecoregions of New Mexico*.

47. Noel, *A Campaign from Santa Fe to the Mississippi*, 28.

48. Ibid., 32.

49. W. J. McGee, "[The Phenomena of Desert Thirst]" (1906), as synopsized in "Desert Thirst as a Disease," *American Medicine* 12 (May 1906): 51–52; Peter Stark, *Last Breath: The Limits of Adventure* (New York, 2001), 254–56, 259, 267, 274, 283; Megan Kate Nelson, "Dying in the Desert," *Civil War Monitor* 2, no. 1 (Spring 2012): 48–53, 71–73.

50. Davidson, "History of the Sibley Brigade," 129, 130.

51. Graydon to Paul, May 14, 1862, *OR* I: 9, 671–72.

52. Truett, *Fugitive Landscapes*, 15.

53. Henry Connelly to General Edward R.S. Canby from Santa Fe, June 15, 1862, in Wilson, *When the Texans Came*, 285–86; Hall, *Sibley's New Mexico Campaign*, 146; Thompson, Introduction to *Civil War in the Southwest*, xx-xxi; Henry H. Sibley Report from Fort Bliss, May 4, 1862, *OR* I: 9, 511–12.

54. Robert H. Schmidt, "Trans-Pecos," *Handbook of Texas Online* (Texas State Historical Association), www.tshaonline.org; "Monthly Weather Data for Fort Davis, TX [Texas]," July 1902–2012, weather-warehouse.com.

55. Stark, *Last Breath*, 139–47; Nelson, "Dying in the Desert."

56. Theophilus Noel, *Autobiography and Reminiscences of Theophilus Noel* (Chicago: Theo. Noel Co., 1904), 64–65; Noel, *A Campaign from Santa Fe to the Mississippi*, 35.

57. On Native American raiding during the Civil War, see Brian DeLay, *War of a Thousand Deserts: Indian Raids and the U.S.– Mexican War* (New Haven: Yale University Press, 2008); Pekka Hämäläinen, *The Comanche Empire* (New Haven: Yale University Press, 2008); Nelson, "Indians Make the Best Guerrillas."

58. Hall, *Sibley's New Mexico Campaign*, 147; Davidson, "History of the Sibley Brigade," 127.

59. Davidson, "History of the Sibley Brigade," 127; Hall, *Sibley's New Mexico Campaign*, 147; Noel, *A Campaign from Santa Fe to the Mississippi*, 35; Noel, *Autobiography*, 65.

60. Davidson, "History of the Sibley Brigade," 127–28.

61. Noel, *Autobiography*, 65–66.

62. Bellville, *Countryman*, June 7, 1862, and Houston *Tri-Weekly Telegraph*, May 28, 1862, as quoted in Hall, *Sibley's New Mexico Campaign*, 145, 149.

63. Sibley Report to Davis from Fort Bliss, May 4, 1862, *OR* I: 9, 511–12.

64. *Austin (Tex.) State Gazette*, June 7, 1862, as quoted in Hall, *Sibley's New Mexico Campaign*, 150.

THREE

Kit Carson and the War for the Southwest

SEPARATION AND SURVIVAL ALONG THE RIO
GRANDE, 1862–1868

Lance R. Blyth
U.S. Northern Command

AS THE REMNANTS OF THE SIBLEY BRIGADE trickled southward, Christopher "Kit" Carson's Civil War was over. In June 1861, Carson had resigned his Ute Indian agency post to answer the call for volunteers. Appointed first as a lieutenant colonel, and then a colonel, Carson had raised the First Regiment New Mexico Volunteers among the plazas of northern New Mexico and trained his Hispano soldiers at Fort Union and Albuquerque. Dispatched south to Fort Craig along the Rio Grande in January 1862, Carson led his regiment at the Battle of Valverde on February 20–21, performing well enough to be mentioned in dispatches. Carson took command of Fort Craig when Brigadier General Edward R. S. Canby led the bulk of the Union forces to harry the Texans out of New Mexico on April 1. Canby returned three weeks later, relieved Carson, and ordered him to Albuquerque. There, in early May 1862, Carson learned that his services would still be needed because—though the Civil War in the Southwest was over—the War for the Southwest continued.[1]

The upper Rio Grande Valley was a borderland of conflict in 1862, its combatants more peoples than armies. Along the river, its tributaries, and westward across the Colorado Plateau lived the Southwest's oldest inhabitants, the Pueblo Indians, who inhabited more than twenty pueblos, "compact permanent settlements" in the archaeological definition. Despite having some twelve linguistic divisions and cleaved internally by political, religious, and social factionalism, the Pueblos did share much in common, practicing intensive agriculture, creating distinctive crafts, and maintaining a comprehensive ceremonial system and worldview. Hispanos, descendants of the territory's original Spanish settlers, inhabited villages and a few towns

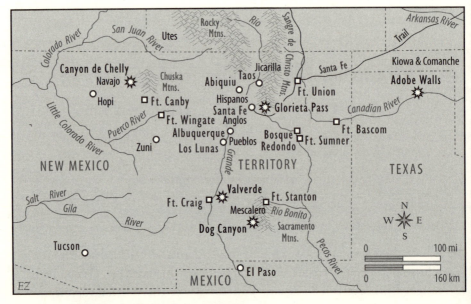

MAP 3.1. The War for the Southwest, 1862–68.

alongside the Pueblos for more than two centuries. Hispanos were nearly uniformly Catholic and Spanish speaking, but socially divided into a handful of *ricos* (wealthy), who made their fortunes in trade and sheep ranching, and the great mass of *pobres* (poor), who scraped out a living as farmers, servants, woodcutters, sheepherders, and day laborers, many in debt peonage. Anglos, white Americans of non-Hispano descent, were recent newcomers and a stark minority in the Southwest. Most were merchants, lawyers, or governmental officials, like Carson, living mainly in the capital of Santa Fe and in the region's largest town, Albuquerque. Not surprisingly, because acquiring the territory at the end of the War with Mexico, the U.S. federal government in the Southwest mostly served the needs of these Anglos, as they sought wealth and the conditions necessary to secure it.[2]

In northern New Mexico, Jicarillas (or *Tinde*) inhabited lands between Pueblo and Hispano villages. The Ollero (potter) band, lived around Taos and on the west bank of the Rio Grande, while the Llaneros (plainsmen) lived in the Sangre de Cristo Mountains in north-central New Mexico, especially the eastern slopes. The Utes (or *Núu-ci*) were far-raiding middlemen between New Mexico and the Great Basin Indians, who sought to secure their trade position in the Rocky Mountains and were thus willing to serve as allies for Hispanos and then Anglos. To the east, on the high southern plains, were the Kiowas (or *Ka'igwu*) and their *Nʉmʉnʉʉ* (or Comanche) allies. Kiowas and Comanches had long conducted far-reaching raids into Mexico and controlled the long-distance trade across the Great Plains. By 1860, however, they were "in desperate straits," as a fifteen-year drought had caused the bison herds to "evaporate" and Anglo migration and expansion turned the northern and southern ends of their territory into "wastelands."[3]

To the east and south of the Rio Grande were the "Mescal People," or *Ndé*. Mescaleros lived in bands under a leader (*nant'á*) and sought subsistence via mobility to roam a large region, using all available resources without any competition, while maintaining the flexibility to hunt large game animals; collect wild foods, particularly their namesake mescal agave plant; negotiate for exchanges with neighbors; or raid for livestock, goods, and captives. Finally, to the west were the Navajos (or *Diné*) inhabiting the *Diné Bekéyah* (Navajo Country), a region centered on Canyon de Chelly, striving to survive on sheep pastoralism. Pastoralism divided Navajo society into those who were wealthy in sheep, called *ricos* (rich) by outsiders though never by the *Diné* themselves, and those who were not. At least two-thirds of Navajos did not have large enough flocks—at least two hundred sheep—to ensure material and social survival.[4]

Pueblos, Hispanos, Jicarillas, Utes, Mescaleros, Navajos, Kiowas, and Comanches were all deeply enmeshed in what historian James Brooks has called a "borderlands political economy," organized around the reciprocal taking and exchanging of captives and livestock, via violent raids and reprisals, and less so by trade. Men of all these peoples recognized that, although livestock—sheep, cattle, horses—provided prestige and power, it was the women and children who were the most important commodity in this economy. Though the capture of livestock, women, and children led to violent retaliation, it also created and ensured exchanges among all sides. Raids and reprisals further redistributed resources from the wealthy to the poor of all societies involved. No government up to this time in the Southwest—whether Spanish imperial, Mexican national, or American territorial—had possessed enough power to control the borderlands political economy.[5]

For example, in May 1862, Kiowas and Comanches were busily raiding cattle and horses from rebel Texas, taking tens of thousands of animals each year. Texan cattleman Charles Goodnight estimated Kiowas and Comanches brought at least 300,000 head of cattle and 100,000 horses out of Texas in the years between 1860 and 1867. Kiowa and Comanche herds burgeoned with stolen livestock, such that each lodge had a string of ten, twenty, or even thirty horses. Texan cattle and horses, replacing the shrinking bison herds, provided subsistence and hides for Kiowas and Comanches. Yet livestock, especially cattle, and Indian and Mexican captives, also provided a "product" for the borderland political economy.[6]

The consumers of these "products" were Hispano and Pueblo traders, called *comancheros* by Anglos. These traders annually followed well-worn paths onto the high plains with convoys of squealing two-wheeled *carretas* in order to meet the Plains Indians at traditional trading sites. There they exchanged foodstuffs (salt, corn, flour, sugar, tobacco) and manufactured goods (knives, hatchets, blankets, occasionally firearms and ammunition) for livestock and captives. By the 1860s, with demand for beef booming in territorial New Mexico to feed the military mobilization, Anglo merchants and officials worked with *comanchero* parties to provide the goods for trade. Pueblos and Hispanos also carried out raids and reprisals, taking Indian women, children, horses, cattle, and especially sheep in self-organized mounted militia units, called *nacajelleses* by victimized Navajos (from the Navajo word for Mexican, *nakai*). *Nacajelleses* added the stolen sheep to their own herds or sold them back to their owners. Young Indian women and children were also either added to the households of the *nacajelleses* as servants or sold to serve as dowries for *rico* Hispano brides. The scale of this borderland trade was significant: in 1860 alone *nacajelleses* stole nearly fifty thousand head of sheep from Navajos and seized more than a hundred Navajos as captives before running off another eight thousand sheep in the next year.[7]

Navajos were also bound to the logic of the borderland political economy, regularly raiding into New Mexico for Hispano and Pueblo livestock and captives in reprisal or to answer their own needs. These raiding parties were often made up of poorer Navajos, called *ladrones* (thieves) by Hispanos, banded together under a war leader, who knew one of the ritual "ways" of going on a raid (Blessing Way, Bear Way, Big Snake Way, Turtle Way, Frog Way). The war leader received a larger share of anything taken on the raid, while the *ladrones* typically distributed their booty to family and friends. Many of the sheep and most of the captives taken from New Mexico ended up being added to the herds and households of Navajo *ricos,* increasing their wealth, status, and responsibility in society. *Ladrones* proved to be prodigious raiders, taking at least twenty-five thousand sheep and eight captives from New Mexico in 1860, another fifty thousand sheep in 1861, and thirty thousand in 1862.[8]

Meanwhile, in the southeastern reaches of the Rio Grande Valley, Mescaleros reentered the borderland political economy. In the six years prior to 1861, many Mescaleros settled near Fort Stanton, below Sierra Blanca Peak, keeping a tentative peace with the Anglos. But when Anglo troops abandoned the post as the Texans occupied El Paso and southern New Mexico in August 1861, Mescaleros resumed raiding for supplies and reprisal. They attacked wagon trains and stagecoaches along the El Paso—San Antonio Road and on September 1 killed three Texans scouting from Fort Stanton before wiping out a party of fifteen Texans who attacked one of their settlements. They also drove off those Hispanos who had settled along the Río Bonito to the immediate east of Fort Stanton. With the Texan retreat, Mescaleros widened their attacks to Hispano settlements along the Pecos River to the north, and took horses, mules, donkeys, cattle, and large numbers of sheep while killing some forty men and six children during the spring and summer of 1862.⁹

Of all the combatants in the War for the Southwest, as a group only Anglos were not full participants in the borderlands political economy, except as individuals around the edges. As governmental officials, military officers, and merchants, Anglos overwhelmingly abhorred the violence and insecurity the cycle of reciprocal raid and reprisal brought to the Southwest. Anglos diagnosed the problem as resulting from the close proximity between Indians and the settled peoples of the Rio Grande Valley, particularly the Hispanos. Even as he awaited the imminent Texan invasion in November 1861, Canby stated that the difficulties with Indians "if they have not been caused by, have at least been greatly aggravated by, the unauthorized and illegal actions of a portion of the Mexican [Hispano] population," *nacajelleses* in other words. Carson certainly agreed with this assessment. A few years later, he attributed Indian hostility to "acts of aggression on the part of the numerous reckless frontiersmen that swarm upon the borders of Indian territory."¹⁰

By 1861, Anglos determined to end the borderland economy by separating Hispanos from Indians, placing the latter onto reservations: one for Utes in the northwestern part of the territory, one for Apaches in the southeastern, and one for Navajos in the west. But as the New Mexico superintendent of Indian affairs J. L. Collins noted in 1862, "No civil authority can be exercised over these hostile tribes and bands until they are thoroughly convinced of the power of the government to enforce its will among them." Thus, Anglos needed forces to carry the war to the Indians, necessitating a field commander and a field force. Carson provided the former and the territory's Hispano inhabitants the latter.[11]

Once Anglo officials were certain the environment had turned the ninety-day Texan invasion into a debacle, as discussed by Megan Kate Nelson in her chapter, they determined they did not need all the volunteer regiments raised for the territory's defense. But they would put these Civil War soldiers to use. Carson received Department Orders No. 44, dated May 11, 1862, directing the reorganization of his regiment. Orders transferred companies of selected men and officers from the First, Second, Fourth, and Fifth Regiments, along with Paddy Graydon's Spy Company to the First Regiment. The resulting First New Mexico Cavalry was thus a combined Anglo-Hispano outfit. Carson's lieutenant colonel was a Hispano, José Francisco Chavez. The two majors, surgeon, and assistant surgeon were all Anglos, as were the adjutant and quartermaster. The chaplain, Father Damaso Taladrid, was a native of Madrid, Spain, who had come to New Mexico in 1854. Of the original twenty-nine company officers, ten were Hispanos, as were four of the ten company commanders. Hispanos also made up the bulk of the enlisted troopers, so that one or more officers in each company, and at least four of the thirteen authorized company noncommissioned officers, had to speak both English and Spanish. Carson's regiment was to serve in Indian country to suppress "bandits and marauders" and restore and preserve order.[12]

The initial plan was for Carson to take the bulk of his new regiment on campaign against the Navajos in the fall of 1862, while Lieutenant Colonel Chavez conducted a holding action in Mescalero Apache country with the rest. However, a change of command overtook these lines of operation. In mid-September General Canby turned command of the Department of New Mexico over to James H. Carleton, who had just arrived at the head of the California Column. Initially called to combat the Texans, Carleton remained concerned to defend against another Texan invasion, which was rumored almost every day. This required building up supplies and maintaining troops in the southern reaches of the territory, where they would be vulnerable to Mescalero raids. Indeed, on the day Carleton started for Santa Fe to take up his new command, Mescaleros clashed with a party of California cavalry scouting an abandoned post southeast of El Paso.[13]

Carleton thus ordered Carson to reoccupy Fort Stanton on September 27, 1862. Mescalero leaders learned of the returning troops and offered to talk peace, but Carson's instructions gave him no authority to make treaties in the field. If Mescaleros wanted peace, "their chiefs and 20 of their principal men

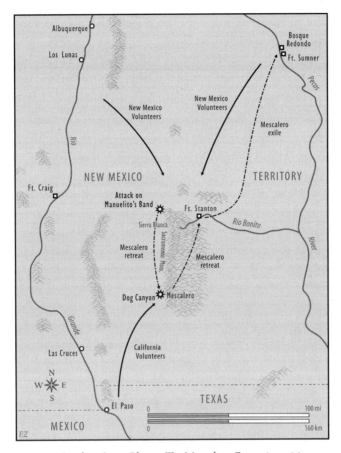

MAP 3.2. South to Sierra Blanca: The Mescalero Campaign, 1862.

must come to Santa Fe to talk here"; otherwise Carson was to "make war upon the Mescaleros... until further orders." Led by Paddy Graydon's spy company, recast as Company "H," the New Mexico Volunteers attacked the bands of Manuelito and José Largo as they attempted to parley at a spring north of Sierra Blanca, killing both leaders along with nine men and a woman. The Hispano troopers took seventeen horses and mules, though Carleton would later order them returned to the survivors of Manuelito's band.[14]

The remaining Mescaleros withdrew to the south, away from Carson's advancing troops. Bands led by Cadete, Chaco, and Estella, along with several others, totaling some five hundred individuals, gathered in Dog Canyon to take revenge for Manuelito's killing. But California volunteer troops ordered up from the El Paso area surprised the gathered Mescaleros and scattered them. The leaders headed for Fort Stanton, now reoccupied by Carson, to sue for peace. Carson sent Cadete, Chaco, Estella, and two other leaders to Santa Fe to talk with Carleton in November. Carleton informed them that those Mescaleros who wished for peace would have to go to the new Fort Sumner at Bosque Redondo on the Pecos River to await the end of Carson's campaign against their brethren. Cadete, called Gian-na-tah (Always Ready) by Mescaleros, accepted Carleton's demand. By March 1863 more than four hundred Mescaleros were at Bosque Redondo, but Carleton changed his mind. Mescaleros would not be allowed to return to Sierra Blanca, but were to remain at Bosque Redondo and become "a pueblo," living in houses, practicing irrigated agriculture, and thus be divorced from the borderland political economy. With this, Carleton declared the Mescaleros "subdued" and determined to "send the whole of Colonel Carson's regiment against the Navajos."[15]

Navajos heard of the Mescalero campaign, and a delegation of eighteen headmen led by Barboncito and Delgadito approached the Anglos at the end of 1862. Carleton told them that if they wished for peace then they should be peaceful, by an Anglo definition. This would prove difficult, as Navajos remained deeply enmeshed in reciprocal retaliatory exchanges. In the last days of February 1863 alone, Navajo *ladrones* took more than ten thousand sheep and three hundred horses and cattle from the Rio Grande Valley. Thus Delgadito and Barboncito made their way to Santa Fe again in April 1863. This time Carleton informed them that any Navajos who wished for peace would have to surrender unconditionally and accept confinement on a reservation. But, for reasons still unclear, Carleton abandoned the plan to place a Navajo reservation in the western part of the territory and instead insisted that all Navajos would have to relocate to Bosque Redondo in the east. Possibly, he thought there was gold in Navajo country. Perhaps he felt that colonization was the best means for separation, as did so many others, as discussed in chapter 5 by Nicholas Guyatt. Or he may have simply wanted to secure the Pecos River corridor against another Texan invasion by placing several thousand Navajos across their route. Whatever Carleton intended, he told Delgadito and Barboncito that any Navajos who wished for peace would have to surrender by July 20 or face the upcoming campaign.[16]

While on home leave in Taos in April 1863, Carson received orders to recruit Ute Indians to serve as "spies and guides" for this campaign against the Navajos. Ten Utes answered Carson's call, but at least four war parties, including one led by Ka-ni-ache, set off on their own for Navajo lands.

Accompanied by his Ute scouts, Carson rendezvoused with his regiment at Los Pinos, sixteen miles south of Albuquerque, where he received his orders, dated June 15, 1863, for the Navajo campaign. Carson was to establish a post with nine companies near Pueblo, Colorado (present-day Ganado, Arizona), on the west slope of the Chuskas, to be called Fort Canby. Lieutenant Colonel Chavez would command four companies at Fort Wingate (east of present-day Gallup, New Mexico) to keep the supply lines open and pressure Navajos from the south. Again, no peace would be granted while on campaign; that could only come from headquarters in Santa Fe.

Carson left the Rio Grande Valley on July 7 for the Pueblo Colorado River. Ka-ni-ache's Ute raiding party joined Carson two weeks into his march, reporting one Ute party was returning to their lands with Navajo captives to sell and at least two other parties were still at large. Carson took on Ka-ni-ache and five of his men as additional scouts. Carson also requested that the Utes be allowed to keep the Navajo captives they took, something Carleton denied, insisting that all Navajos had to go to Bosque Redondo. Failing to find a suitable site on the Pueblo Colorado for his campaign's depot, Carson reoccupied an abandoned fort and renamed it Fort Canby, at the site of present-day Window Rock, Arizona. From there Carson set out on August 5 for Hopi country. After a quarrel over livestock, the Ute scouts departed Carson's campaign. Carson led a second patrol, or "scout" in the parlance of the day, accompanied by more than twenty Zuñi Indians, to search the land between the Pueblo Colorado and the Little Colorado rivers in what is now northeastern Arizona on September 7. Carson's approach march and two scouts yielded very little, encountering only a few Navajo outfits, killing or capturing barely twenty, and taking little livestock. He had mainly worn out his men and, more important, their horses. Coercing the Navajos to surrender would have to be done by others, particularly the Utes.[17]

Although Utes had quit Carson's campaign, they had not quit raiding into Navajo country. Navajo memories of the time are replete with stories of *Nóóda'í* (Ute) depredations. Anglo Indian agents reported that Utes took many captives and much livestock. Hispano *nacajalleses,* often from the frontier village of Cebolleta, also continued to attack the Navajo in parties as few as three or as many as one hundred, killing, capturing children, and taking livestock. Pueblo Indians pursued Navajo raiders, too, and also carried out campaigns into Navajo country on their own. At the time, Carleton found "the alacrity with which the citizens of New Mexico have taken the field to pursue and encounter the Indians is worthy of all praise."[18]

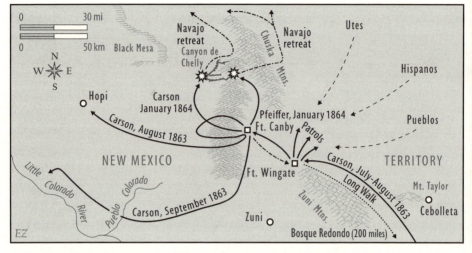

MAP 3.3. West to Canyon de Chelly: The Navajo Campaign, 1863–164.

With Utes raiding from the north, Hispanos and Pueblos attacking from the east, and Carson's troops maneuvering in the south and west, Navajos found themselves beset on all sides and facing a choice: flee or surrender. In mid-October, Sordo, the brother of headmen Delgadito and Barboncito and claiming to represent some five hundred Navajos, approached Fort Wingate to ask for peace and permission to settle a few miles southwest of the fort. He was informed that peace would be granted, but only at Bosque Redondo. Several weeks later Delgadito, accompanied by nearly two hundred Navajos, chose to surrender and accept exile to the east. Then Delgadito, along with three other Navajos and a Hispano interpreter, were sent back to Navajo country to induce others to surrender.[19]

This left several thousand *Diné* still at large, however, and needing to flee, but flee to where? Several of the big outfits, *ricos,* escaped to the north, west, and south as they had the manpower to fend off slavers and possessed large enough flocks to absorb losses from livestock raiders. Smaller outfits were vulnerable to attacks as they could not protect themselves and the loss of even a few sheep could threaten their survival. Many of these therefore abandoned their fields and pastures to band together in *Tséyi'* (Canyon de Chelly), with a few *ricos,* for protection. From there they struck back, raiding to replace lost livestock and labor. In mid-November, mid-December, and early January, Navajo raiding parties set out for the concentration of both at Bosque Redondo and in Northern New Mexico. Though the first two had some success, the last expedition ended in failure and the survivors limped back toward Canyon de Chelly, empty handed and unaware that Carson was heading the same way.[20]

The last months of 1863 saw Carson's dispatch riders killed, supply trains attacked, and critical pack mules driven off by Navajos, while heavy snowfall hampered his few patrols. Furthermore, Carson had no desire to endure the rigors of a winter campaign nor to inflict them on his men and animals. Yet Carleton extended the campaign through the winter months, denied Carson's request for home leave, and ordered him to Canyon de Chelly. The harsh environment of the Southwest would once again play a military role. When Carson set out on January 6, 1864, through a heavy snow that froze his men's feet, they discovered several frozen Navajo corpses.[21]

Upon reaching the western entrance to Canyon de Chelly on January 12, Carson divided his command into two columns: one to scour the northern branch and one to search the southern or main canyon. A third column, under Captain Albert Pfeiffer, had departed Fort Canby four days ahead of Carson and entered the canyon from the eastern entrance. The southern and eastern columns met on January 15, and a day later sixty Navajos surrendered and expressed a willingness to go to Bosque Redondo. When the northern column returned, Carson quickly set out for Fort Canby, having accepted the surrender of two hundred Navajos. But the surrenders were just beginning. Driven by an extended drought, extreme winter weather, the destruction of their crops, the loss of their flocks, and ongoing Ute, Pueblo, and Hispano raids, large numbers of Navajos made the decision to give up. Soldado Surdo and Herrera Grande brought their bands in and, by the end of February 1864, more than fifteen hundred Navajos were at Fort Canby. At the same time, to the east, Delgadito had gone among those bands that chose to hunker down along the slopes of the Chuskas, convincing some twelve hundred to surrender at Fort Wingate.[22]

So as not to interfere with the surrendering Navajos, Captain Asa B. Carey, commanding the campaign with Carson's departure for home leave at the end of January, ordered an end to all offensive actions. However, although the New Mexico Volunteers paused their campaign against the Navajos, Ute raiders, Pueblo warriors, and Hispano *nacajalleses* did not. So dire did the problem become that the territorial governor issued a proclamation in May 1864 prohibiting, "under the severest penalties," any "forays by our citizens of a hostile character" into Navajo lands. But the citizens of New Mexico did not have to range far to engage the Navajos. As convoys of Navajo prisoners crossed the Rio Grande Valley on their way to Bosque Redondo, Hispanos and probably Pueblos ran off livestock and took Navajo children in retaliation. The surrendering Navajos made their long walk over the 300 miles to Bosque Redondo in six main convoys between February and November 1864. Officers reported sending some ten thousand Navajos to the bosque during that time from Forts Canby and Wingate and other points, but reported only some eight thousand as arriving. Nearly two hundred Navajos escaped, another three hundred died along the way, and three Navajo children were stolen. Anglos could not account for another two thousand Navajos; whether escaped, dead, or enslaved is unknown.[23]

By the summer of 1864 Carleton determined to bring the campaign against the Navajo to a close. Driving his decision were the expiring Civil War enlistments of his New Mexican volunteers. But for Anglos, the campaign had been a success, the objective met, as Navajos were separated from the peoples of the Rio Grande Valley, with many—possibly most—now confined on a reservation. While many Navajo *rico* outfits were still free, they were hunted by Anglos, Hispanos, Utes, and Pueblos. The group imprisoned at Bosque Redondo found themselves strangers in a strange landscape, vulnerable to plains raiders and facing the challenge of simply surviving. Ironically, the campaign was the last florescence of the borderland political economy, as Utes, Pueblos, and Hispanos took a rich haul of Navajo captives and sheep on the margins of the U.S. troop action.

By the fall of 1864, the Bosque Redondo reservation was a disaster, as more Navajos had surrendered than Carleton thought existed. Worms destroyed the Navajo corn crop that Carleton counted upon to feed them. Late hail storms and an early freeze wiped out the harvest of Hispano farmers with which Carleton planned to replace the failed Navajo harvest. Navajos and Mescaleros thus relied upon supplies coming into the territory down the Santa Fe Trail. But, Carleton later admitted, "We have been greatly embarrassed in getting their supplies from the States because the Kiowas and Comanches had attacked our trains." The return of the rains in the mid-1860s emboldened Kiowas and Comanches to assault the vulnerable, livestock-rich convoys making their way down the Santa Fe Trail into New Mexico.[24]

Anglos initially responded by reinforcing the trail, but did not possess enough troops to guard it at all points. Too weak to stay on the defense, Carleton opted for an offensive thrust and therefore planned another campaign for Carson to drive the Kiowas and Comanches from New Mexico. Civil War enlistments had expired but many Utes, including Ka-ni-ache,

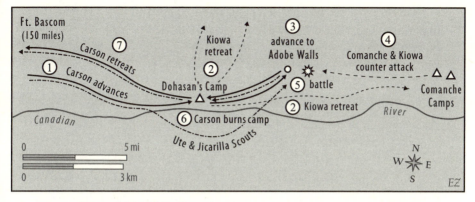

MAP 3.4. East to Adobe Walls, November 1864.

were willing to "go out onto the plains and attack the Kiowas," according to Carson, provided they be furnished with rations and ammunition and be allowed to keep whatever stock "or other property" they captured. So a plan formed, as summer turned to fall, for the remaining Hispano and Anglo volunteers to take the field, joined by Utes. A number of Jicarilla Apaches, who shared an agency with Utes, also agreed to go.[25]

On November 12, 1864, Carson led a force of Anglo and Hispano troopers, two mountain howitzers, and Ute and Jicarilla scouts out of Fort Bascom on the Canadian River in the eastern part of the territory. Carson headed for Adobe Walls (which he knew as Adobe Fort), an abandoned trading post located in the Texas Panhandle, to erect a depot. He had orders to search out and attack the Kiowas and Comanches in their vulnerable winter camps, kill only the men, while avoiding willfully and wantonly killing women and children. Twelve days later, at sundown, his scouts discovered the trail of a large Indian encampment. Carson immediately moved his force through the night, waited several freezing hours until dawn, and surprised the Kiowa camp led by Dohasan (Little Mountain). Carson's troopers pursued the fleeing Kiowas to the Adobe Walls where they encountered a large force of Kiowas and Comanches streaming up from downriver camps. Carson's men dismounted and held off the Kiowas and Comanches thanks to their artillery and the timely return of their Ute and Jicarilla scouts, who had been helping themselves to Kiowa horses. After several hours of fierce combat, Carson fell back, burned what he could of Dohasan's camp, and retreated to Fort Bascom, arriving on December 20. A few days after Christmas 1864, Carson received the order ending his campaign and sending him home to Taos. Elated at first to have survived yet another scrape, Carson claimed to have "taught the Indians a lesson." But as he lay dying in May 1868, recounting his exploits in the West, Carson admitted that, in this last campaign, the Kiowas and Comanches had "whipped him," an assessment that Ka-ni-ache would have shared.[26]

After the battle at Glorieta Pass, after Carson's death, after Appomattox, the separation of peoples in the Southwest went on. Indeed, the question after 1868 was not whether Indians would be separated onto reservations, as it was in 1862, but rather when would they go and where would their reservation be? Neither Mescaleros nor Navajos, however, would be at Bosque Redondo, where Carson had sent them. Mescaleros abandoned the reservation en masse during the night of November 3, 1865, and not until 1871 did they accept a peace allowing them to stay in the Sierra Blanca. Navajos negotiated a treaty in 1868 with an Indian Commission, allowing them to return to *Diné Bekéyah,* but their federally assigned homeland was several hundred miles westward of the best cornfields and grazing lands. Utes gave up land claims in New Mexico, along the Front Range, and in the San Luis Valley in exchange for a reservation in western Colorado and annuities in October 1863, codified in an 1868 treaty (mediated by their old agent, Kit Carson) in a deal to create a 15 million-acre reservation. It did not last, however, and by 1880 Utes were confined to Anglo-determined reservations on the western and southern edges of their old mountain strongholds. Victory at Adobe Walls meant the Kiowa and Comanche challenge would be answered from Texas, not New Mexico, as Greg Downs discusses in his chapter in this volume. The converging columns of the Red River War of 1874, including a second fight at Adobe Walls, drove the surviving Kiowas and Comanches to accept a reservation in Oklahoma, severed from their historic connections to the Southwest. Jicarillas were the last to accept Anglo confinement. In 1883, Anglos moved the Jicarillas to the Mescalero Reservation, but four years later Jicarillas agreed to take a different reservation in northwestern New Mexico, far removed from their historic enclaves.[27]

All these separations allowed Anglos to end the borderland political economy. Anglo officials increasingly harassed the *comanchero* trade with Plains Indians before ending it outright in the 1870s. Anglo removal of Navajos meant Hispano *nacajelleses* were no longer able to raid for sheep and captives, while confinement to a reservation prevented Navajo *ladrones* from raiding Hispanos and Pueblos. The return of federal military forces in the years after 1868 would only solidify the separation of Navajos from Hispanos and Pueblos. Finally,

Anglo courts attacked Hispano debt peonage and Indian slavery, though many freed captives refused to leave their captors' households.[28]

The division of Indians onto reservations, where they would be dependent upon the federal government for their survival, not only ended the borderland political economy, it also forced Pueblos and Hispanos into their own separation. Pueblos, no longer able to raid or trade, retreated to their villages, where they struggled to survive. Hispano *pobres* fell back to their plazas, taking up subsistence farming, stock raising, and seasonal wage labor, while many *ricos* relied upon their social, economic, and political alliances with Anglos. The troop buildup of the Civil War allowed Anglos to win in crucial episodes of the separate War for the Southwest, and by the 1870s Anglos were unchallenged in their control of the region. Yet it was a diffuse domination. No single federal official—territorial governor, military departmental commander, Indian superintendent—held full power in the New Mexico Territory after 1865. Federal outlays went for local purposes, particularly to purchase Indian annuities, which proved to be a profitable regular business. Indeed, New Mexico Territory was as much under the rule of Anglo merchants and lawyers as politicians and Army officers.[29]

The War for the Southwest provided more physical and material security in the region, but it destroyed the borderland political economy, the regular patterns of a multiethnic, violent Southwest that was centuries old. Ethnicities were now concentrated, separated, and subordinated to an Anglo-dominated state, economy, and society. Indian and Hispano cultures became the means to construct exclusive identities, identities deployed to make claims against the Anglo order for survival. The limits of sovereignty had been tested in the Southwest; the answers that emerged during the War for the Southwest, fought concurrently with the U.S. Civil War, would shape the region well into the next century.[30]

NOTES

The views presented are those of the author and do not necessarily represent the views of U.S. Northern Command or the Department of Defense. My thanks to The Latin American and Iberian Institute at the University of New Mexico for supporting the research for this essay.

1. Marc Simmons, *Kit Carson and His Three Wives: A Family History* (Albuquerque: University of New Mexico Press, 2003), 112–19.

2. Marc Simmons, "History of the Pueblos since 1821," and Fred Eggan, "Pueblos: Introduction," *Handbook of North American Indians, Vol. 9: Southwest*, Alfonso Ortiz, ed. (Washington, DC: Smithsonian Institution, 1979), 206–35; Charles Montgomery, *The Spanish Redemption: Heritage, Power, and Loss on New Mexico's Upper Rio Grande* (Berkeley: University of California Press, 2002); Thomas D. Hall, *Social Change in the Southwest, 1350–1880* (Lawrence: University Press of Kansas, 1989), 210–14.

3. Sunday Eiselt, *Becoming White Clay: A History and Archaeology of Jicarilla Apache Enclavement* (Salt Lake City: University of Utah Press, 2012); Ned Blackhawk, *Violence over the Land: Indians and Empires in the Early American West* (Cambridge, MA: Harvard University Press, 2006); Pekka Hämäläinen, *The Comanche Empire* (New Haven: Yale University Press, 2008), quotes 312–13; James Mooney, "Calendar History of the Kiowa Indians," *Seventeenth Annual Report of the Bureau of American Ethnology*, pt. 1 (Washington, DC: Government Printing Office, 1898).

4. Harry W. Basehart, "The Resource Holding Corporation among the Mescalero Apache," *Southwestern Journal of Anthropology* 23 (1967): 277–91; C. L. Sonnichsen, *The Mescalero Apaches*. 2nd ed. (Norman: University of Oklahoma Press, 1973), 57–98; Lynn R. Bailey, *If You Take My Sheep: The Evolution and Conflicts of Navajo Pastoralism* (Pasadena, CA: Westernlore, 1980); Marsha Weisiger, *Dreaming of Sheep in Navajo Country* (Seattle: University of Washington Press, 2011); James F. Brooks, *Captives and Cousins: Slavery, Kinship, and Community in the Southwest Borderlands* (Chapel Hill: University of North Carolina Press, 2002), 293, 377–80.

5. James F. Brooks, "Violence, Justice, and State Power in the New Mexican Borderlands, 1780–1880," in Richard White and John M. Findlay, eds., *Power and Place in the North American West* (Seattle: University of Washington Press, 1999), 23–60, quotes 25.

6. Hämäläinen, *The Comanche Empire*, 315–19; J. Evetts Haley, "The Comanchero Trade," *Southwestern Historical Quarterly* 38 (1935): 157–76, esp. 169.

7. Charles L. Kenner: *The Comanchero Frontier: A History of New Mexican-Plains Indian Relations* (Norman: University of Oklahoma Press, 1994); Brooks, *Captives and Cousins*, 250–57, 341–44, 385; C. C. Marino, "The Seboyetanos and the Navahos," *New Mexico Historical Review* 29 (1954): 8–27.

8. W. W. Hill, "Navaho Warfare," *Yale University Publications in Anthropology*, no. 5 (New Have.: Yale University Press, 1936), 3–19; Brooks, *Captives and Cousins*, 92–93, 380.

9. C. L. Sonnichsen, *The Mescalero Apaches*, 2nd ed. (Norman: University of Oklahoma Press, 1973), 57–102; United States War Department, *The War of the Rebellion: A Compilation of the Official Records of the Union and Confederate Armies* (Washington, DC: Government Printing Office, 1880–1901), series I, vol. 4: 19, 24–26 (hereafter cited as *OR* series, volume); United States Department of the Interior, *Report of the Commissioner of Indian Affairs* (Washington, DC: Government Printing Office, 1861), 122 (hereafter cited as CIA, Year); CIA, 1862: 247.

10. *OR* 1, 4: 76; *Condition of the Indian Tribes: Report of the Joint Special Committee* (Washington, DC: Government Printing Office, 1867), 439.

11. CIA 1861: 19, 125; CIA, 1862: 35, 36, quote 241; CIA, 1863: 14–15, 110.

12. Lee Myers, "New Mexico Volunteers, 1862–1866," *The Smoke Signal* 37 (1979): 138–51, quote 148; Edward L. Sabin, *Kit Carson Days, 1809–1868*, rev. ed. 2 vols. (Lincoln: University of Nebraska Press, 1995), vol. 2, 696–97.

13. Lawrence C. Kelly, *Navajo Roundup: Selected Correspondence of Kit Carson's Expedition against the Navajo, 1863–1865* (Boulder, CO: Pruett., 1970), 3–4, 8; *OR* I, 9: 688, 695. For Carleton's concerns see William I. Waldrip, "New Mexico during the Civil War (continued)," *New Mexico Historical Review* 28 (1953): 266–67 and Glen Sample Ely, "What to Do about Texas? Texas and the Department of New Mexico in the Civil War," *New Mexico Historical Review* 85, no. 4 (Fall 2010): 375–408.

14. Kelly, *Navajo Roundup*, 8–9, 11; *OR* I,15: 579 (quotes); Jerry D. Thompson, *Desert Tiger: Captain Paddy Graydon and the Civil War in the Far Southwest* (El Paso: Texas Western Press, 1992), 51–54; Sabin, *Kit Carson Days*, vol. 2: 703–04.

15. Sonnichsen, *Mescalero Apaches*, 112–15; Sabin, *Kit Carson Days*, vol. 2: 704–5; Kelly, *Navajo Roundup*, 16.

16. Kelly, *Navajo Roundup*, 18, 20; *OR* I, 5: 228.

17. Kelly, *Navajo Roundup*, 18–33, 37–44, 52–56; *OR* I, 26, pt. I: 26, 28; Morris F. Taylor, "Ka-ni-ache," *Colorado* 43 (1966): 275–302.

18. *OR*, I, 26, pt. I: 27–32 (quote 32); Diné College, *Navajo Stories of the Long Walk Period* (Tsaile, AZ: Diné College Bookstore Press, 1983), 109, 127, 137, 139, 151, 161, 167, 171, 182, 210, 219, 225, 246, 255, 258, 267; Marino, "The Seboyetanos and the Navahos"; Kelly, *Navajo Roundup*, 145fn.

19. Kelly, *Navajo Roundup*, 58–59, 70–71.

20. Gerald Thompson, *The Army and the Navajo: The Bosque Redondo Reservation Experiment, 1863–1868* (Tucson: University of Arizona Press, 1976), 22–27.

21. Kelly, *Navajo Roundup*, 80–98.

22. Bailey, *If You Take My Sheep*, 248–49; Kelly, *Navajo Roundup*, 97–113.

23. Kelly, *Navajo Roundup*, 114–25, 131–36, 148–50, 160–63; Frank McNitt, "The Long March: 1863–1867," in Albert Schroeder, ed., *The Changing Ways of Southwestern Indians* (Glorieta, NM: Rio Grande Press, 1973), 145–69.

24. Thompson, *The Army and the Navajo*, 46–67; *Condition of the Indian Tribes*, 201 (quote), 205; *OR* I, 41, pt. I: 212–13; *OR* I, 41, pt. 2: 927–28.

25. *OR* I, 41, pt. 2: 723, 897, 927; *OR* I, 41, pt. 3: 224–25, 400, 525; *OR* I, 41, pt. 4: 99.

26. *OR* I, 41, pt. 1: 939–43, Robert M. Utley, "Kit Carson and the Adobe Walls Campaign," *American West* 2 (1965): 4–11, 73–75; George H. Pettis, "Kit Carson's Fight with the Comanche and Kiowa Indians," *Historical Society of New Mexico* 12 (1908): 8–33; *OR* I, 41, pt. 4: 198–99, 214; Mooney, "Calendar History," 314–15; Sabin, *Kit Carson Days*, II: 747; *OR* I, 48, pt. 2: 186, 344–45.

27. Sonnichsen, *Mescalero Apaches*, 132–33; Opler, "Mescalero Apaches," 422–23; Thompson, *The Army and the Navajo;* John L. Kessell, "General Sherman and the

Navajo Treaty of 1868: A Basic and Expedient Misunderstanding," *Western Historical Quarterly* 12 (1981), 251–72; Blackhawk, *Violence over the Land,* 216–25; Hämäläinen, *The Comanche Empire,* 313–41; Veronica E. Tiller, "Jicarilla Apache," *Handbook of North American Indians,* vol. 10, 451–52.

28. Kenner, *The Comanchero Frontier,* 176–200; Brooks, *Captives and Cousins,* 349–54; Lawrence R. Murphy, "Reconstruction in New Mexico," *New Mexico Historical Review* 43 (1968): 99–115.

29. Simmons, "History of the Pueblos," 214–15; Montgomery, *The Spanish Redemption;* Howard R. Lamar, *The Far Southwest, 1846–1912: A Territorial History,* rev. ed. (Albuquerque: University of New Mexico Press, 2000), 114–17.

30. Brooks, "Violence, Justice, and State Power," 48–49.

FOUR

Scattered People

THE LONG HISTORY OF FORCED EVICTION IN THE KANSAS–MISSOURI BORDERLANDS

Diane Mutti Burke

ON AUGUST 25, 1863, UNION GENERAL Thomas Ewing Jr. the new commander of the District of the Border, issued General Order No. 11. Ewing called for the virtual depopulation of the four Missouri counties—Jackson, Bates, Cass, and a section of Vernon—along the state's unobstructed border with Kansas, south of the bend in the Missouri River. A brutal Confederate guerrilla raid on Lawrence, Kansas, in late August 1863 led Ewing to conclude that the only way to quell the violence along the border was to evict the residents, whose presence, he believed, fuelled the conflict. The order called for the complete removal of the large civilian population in the four counties, allowing only Unionists to relocate within one mile of Army garrisons. After Union forces swept in to enforce the order, little remained but charred remnants of the homes and farms that had lately dotted the countryside. The experience angered Cole Younger; it stiffened his resolve as a Confederate guerrilla, and drove his turn to postwar banditry as part of a gang that included the brothers Frank and Jesse James. As he later observed, because of Order No. 11, the people of the border were "scattered [to] the four winds of the earth."[1]

The forced exodus that followed Ewing's General Order No. 11 was one of the most dramatic—and many would argue egregious—actions by the military against a civilian population during the American Civil War. But merely focusing on the epic events of August 1863 obscures the long history of human tragedies that resulted from the violent struggle over the settling and development of the Kansas-Missouri borderlands. Native Americans, Mormons, and free-soil Kansas settlers were in the crosshairs of proslavery Missourians for decades. When the Confederates fired on Fort Sumter, the war along the Kansas-Missouri border did not begin—it merely continued in more lethal form.

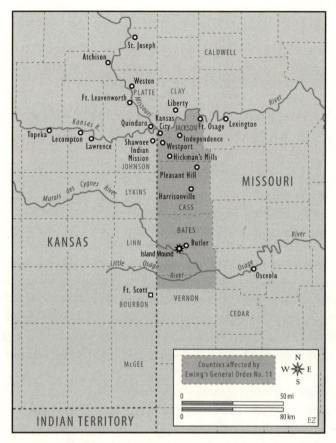

MAP 4.1. The Kansas–Missouri Borderlands during the Era of the Civil War.

During the early years of its history, Missouri was a frontier state serving as the border between the United States and Indian Territory. When granted statehood in 1821, Missouri also became the dividing line between freedom and slavery. Missouri was the border between both East and West *and* North and South. Missourians were thus enmeshed in the political dispute over the status of slavery in the western territories from the beginning. Many Missourians worried that the state's border location rendered slavery vulnerable, with Missouri's unobstructed border with southwestern Kansas of special concern by the 1850s. Western Missourians jealously guarded their rights and their human property by repeatedly attempting to intimidate and drive out those who opposed their proslavery vision for the region.[2]

The long history of violence and displacement in the Kansas-Missouri borderlands began with the eviction of Native Americans. At the time of the Louisiana Purchase, the Osage dominated southwestern Missouri through their alliance with French fur interests out of St. Louis. In addition, a number of emigrant Indian tribes, the Delaware, Shawnee, and Potawatomi, among others, had recently relocated to Missouri from the eastern states. When U.S. settlers flooded into the region, the federal government attempted to confine the Indians to western Missouri in order to make way for the newcomers in the eastern and central parts of the territory. The Osage were forced by treaty—with little compensation—onto a small section of land near the Marais des Cygnes River in southwestern Missouri, and the Iowa, Potawatomi, and Sac and Fox were relegated to a section of land in northwestern Missouri. When white settlers clamored for more land, the U.S. government forced the Osage out of the state in 1825 and acquired the land of those in northwestern Missouri through the "Platte Purchase" in 1836. By the 1840s, the government had virtually completed the "ethnic cleansing of Missouri," making way for the increasing number of migrants, most hailing from the Upper South and many bringing their slaves. Most of the displaced Indians were promised new homes just to the west of the Missouri state line, in the part of Indian Territory destined to become Kansas.[3]

Among those U.S. settlers who recognized the potential of the new lands in western Missouri were the Mormons, members of the Church of Jesus Christ of Latter-day Saints. By 1833, Mormons comprised nearly a third of the residents of Jackson County. Many western Missourians worried that their new Mormon neighbors, who mostly hailed from the Northeast and British North America, held antislavery beliefs and were sympathetic to local Indians. They grew increasingly agitated as Mormon setters purchased large tracts of land, which they believed threatened their economic and political power. When a local Mormon leader made antislavery remarks that were viewed as incendiary, Jackson County citizens found an excuse to force their Mormon neighbors across the Missouri River into Clay and Ray counties.

In 1836, in an effort to alleviate local concerns about the rapid growth of Mormon settlement, the Missouri state legislature voted to carve out the new county of Caldwell for the exclusive residence of Mormons—a reservation of sorts. But as the Mormons expanded their settlement outside of the new county and many began to develop a militant defensive posture, some Missourians demanded action. In the so-called Mormon War of 1838, Missouri governor and Jackson County resident Lilburn Boggs ordered that the "Mormons must be treated as enemies and must be exterminated or driven from the State if necessary for the public peace—their outrages are beyond all description." Within the year, borderland residents had evicted the demonized Mormon "intruders" from the state and restored "law and order" through violence, establishing a pattern of vigilante action that would be repeated over the decades.[4]

When, in 1854, the Kansas Territory was carved out of Indian Territory and the future of slavery was left up to the decree of popular sovereignty, Missouri slaveholders were upset to find free-soil migrants swarming into eastern Kansas, often financed by northeastern abolitionists. Many believed that should Kansas become a free state, "slaves will almost be value less in Missouri." Although not all thought direct action should be taken, some western Missourians attempted to actively influence the political outcome in Kansas by staking land claims in the territory and traveling across the border to illegally vote in territorial elections.[5]

As the conflict over the status of Kansas Territory intensified, proslavery and free-soil advocates along the Kansas–Missouri border increasingly dehumanized their opponents, and their hatred eventually led to bloodshed. Proslavery Missourians made repeated raids into Kansas in order to terrorize free-soil settlers, meddle in the political process, and reclaim runaway slaves. Guerrilla bands organized by Free Soilers, such as James Montgomery, Charles "Doc" Jennison, and John Brown, made similar raids into Missouri to steal farmers' property and occasionally liberate their slaves. But partisans targeted enemy settlers on their own side of the state line as well. Free-soil guerrillas, derisively dubbed Jayhawkers by Missourians, systematically worked to purge southeastern Kansas of proslavery settlers, many who fled eastward into the adjoining Missouri counties. Meanwhile, proslavery organizations in Missouri, such as the Platte County Self-Defensive Association, sought to eradicate a perceived abolitionist threat in the borderlands. In a letter to fellow proslavery sympathizer U.S. Secretary of War Jefferson Davis, Missouri Senator David Rice Atchison drew parallels to an earlier purge as he bragged, "We will be compelled, to shoot, burn & hang, but the thing will be soon over, we intend to 'Mormonise' the Abolitionists." The loss of life was not great during the Bleeding Kansas years; nevertheless, fear compelled many settlers to move out of the region. As a government agent wrote to Missouri's governor in 1858, "A large strip of country within our state is almost entirely depopulated, our citizens driven from their homes and . . . threatened with death should they return."[6]

The animosities engendered by years of strife along the border quickly spilled over into the developing political crisis after Abraham Lincoln's election as president. Missourians were deeply divided over the question of secession. Some Missouri slaveholders reasoned that they could best preserve their way of life if the state remained in the Union, but from the start there were fervent pockets of secessionists in the western Missouri River counties (which boasted the largest slave populations in the state), as well as along the contested Kansas–Missouri border. While much of the dispute over secession was just talk, in some cases partisans employed intimidation and violence against their political enemies. In Cass County, for example, local secessionists held a political meeting in late April 1861 in which they declared the county in support of the Confederacy, and even debated a "resolution recommending the hanging of Union men who should refuse to leave upon notice." Hundreds of Unionist families were pushed out of western Missouri in the early months of the war, many seeking refuge across the state line in Kansas, which had entered the Union as a free state in January 1861. In Kansas, James Montgomery and his fellow Jayhawkers were emboldened by the election of Lincoln, interpreting it as a green light to resume their fight against proslavery settlers. They first targeted individuals who had wronged free-soil settlers, including those who captured and returned fugitive slaves, but they eventually directed their ire at the people living across the border in Missouri, especially those proslavery settlers they had already chased out of Kansas.[7]

In June 1861, pro-Union troops swept in from St. Louis and ousted Missouri's secessionist governor Claiborne Fox Jackson from the state capitol. The invasion forced the administration to flee to western Missouri, where it had a stronger base of support. President Lincoln prioritized securing Missouri for the Union, and Union commanders flooded the state with troops from the surrounding free states in an effort to suppress Confederate aspirations there. Although the secessionists made some military gains in the state during the summer and fall of 1861, by early 1862 Union forces had pushed both Missouri's pro-southern forces and government into northwestern Arkansas. With the exception of a few dramatic Confederate raids into the state, Missouri was under Union military occupation for the remainder of the war. Union troops were strategically scattered in towns throughout the state in an effort to control the countryside and protect the railroad lines.[8]

A pro-Confederate guerrilla insurgency quickly arose to counter the Union military occupation. The Union hold on many areas was fragile and did not expand much beyond a small radius around military garrison towns. Union and guerrilla forces clashed throughout Missouri, but the fight was particularly intense along the Kansas–Missouri border. Union officers quickly determined that containing the guerrillas would be difficult. Often called bushwhackers, the guerrillas rarely fought in the open; they preferred to attack small detachments of soldiers and then melt away into the countryside. Moreover, many civilians in western Missouri reasoned that the guerrillas provided the best protection from the abuses of occupying Union troops and Kansas Jayhawkers and thus they began to actively aid insurgents.[9]

Indeed, Union commanders often enacted harsh measures in an effort to maintain security and enforce the loyalty of the state. Missouri was under martial law starting in the summer of 1861 and a military provost marshal system was established to regulate and prosecute disloyal civilians. Missourians were asked to swear an oath of loyalty to the United States if they wished to benefit from the protection of Union troops, keep their guns, practice their professions, and escape the financial penalties that were levied against disloyal citizens. These assessments were meant to provide "subsistence of the troops, the families of such as are in indigent circumstances, and refugees"; in essence, to underwrite the Union military occupation and aid for Unionists who were displaced by Confederate guerrilla violence. Many Missouri men and women signed loyalty oaths, although Union soldiers and Unionists suspected that they often lied in order to keep from being penalized or harassed. Though this was true in some cases, Missourians argued that soldiers were predisposed to believe that those of southern origin—especially if they owned slaves—were disloyal. In truth, many Missourians, and indeed even some slaveholders, remained loyal to the U.S. government, and these Unionists were essential to the success of the Union cause.[10]

Missouri civilians frequently complained about Union soldiers' harsh tactics. Those deemed disloyal often suffered harassment and risked arrest and imprisonment. In fact, more men and women from Missouri were arrested for disloyalty than from any other state. Prosecuted by the local provost marshal, often on the testimony of Unionist neighbors and escaped slaves, many were imprisoned in local Army encampments, while others were transferred to Union military prisons in St. Louis and Illinois or banished from the state altogether. It was not unusual for soldiers to shoot or hang suspected secessionists without the benefit of a trial.[11]

Kansas troops gained a reputation for the worst brutality. At the start of the war, the irregular Jayhawkers (also called Red Legs in reference to their distinctive hosiery) were folded into the regular Army. While not all were involved in "jayhawking" activities, many of the men who filled the ranks of the Union Army in Kansas held deep-seated resentments toward Missourians and took any opportunity to settle old scores. Jayhawkers were not always discerning in whom they attacked, inaccurately believing that all Missourians were on the wrong side of the war. They made frequent raids across the border from Kansas into Missouri, harassing—and sometimes murdering—Missouri men; confiscating civilian property, including horses, livestock, and personal household items; and liberating Missouri slaves. While some raids served legitimate military purposes, in many cases Jayhawkers served their own agenda. For instance, in late September 1861, Kansas senator James Lane's Jayhawker brigade plundered and torched the western Missouri town of Osceola after a brief skirmish with southern forces. Most of the residents, including Lelia Crutchfield Weidemeyer and her two small children, fled with only the few belongings that they could quickly gather before the Kansans' arrival. Western Missourian Nancy Pitcher reported the actions of Jennison's Jayhawkers in Jackson County during the following winter: "Several of her relations have had thare houses burned by them, thare negros, hoarses and everything they had taken from them. They have taken the lives of boys ten years old."[12]

Missouri bushwhackers often pointed to the desire to protect their families and friends from Union soldiers' and Jayhawkers' deprivations and abuses as their reason for joining the guerrillas. They generally recruited directly from the local population and operated in the vicinity of their own neighborhoods. Familiarity with their surroundings was an asset to these irregular forces, allowing them to hit their targets and quickly disappear into the countryside. Operating locally also allowed them to remain close to their supply networks, which were largely made up of their own relatives and neighbors. Civilian households supplied bushwhackers with food, clothing, horses, fodder, shelter, and military intelligence.[13]

Bushwhackers promoted their cause as noble, but in the end their tactics against Union soldiers and Unionist civilians were every bit as brutal as those of the Jayhawkers. While they focused their attacks on Union soldiers, bushwhackers also targeted local Unionists, especially the German Americans, who were much despised for their fervent free-labor, antislavery commitments. The bushwhackers made "constant raids" across the state line into Kansas, where they "rob our citizens[,] burn their houses and murder prominent men." Guerrillas regularly roused their enemies from their beds at night, set homes and farm buildings aflame, and shot or hanged men and older boys within sight of their families. While many Missourians (even some who sympathized with secession) rejected the bushwhackers' brutal tactics, the strategy of violence and intimidation nevertheless reaped rewards over time. One western Missouri newspaper reported in 1863 that Unionists' circumstances were dire "in this distracted, deserted, destroyed, distressed and destitute country."[14]

The movement of troops and the many partisan raids decimated the farms and towns along the border. Claims filed with the federal government by self-described Unionists for reimbursement for their property taken by the Union Army during a brief military occupation of Cass County in the winter of 1861–62 are a window into the financial dislocation caused by the war. Claim after claim tells the story of repeated visits by soldiers who confiscated the resources accumulated through years of toil. Confederate guerrillas preyed on border farmers as well. In some cases, supporters gladly provided bushwhackers with the resources to continue their fight, but in other instances guerrillas intimidated people into supporting them or stole from them during violent raids. Border residents claimed that the Jayhawkers took from both sides. Andrew Brownlow pleaded with Governor Gamble in 1862, "If you dont do some thing to protect the people on the Border all there [sic] property will all Be taken to Kansas." Over time even those who willingly supplied men fighting for their chosen side felt beleaguered by the incessant demands placed upon them when they had so little to spare.[15]

Midway through the war, burned buildings scarred the landscape; the area was nearly devoid of fence rails; horses, mules, and livestock were in short supply; and in many places fields lay barren. Lizzie Brannock described the devastated landscape: "Our country is desolate, indeed almost entirely a wilderness, robbery is an every day affair so long as their [sic] was anything to take our farms are all burned up, fences gone, crops destroyed no one escapes the ravages of one party or the other." Men and boys often were afraid to plow and plant their fields, fearing that working in the open would leave them exposed, and many routinely hid in the woods with their livestock in an attempt to preserve both their animals and their lives. Believing they would not be physically harmed, men often left women and children to protect and manage the family property the best that they could.[16]

Some men eventually concluded that the risks had become too great and it was necessary to leave their homes. Most who fled did so in great haste and under the cover of night in order to avoid detection by their enemies. Some left to join the Union or Confederate armies or local guerrilla forces, while others sought shelter in nearby towns or in communities far removed from the fighting. There was a strong Union military presence in St. Louis, and Unionists gravitated there, though many secessionists found a safe haven in the city as well. Family and friends in the states of the Old Northwest also harbored men from both sides, while secessionists usually went to Arkansas, Texas, or Kentucky.[17]

Border residents of both political persuasions also looked farther west as they sought a safe haven from the violence and turmoil of the war. Many imagined the West as a place of refuge and restoration, as described in William Deverell's chapter in this volume, while others were likely intrigued by the promise of western land offered by the 1862 Homestead Act and mining prospects. Going west was an attractive and viable option for Missourians; travel routes were well developed, accessible, and familiar to western Missourians. A large number of Missouri men (and some women) took off across the Plains in an attempt to escape wartime violence and evade the Union military draft. Secessionist Charles France left St. Joseph for Denver, where he opened a mercantile business, and the brothers George and John Watkins escaped the violence in Clay County by spending part of the war running freight to Montana Territory, where a gold rush was underway. Similarly, Arvazena "Nan" Cooper claimed that bushwhackers marked her family as "abolitionists" in spite of their moderate Unionist leanings, and when their persecution became unbearable, the family decided to flee to safety in Oregon. Though some Missourians returned home after the situation cooled off, many, such as George Watkins (who purchased a large Montana ranch) and the Coopers, remained permanently in the West.[18]

Men often believed that they could ride out the conflict and quickly reunite with their families, but as the war dragged on and conditions at home became more unbearable, many encouraged their wives and families to leave as well. Few lightly made the decision to abandon their homes and farms. Removal often came at great economic loss. It was nearly impossible to sell farms located in such a hostile environment, and many simply abandoned their property, hoping to eventually return to it. A fortunate few had the benefit of ample time to organize and pack for their trips, but threats of violence forced many to leave in great haste with few of their possessions. Priscilla Hunter expressed the sentiments of many border residents as her family contemplated whether or not to leave their southwestern Missouri home: "I hate to live in such a country and I hate to leave it when I think of the good home we had in it.... I never expect to be as well satisfyed in any other c[oun]try as I was in this."[19]

Refugees found travel extremely difficult as they navigated Missouri's wartorn landscape, negotiating with Union officials for the necessary military passes to move through occupied areas. Most women and children traveled without assistance from men. In the absence of male escorts, some women formed travel partnerships, such as when Partheny Horn and a group of Cedar County women organized a wagon train to move from southwestern Missouri to Texas. The trip was perilous even when accompanied by others. Armed men routinely attacked travelers, and it was often difficult to locate help if it was needed along the way. As the war progressed, border residents became increasingly suspicious of unknown individuals and many were concerned that if they aided the wrong person they would face retribution from their enemies. When a wheel broke on one of the Cedar County women's wagons and they could not fix it themselves, they searched long and hard to find a man who was willing to aid "rebel" women.[20]

Although the wartime turbulence resulted in the displacement of white residents on both sides of the border, it also created opportunities for many enslaved Missourians who began to flee from their owners as the state of affairs deteriorated. Missouri slaveholders frequently accused Jayhawkers of "stealing" their slaves, but most often African Americans actively sought protection from Union soldiers or sympathetic Kansans. During the first years of the war, Union Army officers often returned the slaves of loyal Missouri slaveholders, as mandated by official policy, but by midway through the war, few people—regardless of their loyalties—were able to reclaim their slaves.[21]

Not all black Missourians were refugees by choice, however. Missouri slaveholders forcibly transported a large number of people out of the state during the war. Many decided that the best means of protecting their "property" was to "refugee" their slaves far behind Confederate lines, where they often sold them or placed them under the authority of their family members or friends. Texas was a favored destination of Missouri slaveholders because of their many connections to kin and neighbors who had migrated there during the 1850s. The man holding Esther Easter as a slave sent her to Texas for sale, and Richard Kimmons's owner so feared that Union soldiers would take his slaves that he sent them to his son in Texas, leaving his crops standing in the fields. Others transported their slaves to Kentucky, where they fetched higher sale prices than in wartime Missouri.[22]

Those enslaved Missourians who attempted to run away did so at great risk. As slavery began to disintegrate, Missouri slaveholders became increasingly desperate to maintain labor discipline and keep people working on their farms. Not only did they vigilantly watch their slaves' movements—sometimes even locking slaves up at night to prevent their flight—but they also were aided in these efforts by local slave patrols and later secessionist guerrillas, who filled this crucial role when the local governments ceased to function. Slaveholders had less incentive to protect their slaves from abuse at the hands of patrollers once it became apparent that emancipation was imminent. Bushwhackers became particularly brutal after the Union Army began to recruit enslaved men in Missouri starting in the late fall of 1863. One formerly enslaved Missourian observed, "[I]t was worth a negro's life, almost, to try to get away."[23]

As the number of refugees increased in Missouri and the surrounding states, individuals, communities, and government agencies were forced to reckon with the results of civilian displacement on such an unprecedented scale. The response to the growing refugee crisis was largely driven by political and military concerns. The Union Army's primary military objective in the border region was to contain the guerrilla insurgency. Both the military's official and unofficial policies toward the guerrillas and their supporters ultimately influenced the treatment of refugees. In most cases, individuals only dispensed aid to refugee strangers who shared their politics; government and charitable organizations frequently used this litmus test as well. Also at play was the evolving federal policy regarding the status of Missouri's enslaved population. Unionist refugees and escaped slaves expected protection and assistance from federal troops because of their loyalty to the Union cause. During the early days of the war, mostly adult men fled to the camps to escape both slavery and the political violence in the countryside, but as the war continued, large numbers of women, children, and the elderly sought refuge with the Army.[24]

As the situation unfolded, Army officers forced the federal government to expand its mission and provide direct aid to the many needy loyal citizens (especially white Unionists) who were displaced by the war. Many believed that they could better justify feeding and sheltering people if they were engaged in service to the Union cause. Field officers asked their commanders for permission to put people to work within Army camps and to recruit refugee men into military service. White Unionists regularly enrolled in the Army, but as early as the summer of 1862, James Lane began recruiting the

First Kansas Colored Infantry without official military permission from formerly enslaved refugees congregated around Fort Scott, Kansas.[25]

Some commanders eventually allowed officers to distribute partial military rations and provide shelter to refugees, but in some places the displaced population swelled so large that it overwhelmed attempts to help. African American recruitment exacerbated the refugee problem in military camps, as enslaved women argued that their husbands' military service obligated the Army to aid and protect them and their children. It was reported that many women and children arrived at the camps with "nothing to eat or scarcely wear." The situation became so acute during the last years of the war that it became difficult for the Army to meet the many needs of the displaced population. Overwhelmed by the crisis, military officers in central and western Missouri attempted to solve the problem by pushing the refugees elsewhere. A favored plan was to transport needy freedwomen and children to join "their friends" in Kansas, in yet another phase of borderland eviction. The large number of former slaves who sought refuge in Kansas may explain James Lane's interest in colonizing freedpeople in the Southwest, as described in Nicholas Guyatt's chapter in this volume.[26]

This was the context in which Order No. 11 was promulgated. Given border residents' long history of using violence and forced eviction as a political and security tool, General Thomas Ewing's decision to depopulate western Missouri in the summer of 1863 should not be surprising. After taking command of the newly created District of the Border in June 1863, Ewing systematically set about collecting the names of disloyal border residents, a list made up of households mainly headed by women and elderly men. Midsummer, he began to arrest family members of known bushwhackers and those who had provided substantial material aid to them. On August 13, the makeshift Kansas City prison in which some of the women were imprisoned collapsed, killing four women and girls and maiming many others. Before the dust of the jail barely had settled, Ewing issued two military orders that allowed for the enlistment of enslaved men belonging to disloyal citizens, ordered the destruction of local blacksmith shops, and called for the arrest and eviction of all who supported the guerrillas. This plan was already in place before William Quantrill and nearly four hundred guerrillas attacked Lawrence, Kansas, on August 21, massacred as many as 180 unarmed men and boys, and torched the town.[27]

Ewing believed that the bushwhackers had forced his hand when they made this horrific raid. He had long reasoned that the guerrilla insurgency could not be contained if disloyal citizens remained to support it, but now he also feared that vengeful Kansans would sweep into western Missouri on a bloody, retaliatory raid. Ewing thought the best chance to arrest the violence was to depopulate and destroy the Missouri border counties, leaving nothing for anyone to fight over. On August 25, he ordered the eviction of all residents of Jackson (excluding Kansas City), Cass, Bates, and the northern portion of Vernon counties within fifteen days, allowing only certified Unionists to move into garrison towns scattered throughout the northern part of the military district.[28]

Though some citizens were able to get out ahead of the invasion, others literally had minutes to drag out a few precious possessions and vacate their dwellings before Union troops ransacked and burned them. Union soldiers also torched outbuildings, confiscated livestock, grain, and hay, and commandeered modes of transport that were essential to the conveyance of the now-refugee population. Most border residents lived in reduced circumstances by the summer of 1863; few men and boys remained to assist families as they removed, nor did many possess wagons or draft animals to convey them. A few people resisted eviction, and these shows of defiance often had violent consequences, such as when six such men were rounded up and shot by Union soldiers along a Jackson County road.[29]

The human misery so evident in the long train of refugees portrayed in the background of Missouri artist George Caleb Bingham's painting *Martial Law* was the reality of life on western Missouri roads in the wake of the eviction order. Jackson County resident Frances Fristoe Twyman remembered "the many scenes of misery and distress" as women, children, and the elderly trudged eastward with rattletrap wagons and carts in the extreme heat of late summer. Between the fires set by Union soldiers and the wildfires that were common on the high grass prairies in late summer, vast stretches of western Missouri were turned into a charred wasteland, with only chimneys remaining to mark the spots where homes once stood. Even many Unionists found the sight of the refugees "heart sickening," although many deemed the order necessary to reinstate law and order along the border.[30]

In the wake of the order, refugees scattered in every direction, although Ewing officially restricted them from relocating in the easternmost tier of Kansas counties, fearing that their presence would lead to continued cross-border violence. In a bid to disassociate themselves from the evicted secessionists and to protect their communities from a similar fate, the citizens of Clay and Platte counties, located just north of the affected area, issued a notice

FIGURE 4.1. Martial Law. Engraving from painting by George Caleb Bingham, c. 1869–1870. Library of Congress, Prints and Photographs Collection.

proclaiming that the refugees were not welcome. In spite of nineteenth-century gender conventions, few residents of the border region were inclined to aid refugees simply because they were women and children. Union soldiers and Unionists understood that the guerrilla insurgency could not succeed without support from secessionist women, and many were reluctant to assist those who had served their enemies. Others likely were concerned that their acts of benevolence would mark them as southern sympathizers. Ironically, the Union troops frequently undermined their own military objective to push secessionists out of the border region when they attacked enemy travelers and stole whatever they had—sometimes taking even their wagons and the animals pulling them.[31]

In the months following the order, Union military commanders tried to downplay the severity of the measure by suggesting that a large number of civilians had left the designated counties ahead of the order, and of those who remained, the vast majority were disloyal. Indeed, as early as the fall of 1861 one border resident explained that the western Missouri counties were already "almost entirely depopulated, towns burnt and the whole country laid waste.... the people have nearly all been run off." But in October 1863, Major J. T. Ross of the Eleventh Kansas Cavalry described the appearance of what was already known as the "Burnt District": "[T]he depopulation of the counties of Jackson, Cass, Bates and Vernon, is thorough and complete. The traveler may ride for hours without seeing a single inhabitant. Deserted houses and farms are everywhere to be seen, and the whole is one grand picture of desolation." Regardless of whether the displaced totaled the forty thousand who lived in the region in 1860 or the possibly twenty thousand who remained by 1863, the forced eviction of border residents and the destruction of what was left of their property created immense human suffering.[32]

In November 1863, Ewing's General Order No. 20 removed some of the harshest strictures of General Order No. 11. Loyal border residents were allowed to return to their homes, but most felt unsafe living in the countryside and in many cases their farms had been destroyed. The permanent population of the targeted region shrunk to a few thousand Unionists who huddled during the brutal winter of 1863–64 in the garrison towns of Westport, Kansas City, Independence, Harrisonville, Hickman's Mills, and Pleasant Hill, where they could expect military protection. Although evicting the secessionist women and children disrupted the guerrilla supply chain and achieved Ewing's objective of reducing violence in the borderlands, in the end it merely pushed the problem into central Missouri.[33]

In the ongoing fight over the right to claim and dominate the region, border residents forced out Native Americans, then the Mormons, and finally those with whom they disagreed over slavery. Decades of animosity and violence shattered the society that had developed in the Kansas–Missouri borderlands: men were divided into heavily armed camps; brutality and destruction were the order of the day; people were left with practically nothing; slavery was nearly destroyed; and thousands were displaced from their homes. Ewing's order merely brought this long legacy of violence and eviction to its logical conclusion.

Civilian displacement along the Kansas–Missouri border was a precursor of that which enveloped the southern states during the last years of the Civil War. As with many aspects of the war, developments in the West served as the proving ground for the direction the war would take in the East during its last hard years. When determining the proper response to the emerging civilian crisis, the federal government sought the testimony of border region military commanders at the 1863 commission that was organized to explore the issues of emancipation, displaced people, and black military service. In 1865 Congress created the Bureau of Refugees, Freedmen, and Abandoned Lands to directly address the southern refugee crisis, for whites and blacks. But long before this step was taken, those along the border found their own solutions, however imperfect, to the humanitarian crisis that had plagued the region for many years.[34]

NOTES

The author thanks the Clements/Autry Civil War in the West scholars, especially Adam Arenson and Andrew Graybill, for their insightful comments on earlier versions of this chapter.

1. Cole Younger Letter, August 1, 1880, quoted in Tom A. Rafiner, *Caught Between Three Fires: Cass County, MO., Chaos & Order No. 11, 1860–1865* (Xlibris Corporation, 2010), 505.

2. For discussions of Missouri's border location, see Christopher Phillips, *Missouri's Confederate: Claiborne Fox Jackson and the Creation of Southern Identity in the Border West* (Columbia: University of Missouri Press, 2000); Stephen Aron, *American Confluence: The Missouri Frontier from Borderland to Border State* (Bloomington: Indiana University Press, 2006); Adam Arenson, *The Great Heart of the Republic: St. Louis and the Cultural Civil War* (Cambridge, MA: Harvard University Press, 2011); Stanley Harrold, *Border Wars: Fighting Over Slavery before the Civil War* (Chapel Hill: University of North Carolina Press, 2010); and Jeremy Neely, *The Border Between Them: Violence and Reconciliation on the Kansas-Missouri Line* (Columbia: University of Missouri Press, 2007).

3. The Platte Purchase opened northwestern Missouri to U.S. settlement and included the present-day counties of Andrew, Atchison, Buchanan, Holt, Nodaway, and Platte. Aron, *American Confluence,* quotation on 214. See also Willard H. Rollings, *The Osage: An Ethnohistorical Study of Hegemony on the Prairie-Plains* (Columbia: University of Missouri Press, 1992); Anne Farrar Hyde, *Empires, Nations, and Families: A History of the North American West, 1800–1860* (Lincoln: University of Nebraska Press, 2011); and J. Frederick Fausz, "Becoming 'A Nation of Quakers': The Removal of the Osage Indians from Missouri," *Gateway Heritage* 21 (2000): 28–39.

4. See *The Missouri Mormon Experience,* Thomas M. Spencer, ed. (Columbia: University of Missouri Press, 2010); Stephen C. LeSueur, *The 1838 Mormon War in Missouri* (Columbia: University of Missouri Press, 1987); and Aron, *American Confluence,* 236–38. I am especially indebted to Kenneth Winn for his article about the Mormon War's legacy of violence. See Kenneth Winn, "The Missouri Context of Antebellum Mormonism and Its Legacy of Violence," in *The Missouri Mormon Experience,* 19–26. Gov. Lilburn Boggs, "Extermination Order", October 27, 1838, Missouri State Archives, Jefferson City, Missouri, www.sos.mo.gov/archives

/resources/findingaids/miscMormRecs/eo/18381027_ExtermOrder.pdf. For discussions of vigilantism and concerns about law and order, see: Richard Maxwell Brown, *Strains of Violence: Historical Studies of American Violence and Vigilantism* (New York: Oxford University Press, 1975); Nicole Etcheson, "The Goose Question: The Proslavery Party in Territorial Kansas and the Crisis of 'Law and Order,'" *Bleeding Kansas, Bleeding Missouri: The Long Civil War on the Border,* Jonathan Earle and Diane Mutti Burke, eds. (Lawrence: University Press of Kansas, 2013) [hereafter *BK,BM*], 47–63; Kristen Tegtmeier Oertel, "'Nigger-Worshipping Fanatics' and 'Villain[s] of the Blackest Dye': Racialized Manhoods and the Sectional Debates," in *BK,BM,* 65–80; and Pearl T. Ponce, "'The Noise of Democracy': The Lecompton Constitution in Congress and Kansas," *BK,BM,* 81–96. Emphasis mine in last sentence.

5. Jordan O'Bryan to John Miller, February 6, 1854, Jordan O'Bryan Letter, 1854, State Historical Society of Missouri, Manuscript Collection, Columbia, Missouri [hereafter SHSM]. In many cases the new settlers displaced the Native Americans who recently had been concentrated there. See Kristen Tegtmeier Oertel, *Bleeding Borders: Race, Gender, and Violence in Pre-Civil War Kansas* (Baton Rouge: Louisiana State University Press, 2009); Nicole Etcheson, *Bleeding Kansas: Contested Liberty in the Civil War Era* (Lawrence: University Press of Kansas, 2004); Tony R. Mullis, "The Illusion of Security: The Governments' Response to the Jayhawker Threat of Late 1860," in *BK,BM,* 99–117; Tony R. Mullis, *Peacekeeping on the Plains: Army Operation in Bleeding Kansas* (Columbia: University of Missouri Press, 2004); and Neely, *The Border Between Them.*

6. Platte County Self-Defensive Association, B. F. Stringfellow, chairman, committee report, *Negro-slavery; No Evil, or the North and the South* (St. Louis: M. Niedner & Co., 1854). David Rice Atchison to Jefferson Davis, September 24, 1854, in Jefferson Davis, *The Papers of Jefferson Davis: 1853–1855,* Lynda Lasswell Crist, ed. (Baton Rouge: Louisiana State University Press, 1985), 83–84. Adj. General Gustavus Parsons to Missouri Governor Robert Stewart, Harrisonville, June 16, 1858, as quoted in Neely, *The Border Between Them,* 72–73.

7. For a discussion of the political history of Civil War Missouri, see William Parrish, *Turbulent Partnership: Missouri and the Union, 1861–65* (Columbia: University of Missouri Press, 1963); Christopher Phillips, *Missouri's Confederate;* Mark Geiger, *Financial Fraud and Guerrilla Violence in Missouri's Civil War, 1861–1865* (New Haven: Yale University Press, 2010); and Aaron Astor, *Rebels on the Border: Civil War, Emancipation, and the Reconstruction of Kentucky and Missouri* (Baton Rouge: Louisiana State University Press, 2012). The resolution ultimately did not pass because of the efforts of Cass County Unionist Andrew G. Newgent, who soon after was forced from the county under the threat of violence. See *Journal of the Missouri State Convention, January 6-April 10, 1865* (St. Louis: Missouri Democrat, 1865), 180. For a discussion of politics along the border, see Rafiner, *Caught Between Three Fires,* and Neely, *The Border Between Them.*

8. Missouri's secessionist military force, the Missouri State Guard, was not officially incorporated into the Confederate Army until March 1862, although the

Missourians occasionally fought alongside Confederate troops during the first year of the war. For a military history of Civil War Missouri, see Louis S. Gerteis, *The Civil War in Missouri: A Military History* (Columbia: University of Missouri Press, 2012); William Garrett Piston and Richard W. Hatcher III, *Wilson's Creek: The Second Battle of the Civil War and the Men Who Fought It* (Chapel Hill: University of North Carolina Press, 2000); and James Denny and John Bradbury, *The Civil War's First Blood, Missouri, 1854–1861* (Boonville: Missouri Life, 2007).

9. For discussions of the guerrillas, see Michael Fellman, *Inside War: The Guerrilla Conflict in Missouri during the American Civil War* (New York: Oxford University Press, 1989); Daniel E. Sutherland, *A Savage Conflict: The Decisive Role of Guerrillas in the American Civil War* (Chapel Hill: University of North Carolina Press, 2009); and Thomas Goodrich, *Black Flag: Guerrilla Warfare on the Western Border, 1861–1865* (Bloomington: Indiana University Press, 1995).

10. Brigadier General Loan assessed the disloyal citizens of Lexington, Missouri for $15,000. M. Chapman, A.A.G., Headquarters Sixth Military District E.M.M., Lexington, Missouri, October 29, 1862, Battle of Lexington Historic Site, Lexington, Missouri, www.civilwaronthewesternborder.org/content/order-funding-lexington-missouri. R.C. Vaughan, Proceedings of the Lafayette County Board, SHSM, www.civilwaronthewesternborder.org/content/proceedings-lafayette-county-board. For discussion of assessments and loyalty oaths, see John F. Bradbury Jr., "'Buckwheat Cake Philanthropy': Refugees and the Union Army in the Ozarks," *Arkansas Historical Quarterly*, 57, no. 3 (Autumn 1998): 233–54; LeeAnn Whites, *Gender Matters: Civil War, Reconstruction, and the Making of the New South* (New York: Palgrave Macmillan, 2005), 45–64; and Christopher Phillips, "'A Question of Power Not One of Law': Federal Occupation and the Politics of Loyalty in the Western Border Slave States during the American Civil War," in *BK,BM*, 131–50.

11. For discussions of Union military occupation and civil liberties issues, see William C. Harris, *Lincoln and the Border States: Preserving the Union* (Lawrence: University Press of Kansas, 2011); Dennis K. Boman, *Lincoln and Citizens' Rights in Civil War Missouri: Balancing Freedom and Security* (Baton Rouge: Louisiana State University Press, 2011); Mark E. Neely Jr., *The Fate of Liberty: Abraham Lincoln and Civil Liberties* (New York: Oxford University Press, 1991); and John Fabian Witt, *Lincoln's Code: The Laws of War in American History* (New York: Free Press, 2012).

12. For Kansas troops, see Mullis, *Peacekeeping on the Plains;* Bryce Benedict, *Jayhawkers: The Civil War Brigade of James Henry Lane* (Norman: University of Oklahoma Press, 2009); Rafiner, *Caught Between Three Fires;* and Neely, *The Border Between Them*. John M. Weidemeyer, "Memoirs of a Confederate Soldier [1860–1865],"4, and John M. Weidemeyer Journal—1860–1863, John M. Weidemeyer Papers, Pearce Civil War Collection, Navarro College, Corsicana, Texas, www.ozarkscivilwar.org/archives/4703. Margaret Mendenhall Frazier, ed., *Missouri Ordeal, 1862–1864, Diaries of Willard Hall Mendenhall*, January 30, 1862 entry (Newhall, CA: Carl Boyer, 3rd, 1985).

13. For more on guerrillas and their supporters, see Coleman Younger, *The Story of Cole Younger* (St. Paul: Minnesota Historical Society Press, 2000 reprint); Albert

Castel and Thomas Goodrich, *Bloody Bill Anderson: The Short, Savage Life of a Civil War Guerrilla* (Mechanicsburg, PA: Stackpole, 1998); Sutherland, *A Savage Conflict;* Richard S. Brownlee, *Gray Ghosts of the Confederacy* (Baton Rouge: Louisiana State University Press, 1984 reprint); Mark W. Geiger, *Financial Fraud and Guerrilla Violence in Missouri's Civil War, 1861–1865;* LeeAnn Whites, "Forty Shirts and a Wagonload of Wheat: Women, the Domestic Supply Line, and the Civil War on the Western Border," *Journal of the Civil War Era* 1 (March 2011): 56–78; and Joseph M. Beilein Jr., "Household War: Guerrilla Men, Rebel Women, and Guerrilla Warfare in Civil War Missouri," PhD diss., University of Missouri, 2012.

14. William McCoy to Ellen W. McCoy, June 7, 1863, SHSM, www.civilwaronthewesternborder.org/content/william-ellen-w-mccoy. Samuel R. Ayres to Lyman Langdon, August 24, 1863, Linn County, Kansas, Kansas Historical Society, Topeka, Kansas, www.civilwaronthewesternborder.org/content/samuel-r-ayres-lyman-langdon. Elizabeth Hunter and Priscilla Hunter letters to Margaret (Mag) Hunter Newberry, August 11, 1864, White Oak, Missouri, Hunter-Hagler Collection, State Historical Society of Missouri, Manuscript Collection, Rolla, Missouri [hereafter SHSM-Rolla], www.ozarkscivilwar.org/archives/1044. *Cass County Missouri Families* (Cass County Historical Society, 1976), 59. Kansas City *Daily Journal of Commerce,* May 5, 1863, as quoted in Rafiner, *Caught Between Three Fires,* 291–93.

15. Tom Rafiner conducted a systematic study of loyal Cass Countians' property claims filed with the U.S. government after the war. See Rafiner, *Caught Between Three Fires,* 113–62. Robert Brownlow to Gov. Hamilton R. Gamble, August 2, 1862, Buchanan County, Missouri, Missouri History Museum, St. Louis, Missouri, www.civilwaronthewesternborder.org/content/andrew-brownlow-hamilton-r-gamble. Ann Raab argues that there is archeological evidence of the economic stress faced by border residents. See Ann Raab, "Warfare as an Agent of Culture Change: The Archaeology of Guerrilla Warfare on the 19th Century Missouri/Kansas Border," PhD diss., University of Kansas, 2012.

16. Lizzie Brannock to Brother Edwin, January 13, 1864, Lizzie E. Brannock Letter, 1864, SHSM. See *Cass County Missouri Histories* (Cass County Historical Society, Inc., 1976), 200–201. See also Rafiner, *Caught Between Three Fires,* 98–99.

17. For examples, see Elvira Ascenith Weir Scott Diary, 1860–1887, SHSM; Hunter-Hagler Collection; Isley Family Papers, Wichita State University Special Collections and University Archive, Wichita, Kansas, www.ozarkscivilwar.org/archives/3553; Dorsey-Fuqua Family Collection, 1851–1839, SHSM; Priscilla Thomas Ingram Patton Diary, Patton-Scott Family Papers, SHSM; Louisa Cheairs McKenny Sheppard, "A Confederate Girlhood," History Museum for Springfield-Greene County, Missouri, Springfield, Missouri, www.ozarkscivilwar.org/archives/1122; Partheny Horn Memoir, private collector, www.ozarkscivilwar.org/archives/2699; and John M. Weidemeyer Journal—1860–1863, John M. Weidemeyer Papers.

18. Garland Jefferson Mahan Diaries, 1864–1873, 1961, SHSM. Pauline Stratton Collection, SHSM. Charles B. France Papers, SHSM. Louis Potts and Ann Siglar,

Watkins Mill: Factory on the Farm (Kirksville, MO: Truman State University Press, 2004). Nan Cooper, "Mother's Trip across the Plains," 1901, SHSM and www.nwda.orbiscascade.org/ark:/80444/xv52684.

19. Elizabeth Hunter letter to children and Priscilla Hunter to Dear Brother and Sisters, November 1, 1864, Hunter-Hagler Collection.

20. Mrs. Silliman to My Dear Brother, [1862], Silliman Family Letters, 1862–1865, SHSM. Watts Hays Letters, wattshaysletters.com. Partheny Horn Memoir.

21. For a discussion of enslaved Missourians' wartime flight and Union military policies regarding them, see Diane Mutti Burke, *On Slavery's Border: Missouri's Small-Slaveholding Households, 1815–1865* (Athens: University of Georgia, 2010), 268–307; and Diane Mutti Burke, "'Slavery Dies Hard': Enslaved Missourians' Struggle for Freedom," in *BK,BM,* 151–68. See also Yael A. Sternhell, *Routes of War: The World of Movement in the Confederate South* (Cambridge, MA: Harvard University Press, 2012).

22. Esther Easter interview, *The American Slave,* vol. 7, 88–99, and Richard Kimmons interview, *The American Slave,* Suppl., series, 2, vol. 6.6, 293–98, George Rawick, ed. (Westport, CT: Greenwood, 1972–79). See also Dale Baum, "Slaves Taken to Texas for Safekeeping during the Civil War," in *The Fate of Texas,* Charles D. Grear, ed. (Fayetteville: University of Arkansas Press, 2008), 83–104.

23. Excerpt from testimony of R. A. Watt [November 30, 1863], *The Black Military Experience,* Ira Berlin et al., eds. (Cambridge: Cambridge University Press, 1983), 235–36.

24. For additional information on the military's policies in Missouri regarding contraband slaves and refugees, see Ira Berlin et al., eds., *The Destruction of Slavery* (Cambridge: Cambridge University Press, 1993), 395–412; and Bradbury, "'Buckwheat Cake Philanthropy.'"

25. For recruitment in the border region, see John Blassingame, "The Recruitment of Negro Troops in Missouri during the Civil War," *Missouri Historical Review* 58, no. 3 (April 1964): 326–38; Ira Berlin et al., eds., *The Wartime Genesis of Free Labor: The Upper South* (Cambridge: Cambridge University Press, 1985), 188–89, 236–38. See also Chris Tabor, "The Skirmish at Island Mound" (Butler, MO: Bates County Historical Society, 2001); and Benedict, *Jayhawkers.*

26. Brigadier General Clinton B. Fisk to Jas. E. Yeatman, Esq., March 25, 1865, *The Destruction of Slavery,* 489. Brigadier General E. B. Brown to Major O. D. Greene, March 19, 1864, and Brigadier General Wm. A. Pile to Maj. O. D. Greene, March 29, 1864, *The Wartime Genesis of Free Labor,* 593–95. Capt. J. C. W. Hall to Lieutenant Colonel T. A. Switzler, July 1, 1864, *The Wartime Genesis of Free Labor,* 611. See also James Downs, *Sick from Freedom: African-American Illness and Suffering during the Civil War and Reconstruction* (New York: Oxford University Press, 2012); and Amy Murrell Taylor, "How a Cold Snap in Kentucky Led to Freedom for Thousands: An Environmental Story of Emancipation," *Weirding the War: Stories from the Civil War's Ragged Edges,* Stephen Berry, ed. (Athens: University of Georgia Press, 2011), 191–214.

27. The building in which the imprisoned women were housed was owned by Missouri artist George Caleb Bingham. See Whites, "Forty Shirts and a Wagonload of

Wheat"; and Charles Harris, "Catalyst for Terror: The Collapse of the Women's Prison in Kansas City," *Missouri Historical Review* 89, no. 3 (April 1995): 290–305. See also Thomas Ewing Family Papers, Manuscript Division, Library of Congress, Washington, DC. General Orders No. 9 and 10, Hdqrs. District of the Border, Kansas City, Mo., August 18, 1863, *The War of the Rebellion: A Compilation of the Official Records of the Union and Confederate Armies* (Washington, DC: U.S. Government Printing Office, 1880–1901) [hereafter *OR*], vol. 22, chap. XXXIV, Correspondence, 460.

28. General Orders No. 11, Hdqrs. District of the Border, Kansas City, Missouri, August 25, 1863, *OR*, vol. 22, chap. XXXXIV, Correspondence, 473. See Ann Davis Niepman, "General Orders No. 11 and Border Warfare During the Civil War," in *Kansas City, America's Crossroads: Essays from the Missouri Historical Review, 1906–2006*, Diane Mutti Burke and John P. Herron, eds., 96–121 (Columbia: State Historical Society of Missouri, 2007); Albert Castel, "Orders No. 11 and the Civil War on the Border," *Missouri Historical Review* 57, no. 4 (1963): 357–68; Neely, *The Border Between Them;* and Rafiner, *Caught Between Two Fires.*

29. Mattie Jane Tate to Cousin Mary, December 14, 1864, Lone Jack Historical Society, Lone Jack, Missouri, www.civilwaronthewesternborder.org/content/mattie-jane-tate-cousin-mary. George Miller, *Missouri's Memorable Decade: 1860–1870* (Columbia, MO: E. W. Stephens, 1898), 103–4.

30. See Joan Stack, "Toward an Emancipationist Interpretation of George Caleb Bingham's Order Number 11," *Missouri Historical Review* 107, no. 4 (Summer 2013): 203–11. Missouri Division United Daughters of the Confederacy, *Reminiscences of the Women of Missouri during the Sixties* (Dayton, OH: Morningside House, 1988 rep.), 263. Bazel Lazear to wife, September 10, 1863, and September 17, 1863, Bazel Lazear Papers, SHSM.

31. Willard P. Hall to Hamilton R. Gamble, August 31, 1863, www.civilwaronthewesternborder.org/content/willard-p-hall-hamilton-r-gamble. *Liberty Tribune*, September 11, 1863, SHSM. "Disloyalists Banished from Western Border," ca. August 1863, Missouri History Museum, St. Louis, Missouri, www.civilwaronthewesternborder.org/content/disloyalists-banished-western-Missouri. See also Rafiner, *Cought Between Three Fires*, 398. For descriptions of arrests and attacks on women, see Partheny Horn Memoir; Elvira Ascenith Weir Scott Diary; and Whites, *Gender Matters.*

32. Allen T. Ward to My Dear Sister, October 27, 1861, Kansas Historical Society, Topeka, Kansas, www.civilwaronthewesternborder.org/content/allen-t-ward-my-dear-sister. *Morning Herald of St. Joseph*, October 18, 1863, statehistoricalsocietyofmissouri.org/cdm/compoundobject/collection/stjoemh/id/2579/rec/1. For the number of displaced civilians see Neely, *The Border Between Them;* and Rafiner, *Caught Between Three Fires.*

33. For additional discussions of General Order No. 11 and its aftermath, see Donald Gilmore, *Civil War on the Missouri/Kansas Border* (Gretna, LA: Pelican Press, 2006); and Jay Monaghan, *Civil War on the Western Border, 1854–1865* (Boston: Little, Brown, and Co., 1955). Now called Hickman Mills, in the nineteenth century the community was called both Hickman's Mill and Hickman's Mills.

34. There were a number of aspects of the war that unfolded in Missouri earlier than elsewhere. The Union army grappled with how to subdue a hostile civilian population under military occupation, how to respond to enslaved people seeking their freedom, how to help civilians who were displaced by the conflict, and how to train newly freed men to fight against their former owners. See Captain Richard H. Hinton testimony, December 14, 1863, New York City, American Freedmens' Inquiry Commission, Letters Received by the Office of Adjutant General, M619, reel 201, File 8, National Archives and Records Center, Washington, DC.

PART TWO

The Civil War is Not Over

FIVE

"The Future Empire of Our Freedmen"

REPUBLICAN COLONIZATION SCHEMES IN TEXAS AND MEXICO, 1861–1865

Nicholas Guyatt

IN THE SPRING OF 1862, AS THE CIVIL WAR'S first year drew to a close, the U.S. consul in Havana, Robert Wilson Shufeldt, asked Secretary of State William Seward for a two-month leave of absence. Rather than return to the United States, Shufeldt wanted to visit Mexico, which was in the midst of an extraordinary crisis. The Liberal government of Benito Juárez had emerged triumphant from Mexico's own civil war in January 1861 but had emptied the national treasury in the process. After defaulting on its foreign loans that summer, Mexico had been unable to prevent its European creditors—France, Britain, and Spain—from seizing its biggest port, Veracruz, in December 1861. Shufeldt urged Seward to look beyond the default for a darker design in the invasion. In the late 1850s, he had captained steamers on the first leg of the journey from New Orleans to California, dropping his passengers on the eastern side of the Mexican isthmus of Tehuantepec. A European invasion would surely culminate in the seizure of this lucrative route to the Pacific, unless the United States could secure Tehuantepec before foreign troops reached Mexico City. Beyond national security and commercial advantage, Shufeldt had another use for the isthmian region: it represented "the future home of the emancipated negro."[1]

Seward, who was desperate to avoid giving European governments a pretext to recognize the Confederacy, agreed to let Shufeldt make the trip on the condition that he would observe rather than meddle in Mexican affairs. But on arrival in Mexico City, Shufeldt befriended the U.S. ambassador, Thomas Corwin of Ohio, and pushed ahead with his plan. The two men agreed that the United States would lend money to the Liberals if Mexico allowed

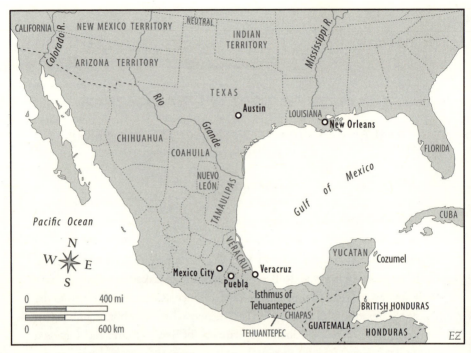

MAP 5.1 Mexico and the U.S. Southwest in the Era of Colonization.

African Americans to settle the lands of Tehuantepec. Acting without authority, Shufeldt reached a provisional agreement on colonization with Mexico's foreign minister. Corwin signed a separate loan treaty, but sent the draft to Washington with an enthusiastic endorsement of Shufeldt's plans—which was circulated to every member of Congress. Colonization wasn't the only reason to approve the loan, Corwin conceded, but it was among the most important: "It will give us an asylum, well adapted in its climate, soil and productions, . . . for the colonization of such people of color as we may wish, from any cause whatever, to get rid of."[2]

Shufeldt's plan for Tehuantepec was only one of a series of colonization efforts directed at Mexico and the southwestern United States during the Civil War years. The familiar narrative of Republican "growth" on the race question holds that Abraham Lincoln and his supporters entertained colonization only until events changed the paradigm: the Emancipation Proclamation broke the link between freedom and racial removal, while the enlistment of black soldiers allowed African Americans to ground their citizenship claims in battlefield courage rather than the largesse of northern philanthropists. But the story of these schemes for settling non-white Americans in Mexico, the Caribbean, or the U.S.–Mexico borderlands suggests that the logic of black belonging was far from obvious to many Republican leaders. Plans for black removal to Texas or Mexico were discussed before and after the Emancipation Proclamation, and one of the most important early boosters of black enlistment, Jim Lane of Kansas, promoted a version of "military colonization" in which black veterans would be rewarded for their service with a homeland in the Southwest. Historians have started to realize that the lure of a geographical partitioning of the races comfortably survived both emancipation and the Union victory at Appomattox. Not for the first time in American history, the West became the canvas for multiplying visions of racial containment and separation.[3]

The idea of a black colony in the American West dates back to the eighteenth century, but it gained momentum under Benjamin Lundy, the abolitionist mentor of William Lloyd Garrison. In the 1820s, like Stephen F. Austin, Lundy was drawn to Texas by its vast and fertile territory and the desire of Mexico's politicians and generals to consolidate the region through Anglo colonists. Though Lundy initially promoted various emigration schemes—including Liberia—in the pages of his antislavery newspaper, *The Genius of Universal Emancipation*, the skepticism of many free blacks toward the American Colonization Society (ACS) persuaded him that a black homeland should be located in North America. On a scouting trip to Texas in 1833, Lundy won tentative approval for a colony from Mexican officials but struggled to close the deal. Austin's Anglo colonists were already estranged from Mexico's central government, and the long-running battle between federalists and centralists in Mexico confounded Lundy's search for a stable negotiating partner. "I am completely baffled in my attempts to establish colonies in Texas," he confided to his journal in 1834. Lundy finally signed an agreement with the governor of the northeastern Mexican state of Tamaulipas in March 1835 and issued advertisements for colonists in northern newspapers. Prominent abolitionists—including David and Lydia Maria Child—agreed to travel to Mexico to help found the settlement. But Lundy's years of work were undone in a matter of months by the Anglo uprising that severed Texas from Mexico.[4]

Many antislavery northerners shared Lundy's view that the Texas Revolution was a conspiracy to transfer the state from an abolitionist authority (Mexico) to a proslavery one (the United States). But during the fractious

1844 presidential campaign, which was dominated by the issue of Texas annexation, the Mississippi senator Robert J. Walker popularized a more emollient view of the region's potential. Developing the old Jeffersonian idea that slaves would be less harmful to the United States if diffused across a wide area, Walker argued that the expansion of slavery in Texas would facilitate abolition in the upper South. With an eye on a northern audience unnerved by the prospect of immediate emancipation (and a northward exodus of freed slaves), Walker pitched Texas as the "safety valve" that would steer African Americans toward Mexico and Central America. Walker's argument won little favor from abolitionists, though Texas landholders soon learned that their slaves could open the safety valve into Mexico themselves. Thousands escaped across the Rio Grande during the 1840s and 1850s, leaving slaveholders to complain bitterly at authorities on both sides of the border.[5]

Despite their hostility toward Liberia and the ACS, free black leaders in the northern states had experimented with a variety of emigration schemes in the 1820s and 1830s: to Haiti and Canada, most notably. In 1851, soon after the passage of the Fugitive Slave Act, the Oberlin-educated brothers Charles and John Mercer Langston wrote their senator, Salmon P. Chase, to propose a black homeland within the territories acquired from Mexico in 1848; Chase thought this impracticable and recommended the Caribbean instead. The following year, John Mercer Langston spoke in favor of colonization at a black convention in Cincinnati, and the pioneering black nationalist Martin Delany counseled emigration to Latin America. (Delany even urged forward-thinking blacks to learn Spanish.) Inadvertently echoing the logic of Robert Walker, Delany suggested that, had the United States absorbed the entire nation of Mexico in 1848 rather than just its northern regions, "no people would have flocked there faster than the colored people from the United States."[6]

White colonization proponents had struggled to gain political traction since the 1820s, partly because the lower South staunchly opposed federal assistance for black removal. The rise of the Republican Party in the 1850s, and the prospect that a northern political bloc could sweep the national government, promised to change this equation. In 1859, during the debate over the proposed annexation of Cuba, Senator James Doolittle of Wisconsin suggested that a key Republican initiative—cheap homesteading in the West—should be adapted for free blacks and emancipated slaves. "A generous homestead policy for both races," he argued, would relocate whites to the Great Plains and blacks to Mexico and Central America. Frank P. Blair Jr., the Missouri congressman, insisted that free-black colonies near the isthmus would provide economic benefits to the United States without the taint of exploitation: they would become "our India, but under happier auspices." Blair's brother, Montgomery, told James Doolittle in 1859 that colonization's moment had finally arrived. A generation of politicians had bemoaned the spread of slavery, "confessed their inability to deal with it," and pointed vaguely toward a future crisis when it might finally be confronted. "The time has come, if ever, when this enabling act must be adopted."[7]

When Republicans looked to the Southwest in the late 1850s, they saw not a blank canvas but a dangerous vacuum. The European invasion of 1861 confirmed their fears, but Republicans had long fretted over the imperial designs of southern slaveholders. The annexation of a slaveholding Texas, a series of overtures toward Cuba, and the murky activities of filibusters in the Caribbean and Central America gave little reassurance that a conflict between North and South would be contained within the bounds of the United States. And so in January 1861, president-elect Abraham Lincoln met with Matías Romero, the Washington representative of Benito Juárez's Liberal government, to enquire whether Mexico's systems of peonage constituted "a more abominable servitude than the Negroes on Southern plantations." Although Romero relieved Lincoln's worries about a natural affinity between Mexico and the Confederacy, the idea that the South would lunge across the Rio Grande continued to circulate.[8]

The threat of a Confederate assault on Mexico strengthened the hand of colonization proponents during the Civil War's first year. Even before the firing on Fort Sumter, Lincoln met with Ambrose Thompson to discuss a colonization plan at the Panamanian isthmus. In a private meeting with Romero in June 1861, Montgomery Blair, now serving in the cabinet as postmaster general, stressed the mutual benefits of colonization. Mexico had underdeveloped territory in its tropical regions; American officials wanted to resettle millions of blacks who were supposedly fitted for tropical labor. Romero appreciated the company of "one of the most influential men in the cabinet, and a Radical Republican," but remained unconvinced by climatic theories of racial ability. And yet he conceded that Mexico needed immigrants, and graciously accepted Blair's head-spinning compliment that Mexicans "believe all human beings are endowed with the same rights without distinctions about their place of birth or the color which nature painted their faces with."[9]

Romero doubted that colonization could take place on a grand scale, but the deepening Mexican economic crisis and the European invasion made him ever more solicitous of his influential friend. When Blair raised colonization again in February 1862, the Lincoln administration was already negotiating with governments throughout the Americas for suitable territory. Blair's latest idea was Cozumel, just off the Yucatan coast. He had heard that the island might be for sale from Domingo de Goicouria, a member of a Mexican economic mission then in Washington. Romero doubted that Goicouria was speaking for his government—as a veteran of Narciso López's attempt to wrest Cuba from Spain in 1851 *and* of William Walker's notorious takeover of Nicaragua five years later, Goicouria was not the most transparent man of the age. (He was also Cuban and, in Romero's estimation, a poor judge of Mexico's best interests.) But, finding Blair typically persistent, Romero conceded that Mexico could allow "some or all of the Southern Negroes" to be resettled there, providing the island remained under Mexican control. Blair pressed for U.S. annexation on altruistic rather than expansionist grounds: "The Negroes do not wish to go anywhere, except under the protection of the United States flag." Romero assured Blair that African Americans could retain their U.S. citizenship and own land on Cozumel while the island remained a part of Mexico, and Blair bent a little. The Lincoln administration had been thinking of buying Cozumel "not precisely to acquire territory," he insisted, "but because it seemed easier to accomplish the colonization in this way." Romero left Blair with the impression that he was "entirely satisfied" with the plan, though he reported his true feelings to his superiors in Mexico City: "Unfortunately, I am not."[10]

The issue of colonization was reaching critical mass among American policymakers in early 1862. Romero had been badgered by William Seward, Montgomery Blair, and James Doolittle. Lincoln's annual address of December 1861 had promised a Latin American home for freed slaves, and Montgomery's brother, Frank, had authored a House bill to fund the purchase of Cozumel or another tropical region. Romero warned the Mexican foreign ministry to be on its guard against a new wave of aggressive aggrandizement. But the threat to the Juárez regime from the European powers was more immediate than the danger posed by U.S. expansionism. When Thomas Corwin and Robert Shufeldt met with Mexican foreign minister Manuel Doblado in the spring of 1862, French troops were closing on the capital, and the U.S. Senate had already rejected the first draft of a loan treaty that might bolster Juárez against the invaders. Corwin and Doblado prepared a new agreement providing Mexico with $11 million in return for the creation of a land board that would sell or apportion Mexican territory until the loan had been repaid. (Three board members would be Mexican, two from the United States.) Corwin framed the deal to Seward as an act of benevolence: Americans would buy land under the new treaty and teach Mexicans "lessons in morals, religion and politicks" that would complete their republican education. Corwin clearly envisaged, though, that the foot soldiers of this altruistic invasion would be black. "If our treaty is ratified," he told a friend, "We have a hold in the future of Mexico, by settling all her immense vacant lands with our people, and room enough in the tierra Caliente for two millions of free negroes, who could live in peace and honor with the only people of the white race known to us, who do, as you know, treat the black man and woman on a footing of perfect equality." Failure to ratify the treaty would squander "the best chance ever presented of colonizing the free negroes, which if not sent somewhere will be a lasting plague to us."[11]

Shufeldt's parallel agreement was more specific. The United States would gain a colonizing concession in Tehuantepec; its settlers would be exempt from Mexican taxes and military service, and protected by U.S. troops. But the hopes of Corwin and Shufeldt ran aground in Washington. Both were accused of bending diplomacy to their private interests—a charge that was hard to dismiss, given their commercial investments in the Tehuantepec region. Seward, meanwhile, feared a proxy war with Napoleon III that might jeopardize the Union cause. If Lincoln bankrolled the Mexican Liberals, would France formally recognize the Confederacy? This anxiety drove the Corwin-Doblado treaty to defeat in the Senate in July 1862. Corwin and Shufeldt had succeeded where Lincoln's many colonization emissaries had failed: they had the outline of a deal that would secure a huge tract of land for colonizing African Americans. But their plan could not be secured without upsetting the delicate diplomatic equilibrium that underpinned the war effort.[12]

. . .

While government officials continued to explore schemes for black resettlement, the idea of southwestern colonization found a champion in Senator Jim Lane, a former Democrat who had risen to national prominence by organizing military efforts in support of the Free State movement in Kansas. (For more on Lane see Diane Mutti Burke's chapter in this volume.) From the war's first months, Lane insisted that slaves should be swept into the Union armies and, at the war's end, settled on the fringes of the United States. On a visit to the White House in January 1862, he asked Lincoln "why you do not ... set apart some territory somewhere in the South, and say to the negroes in the rebel States, 'Here! come out and go over there, and we will protect you in its possession and your own freedom.'" Lane won plaudits throughout the North—even from abolitionists and free blacks—for insisting that the war should become "the mighty engine for the destruction of slavery." But his radicalism was anchored by a commitment to racial separation when the fighting was done.[13]

For Lane, Texas offered the best opportunity to launch his experiment in military colonization. Since its secession in March 1861, Texas had remained out of the reach of Union forces, but Lane proposed to march nearly seventy thousand men—half of them black—from Kansas to the Gulf of Mexico to subdue the rebellion there. Northern audiences were electrified by the idea. At a public reception in Chicago in January 1862, Lane claimed Lincoln's approval for a biracial assault on the Confederacy: "The other day, while I was talking with the President, Old Abe said to me, 'Lane, how many black men do you want to take care of your army?' I told him as my army would number 34,000, I proposed to have 34,000 contrabands in addition to my teamsters and wagonmasters. I consider every one of my soldiers engaged in this glorious Crusade of freedom a knight errant, and entitled to his squire to prepare his food, black his boots, load his gun, and take off his drudgery." But when Lane was interrupted by a shout from the crowd—"What are you going to do with the niggers?"—he elaborated on the full extent of his plan: "Ah, my friend, you are just the man I have been looking for. I will tell you what I am going to do with them. I am going to plant them on the soil of the gulf coast, after we have got through this war, let them stay there and cultivate the land; have government extend a protection to them, as it does to the Indians, and send superintendents and governors among them and pay them wages for their labor. There could be no competition between black and white labor." For Lane's "squires," this would be a one-way trip: "The blacks at no distant day would have possession of that Gulf country, to which they [are] acclimated and physically conditioned." According to the *Chicago Tribune,* Lane's ideas generated "astonishing enthusiasm" throughout the West during the war's first winter.[14]

The idea that the South could be subdued by military colonization became ubiquitous in 1862. In the fall, Massachusetts businessman Eli Thayer—another veteran of the Kansas struggles in the 1850s—proposed the settlement of Florida by white soldiers. The press reported his plan as a blueprint for black removal, and for several months Thayer did nothing to correct the misunderstanding. Even Frederick Douglass, a reliable opponent of removal schemes, thought that a black Florida "would cost nothing in comparison to the expensive scheme of Central American colonization." Frank Blair wrote to Secretary of War Edwin Stanton in July 1862 urging "the military occupation and colonization of the state of Texas." Blair saw the U.S. Southwest as a beachhead for the establishment of a black colony in "the tierra caliente of Mexico," which would in turn encourage blacks still in slavery to emancipate themselves "without formal proclamations of freedom." (Frederick Douglass had been willing to entertain a Florida colony for the same reason.) Blair's father, Preston, discussed the plan directly with Lincoln in August 1862, the same month that Lincoln conducted his infamously maladroit colonization interview with a delegation of free-black representatives from Washington. While the president equivocated that fall, the following summer Frank Blair still believed that he would imminently take command of a huge army "for the occupation and military colonization of Texas."[15]

Did Lincoln consider a massive black migration to the borderlands with Mexico? A clue comes from the 1891 memoir of Lucius Chittenden, a Vermont politician who served in the Treasury during the war. According to Chittenden, Lincoln visited his office in late 1862 or early 1863 "buried in thought over some subject of great interest." The president planned "to remove the whole colored race of the slave states into Texas," and asked Chittenden to suggest a contractor who might be able to help. Chittenden summoned John Bradley, a fellow Vermonter who owned a mercantile firm with wharves in Boston and New York. After a two-hour meeting with the president, Bradley reported that Lincoln wanted to give African Americans "a republic of their own" in the Southwest. If Lincoln were serious about "this wholesale transfer of the colored race," thought Bradley, "they will be in Texas within a year." Regardless of Bradley's logistical guarantees, however, the president must have realized that a massive "transfer" plan would struggle to win black support.[16]

The reluctance of black individuals and organizations to countenance colonization persisted through the war. Frederick Douglass, who had flirted with Haitian emigration during the first months of 1861, denounced the Republican embrace of tropical homesteading as "unjust and revolting." The entanglement of colonization with black military enlistment intrigued Douglass, and his newspaper closely followed Jim Lane's various plans in 1862 and 1863. Most African Americans, however shared the sentiments of the *Christian Recorder*, which urged its readers to avoid Lane's mooted black army, "to stay in their own State, and let the whites battle away at their pleasure." The only mainstream black organization that actively promoted emigration during the Civil War was the African Civilization Society, founded in 1859 by Henry Highland Garnet. The society's principal interest was in Africa rather than Central America, but it agreed at its September 1863 meeting to form a "standing committee on Texas, Florida and Mexico." Northern blacks—and even freed slaves in the contraband camps of the upper South—remained reluctant to leave the United States. While white proponents of a sweeping separation of the races predicted a "great change among the free blacks on this subject," black resistance remained the crucial obstacle to colonization.[17]

. . .

Throughout all of these debates about resettling black people in the Southwest, Mexico remained the most tantalizing destination. Its contiguity and relatively small population made it an obvious candidate for emigration proposals even before the European invasion of December 1861. For James Mitchell, the Indiana clergymen who would become Lincoln's colonization commissioner in 1862, Mexico's difficulties represented an opportunity for the United States. He urged the president to offer "passive submission" to the Europeans in return for "a home for our mixed races." (Intriguingly, Mitchell also envisaged Mexico as "a proper receptacle for the defeated rebels.") Most Washington observers, more faithful to the Monroe Doctrine, cheered the withdrawal of British and Spanish troops from the expeditionary force in the spring of 1862, and the ensuing defeat of the French Army at Puebla, southeast of the Mexican capital, on *el Cinco de Mayo*. But Napoleon III quickly dispatched reinforcements to Veracruz, with orders to unite the "Latin races" of the continent and make Mexico a bulwark against Anglo-Saxon expansionism. To achieve this goal, Napoleon proffered the Austrian Archduke Maximilian as the new emperor of Mexico.[18]

These plans were offensive to all manner of American assumptions. The characterization of U.S. expansion as a malevolent force was bad enough, but the French promotion of a European nobleman wounded the American republic's oldest vanity: that it had destroyed the mythos of monarchy in the Western Hemisphere. While Matías Romero struggled to convert the sympathy of administration officials into concrete support for the Mexican Liberals, American newspapers and public figures urged military intervention. Andrew Jackson Hamilton, whom Lincoln had appointed as military governor of Texas ahead of the long-delayed Union assault on the state, urged the president in August 1863 to send African Americans to fight Napoleon's forces. At the heart of his appeal was a conspiracy theory: France was planning a merger of Mexico's northern states with Confederate-controlled Texas, spawning "a new government under the imperial sanction and favor of Louis Napoleon." An African American army would not only be "an immense power on the side of nationality," but would provide "the only security" against the French plot.[19]

A few weeks later, the *Christian Recorder* published a letter from Henry McNeal Turner, the Episcopal preacher-turned-soldier who acted as a key promoter of black enlistment in Washington, D.C.: "Is it right to stand by and see republican *Mexico* shattered to pieces, and Maximilian, the Austrian prince, erect an imperial throne upon the ruins thereof? Should he not be warned to keep off of the American continent?" Black troops would enable the Lincoln administration both to win the Civil War and to keep America's republican promises: "I believe this government can drown Jeff. Davis and his hosts in the Red Sea, and send three hundred thousand men to Mexico to welcome Maximilian to his imperial throne, with as much canister and grape as would blow him into another region. . . . I would like to see an army of colored men, equal to that which was under Gen. McClellan, well drilled, over in Mexico when the contemplated king or emperor makes his appearance. I think France and he both would be glad to get away faster than they came." In the spring of 1864, Abraham Lincoln received similar advice from the Czech immigrant Anthony Dignowity, a longtime Texas resident who was nearly lynched for his unionism in 1861. Dignowity proposed that "as many as possible of the Negro regiments" should "clear out the Whole of Mexico of the French and other auxiliaries of theirs."[20]

Dignowity's inspiration was Jim Lane, who in February 1864 introduced a bill in the Senate "to set apart a portion of the State of Texas for the use of persons of African descent." Black soldiers would be mustered out in Texas, as white soldiers had been in California after the Mexican War, and their families would join them there. "Four millions of good citizens" in Texas would "cultivate friendly relations with the people of Mexico" and, before long, would persuade Mexico's northern states to "seek an annexation to our then glorious free republic." Lane's confidence that blacks would renovate the border region was grounded in climate theory. When African Americans reached the "tropical or semi-tropical lands" that best suited their constitution, they would become "lords of the soil." "The destiny of the whole tropical belt," he assured Congress, "is to pass under the future empire of the educated and civilized children of our freedmen." At a public meeting in New York, he promised that his "500,000 negro troops" would "crush" the Confederacy, "assert the Monroe Doctrine, and drive Maximilian out of Mexico."[21]

After Maximilian's coronation in the spring of 1864, black soldiers seemed uniquely suited to the task of advancing both the Monroe Doctrine and manifest destiny. The *Liberator*, in a departure from its usual hostility to colonization, published a proposal for 250,000 black soldiers to expel Napoleon. "Let Mexico become the home of the Freedmen," it urged, "and give to *our* race the wide-spread fields for fruits and flowers and human happiness, afforded by the Southern States." Similar sentiments were expressed in the congressional debates over the Thirteenth Amendment and the readmission of Louisiana. Even William Kelley, the celebrated Pennsylvania radical, envisaged the transfer of black Americans into "the tropical and malarious regions of Central America." Kelley was an opponent of streetcar segregation in Philadelphia and a supporter for black suffrage, but saw no contradiction between racial progressivism and these settlement plans. If blacks could be given suffrage and education at home, they would quickly acquire the skills and experience required for the "ultimate Americanization" of Mexico and Central America.[22]

The most outlandish plan for a march on Mexico during the war's final winter emerged from the peace overtures that produced the Hampton Roads conference. Predictably, it involved the paterfamilias of Republican colonization, Preston Blair. With Lincoln's blessing, Preston met secretly with Jefferson Davis in Richmond in January 1865 to suggest that North and South should unite to drive Napoleon from the continent. Davis would move "portions of his Army" to Texas, where they would rally with the forces of Benito Juárez and, if required, "multitudes of the army of the North." Juárez was already on board: Preston's son, Montgomery, had confirmed with Matías Romero that the Liberals would offer Jefferson Davis anything to recover and stabilize their country; even "a dictatorship if necessary." When this daring mission was complete, Preston continued, the army of deliverance could easily remake the states of Mexico "in form & principle to adapt them to our Union." Preston's plan made no reference to colonization but, given the Blairs' involvement and the heightened interest in a southwestern colony during this moment, it seems very likely that an ancillary benefit of the proposal would be the opening of territory that could be colonized by African Americans. As Matías Romero nervously told his superiors, at the conclusion of this adventure the United States would expect reimbursement from liberal Mexico "with unoccupied land."[23]

Alexander Stephens, the Confederacy's vice president, pressed Lincoln at Hampton Roads to agree to the grand alliance against Napoleon and Maximilian, suggesting (rather mischievously) that the Union might be restored after Confederate and Union troops had marched into Mexico to defend the principle of "local self-government." But Lincoln demanded a promise of restoration before any military expedition, and the talks came to nothing. Instead, the collapse of the Confederacy prompted thousands of southerners to contemplate their own exodus to Mexico.

Surprisingly, perhaps, given the long involvement of southerners in the U.S. erosion of Mexican sovereignty, the imperial government in Mexico City welcomed Confederate exiles. In part, this reflected Maximilian's unexpectedly engaged and technocratic view of Mexico's economic development, and his belief that immigration and colonization were crucial to the nation's future. In March 1865, he created a colonization *junta* with a cosmopolitan membership that included Nathaniel Davidson, an English agent of Rothschild's bank, and Enrique Sauvage, a French nobleman who had lived in South America before moving to Mexico. Throughout 1865, the court newspaper *El Diario del Imperio* ran dozens of articles on colonization. Impresarios promised to lure settlers from France, the United States, and even from Asia, while the government issued concessions and land grants. And yet, given the nation's instability, very few immigrants had actually materialized. The Confederates who made their way to the capital therefore had two pieces of good fortune: they arrived in Mexico amid a grand colonization drive and, for the most part, they had the place to themselves.[24]

Amid the flurry of colonization proposals circulating in Mexico City in the spring and summer of 1865, the businessman and railroad magnate Abdón Morales Montenegro looked to bring 100,000 "African and Chinese colonists" into Mexico—an idea that was formally debated by the colonization *junta*. Enrique Sauvage admitted that Chinese workers in Cuba had become a "moral cancer" on the island's cities, but denied that black or South Asian workers would contaminate Mexican morals. Their numbers would be small, and they would settle in areas "only really habitable by men of color." Sauvage shared the same basic assumption about black colonization as his American counterparts: it would consolidate peripheral areas without the risk of amalgamation. But the rest of the *junta* narrowly rejected the Abdón Morales concession, with the president warning of the threat posed by "germs" and "heterogeneity" to the purity of the Mexican populace. (Sauvage had already pointed out, to no avail, that Mexico's existing population was a mixed-race one.)[25]

By the fall of 1865, Maximilian's Liberal opponents were on the march from their stronghold in the northern states of Mexico, and the emperor was desperate to plant loyal settlers in their way. In September he revised the laws on peonage, strengthening the rights of landholders to apprentice the children of their workers. The colonization *junta* simultaneously approved land grants north of Veracruz for exiled Confederates. Although the peonage decree codified practices that were already applied to Mexican Indians, American officials were outraged. William Seward ordered the U.S. ambassador to France to make a formal protest to Napoleon III. Thomas Corwin, who remained U.S. ambassador to Mexico, fretted privately to Seward that "only the best and most industrious negroes will come here with their old masters," a development that would saddle the United States with the "idle and vicious" remnant who refused to move south. To avert this outcome, Corwin told the secretary of state to play up the threat of Mexican re-enslavement among southern blacks. Having lost control of the colonization agenda, Corwin now wanted the U.S. government to persuade African Americans to stay put.[26]

. . .

More than twenty thousand black Americans gathered on the northern bank of the Rio Grande in the summer and fall of 1865, but not for the reason Thomas Corwin had dreaded. U.S. commanders Ulysses S. Grant and Philip Sheridan insisted on increasing the military presence on the Mexican border, both to show support for the Liberals and to slow the movement of ex-Confederates southward. Nearly half of the forty-five-thousand-man force was black, partly because African Americans had enlisted at a later stage of the war, but also because commanders thought that black soldiers could be kept in uniform more easily than "dissatisfied Volunteers" from white regiments. Having welcomed Confederates and their slaves the previous fall, Maximilian and his officials now dreaded an invasion by black troops in Union colors. When, in January 1866, American and Mexican troops began shooting at each other in the border town of Bagdad, Texas, observers in Mexico City fell into a panic. The newspaper *La Nacion* concluded that white Americans had already realized the danger of living alongside blacks in freedom and were now looking to "get rid of them" by creating an army that would conquer northern Mexico. Though the Bagdad incident was an isolated one—and had been engineered by Mexican Liberals rather than American colonizationists—it reinforced the view in Mexico City that a black army on the border promised "the extermination of the white race" in northern Mexico.[27]

Beyond the occasional article in the black press, African American interest in colonization failed to ignite in the war's aftermath. Although the quickening pace of white resentment in the former Confederacy may have clouded black hopes of peaceful coexistence, the Union victory had created a new calculus of racial belonging in the South. The journalist Whitelaw Reid, who traveled through Georgia and Louisiana in 1865, thought that even those blacks who accepted the need for racial separation had a novel understanding of how it would work: "Their idea of accomplishing it is, not to remove the blacks, but to have the whites remove from them."[28]

In Mexico, the idea of colonizing undeveloped regions with black labor was undermined by the prejudices of Mexican officials and the worsening position of the imperial regime. In the fall of 1865, Maximilian appointed colonization agents to promote Mexican settlement in Tennessee, Louisiana, and Texas, and chose Matthew Maury—a former U.S. Navy officer and a defeated Confederate—as his "imperial colonization commissary." But Maury's paeans to Mexico's ruined haciendas—which he styled as more promising than the "deserts" of the U.S. West—were aimed at Europeans rather than African Americans. Although a trickle of ex-Confederates continued to settle in Mexico, the news in January 1866 that Napoleon was withdrawing his troops made political stability seem more distant than ever.[29]

Despite the darkening prospects for colonization among politicians on both sides of the Rio Grande, its advocates found it hard to relinquish. Senator James Doolittle, one of the pioneers of tropical homesteading, wrote to President Andrew Johnson in September 1865 asking him to create a "freedman's territory" in Texas. (Johnson raised the idea in a private meeting with Salmon Chase that same month.) Montgomery Blair, increasingly estranged from the Radical Republicans in Congress, told a Democratic rally in October 1865 that the United States should condition support for Benito Juárez on the provision of "a place of refuge" within Mexico for freed slaves. Preston Blair asked Freedmen's Bureau commissioner Oliver O. Howard to create black colonies in Texas; and, more than two years after the surrender at Appomattox, Blair made a similar pitch to General Grant. Blacks should be given "a state on either side of the Rio Grande where they could exercise sovereignty"; with this bright offer in hand, they could be legitimately subjected to "white legislative supremacy" if they declined to go. Blair hoped blacks would establish an exclusive zone around the Gulf of Mexico, and congressional radicals would agree to their removal as a "compromise plan" for Reconstruction. At some point, Blair noticed that Grant was saying nothing, and that his expression had changed. "*He looked aghast*," Blair later wrote his son, "and I left him."[30]

With the cause of southwestern colonization left to its diehard supporters by 1866, it would be tempting to conclude that the idea had become an anachronism: a smudge of moral evasion that had been washed away, for the most part, by the rising tide of emancipation. But sweeping visions of racial separation lingered in the white imagination long after the passage of the Thirteenth Amendment. Andrew Johnson invoked colonization as a fallback plan if Reconstruction ran into difficulties. When Ulysses S. Grant launched his bid to annex the Dominican Republic in 1870, he combined the promotion of nonwhite citizenship with a tacit avowal of racial separation: an American state of Dominica would function as both the capstone of Reconstruction and as a lifeboat for black people fleeing racialized violence in the southern states. The idea that African Americans would ultimately move elsewhere had a romantic vagueness for liberal whites, but it was strong enough to survive the upheavals of the war and the collapse of countless schemes for black removal. In fact, for some Republicans the war's successful outcome cleared the way for more extensive experiments in racial realignment. What kept these experiments in check was not the moral epiphany of emancipation but the steadfast refusal of most black people to consent to their expatriation.[31]

In 1871, Robert Shufeldt looked back on his plans for Mexican colonization with pride and regret. He recalled that Lincoln had given serious consideration to "settling the river-bottoms of [the] Isthmus with negroes from our Southern States," and he remembered his own role in securing the Mexican government's approval for that plan. Only "the march of events at that time"—the wars on either side of the Rio Grande—had thwarted his designs. Shufeldt had recently returned to Mexico to survey the Tehuantepec region for an isthmian canal, and in his report to Congress he threaded his reflections on wartime colonization through an accounting of the labor required to unite the oceans. On this latest trip, he had even met a black American who moved to Mexico in the 1850s and who had recently toured the southern states amid the turmoil of Reconstruction. His informant was "emphatically of the opinion that there are many discontented men of his own race in that part of our country who would willingly emigrate to Mexico if any such public work would be undertaken." In spite of this promising intelligence, and his long-standing fascination with black removal, Shufeldt had, finally, learned something from his disappointments: "The main body of laborers, however, would probably have to come from China."[32]

NOTES

1. Frederick C. Drake, *The Empire of the Seas: A Biography of Rear Admiral Robert Wilson Shufeldt, USN* (Honolulu: University of Hawaii Press, 1984), 14–18, 55–58.

2. Ibid., 58–69. Thomas D. Schoonover, *Dollars over Dominion: The Triumph of Liberalism in Mexican-United States Relations, 1861–1867* (Baton Rouge: Louisiana State University Press, 1978), 70–71, 105. Marcela Terrazas Basante, *Los Intereses Norteamericanos en el Noroeste de México* (Mexico City: Universidad Nacional Autónoma de México, 1990), 83–85. "Mexican Affairs," *New York Times,* June 30, 1862, p. 8.

3. On the colonization of blacks in the Southwest, see Thomas Schoonover, "Misconstrued Mission: Expansionism and Black Colonization in Mexico and Central America during the Civil War," *Pacific Historical Review* 49, no. 4 (November 1980): 607–20; and Rachel Adams, "Blackness Goes South: Race and Mestizaje in Our America," in Sandhya Shukla and Heidi Tinsman, eds., *Imagining Our Americas: Towards a Transnational Frame* (Durham, NC: Duke University Press, 2007), 214–48. On colonization more generally, see Mark E. Neely Jr., "Colonization and the Myth That Lincoln Prepared the People for Emancipation," in William A. Blair and Karen Fisher Younger, *Lincoln's Proclamation: Emancipation Reconsidered* (Chapel Hill: University of North Carolina Press, 2009), 45–74; Eric Foner, *The Fiery Trial: Abraham Lincoln and American Slavery* (New York: Norton, 2010); Phillip W. Magness and Sebastian N. Page, *Colonization After Emancipation: Lincoln and the Movement for Black Resettlement* (Columbia: University of Missouri Press, 2011); and Nicholas Guyatt, "'An Impossible Idea?' The Curious Career of Internal Colonization," *Journal of the Civil War Era* 4, no. 2 (June 2014): 234–63. The most famous proponent of the "growth" theory is Eric Foner; see especially *Fiery Trial,* xix-xx.

4. Benjamin Lundy, *The Life, Travels and Opinions of Benjamin Lundy, Including his Journeys to Texas and Mexico* (Philadelphia: William D. Parrish, 1847), 128. Benjamin Lundy, *A Circular . . . on the Subject of Mexican Colonization* (Philadelphia: J. Richards, 1835). Lydia Maria Child to Ellis Gray Loring, January 30, 1836, and Child to Louisa Loring, May 3, 1836, in Milton Meltzer and Patricia G. Holland, eds., *Lydia Maria Child: Selected Letters, 1817–1880* (Amherst: University of Massachusetts Press, 1982), 43–44, 49. Randolph B. Campbell, *Empire for Slavery: The Peculiar*

Institution in Texas, 1821–65 (Baton Rouge: Louisiana State University Press, 1991), 35. See also Gregg Cantrell, *Stephen F. Austin: Empresario of Texas* (New Haven: Yale University Press, 2001); Michael A. Morrison, *Slavery and the American West: The Eclipse of Manifest Destiny and the Coming of the American Civil War* (Chapel Hill: University of North Carolina Press, 1997), 13–38; Joel H. Silbey, *Storm over Texas: The Annexation Controversy and the Road to Civil War* (New York: Oxford University Press, 2005); and Thomas R. Hietala, *Manifest Design: American Exceptionalism and Empire*, rev. ed. (Ithaca, NY: Cornell University Press, 2003), 10–54.

5. Robert J. Walker, *Letter of Mr. Walker of Mississippi, Relative to the Annexation of Texas* (Washington, DC: Printed at the Globe Office, 1844). Campbell, *Empire for Slavery*, 62–64. Ronnie C. Tyler, "Fugitive Slaves in Mexico," *Journal of Negro History* 57, no. 1 (January 1970): 1–12. Sarah E. Cornell, "Citizens of Nowhere: Fugitive Slaves and Free African Americans in Mexico, 1833–1857," *Journal of American History* 100, no. 2 (September 2013): 351–74. See also Sean Kelley, "'Mexico in His Head': Slavery and the Texas-Mexico Border, 1810–1860," *Journal of Social History* 37, no. 3 (2004): 709–723; Brian DeLay, *War of a Thousand Deserts: Indian Raids and the U.S.-Mexican War* (New Haven: Yale University Press, 2008); and Rosalie Schwartz, *Across the Rio to Freedom: U.S. Negroes in Mexico* (El Paso: Texas Western Press, 1975).

6. William Cheek and Aimee Lee Cheek, *John Mercer Langston and the Fight for Black Freedom, 1829–65* (Champaign: University of Illinois Press, 1989), 170–71. "Convention of Colored Persons in Ohio," *Baltimore Sun*, January 20, 1852, p. 2. Martin R. Delany, *The Condition, Elevation, Emigration and Destiny of the Colored People of the United States, Politically Considered* (Philadelphia: Published for the Author, 1852), esp. 178–89.

7. Cong. Globe, 35th Cong., 2d sess., February 9, 1859, 907. App. to the Cong. Globe, 37th Cong., 2d sess., April 11, 1862, 94–101; 98. Frank P. Blair Jr., *The Destiny of the Races of this Continent* (Washington, DC: Buell & Blanchard, 1859), 23, 27. Montgomery Blair to James Doolittle, November 11, 1859, in "Negro Colonization," *Publications of the Southern History Association*, 10, no. 5 (September 1906): 288.

8. Thomas D. Schoonover, *Mexican Lobby: Matías Romero in Washington, 1861–1867* (Lexington: University Press of Kentucky, 1986), 2–3. On southern expansionism, see Robert E. May, *The Southern Dream of a Caribbean Empire, 1854–1861*, 2nd ed. (Gainesville: University Press of Florida, 2002); Matthew Pratt Guterl, *American Mediterranean: Southern Slaveholders in the Age of Emancipation* (Cambridge, MA: Harvard University Press, 2008), 12–78; David C. Keehn, *Knights of the Golden Circle: Secret Empire, Southern Secession, Civil War* (Baton Rouge: Louisiana State University Press, 2013); and Walter Johnson, *River of Dark Dreams: Slavery and Empire in the Cotton Kingdom* (Cambridge, MA: Harvard University Press, 2013), 330–94. For a sense of the constraints facing Confederate expansionists, see Thomas D. Schoonover, "Napoleon Is Coming! Maximilian Is Coming? The International History of the Civil War in the Caribbean Basin," in Robert May, ed., *The Union, the Confederacy, and the Atlantic Rim* (West Lafayette, IN: Purdue University Press, 1995), 101–30; and Guterl, *American Mediterranean*, 55–78.

9. Foner, *Fiery Trial*, 185. S. N. Page, "Lincoln and Chiriquí Colonization Revisited," *American Nineteenth Century History* 12, no. 3 (2011): 289–325. Schoonover, *Mexican Lobby*, 5–6.

10. Schoonover, *Mexican Lobby* 6, 16–19. On Goicouria, see Stephen Dando-Collins, *Tycoon's War: How Cornelius Vanderbilt Invaded a Country to Overthrow America's Most Famous Military Adventurer* (Boston: Da Capo Press, 2007), 170; and T. J. Stiles, *The First Tycoon: The Epic Life of Cornelius Vanderbilt* (New York: Knopf, 2009), 290. Romero notified Mexico City in May 1862 that Goicouria had recently met with Caleb Smith, Lincoln's interior minister, to discuss the transfer of two thousand contrabands to a railroad project near Veracruz. *Correspondencia de la Legación Méxicana en Washington durante la Intervención Extranjera, 1860–1868*, 10 vols. (Mexico City: Imprenta del Gobierno, 1870–92), 2: 181. Schoonover, *Mexican Lobby*, 18–19.

11. Terrazas, *Los Intereses Norteamericanos*, 67. Romero sent James Doolittle's long April 11 Senate speech on colonization back to Manuel Doblado, with a note that Doolittle "expresses the ideas of the President" on the topic: *Correspondencia* 2: 224. Corwin's letter to Seward of April 16, 1862, is reprinted (along with the treaty itself) in "The Corwin-Doblado Treaty April 6, 1862," *Hispanic American Historical Review* 17, no. 4 (November 1937): 499–506. Corwin to A. C. Allen, May 18, 1862, in Lincoln Papers, Series 1, General Correspondence, 1833–1916, Library of Congress, Washington, DC. (The location of this letter in the Lincoln Papers suggests that Allen, Corwin's friend and emissary, succeeded in his mission of conveying the minister's views directly to the president.) On the backdrop to the Corwin-Doblado treaty, see Schoonover, *Dollars over Dominion*, 48–77.

12. Drake, *Empire of the Seas*, 58–69. On Corwin's commercial interests in Tehuantepec, see Schoonover, *Dollars over Dominion*, 73; and "Synopsis of the Mexican Treaty," *New York Times*, June 30, 1862, p. 8. The House version of the confiscation bill, which passed in June 1862, specified that Lincoln would seek land for colonization in "Mexico, Central America or South America, or in the islands of the Gulf of Mexico." The final Act of July 1862 spoke more vaguely of "some tropical country beyond the limits of the United States." *The Statutes at Large, Treaties, and Proclamations of the United States of America* (Boston: Little, Brown, 1863), 12: 592. The House bill was reprinted in "Passage of the Confiscation Bill," *Christian Recorder*, June 28, 1862.

13. "An Interesting Declaration," *New York Tribune*, January 21, 1862, p. 5. "Lane's Brigade," *White Cloud Kansas Chief*, November 28, 1861, p. 2. "Jim Lane's Speech at Springfield, Missouri," *Smoky Hill and Republican Union*, November 28, 1861, p. 1. Robert Collins, *Jim Lane: Scoundrel, Statesman, Kansan* (New Orleans: Pelican Publishing Company, 2007); and Ian Michael Spurgeon, *Man of Douglas, Man of Lincoln: The Political Odyssey of James Henry Lane* (Columbia: University of Missouri Press, 2008).

14. "Gen. Lane in Chicago," *Chicago Tribune*, January 21, 1862, p. 4. "Gen. Lane on His Way Westward," *New York Times*, January 29, 1862, p. 3. "Our Washington Letter," *Chicago Tribune*, February 26, 1862, p. 2. Western newspapers reported that

Lane's force would be truly multiracial: in addition to blacks recruited from Missouri and drawn to Lane's brigades during the march through slave territory, the intrepid general would attract Native Americans both from Kansas and during the traversal of the Indian country north of Texas. "Jim Lane's Great Expedition," *Chicago Tribune,* January 8. 1862, p. 1.

15. Guyatt, "An Impossible Idea?" "Lane and Hunter," *New York Times,* March 14, 1862, p. 3. Spurgeon, *Man of Douglas, Man of Lincoln,* 193–98. Francis P. Blair Jr., to Edwin M. Stanton, July 14, 1862, in Lincoln Papers, Series 1, General Correspondence, 1833–1916. Francis Blair Sr., to Francis Blair Jr., August 22, 1862; and Blair Jr. to Montgomery Blair, September 24, 1863, in Blair Family Papers, Library of Congress, Washington, DC. The Union assault of Texas eventually took place in November 1863, though without lasting success. See Stephen A. Townsend, *The Yankee Invasion of Texas* (College Station: Texas A&M University Press, 2006). On Lincoln's unfortunate colonization interview with free-black Washingtonians, see Kate Masur, "The African American Delegation to Abraham Lincoln: A Reappraisal," *Civil War History* 56, no. 2 (June 2010): 117–44.

16. L. E. Chittenden, *Recollections of President Lincoln and his Administration* (New York: Harper & Brothers, 1891), 336–40.

17. "Lecture to the Emancipation League of Boston," in John W. Blassingame, ed., *The Frederick Douglass' Papers, Series One: Speeches, Debates and Interviews,* five vols. (New Haven: Yale University Press, 1979–92), 3, 489–508. "The War," *Christian Recorder,* August 16, 1862. "Speech of General Jim Lane," *Douglass' Monthly,* December 1861; "General James H. Lane of Kansas," *Douglass' Monthly,* February 1862. "African Civilization Society," *Christian Recorder,* November 14, 1863. Robert J. Walker, "The Union," *Continental Monthly* 2, no. 5 (November 1862): 572–79. On black proponents of colonization, see Wilson Jeremiah Moses, *The Golden Age of Black Nationalism, 1850–1925* (New York: Oxford University Press, 1988); Floyd J. Miller, *The Search for a Black Nationality: Black Emigration and Colonization, 1787–1863* (Urbana-Champaign: University of Illinois Press, 1975); and James T. Campbell, *Middle Passages: African American Journeys to Africa, 1787–2005* (New York: Penguin Books, 2006). The Haitian Emigration Bureau organized black migration to Haiti between 1860 and 1862 but was directed by the white abolitionist James Redpath: Chris Dixon, *African America and Haiti* (Greenwood, CT: Westport, 2000), 129–205.

18. James Mitchell to Abraham Lincoln, December 13, 1861, in Lincoln Papers, Series 1, General Correspondence, 1833–1916, Library of Congress. On the international/diplomatic context of the Mexican intervention, see Howard Jones, *Abraham Lincoln and a New Birth of Freedom: The Union and Slavery in the Diplomacy of the Civil War* (Lincoln: University of Nebraska Press, 1999), 70–76; Alfred Jackson Hanna and Kathryn Abbey Hanna, *Napoleon III and Mexico: American Triumph over Monarchy* (Chapel Hill: University of North Carolina Press, 1971); and Patrick J. Kelly, "The North American Crisis of the 1860s," *Journal of the Civil War Era* 2, no. 3 (September 2012): 337–68.

19. "Letter of General A. J. Hamilton," *New York Tribune,* August 24, 1863, p. 2.

20. "Republican Form of Government," *Christian Recorder,* October, 3 1863. Anthony M. Dignowity to Abraham Lincoln, April 8, 1864, in Lincoln Papers, Series 1, General Correspondence, 1833–1916, Library of Congress.

21. Cong. Globe, 38th Cong., 1st sess., February 16, 1864, 672–75. "Report to Accompany Senate Bill No. 45," Senate Committee on Territories Report No. 8, 38th Cong., 1st sess., February 4, 1864. Cong. Globe, 38th Cong., 1st sess., 673. *Speeches of Hon. James H. Lane, in the Cooper Institute, New York* (Washington, DC: William H. Moore, 1864).

22. "Letter to a California Senator," *Liberator,* November 25, 1864, 192. Cong. Globe, 38th Cong., 2d sess., January 12, 1865, and January 16, 1865, 236–37, 281–91. Kelley had been promoting tropical colonization since 1862. See, for example, ibid., 37th Cong., 2d sess., January 31, 1862, 596.

23. Francis P. Blair Sr., "Suggestions Submitted to Jefferson Davis," January 12, 1865, in Lincoln Papers, Series 1, General Correspondence, 1833–1916, Library of Congress. "Conversation with Francis Preston Blair," January 12, 1865, in Haskell M. Monroe Jr. et al., eds., *The Papers of Jefferson Davis,* 13 vols. (Baton Rouge: Louisiana State University Press, 1971–2012), 11: 315–23. Schoonover, *Mexican Lobby,* 51–52. See also William C. Harris, "The Hampton Roads Peace Conference: A Final Test of Lincoln's Presidential Leadership," *Journal of the Abraham Lincoln Association,* 21, no. 1 (Winter 2000): 30–61.

24. Harris, "Hampton Roads," 48. Alexander Stephens, *Constitutional View of the Late War between the States,* 2 vols. (Philadelphia: National Publishing Company, 1868–70), 2: 600–609. "Decreto imperial," *El Diario del Imperio,* March 29, 1865, 293. On Confederate refugees from the collapsing Confederacy, see Guterl, *American Mediterranean,* 79–113; Eugene C. Harter, *The Lost Colony of the Confederacy* (College Station: Texas A&M University Press, 2000); Anthony Arthur, *General Jo Shelby's March* (New York: Random House, 2010); and Andrew Rolle, *The Lost Cause: The Confederate Exodus to Mexico* (Norman: University of Oklahoma Press, 1965). On the surprisingly technocratic makeup of Maximilian's government, see Erika Pani, "Dreaming of a Mexican Empire: The Political Projects of the 'Imperialistas,'" *Hispanic American Historical Review* 82, no. 1 (2002): 1–31. On Davidson's involvement in Mexico, see Niall Ferguson, *The House of Rothschild: The World's Banker, 1849–1999* (New York: Viking, 1999), 118.

25. Ulysses S. Grant to Andrew Johnson, June 19, 1865, in John Y. Simon, ed., *The Papers of Ulysses S. Grant,* 32 vols. (1967–2012), 15: 156–58. On the Gwin scheme, see Hanna and Hanna, *Napoleon III and Mexico,* 167–80. Grant to Irvin McDowell, January 8, 1865, in Simon, ed., *Papers of Ulysses S. Grant,* 13: 250; Lewis Wallace to Grant, May 16, 1865, in Simon, ed., *Papers of Ulysses S. Grant,* 13: 290; Philip Sheridan to Grant, July 18, 1865, in Simon, ed., *Papers of Ulysses S. Grant,* 15: 260–61. Corwin to Seward, September 10, 1865, in *Message of the President of the United States of March 20, 1866, Relating to the Condition of Affairs in Mexico,* Executive Document No. 73, 39th Cong., 1st sess. (Washington, DC: Government Printing Office, 1866), 1: 470–71. Grant and Sheridan nursed anxieties about a mass removal of Confederates to Mexico into 1866: see Sheridan to Grant, February 7, 1866, in

Simon, ed., *Papers of Ulysses S. Grant*, 15: 426. Colonizacion," *El Diario del Imperio*, June 10, 1865, 545–47. Rolle, *Lost Cause*, 110. On the challenges facing colonization proponents in Mexico, see Luis Robles Pezuela, *Memoria Presentada á S.M. El Emperador Por El Ministro de Fomento* (Mexico City: J. M. Andrade and F. Escalante, 1866), 99–100, 108; and Alfred J. Hanna and Kathryn Abbey Hanna, "The Immigration Movement of the Intervention and Empire as Seen through the Mexican Press," *Hispanic American Historical Review* 27, no. 2 (May 1947): 220–46.

26. Corwin to Seward, September 10, 1865, in *Message of the President of the United States of March 20, 1866, Relating to the Condition of Affairs in Mexico*, Executive Document No. 73, 39th Cong., 1st sess. (Washington, DC: Government Printing Office, 1866), 1: 470–71. Seward to John Bigelow, November 2, 1865, in *Condition of Affairs in Mexico*, 479–80. Romero to the Foreign Ministry, October 1, 1865, in *Correspondencia*, 5: 660.

27. Grant to William T. Sherman, October 31, 1865, in Simon, ed., *Papers of Ulysses S. Grant*, 15: 377. The article in La Nacion was reprinted as "La Cuestion de las Razas" in *El Diario del Imperio*, February 6, 1866, 156. See also William E. Hardy, "South of the Border: Ulysses S. Grant and the French Intervention," *Civil War History* 54, no. 1 (2008): 63–86; James N. Leiker, *Racial Borders: Black Soldiers along the Rio Grande* (College Station: Texas A&M University Press, 2002), 27–30; and William A. Dobak, *Freedom by the Sword: The U.S. Colored Troops, 1862–1867* (Washington, DC: U.S. Army Center of Military History, 2011), 434–54. On the Bagdad raid, see Dobak, *Freedom by the Sword*, 448–50; and Jerry D. Thompson, *Cortina: Defending the Mexican Name in Texas* (College Station: Texas A&M University Press, 2007), 167–70.

28. "What Shall Be Done with the Negro?" *Christian Recorder*, August 19, 1865. Whitelaw Reid, *After the War: A Southern Tour* (Cincinnati and New York: Moore, Wilstach and Baldwin, 1866), 146–47.

29. M. F. Maury, "A todos los que quieran establecerse en México," ["To all that wish to settle in Mexico"], *El Diario del Imperio*, December 5, 1865, 626. "Junta de Colonizacion," *El Diario del Imperio*, January 24, 1866, 115.

30. James Doolittle to Andrew Johnson, September 9, 1865, James R. Doolittle Papers, Wisconsin Historical Society, Madison, WI. Salmon P. Chase to William Sprague, September 6, 1865, in John Niven, ed., *The Salmon P. Chase Papers, Vol. 5, Correspondence, 1865–73* (Kent, OH: Kent State University Press, 1998), 67–68. "Ratification Meeting at Cooper Institute," *New York Times*, October 19, 1865, p. 1. Matías Romero to the Minister of Foreign Affairs, October 20, 1865, in *Correspondencia*, 5: 711–13. Francis P. Blair Sr. to Francis P. Blair Jr., October 5, 1866, in Blair Family Papers, Library of Congress. Blair Sr. to Blair Jr., December 8, 1867, in Blair Family Papers. See also Guyatt, "An Impossible Idea?"

31. Guyatt, "An Impossible Idea?," 262–63. Kenneth Rayner, *Life and Times of Andrew Johnson, Seventeenth President of the United States* (New York: D. Appleton and Company, 1866), 15–17. Guyatt, "America's Conservatory: Race, Reconstruction, and the Santo Domingo Debate," *Journal of American History* 97 (March 2011):

974–1000. As late as 1891, a U.S. senator introduced a bill for the colonization of African Americans in Baja California. "A New Negro Colonization Project," *New York Tribune*, January 8, 1891, p. 5. See also Karl Jacoby, "Between North and South: The Alternative Borderlands of William H. Ellis and the African American Colony of 1895," in *Continental Crossroads: Remapping U.S.-Mexico Borderlands History*, ed. Samuel Truett and Elliot Young (Durham, NC: Duke University Press, 2004), 209–40.

32. Robert W. Shufeldt, *Reports of Explorations and Surveys to Ascertain the Probability of a Ship-Canal between the Atlantic and Pacific Oceans by way of the Isthmus of Tehuantepec*, Executive Doc. No. 6, 42nd Cong., 2d sess. (Washington, DC: Government Printing Office, 1872), 18. Drake, *Empire of the Seas*, 125–52.

SIX

Three Faces of Sovereignty

GOVERNING CONFEDERATE, MEXICAN, AND INDIAN
TEXAS IN THE CIVIL WAR ERA

Gregory P. Downs

IN THE SPRING OF 1865, THE CIVIL WAR SEEMED at last to grind to an end in Texas. Weeks earlier Confederates had surrendered at Appomattox Court House, Virginia, and Durham, North Carolina, but in Texas the war had not yet concluded. At the battle of Palmito Ranch, on May 12 and 13, 1865, the Sixty-Second U.S. Colored Infantry and other volunteers encountered active Confederates who ambushed them and fought them back from the mainland, taking a hundred prisoners and killing or wounding another thirty U.S. soldiers. It was not until June that Confederate General Edmund Kirby Smith finally surrendered Texas and the Trans-Mississippi West to U.S. forces.[1]

If we think of the Civil War as a series of battles between organized forces, its final acts in Texas seem like insignificant echoes, and the battle of Palmito Ranch merely the answer to a carefully worded trivia question. But contemporaries did not think of the war in such tidy categories. This conflict in Texas was both the end of uniformed skirmishes and the beginning of a post-surrender effort to finish the war by consolidating national power over troubled peripheries.

In October 1865, the *Army & Navy Journal* argued that three "trouble spots" posed significant threats to the nation's stability: "The South, Indian frontiers, and Mexico."[2] In a rhetorical move common at the time, this military newspaper asserted both that the Civil War had ended and that it endured. Surrender had simultaneously concluded and continued the war. The clash between armies had ended, but the series of challenges to the nation's authority over its peripheries was not over—that civil war continued. How much power would the national government be able to exert over its borderlands and throughout the countryside? On that question, the battles in both western and southern states endured in the years after surrender.

Although the relationship between the *Army & Navy Journal*'s "trouble spots" could be traced in any number of areas, in Texas the threats to federal authority were multiple and intertwined: ex-Confederates who continued to hold slaves; Indian tribes who raided white settlements; and, as Nicholas Guyatt discusses in this volume, imperial Mexican sympathizers who sought once again to steer Texas, or at least Texans, back to Mexico. Placing the U.S. efforts to pacify Texas within a broader set of sovereignty tests helps broaden our understanding of the Civil War era's trials of both the national government's resilience (the typically southern question) and its reach (a question more central to western historians). By examining competing visions of how to impose sovereignty within Texas—against Mexico, rebels, and Indians—this chapter examines how these civil wars could only be resolved in the West.[3]

If scholars assert that the Civil War began in Texas and the Southwest (because of the annexation question following the U.S. war with Mexico), they have been slower to consider seriously how it continued there after the eastern surrenders.[4] Even though Palmito Ranch is cited as the last significant skirmish of the war, and President Andrew Johnson attempted to end the Civil War with a special proclamation terminating the rebellion in Texas, scholars have been slow to think about how the civil wars and reconstructions in the South and West were inherently intertwined. The problems of ending slavery, subduing Confederate disloyalty, creating defensible space for settlers in Indian lands, and asserting control over a previously foreign region each tested the government's capacity to make itself felt and to stabilize a deeply fractured nation. Rather than a place apart, Texas was a place embedded within broader struggles for spatial control, waged between settlers and Indians, between Mexican imperialists and Liberals on the border, and between planters and freedpeople in the plantation belt. Contemporaries captured the fluidity of Texas as borderland, rebel land, Indian land, and Mexican land as they advanced different visions for the postwar nation; in free-floating comparisons, Texas became a place for the potential reenactment of Missouri's guerrilla warfare, Virginia's Shenandoah Valley counterinsurgency Army campaigns, and Mexico's ongoing civil war. Through these analogies, observers at the time asked whether the territories obtained in the annexation of Texas and the Southwest could be thoroughly incorporated into a postwar nation. Could Comanche and other Indians be geographically confined to make safe routes of passage and zones of residence for the burgeoning numbers of westward-bound white settlers?

In Texas, as in the rest of the country, the United States faced these crises with only the bluntest of tools: the understudied and understaffed—but still formidable—postsurrender Army. The most visible and often most effective arm of the federal government, the Army was the largest part of what was in turn a surprisingly robust, ambitious, and geographically widespread occupation of the ex-Confederacy. At the same time, in Texas, it was also part of the national government's efforts to undermine the imperial government in Mexico and to force Indians onto increasingly narrow reservations. After holding only a tiny sliver of Texas in the spring of 1865, the United States rolled inland slowly but forcefully as Confederate armies surrendered in the east. After Confederate General Edmund Kirby Smith's surrender, the Army occupied eight cities and forts in June, and twenty-two more in July, declaring emancipation as they went. In August 1865, the state held nearly fifty thousand U.S. soldiers, more than 20 percent of all those located in the ex-Confederacy (and by far the largest contingent in any former rebel state). In these years around 30 percent of all troops stationed in the ex-Confederacy were in Texas, where they held at various times between fifteen and thirty-six different outposts.

At first the Army clustered along the Texas–Mexico border, the rivers that ran into the plantation belt, and along the border with Indian Territory to the north, holding down three fronts in the quest for enforceable authority. Over time the size and allocation of those forts would become the source of many Texans' pleas and complaints. If the federal government were going to keep troops in Texas, what constituted the direst threat? And who should determine these priorities? This Army presence served as both a focal point and source of conflict as the government sought to use similar strategies of pacification to different ends over the three problems that Texas posed: continental, Confederate, and frontier.

Viewed from far above, the most dramatic and consistent assertion of federal power in Texas was the shift of tens of thousands of troops to the Mexican border. As Nicholas Guyatt has discussed in his chapter, from the beginning of the European attacks upon Veracruz in December 1861, U.S. politicians articulated the interconnection between the two conflicts. After France's Napoleon III installed Maximilian as emperor with French-backed forces, the United States continued to recognize Benito Juárez's beleaguered Liberal government. Fearful of engaging in multiple wars, Secretary of State William Seward had refused to fight directly against Maximilian, but with Confederate surrenders, these restraints no longer mattered.[5] Drawing upon the propaganda work of Mexican Liberals aiming to gain U.S. supporters, many Republicans came to analogize the Mexican and U.S. conflicts as a common struggle between liberals and landed reactionaries, testing the endurance of a republican or American model of governance against an increasingly resurgent European monarchism.[6] By this view, a war over the survival of republics could not end in Virginia but only across the Texas border because the United States and Mexico were joint fronts in an ideological and geographical contest. "Our duty as a people will not end with the suppression of the rebellion," Congressman Godlove S. Orth said in January 1865. "In the first glimmering of success to our arms the minds of our people are instinctively turned to Mexico."

By tying the Mexican and U.S. wars to conflicts between republicanism and monarchy, Orth's thinking mirrored that of many of his contemporaries in both nations, though his solution was a drastic and imperialistic one: a consolidated continental republic. "The war is shaking North and South, East and West, to their centers," Orth said. "The nation is being born again, and from the fire and smoke of battle, from its death groans of agony.... The lines which you now see on the map of North America as dividing one national possession from another will disappear, they will be sponged out by our people, and our children will see, if we do not live to see, the American flag flying over every foot of this continent, and the American Constitution protecting every human being on its soil."[7]

Although Orth's vision of a continental republic was fanciful, he captured both the sense of dislocation and the idea that the Civil War that began in South Carolina would in some way end at the border with Mexico.[8] This association of the United States and Mexican conflicts transcended political alliances. Permitting "the potentates of Europe to plant a monarchy in the middle of our Continent... to array a great military Power on both flanks of our Republic wielded by a despot" threatened a never-ending dissolution in wars meant to divide the United States "or dissolve it entirely & partition it like Poland," Missouri powerbroker Francis Blair Sr. wrote.[9] Six months later, General Ulysses S. Grant wrote to President Johnson that the establishment of a French-backed monarchy in Mexico was "part and parcel of the late rebellion in the United States, and a necessary part of it to suppress before entire peace can be assured."[10] The war could not end without resolution of the Mexican problem because a Mexican monarchy would eventually prompt a "long, expensive, and bloody war."[11] Peace then would be found not at Appomattox Court House but upon the Rio Grande.

These broad visions of the civil war in Mexico as a threat to a hemispheric, republican order (and to the U. S. power that undergirded that order against European encroachment) took concrete form in the flow of soldiers to the Rio Grande. There they conducted several missions, aiming simultaneously to solidify and undermine the border between the United States and Mexico. They sought to stop trade with imperial-held cities in Mexico, and hence to assert the power of the border to end the cross-boundary spillover by undermining imperial control of northern Mexico and aiding Juárez's armies. As Guyatt argues, one could see the interplay between the two wars in the movement of Confederate soldiers, sympathizers, and materiel in the spring of 1865. Heading south, they either fled from or continued their war by crossing into Mexico. "Everything on wheels, artillery horses mules +c +c have been run over into Mexico," General Philip Sheridan complained. "Large + small bands of rebel soldiers + some citizens, amounting to about 2000 have crossed the Rio Grande."[12] In the border town of Matamoros, Confederate flags flew.

By August 1865, nearly fifty thousand U.S. troops had arrived in Texas, with the largest concentrations in Galveston, Brownsville, and Brazos Island. As ex-Confederates tried to cross into Mexico, Sheridan sent troops up and down the river to frighten them and seized Confederate artillery and property from imperial forces in Matamoros. "If the demand is not complied with go and take it and all those engaged in its transfer," Grant ordered, though he also cautioned Sheridan not to "proceed to hostilities" without "further instructions."[13]

The expansion of the war thus at once inscribed and nearly erased the border. There, men under General Sheridan dumped weapons, ammunition, and supplies on the far side of the river for republican forces. "A War on the part of the United States is to be avoided, if possible, but it wil[l] be better to go to war now when but little aid given to the Mexicans will settle the question than to hav[e] in prospect a greater war shure to come," Grant wrote to Sheridan.[14] By the spring of 1866, Sheridan estimated that he had smuggled thirty thousand muskets from Baton Rouge Armory alone to Juárez's forces.[15]

The movement of soldiers into Texas posed logistical, economic, and political problems. Getting troops quickly from the east to west taxed the capacity of the United States, as soldiers shuttled to seaports and railroad hubs and then languished in tents waiting for ships to Texas. Two divisions of cavalry in Louisiana marched 425 miles over thirty days to reach Texas in July 1865.[16] Beyond the logistics were problems of finance. The Army sent $10 million in cash in the summer of 1865 to paymasters in Texas, and each month that volunteers stayed in service there raised the war's costs.[17] Finally, the time in Texas taxed men's morale. Volunteers who had served willingly, even eagerly, during battles now found it perplexing to still be in the service after the conflict seemed over. Although the U.S. Army ruled that volunteer enlistments would continue until the president proclaimed the war over, soldiers saw it differently and pressed their families and politicians for assistance in returning home. From Galveston, James Rowe wrote in July 1865, "One month ago to day I was rejoicing in the thought of spending this day at home but my hopes were flighted and here I am in Texas.... I am very anxious to go to a land where the sun does not come down with so intense heat.... We have no duty to perform and why we were brought here is a mystery to me."[18] Charles Johnson likewise complained that in his post near Texana "we have been lying here now in Camp almost a month, doing nothing but fighting mosquitoes."[19]

Some soldiers kept fighting by going south to serve in the republican army once they were mustered out by the United States. Having assembled a large cavalry, in June 1865 Sheridan hoped to cross the Rio Grande and help Juárez create a government.[20] In August Sheridan still hoped for a crossing, but a more limited one into northern Mexico to demoralize imperial troops and to prop up Juárez's support there. With U.S. forces massed near the Rio Grande, French and Austrian soldiers shrank away from the border countryside, leaving much of the frontier in Juárez's hands, though imperial soldiers continued to control the river cities of Matamoros and Bagdad. Sheridan also hoped to launch an attack with six to eight thousand cavalry to chase former Confederate General Joseph Shelby, who had established an American colony in Mexico. Beyond that, he expected the United States to provide basic support to Juárez's depleted forces.[21] For a while, Grant hoped to send General John Schofield across the border with a force of voluntary emigrants to assist the Mexican Liberal Army, but Secretary of State Seward deflected this possibility by sending Schofield instead to peace negotiations in Paris. Later, the administration later also blocked George Custer's efforts to join the republican cause. As late as September Grant hoped to sell vast supplies of munitions to Mexico on credit "with officers to Command troops."[22] By

November Sheridan had narrowed his military ambitions to the city of Matamoros. By undermining imperial control of that city, Sheridan hoped to prompt a rebellion across northern Mexico because Maximilian had no functional government in the region.[23]

Within months, the potential for a two-front, two-nation war dissipated as demobilization and diplomacy moved the United States toward a peace footing. As early as July 30, 1865, Grant prepared to muster out the large number of cavalry in Texas to cut military expenses, though he allowed them to refuse transportation home if they wished to go south to Mexico.[24] By August and September, the Army authorized Sheridan to demobilize all white troops he did not need, leaving Texas primarily to black troops and Regulars. From about 50,000 soldiers in August, the number shrank to 23,000 in December and 11,500 in March 1866.[25] Texas had moved, the *Army & Navy Journal* revealingly wrote, to a "peace basis," though the peace it defined was far different than the prewar status quo, as the Army still included thousands of troops spread over almost two dozen outposts. What had changed, however, was the potential for border war.[26] Tens of thousands of troops had marched "to the very brink of the Rubicon, there paused, and the major part of it was faced about and marched quietly homeward," the *Army & Navy Journal* opined.[27] The growing fears of national debt and the hopefulness that Seward's diplomacy would pay off had cooled the calls for war. "We are in no condition to go to war with France," the *Army & Navy Journal* editorialized. "We are plunged to the neck in debt. . . . We have the country to save."[28] To the consternation of congressional Republicans and General Grant, Seward instead relied upon diplomatic pressure to convince Napoleon III to withdraw his support for Maximilian's government. Congressmen, sparked by the lobbying of Mexican Liberals, introduced but then tabled resolutions to create a continental alliance of republics to fight for Mexico.[29]

The border remained porous as Juárez's Liberal government struggled to exert control. In 1866, the United States dispatched two companies of cavalry to Matamoros to preserve order until Liberal forces arrived.[30] In April, Grant asked for permission to pursue hostile Indians into Mexican Territory, because Sheridan believed it was "impossible to protect the Rio Grande frontier effectually against the small bands of Indians who infest certain portions of it, so long as they are permitted to obtain complete safety by crossing the river."[31]

In the summer of 1866, the imperial collapse and the incomplete Liberal victory spurred the creation of a more direct and enduring comparison of

Mexico and the United States as sites of anarchy. Once depictions of the Mexican conflict shifted in the U.S. press from a battle between contesting armies to a Liberal struggle to exert control over the country, Mexico became less a symbol of monarchy and more of instability. "Rival chiefs, at the head of bands of desperadoes, calling themselves, 'liberals' or 'patriots,' plunder the towns and keep the unarmed population in constant terror," the *Army & Navy Journal* wrote. What the guerrilla war revealed in this analysis was not the complex ends of war but the role of culture in preserving stability. "Years of internal dissension have almost obliterated the sentiment of nationality in Mexico."[32] During this period, Republicans and Democrats each turned to Mexico to explain the disorder in Reconstruction in the South. Republicans blamed the private violence of warlord-style planters and Democrats pointed to the role of military intervention, but each found Mexico growing in the soil of the American South.[33] As Republicans considered impeaching President Andrew Johnson in 1867, opponents denounced this as proof that the United States was "rapidly becoming Mexicanized."[34] With the collapse of the imperial forces in 1867, General Sheridan noted that Mexican soldiers who fled to New Orleans "stirred up" the "old rebel feeling."[35] By these lights, a war over the future of republics in the hemisphere could only be resolved when neither the United States nor Mexico faced internal dissolution.

Even as the United States secured its border with Mexico, internal violence in Texas pointed to a second front in the war's resolution: the ultimate suppression of disloyalty and slavery. U.S. goals in Texas's southeastern interior were both completely in keeping with broader wartime methods of suppression and also deeply novel in a period of alleged peacetime. The Army faced these challenges because the state lacked any basic governmental structure to rely upon in the months after Confederate surrender. When provisional Governor Andrew Hamilton arrived, he could not even establish contact with, much less oversight of, large parts of the state. Texans "had been for nearly two months not only without Government but singularly ignorant it seems as to the designs and purposes of the Government," Hamilton wrote. Additionally, the state itself was almost ungovernable because of the "immense territory over which our people are scattered and the entire absence of mail facilities."[36] By the fall of 1865, Texas was the only state not to have begun reorganization, and Hamilton resisted Andrew Johnson's importuning through the early part of the winter on the grounds that he had not yet been able to establish effective authority. Here, the national government's goals of securing the border and reorganizing the South conflicted. While troops were stationed up and down the Rio Grande, "the whole of the immense territory of the state, where our people actually reside" was at first barely covered.[37] Hamilton simply refused to call a constitutional convention, which kept Texas in limbo into the fall and winter of 1865.

Although white loyalists and freedpeople gave the most heart-rending pleas for a federal presence, the clearest and least ambiguous visions for suppressing Confederate Texas emerged in the U.S. officers' testimony to the Joint Committee on Reconstruction in early 1866. Meant to counter President Andrew Johnson's claims that the South was stabilizing, this testimony both recorded and strengthened Republicans' view of the still-rebellious South and characterized the war in Texas as ongoing. What emerged from their accounts was a sense of Texas as a state spotted with different regions of control, where the federal government could be triumphant within narrow boundaries around its outposts but utterly helpless in the state's vast hinterlands. In an inspection report presented to the committee, General W. E. Strong contrasted the "strict military discipline" and quiescence of cities like Galveston, Houston, San Antonio, and Austin with the "fearful state of things" in the interior counties "away from the influence of federal troops and federal bayonets, at points where our army has never penetrated, and where the citizens have but little fear of arrest and punishment." There, "the freedmen are in a worse condition than they ever were as slaves." In many parts of the interior, he believed, two-thirds had never been paid. Other regions, especially east of the Trinity River, and in the area between the Neches and Sabine Rivers, were so isolated from events that freedpeople did "not know that they were free until I told them." What Texas needed, Strong argued, was a continuation of the war. "One campaign of an army through the eastern part of the State, such as was made by General Sherman in South Carolina, would greatly improve the temper and generosity of the people."[38]

Texans posed particular threats because they lived far apart and were thus hard to manage, like other westerners, but also because they were the ultimate southerners, having never truly surrendered the Confederate cause. While proximate destruction, defeat and occupation taught Virginians and Tennesseans to acquiesce to the federal government, Texas's isolation allowed its rebels to maintain confidence in their power. "I consider Texas in a worse condition than any other State, for the reason that they never were whipped there," General David Stanley concluded.[39] White Union loyalists "could not plant crops even around their own houses with safety," Lieutenant Wilson Miller declared, because Texas combined southern disloyalty with ample "opportunity to escape" into the western landscape.⁴⁰

The relationship between federal troops and conditions on the ground was self-evident to a Freedmen's Bureau agent stationed in Marshall, Texas. "Judging from the state of the country in counties where there is no military force," Lieutenant Colonel H. S. Hall testified, "I can say there would be neither safety of person nor of property for men who had been loyal during the war; and there would be no protection whatever for the negro." Without a military force to restrain them, white Texans launched disorganized but effective paramilitary campaigns, using violence to inspire terror. Although ex-rebels claimed that the troops "excited" outrage and disloyalty, in fact a white southern insurgency had grown in the absence of federal authority. Although the presence of U.S. troops might inspire fury, they also provided the only counterweight to what seemed like a privatized continuation of the war, pitting ex-Confederates against freedpeople and isolated Unionists.⁴¹

In these counties, whites claimed pockets of private sovereignty over freedpeople. In December, a freedwoman named Lucy Grimes refused to whip her child when her white employer ordered her to. In retaliation, two former rebel soldiers carried her into the woods, stripped her, and beat her to death. What was galling to the Bureau agent was less the violence than the fact that the murderers could get away with it with impunity; the county magistrate refused to issue a warrant. One hundred miles west in Navarro County, south of Dallas, two whites flogged a black man to death. When Hall applied for soldiers to arrest the perpetrators, he was unable to obtain any troops. Although the Army could assist in arresting outlaws and collecting wages in nearby Upshur, Cherokee, and Panola counties, "it was impossible" for even sympathetic judges in Navarro County to "arrest anybody or hold anybody accountable for acts committed against the negroes" without a "military force." When four discharged U.S. soldiers were murdered, a twenty-man cavalry detachment pursued the killers to Rusk County, just south of Marshall, but were driven away by a mob. A former Confederate captain testified that in a "tier of thirty-three counties" beyond Marshall, "no American flag has been seen since the surrender" and Union men are "under ban among the people."⁴² This bifurcated power was common to the regions the Army occupied. General Christopher Andrews found "more expressions of loyalty" near posts at Beaumont, Brenham, Liberty, and Columbus, but open talk of disloyalty farther away.⁴³

For modern historians perhaps the most confounding testimony came from General George Custer, who led a cavalry force on a grueling march through Texas in 1865. Custer has been justifiably critiqued as a brutal and foolish commander on the Plains, especially for his conduct at the so-called Battle of the Washita in November 1868. Placing his Reconstruction work alongside his role on the Plains shifts the picture, creating a unified picture of a man determined to forcefully exert national control over regions and peoples he saw in rebellion. Toward Confederate Texans, Custer barely evinced more mercy than he would later show to Plains Indians. Custer's cavalry attempted to subdue a wide swath in the center of the state by sending frequent detachments to enforce order. Although Custer did not deny the possibility that there existed a good white man in Texas, he was skeptical. "The people of the north have no conception of the number of murders that have been committed in that State during and since the war," Custer said, considering the plight of Union loyalists. Although loyalists had returned to the state during the occupation, their presence depended upon the soldiers. "The feeling of hostility towards loyal men is carried to such an extent that a loyal man engaged in business receives no patronage except from loyal men."

Buoyed by what they saw as support from President Andrew Johnson, a "majority" of white Texans openly expressed their disloyalty to the government. Around Austin, outlaws systematically murdered loyalists who had joined the U.S. Army and then returned home upon Confederate surrender, killing six in one county. Other bands shot a man for refusing to take down his U.S. flag. In Fannin County, northeast of Dallas, locals attacked a procession of Unionists, took their flag, tore it to pieces, and ordered them not to meet again. The only solution was force. Where soldiers were "in sufficient numbers to control the section of country," the people are "very respectful to them," but if alone they insulted soldiers frequently. Custer urged efforts to teach rebels "the enormity of the crime they have committed" as part of a broader, military-led effort to "foster and encourage throughout the southern States a proper regard and affection for the national authority."

Like almost all the generals, Custer equated harsh treatment of freedpeople with disloyalty, binding together the two projects of completing emancipation and subduing the Confederates.[44] Custer learned to equate emancipation and union by watching the rebels. According to Custer, "The great mass of the people there seem to look upon the freedman as being connected with, or as being the cause of, their present condition, and they do not hesitate to improve every opportunity to inflict injuries upon him in order, seemingly, to punish him for this." Ending the war could only mean submitting to the dual goals of national power: unification and a defensible emancipation. For Custer, this turned local white efforts at oppressing freedpeople into disloyalty. Custer reported that five hundred men had gotten away with murdering disloyal people, but freedmen were punished all the time for minor offenses.

Although Custer shared some of his fellow officers' skepticism about black equality, he had no doubts about their loyalty, arguing that they were "loyal without a single exception.... They realize, as all Union men in the State do, that their only safety and protection lies in the general government; and they realize, too, that if the troops are withdrawn, they will be still more exposed than they are now." If soldiers left, white Texans would create "a system of oppression that would be equally as bad as slavery itself." Custer believed freedpeople "manifest a very great interest" in politics but were "very quiet" about suffrage, perhaps reflecting either Custer's own skepticism or their awareness of political opposition. Although some claimed that freedpeople would be lured into voting with their masters, Custer dismissed that idea. "The vast majority of them would co-operate with Union men..... They could discern more quickly who are their friends and who are their enemies than many of the white inhabitants."[45]

In this testimony and like-minded reports sent back from officers and agents as well as freedpeople in Texas, the problem was that of violent disorder, one that surrender had slowed but not stopped, much as Lance Blyth has discussed for the various nations of New Mexico. Read in these lights, Sheridan's and Custer's future wars on the Plains fit the patterns both of the West and the South in this era.

Even though the military increasingly dispersed troops up the rivers and highways of the eastern section of the state in the fall and winter of 1865, remaking Texas proved difficult. What emerged were increasingly open confrontations between soldiers and citizens, as in a September 1866 clash in Brenham, in the eastern part of the state, where soldiers set fire to the town after citizens shot two soldiers.[46] In Brownsville in January 1867, white policemen shot black troops openly.[47] The Brownsville incident prompted Grant to write to Secretary of War Edwin Stanton in January 1867 about the "powerlessness of the military in the present state of affairs.... Even the moral effect of the presence of troops is passing away." Texas was "practically" in a "state of insurrection" by refusing to investigate murders of Unionists and freedpeople.[48] Texas, he concluded, revealed the "real sentiments of disloyalty to the Government of the United States" latent throughout the defeated but not cowed former Confederacy.[49]

Texas's disorder and political resistance slowed its path to restoration. When Andrew Johnson proclaimed the end of the insurrection in April 1866, Texas's commander at first ended military commissions and restored civil law. Only afterward did he realize that Johnson had specifically exempted Texas from the proclamation.[50] For the next several months, the war legally continued in Texas, even as it seemed to end in other Confederate states.[51] When Johnson extended his proclamation to include Texas in August 1866, this marked what would become known as the legal (and by some measures fictional) end of the conflict.[52] Quickly, Texas commanders stopped military commissions, and civil courts were flooded with lawsuits against officers and agents.[53]

Nevertheless, military powers were not so easily curbed. In October 1866, Texas's elected governor complained that the military continued to override civil officers in order to enforce the law or protect freedpeople, and the state commander continued to support exempting soldiers from writs of *habeas corpus*. Frustrated, the governor asked "how far State laws, and the laws and Constitution of the United States are to be looked to for protection; and whether the military are to regard the President's Proclamation . . . or are to continue to disregard and override the rights of the loyal citizens of the United States, leaving them powerless and at the mercy of every petty military upstart who may chance to have bayonets to enforce his edicts."[54] A federal attorney, however, saw the situation differently. The state of war continued not because of military tyrants but because of the chaos evident on the ground throughout the state. "It is a fatal mistake, nay a wicked misery to talk of peace or the institutions of peace. We are in the very vortex of war, where the disadvantages are all in favor of the violent and lawless and against the law abiding and peaceful. . . . We need help as a people. . . . It takes military energy and military skill to catch and hold and military justice to execute" the law.[55]

Once and future Texas governor Elisha Pease visited Washington to call for federal protection of Unionists in a long, frank discussion with conservative Navy secretary Gideon Welles. This request for constant, everyday protection was, Welles said, "asking too much." People in "danger must look to the local, municipal and State authorities for protection" and if a majority approved of injustice, "is it wise for the one sixth to come forward and place themselves in direct antagonism to the five sixths [and ask the Federal

Government to sustain them by force]? Would it not be better to remain passive and quietly and patiently strive to modify public opinion." Welles described a nation unable to exert itself, helpless in the face of settler attitudes. "This Government is not one of force." The federal government would not, he claimed, "put down the majority by the bayonet."[56]

In fact Congress turned to force to put down the violent insurgency by expanding military powers and enfranchising freedpeople in the congressional Reconstruction acts passed beginning in February 1867. Texas once again was a testing ground for national power. Frustrated, the military commander removed the elected governor and appointed a new provisional chief executive.[57] As generals on the ground empaneled black jurors and dispossessed additional state officers, Texas became a key battleground for conflicting visions of Reconstruction. The deposed state treasurer complained that the army there "usurped all power to Africanise and Radicalise our state."[58] Instead of quieting in the face of national authority, white Texans fought back, murdering officers and Bureau agents.[59] Texas also tested the endpoints of congressional Reconstruction as it, like Virginia, fell behind the other Confederate states, failing to enact a new constitution in 1868. Texas finally ratified the new constitution in December 1869 and became the second-to-last state to be seated in Congress in 1870.[60] Although Georgia managed to become the final state to be seated in Congress, there is something symbolically telling about Virginia and Texas being the final two to pass new state constitutions. Each represented different ways of thinking about the problems the war had raised, and each place challenged efforts to declare the war at an end.

As Lance Blyth describes for New Mexico, the civil wars and reconstructions of Texas also meant the struggle for control between white settlers and Indians, as violent attacks and counter-attacks increased after the eastern surrenders. Both across the Plains and in Texas, the Civil War had freed Indians, especially the Comanche, to exert greater control over regions that the United States had largely ignored during the conflict. The Confederate surrender and the massive demobilization of both U.S. and Confederate troops unleashed a torrent of unruly white settlers into Indian lands.[61] Yet, unlike in New Mexico or on the Plains, in Texas military officers and freedpeople argued against moving troops to fight Indians, fearful that drawing forces away from the plantation districts would leave planters in complete control. Meanwhile, Confederate sympathizers and white settlers on Comanche lands argued that soldiers should be sent to the frontier precisely to both drive out the Indians and to eliminate the check on planter power. In Texas, the various control strategies collided because they relied upon the same tools and strategies, and drew upon the same limited resource in federal troops.

As generals deemphasized the Indian violence in order to concentrate on the problem of planter attacks, whites in Comanche County in central Texas complained in 1866 that conditions were "absolutely intolerable" and that "every citizen of this Government is entitled to protection for his life and property, but here whole communities are being warred upon."[62] General Sheridan reluctantly shifted troops to cover what the governor called "proper points to cover exposed localities."[63] Instead of resolving the problem, however, these minor moves prompted more intensive lobbying for post coverage.[64] In response, Sheridan tried to protect both white settlers and freedpeople by scattering posts broadly across the state to cover the northern frontier, the Rio Grande, the route from Indianola to San Antonio, and routes near Austin and from Brenham to Galveston, for the "moral influence they may exercise in giving security to union men and freedmen."[65] By doing so, however, Sheridan thinned out his coverage, as posts dropped to fairly small numbers, many holding only a single company of infantry, and some mere detachments.

By January 1867, Texas had 60 percent more posts than any other state in the former Confederacy—and as many as Tennessee, Mississippi, Georgia, and Alabama combined. Still the governor pressed Sheridan to evacuate the interior districts and concentrate more forces on the frontier, since the interior was no more violent than northern states.[66] Flustered, by April 1867, General Sheridan denounced reports of Indian massacres, which, he claimed, "are now manufactured wholesale to affect the removal of troops from the interior to the frontier." By luring the Army to attack Indians, planters hoped to draw them away from freedpeople.[67] But even General William T. Sherman wished to "let these Indians alone" until the Army in Texas was finished with "this civil business."[68]

In outlying areas of Texas, as in parts of the Plains, settlers simultaneously transgressed lines drawn by the federal government and demanded that the Army protect them. They could at once be, by their lights, in the heart of a United States where a citizen expected protection and beyond the boundaries of protection that the Army recognized. These struggles for force were thus in part struggles to define the imagined geography of the nation.[69] The same people who wished to restrain national intervention in the plantation belts imagined an omnipresent and omnipotent nation on Indian lands, ready to protect any white settler, however remote.

Rather than an anomaly, Texas presented an unusual combination of otherwise widespread challenges to federal authority. The problem of silencing Confederates only opened up additional problems concerning the limits of federal control over vast spaces governed in patchwork ways by Indians, settlers, and bands of outlaws. This meant that Civil War surrenders could not inherently bring peace. Unionists in Texas and elsewhere wished for a return to a fabled, if elusive, sense of prewar stability, yet recognized that order would require practices of occupation and regulation, "impossible to do before the war, and indeed scarcely attempted."[70]

In March 1866, Governor Hamilton in Texas again asked for assistance against horse-raiding Indians and white outlaws in the "frontier Counties," especially bordering the Red River and Indian Territory.[71] Over time the military gave in to the calls to move into Comanche territory: between 1866 and 1870, the Army reconfigured its spatial control over Texas, moving forces from the Rio Grande into plantation districts and to the Indian frontier. Prompted by lobbying from both the state's governor and the beleaguered postmaster's office, Grant asked his commander to plan new lines of posts from the Rio Grande to the Red River along the northwestern frontier within the state.[72] By the time Texas was readmitted in 1870, there were few soldiers in the plantation belts. Defending freedom relied upon the influence of freedpeople with local governments. Not coincidentally, the end of the military operations to protect freedpeople marked the beginning of a bold new campaign against Indians in the state's panhandle.

All three sovereignty tests in Texas lasted long after the formal Confederate surrenders. Texas would continue to be a flashpoint for intrigue and border crossing until at least the late 1870s. As a site of disloyalty and an ongoing effort to sustain slavery, Texas was the final state restored under President Johnson's proclamation, the second-to-last state restored by Congress, and a place of enduring labor exploitation and racist violence. As a site for trying to assert settler control over Indians, the conflict in Texas would last until at least the 1870–75 wars with the Comanche, when the Army—led by Reconstruction stalwarts such as Philip Sheridan and Nelson Miles—fought dozens of battles with Comanche and Kiowa in northern Texas and forced the organized bands of Comanche to surrender. The Comanche battle was simultaneously a western, southern, and continental war, as Comanche captive taking inspired claims that slavery itself could only die in Texas with the defeat and containment of Comanche who had for centuries thwarted national sovereignties in the region.

The end of war footing in Texas came not with the conclusion of border conflicts, federal oversight of state politics, or the Indian threat, but with the ultimate drawdown of military force in the state, as the number of soldiers and their zones of coverage shrank. Even as they fought over the allocation of military resources, Texans did not fight over whether those soldiers were necessary—the argument was over where they could best be utilized. Beyond their conflicts over those proper purposes, postsurrender Texans seemed to share a vision, newly created by the war, that the national government could intervene in efficacious but highly geographically constrained ways, and in the process create islands of nationally defensible space in the midst of a sea of home rule. Even though these forces had never been able to regulate Texas, they had created a set of eyes upon the ground, an access point, and a counterweight. Without them, Texas was left largely to its own devices.

The victories in Texas in the late 1860s belonged to the tenacious, if unappealing, claims of local power by white settlers. These claims grew naturally from the state's history, as a place where people had been able for decades to hold off Mexican, British, and U.S. efforts at oversight. Settler power remained the most significant force upon the ground, and the state was stubbornly localized in its governing structures. The national government could accomplish short-term goals—the completion of emancipation, the regulation of the border, the clearing of Comanche—but could not or would not sustain that authority. The federal presence in Texas can seem illusory, evanescent, even more fictional than most sovereignty claims. From the bleakest viewpoint, Texas had been a crucible of whether the federal government could enforce its will over the populace through civil wars and reconstructions, and the answer had largely been no.

NOTES

Thanks to Adam Arenson and Andrew Graybill for patiently and indulgently reading and rereading (and sometimes rewriting) this chapter, and, for advice and inspiration, to Sherry Smith, James Jewell, Megan Kate Nelson, Lance Blyth, Diane Mutti Burke, Nicholas Guyatt, Fay Yarbrough, William Deverell, Martha Sandweiss, Joshua Paddison, Virginia Scharff, Stephen Kantrowitz, Stephen Aron, and Steve Hahn.

1. *The War of the Rebellion: A Compilation of the Official Records of the Union and Confederate Armies* (Washington, DC: Government Printing Office, 1896); vol. 48, pt. 1, 267–69; Jeffrey W. Hunt, *The Last Battle of the Civil War: Palmetto Ranch* (Austin: University of Texas Press, 2002).

2. *Army & Navy Journal*, October 28, 1865: 152.

3. On the broader notion of extending sovereignty over peripheries as a central nineteenth-century challenge of statecraft, see, especially, C. A. Bayly, *The Birth of the Modern World, 1780–1914: Global Connections and Comparisons* (Malden, MA: Blackwell, 2004); Charles S. Maier, "Consigning the Twentieth Century to History: Alternative Narratives for the Modern Era," *American Historical Review* 105, no. 3 (June 1, 2000): 807–31. Elliott West has worked to place western and southern history into a broader framework of threats to an increasingly ambitious and beleaguered national state as part of a "Greater Reconstruction" in Elliott West, *The Last Indian War: The Nez Perce Story* (Oxford and New York: Oxford University Press, 2009). On the geographically complex and often fictional nature of sovereignty claims, see, especially Lauren A. Benton, *A Search for Sovereignty: Law and Geography in European Empires, 1400—1900* (Cambridge and New York: Cambridge University Press, 2010).

4. Despite fine work on postwar Texas, the state has not played a significant role in broader histories of Reconstruction. For Reconstruction Texas, see Barry A. Crouch, *The Freedmen's Bureau and Black Texans* (Austin: University of Texas Press, 1992); James M. Smallwood, Barry A. Crouch, and Larry Peacock, *Murder and Mayhem: The War of Reconstruction in Texas* (College Station: Texas A&M University Press, 2003); Barry A. Crouch, ed., *The Dance of Freedom: Texas African Americans during Reconstruction* (Austin: University of Texas Press, 2007); Carl H. Moneyhon, *Texas after the Civil War: The Struggle of Reconstruction* (College Station: Texas A & M University Press, 2004); William L. Richter, *The Army in Texas during Reconstruction, 1865–1870* (College Station: Texas A & M University Press, 1987); Charles W. Ramsdell, *Reconstruction in Texas* (Gloucester, MA: P. Smith, 1964); Randolph B. Campbell, *Grass-Roots Reconstruction in Texas, 1865–1880* (Baton Rouge: Louisiana State University Press, 1997); Patrick G. Williams, *Beyond Redemption Texas Democrats after Reconstruction* (College Station: Texas A & M University Press, 2007).

5. Gregory P. Downs, "The Mexicanization of American Politics: The United States' Transnational Path from Civil War to Stabilization," *American Historical Review* 117, no. 2 (April 2012): 387–409.

6. Cong. Globe, 38th Congress, 2d sess., 141–44.

7. Thomas Schoonover, "Napoleon Is Coming! Maximilian Is Coming?: The International History of the Civil War in the Caribbean Basin," in Robert E. May, ed., *The Union, the Confederacy, and the Atlantic Rim* (West Lafayette, IN: Purdue University Press, 1995), 101–30.

8. Paul H. Bergeron, ed., *The Papers of Andrew Johnson* (Knoxville: University of Tennessee Press, 1967–2000), vol. 8, 516–17, 522.

9. Ibid., 410.

10. Ibid., 258–59.

11. Sheridan to Grant, June 28, 1865, Container 36, N. P. Banks Papers, Library of Congress (hereafter LoC).

12. John Y. Simon, ed., *The Papers of Ulysses S. Grant* (Carbondale: Southern Illinois University Press, 1967–2009), vol. 15: 139, 146.

13. Ibid., 285–86.

14. Philip Henry Sheridan, *Personal Memoirs of Philip Henry Sheridan, General United States Army* (New York: Charles L. Webster and co., 1888), vol. 2, 224–26.

15. *Army & Navy Journal,* August 5, 1865, 786.

16. Ibid., August 19, 1865, 817.

17. James Rowe to My Own Beloved Sister, July 4, 1865, Box 2, Folder 152, MS 10014, Carlos W. Colby Papers, Newberry Library, Chicago.

18. Chas Johnson to Daniel E. Barnard, August 23, 1865, Box 79, Folder 1073, Howe-Barnard Family Papers, Midwest MS-Howe-Barnard, Newberry Library, Chicago.

19. Sheridan to Grant, June 29, 1865, Series 10, Box 3, Ulysses S. Grant Papers, LoC.

20. Sheridan to Grant, August 2, 1865, Series 10, Box 4, Ulysses S. Grant Papers, LoC.

21. Bergeron, ed., *Papers of Andrew Johnson,* vol. 9: 46.

22. Sheridan to Grant, November 5, 1865, Series 10, Box 4, Ulysses S. Grant Papers, LoC.

23. Simon, *Papers of Ulysses S. Grant,* vol. 15: 289.

24. *Army & Navy Journal,* August 12, 1865, 801.

25. Ibid., August 26, 1865, 8–9.

26. Ibid., October 7, 1865, 97.

27. Ibid., September 16, 1865, 56; September 30, 1865, 88.

28. Ibid., February 24, 1866, 422, 429.

29. Thomas Sedgwick to Captain G. C. Jotwin, December 24, 1866, LRE T 7 1867, Box 17, Entry 1756, Letters Received Department of the Gulf 1867, RG 393, Part 1, National Archives, Washington D.C. (hereafter NA, DC.)

30. Simon, *The Papers of Ulysses S. Grant,* vol. 17:427.

31. *Army & Navy Journal,* October 20, 1866, 141.

32. Downs, "The Mexicanization of American Politics."

33. New Orleans *Daily Picayune,* April 4, 1868, 2.

34. Simon, *Papers of Ulysses S. Grant,* vol. 17, 208.

35. Bergeron, *Papers of Andrew Johnson,* vol. 8: 674–79.

36. Ibid., vol. 9: 436–39.

37. *Report of the Joint Committee on Reconstruction* (Washington, DC: Government Printing Office, 1866), 4:37–39.

38. Ibid., 39–42.

39. Ibid., 43–45.
40. Ibid., 130.
41. Ibid., 160.
42. Ibid., 124.
43. And along the way raising grave doubts about recent work that has argued that the United States sought Union, not freedom, as its primary or even sole war aim, especially Gary W. Gallagher, *The Union War* (Cambridge, MA: Harvard University Press, 2011); Marc Egnal, *Clash of Extremes: The Economic Origins of the Civil War* (New York: Hill and Wang, 2009).
44. *Report of the Joint Committee on Reconstruction*, 4: 72–78.
45. E. C. Mason, Report of the Board of Inquiry, October 2, 1866, M 140 DG 1866, Box 15, Entry 1756, RG 393, Part 1, NA, DC.
46. J. J. Reynolds to Gen. Hartsuff, January 19, 1867, R 20 DG 1867, Box 16, Entry 1756, RG 393, Part 1, NA, DC.
47. Simon, *Papers of Ulysses S. Grant*, 17:38–39.
48. Chas Griffin to Gen. Hartsuff, April 5, 1867, LRA T 10 FMD 1867, Box 1, Book 15, Entry 4498 Fifth Military District Letters Received 1867–1870, RG 393, Part 1, NA, DC.
49. *Army & Navy Journal*, June 16, 1866, 678.
50. Ibid., June 30, 1866, 710.
51. Ibid., August 18, 1866, 6.
52. Joseph Holt to Sheridan, November 14, 1866, Box 16, Entry 1756, RG 393, Part 1, NA, DC.
53. Throckmorton to Henry Stanbery, October 12, 1866, enclosed in Throckmorton to Stanbery, October 15, 1866, Folder 8, Box 135 Texas 1848–1870, Entry 9 Letters Received 1809–1870, RG 60 Department of Justice Office of the Attorney General, National Archives, College Park, Maryland.
54. D. J. Baldwin to Stanbery, February 2, 1867, Folder 1, Box 135, Entry 9, RG 60, NA II, College Park.
55. Gideon Welles, *Diary of Gideon Welles: Secretary of the Navy under Lincoln and Johnson*, ed. Howard K. Beale (New York: Norton, 1960), 2:568–69.
56. Chas Griffin to Sheridan, July 20, 1867, LRB T 121 FMD 1867, Box 1, Entry 4498, RG 393, Part 1, NA, DC.
57. Bergeron, *Papers of Andrew Johnson*, 13:87–89.
58. Joseph Reynolds to Major Geo. W. Smith, November 15, 1867, LR (C) T 200 FMD 1867, Box 3, Entry 4498, RG 393, Part 1, NA, DC.
59. General Orders No. 24, March 15, 1869, Military District State of Virginia, February 18, 1869, Entry 5271, RG 393, Part 1, NA, DC.
60. Gary Clayton Anderson, *The Conquest of Texas: Ethnic Cleansing in the Promised Land, 1820–1875* (Norman: University of Oklahoma Press, 2005); Andrew R. Graybill, *Policing the Great Plains: Rangers, Mounties, and the North American Frontier, 1875–1910* (Lincoln: University of Nebraska Press, 2007).
61. R. M. Morris to the A. A. Genl. Dept. Texas, August 7, 1866, M 10 DG 1866, Box 15, Entry 1756, RG 393, Part 1, NA, DC.

62. Throckmorton to Sheridan, October 26, 1866, T 42 1866, Box 15, Entry 1756, RG 393, Part 1, NA, DC.

63. Throckmorton to Sheridan, n.d. [December 1866], LRE T 9 1866, Box 17, Entry 1756, RG 393, Part 1, NA, DC.

64. Sheridan to George Leet, January 7, 1867, G 2 1867 DG, Box 16, Entry 1756, RG 393, Part 1, NA, DC.

65. Throckmorton to Sheridan, January 28, 1867, L R E T 18 1867, Box 17, Entry 1756, RG 393, Part 1, NA, DC.

66. Simon, *Papers of Ulysses S. Grant,* 17:91–93.

67. Ibid., 243.

68. Bergeron, *Papers of Andrew Johnson,* 13:476–79.

69. *Army & Navy Journal,* August 19, 1865, 821.

70. Bergeron, *Papers of Andrew Johnson,* 10:202–3.

71. Special Orders No. 27, February 6, 1868, enclosed in Gen. J. J. Reynolds to Gen. Hartsuff, March 13, 1868, T 268 (d) FMD 1868, Box 7, Entry 4498, RG 393, Part 1, NA, DC.

72. Special Orders No. 27, February 6, 1868, enclosed in Gen. J. J. Reynolds to Gen. Hartsuff, March 13, 1868, T 268 (d) FMD 1868, Box 7, Entry 4498, RG 393, Part 1, NA, DC.

SEVEN

Redemption Falls Short

SOLDIER AND SURGEON IN THE POST–CIVIL WAR FAR WEST

William Deverell

WOUNDED SOLDIER

ICONOCLASTIC TO A FAULT, AND RENDERED even more temperamental by way of a grievous wartime injury, noted nineteenth-century writer Ambrose Bierce seems to fit a profile of the wounded Civil War warrior searching for, if not finding, redemption, recovery, or renewal in the far West after the fighting had ended. But Bierce is a tough fit with any model or template of personality, profile, or experience. His postwar experience demonstrates how, for so many soldiers, the Civil War never ended.

Born into a hardscrabble Ohio farm family in 1842, the tenth of thirteen children, Bierce was deeply influenced as a boy by his uncle, "General" Lucius Verus Bierce.[1] As a young man, Lucius Bierce walked across the slaveholding South, an experience that transformed him into an ardent abolitionist.[2] Later, as a lawyer, Lucius Bierce served as counsel in several cases regarding the status of fugitive slaves who had escaped bondage and fled to Ohio. He was also a close friend of John Brown. He supported Brown's antislavery campaigns in Kansas, and he apparently passed on arms and ammunition from a disbanded militia company to the famous abolitionist.

According to the journalist and historian Carey McWilliams, who wrote a fine biography of Ambrose Bierce in the 1920s, this weaponry probably also included a set of swords from Lucius Bierce's secret abolitionist society, which may have been the same ones that Brown and several of his sons wielded with awful and deadly efficiency at the notorious Pottawatomie massacre in the spring of 1856, where they hacked several proslavery men to death.[3]

On the day of John Brown's execution ("his translation," as Henry David Thoreau memorably called it), Lucius Bierce requested that the court in

Akron adjourn in commemoration. Later that night, the town followed up with a mass meeting, and Bierce delivered a brimstone speech. "Thank God I furnished him arms," Bierce thundered, "and right good use did he make of them."[4]

When President Abraham Lincoln called for a volunteer military force to defend the Union in April 1861, Lucius Bierce enlisted. He supplied and trained two companies of marines at his own expense and personally escorted them to Washington. McWilliams writes that his uncle's abolitionism undoubtedly influenced the young Ambrose Bierce, "for the General left doubt in the minds of none as to where he stood on the issue of slavery."[5] Fired by his uncle's fervent ideology and abolitionist exuberance, Ambrose Bierce, still a teenager, enlisted in the Union Army on April 19, 1861, and left his family (including siblings Abigail, Amelia, Ann, Addison, Aurelius, Augustus, Almeda, Andrew, Albert, Arthur, Adelia, and Aurelia) for the war.

According to McWilliams, Bierce was the second person in his county to enlist after Fort Sumter (his uncle may have been the first). He was assigned to Company C of the Ninth Indiana Infantry which, over the course of the war, famously became known as the "Bloody Ninth" for fighting in some of the fiercest battles and for its high casualty rates.[6] For much of the war, Bierce worked as a topographical engineer for General William B. Hazen, with whom he became close. His job often required him to explore territory on his own and to prepare maps. He also fought in the second day of Shiloh, the siege of Corinth, at Stone River, Chickamauga, Chattanooga, Missionary Ridge, and at Pickett's Mill.[7]

Bierce took a bullet to the head at Kennesaw Mountain on June 23, 1864. According to Hazen's report of the incident, the Army of the Cumberland encountered Confederate forces along the slopes of a hillside, and he sent Bierce, by then a lieutenant, to advance the skirmish line. A Confederate musket ball pierced Bierce's skull. Hazen's account noted that the shot "caused a very dangerous and complicated wound, the ball remaining within the head from which it was removed sometime afterwards. This wound caused Lieut. Bierce to be unfit for and absent from his duties for a considerable period of time."[8] The bullet entered Bierce's scalp near his temple and lodged on the side of his head. After several months convalescing at home, Bierce eventually returned to his company.

It is abundantly clear that Ambrose Bierce was never the same after having his head, as he described it, "broken like a walnut."[9] According to biographer William McCann, Bierce's injury bothered him for the rest of his life. At least some of his many brothers attributed Bierce's acerbic temperament after the war to his traumatic head wound. In an application for a pension in the later part of his life, Bierce reported that he had experienced "violent headache and vertigo" as a result of his injury.[10] It seems at least plausible that his own wounding was at the root of Bierce's obsessive fascination—ever abundant in his writing—with the damage wrought by war on the bodies of those who fight and die. Bierce's fiction is replete with wounds and bodily trauma, and it is this realistic portrayal of the war's costs that makes his writing stand apart from any of his contemporaries.

At the close of the war, Bierce resigned his Army commission and accepted a low-level job with the U.S. Treasury Department, which stationed him in Alabama and placed him in charge of collecting abandoned and stolen cotton and other property. He spent only a few months there. In the fall of 1865, Bierce received a letter from Hazen, his old commander and friend, offering him a job as the engineering attaché on a military surveying expedition of Indian Territory. According to McWilliams, Bierce "dropped all former associations and jumped at the chance to go west." He quickly left Alabama for Nebraska, where he met up with Hazen and the rest of the expedition. McWilliams also suggests a convalescent purpose: "The trip gave him a chance to recover his health, too, for he suffered from the disease of asthma which he had inherited from his mother. It had not bothered him much during the war, but it had sorely harassed him in the South. No sooner had the expedition started west than he began to feel better with every change in climate," though we can assume that the head wound still bothered him physically and otherwise. McWilliams connects the war, the West, and Bierce's future, writing that "the war saved Bierce from Indiana and turned his face westward."[11]

As with other postwar surveys, the Hazen effort was ambitious in time, space, and purpose. The expedition took Bierce from Omaha through the Platte Valley and on to Fort Kearney in central Nebraska. The surveyors passed the Missouri River en route to the Big Horn Mountains. From there they headed to Fort Smith, then to Fort Benton on the upper Missouri in Montana Territory. They then followed the Missouri River, passed south through the Rockies, and stopped at Salt Lake City. From Utah, they followed Gold Rush and Oregon Trail routes into Nevada, over the Sierras to Sacramento, and ended up in San Francisco in 1867.[12]

Carey McWilliams describes the trip and, especially, the impact the far West had on the wounded warrior. In his reading of Bierce and his notes and drawings, McWilliams connected region and redemption—or, at least, region and putative recovery:

> It was not long before the Dakotas were lost and they entered a region that was new, and therefore marvelous, to them all. Something of the exuberance of their spirits is indicated by the sketches and drawings, and data for maps, recorded in the journal that Bierce kept. These blurred lines on fading paper were symbols to Bierce and represented the wild grandeur of the Rockies.... These months of camping and riding, from Omaha to San Francisco, were for Bierce an introduction to the western manner. He was still young enough to be impressed with the feeling of liberation that the fresh and untrammeled life of the West created.... The West gave such a character elbow-room and if he became an excessive individualist it should not be too seriously deplored. His enormous energy, personal bravery, forceful directness; his impatience with pettiness and disdain for social fetishes, all these qualities were Western. Of course it is always difficult, if not specious, to localize a virtue. But the West did emphasize certain values which have come to be called Western. Bierce's best work was done in San Francisco, and it was to San Francisco that he was now journeying.[13]

Although our romanticism about the West may have faded some since McWilliams's day, we recognize the attraction of the region for him and for his portrait of Bierce. Yet we make a grave mistake if we excise the Civil War, and Bierce's travails in it, from the West as Bierce experienced it.

As they traveled, Bierce and Hazen petitioned military authorities for Bierce to receive a commission as captain in the U.S. Army upon their arrival in San Francisco. Once there, however, they discovered that he had been promoted only to second lieutenant, a rung below the expected appointment. Piqued, Bierce rejected the commission and an army career. "I resigned," he wrote, "parted from Hazen more in sorrow than in anger and remained in California."[14] Thus was the literary history of the American West, the Civil War, and the nation as a whole, forever changed.

McWilliams well understood the impact of the Civil War on Bierce. "The war was a troubling memory. It never left him; he mused and puzzled about it all his life."[15] And of the writer's darkness and gothic sensibilities, McWilliams looks to 1864 for their genesis. "Death had marked him at Kennesaw Mountain and had left a question in his mind about which he was to puzzle all his life."[16] It is abundantly clear that Bierce never "got over" the war. It had entered his psyche as bluntly and powerfully as the Confederate bullet that had crashed into his skull. Hardly one to fraternize in postwar

Bay Area Grand Army of the Republic bonhomie, Bierce wallowed for half a century in talented misanthropy. He wrote throughout the rest of his life about his war experiences—in the forms both of memoir and fiction.

In recounting his experiences at Shiloh, for example, Bierce wrote candidly and well ahead of the conventions of his era, about the horror of it all. Again, his focus on the wounds of the fallen is startling, especially for the age:

> There were men enough; all dead apparently, except one, who lay near where I had halted my platoon to await the slower movement of the line—a Federal sergeant, variously hurt, who had been a fine giant in his time. He lay face upward, taking in his breath in convulsive, rattling snorts, and blowing it out in sputters of froth which crawled creamily down his cheeks, piling itself alongside his neck and ears. A bullet had clipped a groove in his skull, above the temple; from this the brain protruded in bosses, dropping off in flakes and strings. I had not previously known one could get on, even in this unsatisfactory fashion, with so little brain. One of my men whom I knew for a womanish fellow, asked if he should put his bayonet through him. Inexpressibly shocked by the cold-blooded proposal, I told him I thought not; it was unusual, and too many were looking.... Along a line which was not that of extreme depression, but was at every point significantly equidistant from the heights on either hand, lay the bodies half buried in ashes; some in the unlovely looseness of attitude denoting sudden death by the bullet, but by far the greater number in postures of agony that told of the tormenting flame. Their clothing was half burnt away—their hair and beard entirely; the rain had come too late to save their nails. Some were swollen to double girth; other shriveled to manikins. According to degree of exposure, their faces were bloated and black or yellow and shrunken. The contraction of muscles which had given them claws for hands had cursed each countenance with a hideous grin. Faugh! I cannot catalogue the charms of these gallant gentlemen who had got what they enlisted for.[17]

As literary scholars Russell Duncan and David Klooster have written, "No one had ever written this kind of war story, one eschewing patriotism and glory to focus on terror and death."[18]

Like many a veteran, Bierce returned to the sites of war late in life. In his sixties, he went to many of the battlefields where he had fought before getting shot. The overland trip back East at least suggested convalescence to the aging Bierce. "My trip through the mountains has done my health good—and my heart too." But no amount of healing could tamp Bierce's dark, entirely unsentimental view of the war, a view which so often touched upon the wartime wounded and dead: "My friends have returned to Washington, and I'm having great times climbing peaks (they are knobs) and exploring gulches and canons—for which these people have no names—poor things. My dreamland is still unrevisited. They found a Confederate soldier over there the other day, with his rifle alongside. I'm going over to beg his pardon."[19] A year later, Bierce wrote an address, which he did not deliver in person but sent in the form of a letter, for the Twenty-Fourth Annual Reunion of the Bloody Ninth. He titled the piece "Battlefields and Ghosts," and his sardonic fatalism had, if anything, only increased:

> After forty-odd years there are neither enemies nor victories, but only gracious mountains and sleepy valleys all aflame with autumn foliage . . . hazy and dim as old memories.[20]
>
> Philipp, where we had our first affair with the enemy, is now a considerable town. It was easy to identify the road by which we entered in the belief that we had the enemy's camp surrounded. The high hill from which a battery of our pitched shells into the startled Confederate camp (and I believe flung a few at us by mistake) is still there, as is the way of hills, and looked quit familiar. We afterward camped on it, among the trees in a field. It is still a field, but the trees are mostly gone. By the way, that battery of ours did nothing worse than take off a young Confederate's leg. He was living near there a few years ago, a prosperous and respectable gentleman, but still minus the leg; no new one has grown on.[21]
>
> I found a number of opened graves besides that of Abbott, and a few undisturbed ones which had apparently been overlooked. Back of the fortifications is the burial ground of the Confederates. It is nearly obliterated. The graves are in rows that can hardly be traced in the dense undergrowth. Persons living within a mile did not know of its existence. I made out between eighty and a hundred graves—depressions that had been mounds. Fallen into them were eight or ten rude headstones with inscriptions that I copied. It did not seem quite fair that these poor fellows should lie there under the forest leaves, their graves forgotten even by their own people, while our dead were so well housed under the flag at Grafton, with monuments and flowers music and Memorial days.[22]
>
> But the whole region is wild and grand, and if any one of the men who in his golden youth soldiered through its sleepy valleys and over its gracious mountains will revisit it in the hazy season when it is all aflame with the autumn foliage I promise him sentiments that he will willingly entertain and emotions that he will care to feel. Among them will be, I fear, a haunting envy of those of his war comrades whose fall and burial in that enchanted land he once bewailed.[23]

To envy the dead, and how ever to put wartime experiences behind one's self? The suggestion of post-traumatic stress disorder (or more blunt brain injury by gunshot) is all too obvious in Ambrose Bierce's life and writings. Bierce's depictions of the war are gruesome and harrowing, with little melodramatic leavening.[24] From his perch in postwar San Francisco, where he rose to some fame, where he steeped his Civil War traumas in story, Bierce's later life suggests that neither time nor distance could heal what the awful conflict had wrought. No matter how recuperative or redemptive in theory, the West could not possibly redeem a warrior so wounded as Ambrose Bierce. His war stories rang with gothic truth, but at terrible cost.

WOUNDED SURGEON

In 1864, San Franciscan Bret Harte, whom Bierce would eventually befriend, wrote a poem in commemoration of California's admission to the Union fourteen years earlier. His was a poem of contrasts between war in the East and the pastoral tranquility of the far West. At its conclusion, Harte compared California's "full harvest and the wain's [wagon's] advance" to the bloodied battlefields of Civil War: "there the Grim Reaper and ambulance."

A great poet Harte was not. But that is beside the point: in this little couplet, he's cleverly tied together in just a few words what struck so many Americans in the era—seeing the country as cleaved in two twice, once at latitude, once at longitude. Harte spoke first of the new division between North and South, then of the older divide between eastern theaters of war and the Pacific landscapes of the Trans-Rocky Mountain West, California preeminent among them. In the East, war. In the West, peace. Here death, there life. Here injury, blood, surgery, and amputation—in Biercean gruesomeness—there convalescence and healing.

> Strange was the contrast that such scenes disclose
> From his high vantage o'er eternal snows;
> There War's alarm the brazen trumpet rings—
> Here his love-song the mailed cicala sings;
> There bayonets glitter through the forest glades—
> Here yellow cornfields stack their peaceful blades;
> There the deep trench where Valor finds a grave—
> Here the long ditch that curbs the peaceful wave;
> There the bold sapper with his lighted train—
> Here the dark tunnel and its stores of gain; . . .

"Wain's advance" and "ambulance" make for a poor rhyme. No matter. Harte was on to something he did not know at the time, and his verse invites us to contemplate the Civil War and postwar life of another individual who sought solace, healing, and escape in the West.

The Union Army's ambulance corps during the Civil War was something new in medical and military history, at least insofar as U.S. battlefields and troops were concerned. The military ambulance was the inspiration of a physician named Jonathan Letterman, whose short, hard, and unhappy life is, in its own way, a mirror of the more famed Civil War-induced darkness of Ambrose Bierce's postwar western life and work. As we explore Jonathan Letterman's life and attempts to start anew in the West, think of a less erratic Ambrose Bierce. Bierce's misanthropy is Letterman's melancholy.

A Pennsylvanian by birth, Jonathan Letterman trained as a physician at Jefferson Medical College in Philadelphia before the war.[25] Following completion of his medical training, he joined the antebellum medical corps of the Army and was assigned to a rotation of installations in the Southeast and the far West, including a California assignment at Fort Tejon northeast of Los Angeles. These pre–Civil War assignments put Letterman at a series of western forts in Indian country, and he began his military medical work pulling arrows out of the bodies of frontier soldiers.

When the Civil War broke out, the Army hurriedly transferred Letterman back east to the theaters of battle. Rising rapidly in the wartime phase of his career, Letterman was soon made medical director of the Army of the Potomac. He is known as author of the famed Letterman Plan, a revolutionary reorganization of Union hospitals and medical care constructed around a set of convalescent principles including fresh air for the wounded, efficient battlefield triage, systems of tent hospitals, and the creation and efficient use of an ambulance corps. This latter innovation was neither easy nor trivial. Previous to Letterman's insights and efforts, care of the battlefield wounded could best be described as chaotic, if not hopeless. Supplies and transport vehicles could easily be hijacked—if they were available at all—by field or command officers for other uses. Battlefield needs invariably took precedent over treatment of the wounded, and military discipline among medical personnel often proved wanting. The end result, inevitably, was untold suffering by the wounded, so many of whom died in agony on the fields where they lay utterly untended for hours or even days after falling.

Jonathan Letterman changed all that. Efficiency, organization, discipline, and adequate supply were all brought to bear on a previously jumbled mess.

Systemic clarity came in the form of field hospitals put up near battlefields, medical aid stations on the battlefields themselves, and ambulances moving back and forth between them and the further-away general hospitals. The ambulances proved especially critical. With these vehicles, usually big wagons pulled by men or horses, the battlefield wounded could be hastily fetched from where they fell, put into a system of care, and assigned to their next destination, whether that was a general hospital, home, or back to their units. Atop it all, Letterman established military discipline within his medical corps, including rotating triage and administrative duties for the doctors serving under him. It worked. As Letterman's biographer shows, the Army of the Potomac's "sick rate" dropped precipitously, and the mortality rate fell from a whopping 26 percent in the early years of the war to 10 percent in the latter years of fighting.[26]

Advances in care and recuperation notwithstanding, Jonathan Letterman knew the Grim Reaper of Bret Harte's 1864 poem. And he knew the wounded and their wounds that so mesmerized Ambrose Bierce. Any surgeon—any soldier—in the Civil War would have. And, unlike the ever sardonic Bierce ("nothing matters"), Letterman was appalled by the carnage of the war, both that wrought by the hostilities and by the surgeons who worked for him. As he wrote following one engagement, "The Surgery of these battle fields has been pronounced butchery."[27]

In 1864, this famed medical director of the Army of the Potomac quit his job. Jonathan Letterman briefly took up new duties with the Army's Department of the Susquehanna—charged with protecting the capital from attack and preventing Confederate crossings of the Susquehanna River—and began inspecting Union hospitals. But then Letterman quit the Army altogether. Friends tried to keep him in the service, but to no avail. His departure was made official at the very end of the year, with President Lincoln's acceptance of his resignation.

Had the physician grown weary of the war and of the carnage? Who wouldn't have? As Scott McGaugh writes in his excellent biography of Letterman, the war had indeed taken its toll. Letterman was sick and tired: "His face had grown gray as the war's toll became evident in the darkened bags that developed under his eyes." Letterman was spent, and "gave every appearance of exhaustion after three years of war, after experiencing some of the war's most devastating battles."[28]

Dr. Letterman could have returned full time to Philadelphia, where he had trained, where through contacts and networks he knew many important people, and where he had spent much of 1864 in fulfillment of his Army

FIGURE 7.1. Photograph of Jonathan Letterman, n.d, National Library of Medicine.

administrative duties. Philadelphia was not only the capital city of American medicine; it was also ground zero of Civil War convalescence, for the wounded and those that cared for them. A physician of Jonathan Letterman's talents and experience would have no difficulty securing work in one of literally dozens of hospitals bursting with Civil War wounded, so many of whom would need care well beyond however long the war lasted.

But he did not stay. He did not take up civilian medical work. On the contrary, Letterman embarked on something entirely surprising. He came back to Southern California. From Philadelphia, Letterman boarded a ship with his wife and young daughter and sailed all the way to California, as if answering the call of the Gold Rush. He disembarked at San Francisco, but instead of roaring off to the gold fields of the Sierra Nevada, he made his way south seeking something else. Forsaking his tent hospitals, battlefield triage, and ambulance corps, Dr. Letterman made his way to what was then called Buena Ventura, what we now call Ventura, on the coast north of Los Angeles. Buena Ventura, in the early months of 1865, was hardly any bigger than one of Jonathan Letterman's prewar frontier forts, and it was a long ways from Philadelphia. What pulled him there?

To get at the mystery, we have to go back to Philadelphia. There, Letterman must have had an exchange, or several, with Thomas A. Scott, one of the era's best-known and wealthiest Pennsylvanians, a railroad titan, land speculator, and would-be oilman. Oil had been recently discovered in Pennsylvania, but Scott had his petroleum sights on the far West. Would Dr. Letterman, Scott offered, like to return to California, this time in a very different pursuit than medical care of frontiersmen or Union soldiers? Would he like to look for oil in Southern California, and would he like to organize the men and materiel to do so?

The Civil War raged on in 1864, but Southern California—especially in the foothills and ravines between Santa Barbara and Los Angeles, was in the grip of oil fever. There, seeps of oil and "asphaltum" came straight up through the earth, bubbling at the surface of oily patches, much as they yet do today. Word about *la brea, la cienega*—the tar, the (oily) swamp—had gotten out: going after the stuff deep into the earth could yield lucrative results.[29]

Scott, the secretive Pennsylvania entrepreneur and railroad man—and assistant secretary of war—had already sent several agents to California to investigate oil prospects on land he owned or might soon own.[30] One of these representatives was Thomas A. Bard, a young attorney with Scott's Pennsylvania Railroad who had served as a volunteer scout for the Union Army at Antietam and other battles early in the war. In later years, Thomas Bard would be a founder of Union Oil Company, become very rich, and serve as a U.S. senator from California. Bard's brother Cephas was a surgeon in the Army of the Potomac, meaning that he worked for fellow Philadelphian Jonathan Letterman. And Letterman was well known (especially in Pennsylvania) as an administrator and innovative institutional organizer and leader. It may be that Cephas Bard introduced Letterman to his brother

Thomas, and from there Letterman met Scott. It also appears that Letterman's wife was known to both Bard brothers; her family was Philadelphia gentry, and these were small, tight-knit circles.[31] Somehow, a connection was made. With a whopping $16,000, Letterman became an investor in a scheme to mine Southern California oil.

In 1864, Jonathan Letterman, author of the famed Letterman Plan, and a man whose battlefield treatment and triage methods saved thousands of lives in the Civil War, left for California, site of Thomas Scott's oil schemes. His own convalescence played a role in Letterman's thinking as well. Clearly exhausted by the war, he was also plagued by gastrointestinal ailments of one sort or another, dysentery and chronic diarrhea among them.[32] But he was now away from the conflict, serving as the general superintendent of the Philadelphia & California Petroleum Company. What followed were a couple of hardscrabble years of effort to wrest oil and sticky tar from the seeps and soils of the area around Santa Paula, Buena Ventura, and Santa Barbara. As improbable as it was, Dr. Jonathan Letterman supervised the drilling of the very first oil well in California, an exercise that failed miserably.

Much as he might try to flee it, the Civil War went west with Jonathan Letterman, just as it had with Ambrose Bierce and legions of other veterans who demonstrated the fallacy of Bret Harte's easy contrasts of East and West, North and South. Letterman's unlikely journey to the opposite shores of the continent seems to have done little to shake off the stress, the blood, and the worry of wartime medicine and wartime experience. One event brings home with glaring clarity the ties that still bound Jonathan Letterman, living on the Pacific coastline of Southern California, to the most famous battle and battlefield in American history.

Gettysburg returned to Letterman at the hands of Stephen Peckham. Raised a Quaker in Rhode Island, Peckham studied chemistry and pharmacology at Brown College in the years just before the outbreak of the Civil War. After graduating, he worked as a pharmacist and then became one of the nation's first petroleum refiners, working with oil coming out of Pennsylvania's early oilfields beginning in the late 1850s.[33] When the war broke out, Peckham volunteered with a Rhode Island unit, serving as a hospital steward with Jonathan Letterman's medical corps of the Army of the Potomac; Peckham attended in surgeries and performed administrative tasks. He served in and around thick combat, including the Battle of the Wilderness, before being sent back to Philadelphia to work as a researcher with the Army Medical Laboratory.

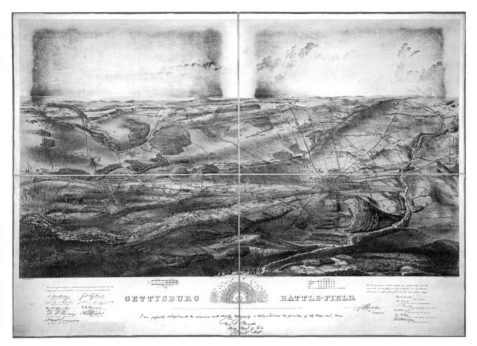

FIGURE 7.2. "Gettysburg Battle-Field," hand-colored lithograph by John B. Bachelder, 1863. Courtesy of the Huntington Library, San Marino, California.

Stephen Peckham's move to California was not quite as doubtful as Jonathan Letterman's. He had at least worked in the oil business before the blood of Civil War field hospitals and surgical tents. As with Letterman, Thomas Scott hired Peckham and sent him to California in 1865. There, in the spring of that year, the spring of Abraham Lincoln's assassination, the two early oilmen crossed paths. Only a few months earlier, amid the hospitals and the wounded of the war, Letterman would have moved in a world far above that of Peckham's status as a medical volunteer. The speculative oil business and frontier California leveled flat the medical and military hierarchies of wartime.

On the evening during which they made a tense acquaintance (the men would be antagonists before later building a friendship), Jonathan Letterman revealed the depths to which war and the wounded still hung around him as a pall. The physician had just, perhaps that very day, acquired a new bird's-eye rendering of the battle of Gettysburg. This was almost certainly John Badger Bachelder's beautiful 1864 panorama.

This is a justly famous work, with a dramatic backstory. Committed to chronicling the Civil War even as it raged, John B. Bachelder arrived at

Gettysburg within a week of the battle and began interviewing survivors and the wounded so as to plot the position of troops and engagements. The map explores the conflict over the three days of fighting. Bachelder sold what he called his "drawing" of the battle through subscription agents, usually disabled or wounded Civil War soldiers, and it went through several editions. He distributed it free to officers from the war, probably in part as a way to thank them for the many and long interviews. It was, he often declared, "well adapted to framing, and forms a suitable ornament for the Library, Hall, dining or sitting room according to taste."[34]

That spring night in 1865, in a small, rustic outpost of the fledgling Philadelphia and California Petroleum Company, 2,600 miles and nearly two years removed from the great battle, Jonathan Letterman spread the big, colorful isometric drawing on the floor and painstakingly went over the battle with Peckham. He dwelled on the final day, on Pickett's fated charge up to Cemetery Ridge that started in wishful glory (the "high water mark of the Confederacy," as Bachelder himself would famously term it) and ended in mortal disarray and infamy.

The evening event is an odd one. Letterman had never before met Stephen Peckham, and they did not at first like one another. Yet upon their meeting, Dr. Letterman immediately proceeded to unfurl or unroll a large, beautiful, and just-arrived (one wonders how it got to him) map, spread it upon the floor, and reveal his still-raw feelings about the most famous battle in all of American history. As he narrated the details of map and fight, Peckham recalled, Letterman lingered on the wounded and what had happened to them. The Gettysburg death rate, as well as the severity of the wounds, had proven unusually high, even as measured against typical Civil War brutality.[35] Letterman clearly remained troubled by it, all the more so because he had created and supervised the triage and care system that was not allowed to fully execute or do its work across those three days of fierce fighting.

Peckham remembered Letterman telling him that, throughout the battle, General George Gordon Meade, commanding the Union forces, had been so sure that he would be routed from the field that he had not brought up Letterman's ambulances or field supply wagons any closer than three miles from his troops, and Letterman was stymied in his attempts to disobey. The distance ensured that the presence of ambulances would be worthless. The surgeons Letterman had on the battlefield had only the tools they carried in their small leather kits. Meade also seemed to fear that Letterman's medical gear might end up in the enemy's hands; how to protect them other than by keeping them very, very far away?[36]

Letterman bitterly told Peckham how, on the third and most important day of Gettysburg fighting, Confederate artillery assaulted the entrenched Union line on Cemetery Ridge, thus exhausting their ammunition and doing little damage. Union artillery commander General Henry Jackson Hunt cleverly held his fire. Thinking that the Union cannon had either been destroyed or had run out of ammunition, Robert E. Lee ordered General George Pickett to move across the open expanse and take the hill. Hunt's artillery mowed the Confederates down, and Meade and the Union carried the day. But the victory had been Pyrrhic; the wounded (of both sides) lay everywhere, beyond care, beyond supplies, beyond hope.[37]

Modesty and his soft-spoken, melancholy demeanor notwithstanding, Letterman's view on the matter was as poignant as it was curt. From the vantage of twenty-six hundred miles and several years, Letterman could yet see, and could certainly feel, Gettysburg and all that it represented to him, spread out as it was upon his floor. "Even should an army be defeated, it is better to have the supplies for the proper care and comfort of the wounded upon the field, and run the risk of their capture, than that the wounded should suffer for want of them. Lost supplies can be replenished, but lives lost are gone forever," he said.[38] At Gettysburg, thousands and thousands of wounded lay mostly where they fell, the hospital tents furled and packed away. And then the weather changed on July 4, mixing rain with all the blood and bacteria and body parts. Where order and science and care could have at least partially redeemed the battlefield and its warriors, Letterman found only a "field of Blood on which the Demon of Destruction reveled."[39]

Nearly two years later, at the edge of the Pacific Ocean, speaking to a man he had only just met and did not like—but a man who also knew his way amid wartime wounded—Letterman's ire seems not to have cooled. And why, as he looked at the best visual rendering of the Civil War's climactic engagement, would it? Letterman must have felt as another soldier did as he looked upon the Bachelder drawing, suitable though it was, the artist said, for framing. "The battle is a huge nightmare to me.... A terrible panorama of tremendous events piled up in that 36 hours."[40]

The next chapters in Jonathan Letterman's story are anything but happy. Following his oil hunting failures, he moved north to San Francisco and became the city and county coroner in 1867 and shortly thereafter was named surgeon general of California. He was joined in San Francisco by former

Jefferson Medical College colleague LaFayette Gould, who had been Letterman's counterpart in the Confederacy. Their reunion proved fleeting. Gould worked briefly as a surgeon for San Francisco's Board of Health before dying young in 1870, at forty-four.

Not long after moving north, Letterman's wife Mary took ill and died, leaving Letterman to raise their two young daughters alone. He then somehow broke his leg, badly, which only exacerbated his health woes. Shattered by Mary's death and seemingly prone to reclusiveness anyway, Letterman died in 1872 at forty-seven, sick, nearly broke, and crushed in spirit. The military hospital at the Presidio Army installation in San Francisco was named for him in the early twentieth century.

If Jonathan Letterman is known at all today—and mostly he is not—it is for that and also for a book entitled *Medical Recollections of the Army of the Potomac,* which he wrote in the last, far West period of his short life. Another medical history of the war was written in the lives and bodies of the thousands of veterans, Union and Confederate alike, who, alongside countless others, came west following the war, hoping that relocation would allow them to renew their lives, if not also heal them. But for Jonathan Letterman, Ambrose Bierce, and so many others, neither recollections nor consequences of the war were softened or healed in California. In aches and pains, nightmares and anxiety, the war went on.

NOTES

1. Carey McWilliams, *Ambrose Bierce: A Biography* (rpt. ed., Hamden, CT: Archon Books, 1967), 24.
2. See Lucius Bierce, *Travels in the Southland, 1822–1823 the journal of Lucius Verus Bierce.* Edited by George W. Knepper (Columbus: Ohio State University Press, 1966).
3. McWilliams, *Ambrose Bierce,* xxii-xxiii.
4. See ibid., at pp. 29 and xxii.
5. Ibid., 28.
6. Ibid., xxi.
7. William McCann, "Introduction," in Ambrose Bierce, *Ambrose Bierce's Civil War* (Chicago: Gateway Editions, 1956), v-vi.
8. Quoted in McWilliams, *Ambrose Bierce,* 55.
9. Quoted in ibid., xx.
10. McCann, "Introduction," vii.
11. See McWilliams, *Ambrose Bierce,* especially 65–72.

12. Paul Fatout, *Ambrose Bierce: The Devil's Lexicographer* (Norman: University of Oklahoma Press, 1951), 67–72.

13. McWilliams, *Ambrose Bierce*, 72–76. See also Robert A. Murray, "The Hazen Inspections," *Montana: The Magazine of Western History*. 18, no. 1 (Winter 1968), 24–33.

14. "Across the Plains," *Works, I*, 364.

15. McWilliams, *Ambrose Bierce*, 63.

16. Ibid., 81. In the 1967 reprint of his Bierce biography, McWilliams stated the point clearly:

I stand by the essential theme—the basic interpretation. In a sense the theme is that Bierce was not essentially a cynic or skeptic but rather an idealist, more accurately perhaps a moralist, who, at an early and impressionable age had been exposed to a frightful baptism of fire—an ordeal of suffering and horror—that had shaped his character and outlook. In an introduction that I did for a paperback edition of *The Devil's Dictionary* in 1957, I tried to suggest what Bierce was really like by comparing him with Oliver Wendell Holmes, Jr. (as did Edmund Wilson in *Patriotic Gore*). Bierce and Holmes were both born in 1842. Both were exposed to the fires of a cruel and horrendous Civil War when they were young men. Both participated in some of the heaviest fighting of the war and both were wounded. Both were intense idealists when they enlisted; they emerged from the war in a different mood. Neither ever forgot or, for that matter, fully recovered from the effects of the war. Both were proud, sensitive, and extremely intelligent; after the war both took a frosty and detached view of human affairs and were somewhat Olympian in outlook. Both were men of rare courage; both looked out at life in a clear-eyed way. Both took an extremely bleak view of the corruption of the post-1865 decades and yet, as Edmund Wilson notes, were too much old-fashioned Americans to identify with the ideals of social justice which began to be voiced near the turn of the century.

See McWilliams, *Ambrose Bierce*.

17. Ambrose Bierce, "What I Saw at Shiloh," in *Ambrose Bierce's Civil War*, 23–27.

18. Ibid., 27.

19. Ambrose Bierce, *The Letters of Ambrose Bierce* (San Francisco: Book Club of California, 1922), 75.

20. Ambrose Bierce, *Battlefields and Ghosts* (Palo Alto, CA: Harvest Press, 1931), title page.

21. Ibid., 6–7.

22. Ibid., 12–13.

23. Ibid., 16–17.

24. See, generally, Michael Schaefer, *Just What War Is: The Civil War Writings of De Forest and Bierce* (Knoxville: University of Tennessee Press), 1997; Brian Thomsen, *Shadows of Blue and Gray: The Civil War Writings of Ambrose Bierce* (New York: Tom Doherty Associates), 2002; Sharon Talley, *Ambrose Bierce and the Dance of Death* (Knoxville: University of Tennessee Press), 2009; David M. Owens, *The Devil's Topographer: Ambrose Bierce and the American War Story* (Knoxville:

University of Tennessee Press, 2006); Russel Duncan and David J. Klooster, eds., *Phantoms of a Blood-Stained Period: The Complete Civil War Writings of Ambrose Bierce* (Amherst: University of Massachusetts Press, 2002); Ambrose Bierce, *Tales of Soldiers and Civilians* (San Francisco: E. L. G. Steele, 1891); Ambrose Bierce, *Ambrose Bierce's Civil War* (Chicago: Gateway Editions, 1956); Donald T. Blume, *Ambrose Bierce's Civilians and Soldiers in Context: A Critical Study* (Kent, OH: Kent State University Press, 2004); Martin Griffin, *Ashes of the Mind: War and Memory in Northern Literature, 1865–1900* (Amherst: University of Massachusetts Press, 2009).

25. LaFayette Gould, a year ahead of Letterman at Jefferson, would become the chief medical officer of the Confederacy. He, too, was stationed in California before the war and was dismissed at the outbreak of the Civil War for refusing to swear an oath of allegiance to the Union.

26. See Scott McGaugh, *Surgeon in Blue: Jonathan Letterman, the Civil War Doctor Who Pioneered Battlefield Care* (New York: Arcade, 2013), 11. Other factors would influence these figures as well, including a fitter and more experienced fighting force as the war went on, but the Letterman revolution in care of the wounded undoubtedly played a significant role.

27. This was a comment seemingly aimed at inelegant and poorly executed surgical work. Letterman did not argue strongly against the frequency—amazing frequency—of amputations themselves. On the contrary, he believed, as did many of his peers and medical colleagues, that amputation helped prevent gangrenous and other infections coming from dirty wounds. "From my observations," he wrote, "I am convinced that if any fault was committed it was that the knife was not used often enough." Quoted in McGaugh, *Surgeon in Blue,* 274.

28. McGaugh, *Surgeon in Blue,* 224.

29. See, for example, Brian Frehner's fine study, *Finding Oil: The Nature of Petroleum Geology, 1859–1920* (Lincoln: University of Nebraska Press, 2011) for an overview of the science, funding, and fieldwork involved.

30. McGaugh notes that Scott had already played an important, if indirect, role in Letterman's revision of the care of wounded Union soldiers. He had, at the request of the federal government, constructed a railroad from Philadelphia to Washington, DC, to bring the wounded to new hospital facilities being built as the war proved no flash in the pan sectional spat.

31. William H. Hutchinson, *Oil, Land, and Politics: The California Career of Thomas Robert Bard,* vol. 1, (Norman: University of Oklahoma Press, 1965), 78–102.

32. Civil War soldiers remained some fifty times more likely to suffer from postwar intestinal illness and distress than the general population. See McGaugh, *Surgeon in Blue,* 274.

33. See Gerald White, *Baptism in Oil: Stephen F. Peckham in Southern California, 1865–66* (San Francisco: Book Club of California, 1984).

34. John B. Bachelder, quoted from a letter to C. F. Johnston, July 10, 1876; Huntington Library, Manuscripts Department.

35. See Mary C. Gillett, *The Army Medical Department, 1818–1865* (Washington, DC: Government Printing Office, 1987), 214. Gillett ascribes this mortality spike in

part to the heat before and during the battle, as well as the fast march many of the troops engaged in before the clash.

36. McGaugh's Letterman biography quotes Letterman in regards to battlefield inefficiencies in care of the wounded; merely piling up supplies in the rear lines or near a battle was worthless without officer accountability brought to bear; without it, such supplies (270) "were lost, and in various ways wasted; and not unfrequently [sic] all the supplies of a regiment were thrown away by commanding officers, almost in sight of the enemy; that the wagons might be used for other purposes." See also Gabor Boritt, *The Gettysburg Gospel: The Lincoln Speech That Nobody Knows* (New York: Simon and Schuster, 2008), 10.

37. To fathom the scale of Gettysburg, it is well here to quote Pat Leonard in "The End of the Gutbuster," *New York Times,* July 5, 2012: "It is difficult to grasp the extent of the carnage that Letterman's corps had to deal with at Gettysburg, but one way to envision it is through a modern example: the number of men treated for battle wounds—nearly 21,000 Union soldiers and Confederate prisoners—would fill up every bed in the 14 largest hospitals in America today. And that figure does not include thousands more Confederate wounded who were evacuated with Lee's retreating army." http://opinionator.blogs.nytimes.com/2012/07/05/the-end-of-the-gutbuster/.

38. Jonathan Letterman, *Medical Recollections of the Army of the Potomac* (New York: D. Appleton, 1866), 157. See also Noah Andre Trudeau, *Gettysburg: A Testing of Courage* (New York: Harper Collins, 2003), 538.

39. Ibid.

40. Quoted in Jim Weeks, *Gettysburg: Memory, Market, and an American Shrine* (Princeton: Princeton University Press, 2009), 23. Weeks noted an opposite line of thinking, suggesting—as the artist himself must have suggested—that Bachelder's great drawing had the "potential to accelerate national healing." See Weeks, 24.

EIGHT

Still Picture, Moving Stories

RECONSTRUCTION COMES TO INDIAN COUNTRY

Martha A. Sandweiss

THE PHOTOGRAPH PUTS US IN INDIAN COUNTRY, in early May 1868. Alexander Gardner had been here at Fort Laramie for more than two weeks, photographing the Indians and government agents assembled at this windswept military outpost on the plains of Dakota Territory. The grass had not yet greened up, and nature's bleak aspect matched the mood of the assembled Lakota Sioux chiefs and federal Peace Commissioners.[1]

The picture focuses our attention. It introduces us to the Peace Commission, created by Congress in July 1867 to "establish peace with certain hostile Indian tribes," "remove the causes of war," secure the frontier settlements and railroad lines, and come up with a plan for civilizing the Indians.[2] In this era of photographic firsts, it documents a near last: the penultimate moment the federal government would negotiate with Indian nations as independent sovereign powers. And in an era of seeming resolutions—not just at Appomattox, but in Mexico, and the troubled borderlands of the Middle West and Southwest—the photograph marks a moment of flux. The entire premise of federal–Indian relations was about to change.

The photograph pinpoints a moment, but it can disperse our attention, as well. If we follow its subjects back into the archives, we find a much larger story about how events in the West fit into the swirling national debates about race, citizenship, and federal power in the nineteenth-century United States. With his Gettysburg Address in November 1863, President Abraham Lincoln recast the Civil War not simply as a fight between Union and Confederate troops, but as a sacred struggle for "a new birth of freedom."[3] After Appomattox, the newly powerful federal government moved to consolidate that reimagined nation, reintegrating the Confederate states into a national political order and extending rights and citizenship to the freedmen. But the meanings and limits

FIGURE 8.1. Alfred H. Terry, William S. Harney, William T. Sherman, Arapaho, John B. Sanborn, Samuel F. Tappan, Christopher C. Augur. Albumen silver print by Alexander Gardner, 1868. Courtesy of the Minnesota Historical Society.

of federal power and personal rights in Indian Country remained far from resolved, the question of who could be a citizen still up in the air. The stories embedded in this photograph, in the messy and complicated trajectories of individual lives, remind us that ideas and experiences forged in the crucible of the antebellum debates about slavery and freedom, the violence of the Civil War, and the political agendas of Reconstruction all cascaded west. As William Deverell argues in his chapter in this volume, the postwar West became a national symbol of healing. During the early years of Reconstruction, however, Indian Country remained a place where the shape of the new American nation looked far from clear. Gardner's photograph offers a concise visual metaphor for that: everything was under negotiation.

Gardner set his two cameras side by side in the midday sun and summoned his subjects. The six commissioners arranged themselves symmetrically on either side of a young Indian girl. The two men on the ends gazed toward the child, their arms held behind their backs. Next to them, two men faced out toward the photographer. The commissioners flanking the girl faced her. Because she barely reached their shoulders, they stared at one another over her head. The men had all been photographed before back East, but they held themselves awkwardly here, far from the familiar comforts of studio chairs and props. Only the child—who had never before seen a camera—looked at ease. She hugged her dark stroud cloth blanket around her shoulders and looked straight into the camera lens.[4]

Gardner made one exposure with his larger view camera, another with his smaller stereographic device. Then he slipped the plate holders from his cameras and ducked back into his dark tent to develop, wash, and dry the negatives. Weeks later, back in his Washington, D.C., studio, he made his prints for the commissioners. In a neat nineteenth-century hand, he named them from left to right: General Alfred Howe Terry, General William S. Harney, General William Tecumseh Sherman, John B. Sanborn, Colonel Samuel F. Tappan, General Christopher C. Auger. He did not know the girl's name, or if he had, he could no longer recall it. He just called her "Arappaho." Later, before he deposited his negative in a Washington archive, he changed his mind. On the glass plate itself, he (or someone close to him) inscribed the word "Dakota." At some point, the glass negative cracked, and a thin black lightning strike of a line smote General Terry in the chest.[5]

The photograph puts us on the northern Plains, far from the large Civil War battlefields of the East and the southern cities and towns where freedmen and women were stepping tentatively into their new post-emancipation worlds. But in the stillness of the photograph, we glimpse the dynamism of the larger national story. The commissioners, all men whose lives had been shaped by the war and the attendant debates about slavery, understood their work out West was intimately tied to the recent struggle between North and South and to these larger contests over freedom, citizenship, and federal power. The former Union commander William T. Sherman, the most recognizable man in the picture and now the commander of the territory between the Mississippi River and the Rockies, put it this way: the "strong, vigorous men" mustered out of the military naturally looked for new opportunities in the far West. There, they would substitute "for the useless Indians the intelligent owners of productive farms and cattle-ranches."[6]

As these veterans and other settlers pushed westward after Appomattox, so too did the railroad lines. With the slavery issue resolved, construction moved forward without the fractious sectional debates that marked earlier struggles over the routes. And the enabling legislation for the Peace Commission addressed head-on the tangled challenges of dealing with settlers, railroads, and Indians. It directed the commissioners to "establish security for person and property along the lines of railroad now being constructed to the Pacific ... [and] insure civilization for the Indians and peace and safety of the whites." Commissioner John B. Sanborn told the Oglala Lakota they would have to move to a reservation: "You are too near to the railroad and trouble might arise at any time."[7]

The commercial interests of the railroads and the safety of the settlers dovetailed with the diplomatic concerns of the commissioners. General Augur, who once had the sad task of guarding access to the boarding house where President Abraham Lincoln lay mortally wounded, now served as commander of the Department of the Platte (as well as a member of the Peace Commission). He protected work parties on the Union Pacific Railroad line. His fellow commissioner, Alfred Terry, a former Union officer, now led the Department of Dakota, where he oversaw the safety of the workers along the Northern Pacific route.[8] At Fort Laramie, they hoped to make the assembled bands accept a Great Sioux Reservation, the northern counterpart to the reservation they'd compelled the tribes of the southern Plains to accept the year before at Medicine Lodge Creek. With the southern Plains tribes confined to Indian Territory and the people of the northern Plains forced to stay north of the North Platte River, a central corridor across Kansas and Nebraska would be free of Indian threats. Then the transcontinental railroad, like one long black stitch of iron, would pull East and West together into the seamless fabric of a post–Civil War nation.

Gardner arrived at Fort Laramie in a roundabout way. He had immigrated from Scotland in 1856 to join a utopian community of like-minded countrymen in eastern Iowa, where they planned to pool their resources to create a "comfortable home for themselves and families where they may follow a more simple, useful and rational mode of life than is found practicable in the complex and competitive society from which they have been anxious to retire."[9] But in the wake of a tuberculosis outbreak, the project collapsed before Gardner arrived. Once a jeweler, later a journalist, and then a would-be cooperative farmer, Gardner became a photographer. He had dreamed of a quiet rural life, but found himself an eyewitness to America's bloodiest decade. He photographed the carnage of Antietam and Gettysburg, made portraits of Abraham Lincoln, then documented the execution of the men who conspired to assassinate the president. He photographed visiting Indian delegations in his Washington, D.C., studio, and headed west himself in 1867 to document the construction of the Kansas Pacific Railroad lines as they stretched out across the central Plains.[10]

Gardner understood that photographs could record events, tell stories, or transport viewers to distant places. He drew on all of these ideas for his monumental *Photographic Sketch Book of the War* (1866), one of the earliest histories of the conflict. With a hundred mounted photographs paired with long narrative captions, he told a tale of Union bravery and Confederate futility. He concluded with an image of the dedication of the memorial on the Bull Run battlefield in June 1865. The tall stone plinth closed the *Sketch Book* like an enormous exclamation point. That war was over; a tragic and breaking news story already transformed into the subject of sentimental memory.[11]

But the wartime debates about race and violence, citizenship and governance still echoed in Indian country, not so easily silenced by the books and treaties that declared the war done. No one here at this Army post, not even the girl, remained untouched by the nation's recent past or isolated from the robust Reconstruction-era government programs designed to consolidate the nation. We can see that now, in hindsight, as Gardner could not.

Take slavery, for example. No African Americans appear in this photograph, but Gardner and the Peace Commissioners all brought to Fort Laramie a deep familiarity with America's peculiar institution. Gardner was a lifelong abolitionist.[12] The commissioners, a mix of pro- and antislavery men, trailed long and varied histories as slaveholders and as abolitionists, as men who championed the rights of freedpeople and men who feared what would happen if former slaves moved into positions of power. Their impulses toward one group tended to shade over to the other; strong racial antipathies toward African Americans tracking anti-Indian sentiment, deep antislavery feelings shading into humanitarian impulses toward the western tribes.

General William S. Harney (1800–1889) had been a slaveholder, a rarity among the top officers of the Union Army, whose suspected pro-Southern sympathies contributed to his dismissal as the commander of the Army's Department of the West in 1861. In 1863, he retired from the military, after forty-five years and service in a string of battles that echo a long, sad history of American expansionism, including campaigns against Seminoles and Sauks, Mexicans and Lakotas. After the 1855 Battle of Ash Hollow in what is now western Nebraska, when Harney led six hundred soldiers in an assault on a Brulé Lakota village, killing eighty-six and capturing seventy-six women and children, the Brulé gave him a name: *Winyan Wicakte,* Woman Killer.[13]

The name was more apt than the Lakotas could have known. As a newly married Army major in St. Louis in 1834, Harney had whipped to death one of his own slaves, a young mother named Hannah. He accused her of losing a key and flayed her with a piece of cowhide "until her flesh was . . . lacerated and torn."[14] His brutality stunned the citizens of that slaveholding city. After a coroner's jury ruled that Harney killed Hannah, the military officer fled for his life as a mob moved toward his house to demand justice. He was still on the lam when a grand jury indicted him for murder. He returned after four months and used his political pull to move the trial to a rural county. No one challenged the fact of the beating, but the country jury acquitted Harney of murder, affirming for him the power that came with being a white man and a military officer. Vindicated, if not exactly redeemed, he moved up the military ranks and was breveted to major general in 1865 in recognition of his distinguished career. Soon afterward, President Andrew Johnson appointed the short-tempered Harney to the Peace Commission.[15]

Samuel F. Tappan (1831–1913), cousin to the celebrated abolitionists Arthur and Lewis Tappan, grew up in Boston on the other side of the slavery issue. Strongly antislavery as a young man, he moved to Kansas in 1854 to join the Free State movement, just after Congress passed the Kansas-Nebraska Act. In 1860 he followed the Pike's Peakers west to Denver, and with the outbreak of war the next year he received a commission to organize a regiment of Union volunteers.[16]

Tappan's military service, coupled with his strong humanitarian ideals, led to his appointment as chief military investigator into the Sand Creek Massacre. On November 29, 1864, soon after their participation in the Union victories in the New Mexico deserts that Megan Kate Nelson describes in her chapter in this volume, Colonel John M. Chivington and his Colorado militiamen had attacked a peaceful encampment of Southern Cheyenne and Arapaho on the plains of eastern Colorado. They murdered some 150 Indians, including many women and children, and afterward brandished their war trophies—which included severed body parts—in a Denver theater. The brutal assault stirred patriotic fervor, widespread horror, and a deepening anxiety about the future of the western Indians. Tappan made no secret of his views: he thought the attack morally wrong and "the greatest military blunder of the age," but he maintained that he could be a fair-minded investigator.[17] During the early months of 1865, he gathered eyewitness testimony. When one Chivington supporter killed an anti-Chivington witness in April 1865, Tappan drew a direct connection to events back East. "The barbarism of slavery culminated in the assassination of Mr. Lincoln, the barbarism of Sand Creek has culminated in the assassination of Capt. Soule."[18] The damning evidence Tappan gathered informed the congressional report that found the Colorado militiamen guilty of "murder" and indiscriminate slaughter "of the most revolting character," and pronounced their officers men of "fiendish malignity and cruelty."[19] The report triggered a congressional investigation into the condition of the Indian tribes, headed by Wisconsin senator James R. Doolittle, that found the western Indians in dire straits, blamed most Indian hostilities on white provocations, and identified the reservation system as the only sound way to move forward. That report, in turn, spurred the creation of the Peace Commission on which Tappan, a humanitarian outlier among the career military officers, now served.[20]

During his tenure on the Peace Commission, Tappan put his humanitarian principles into action by unofficially adopting one of Sand Creek's young survivors. When the killing stopped, Colorado militiamen had pulled a six-year-old Cheyenne girl from a sand pit piled deep with corpses, including the bodies of her mother and father. They claimed her as a mascot, took her to Central City, Colorado, and renamed her Minnehaha, in one bold stroke replacing her real identity with the sentimentalizing name from Longfellow's *Hiawatha*. During the three years her tribe petitioned unsuccessfully for her return, she lived with a white family, attended school, went to church, and was baptized in the Episcopal faith.

In the summer of 1867, as the Peace Commission negotiated with the Cheyenne and some of the other tribes of the southern Plains, the commissioners sent an emissary to Central City to collect "Minnie" and return her to her extended family in fulfillment of their existing treaty obligations. The girl refused to go. Tappan understood how much her return would mean to the Cheyenne and went to plead with her himself. Although she refused to return to her tribe, she accepted his offer to be schooled in Boston. Tappan delivered her there, renamed her Minnie Tappan, enrolled her in public schools and sent her to a Sunday school connected to his own Spiritualist faith.[21] In the winter of 1868 she sat on a Boston stage with the abolitionist Wendell Phillips as he delivered a fiery oration about the massacre at Sand Creek.[22] Tappan might have exemplified abolitionist ideals gone west, but his ward personified the ways in which evidence of the humanitarian crises in Indian Country rippled back east to intersect with the evolving landscape of African American rights. The Thirteenth and Fourteenth Amendments, coupled with the programs being developed by the Freedmen's Bureau, laid out a map for the ex-slaves to be integrated into the nation. But the path forward for the western Indians seemed far less settled.

Neither a slaveholder like Harney nor an abolitionist like Tappan, General William T. Sherman (1820–91) likewise held views toward the Indians that mirrored his attitudes toward African Americans. He had never disguised his mildly proslavery sentiment: "It is certain that he did not enter the military service on account of slavery," his brother said with some understatement. "His sympathies and friendships were largely with the South."[23]

In the fall of 1854, shortly after the passage of the Kansas–Nebraska Act, Sherman advised his brother John (R-Ohio), just elected to the House of Representatives, not to be "too forward" on the slavery question. Citing a familiar argument invoked by defenders of slavery, Sherman explained that Negroes thrived in the southern heat as whites could not, and played a key role in the southern economy. "Negroes free won't work tasks of course, and rice, sugar and certain kind of cotton cannot be produced, except by forced negro labor."[24] After emancipation General Sherman continued to question the fundamental capacities of the freedmen, preferring them as laborers, not soldiers.[25] All the new talk about social equality bothered him. Some wanted "to make negroes voters, and even, with the legal right encouragement, to commingle their blood with ours ... ," Sherman wrote. "I for one would be slow in going to such extremes."[26]

As a Union commander, Sherman thus fought a war to free the slaves while doubting the inherent abilities of African Americans. And now he served on a Peace Commission though he personally sought a military defeat of the Indians. "I never expect to make of Indians good citizens," he wrote, as he served on a government commission that in fact held out Indian citizenship as a possible outcome of the treaty negotiations.[27] As he explained to Tappan in September 1868, he had agreed to the Peace Commission's final report only because he thought the entire project would fail anyway. "I deemed it a necessary concession ... that the United States should make the

Indians a generous offer, before proceeding to extremities. I have no hope of civilizing the Plains Indians.[28]

Other Peace Commissioners in the photograph also understood, in their own ways, the challenges involved in integrating nonwhite peoples into the new postwar nation. As commander of the Department of Virginia in 1866, General Alfred H. Terry (1827–90) urged Congress to offer military protection to the emancipated slaves. The majority of white people treat them with "great harshness and injustice," he said, and it would not be safe to commit them to the care of local authorities or institutions.[29] Attorney and brevet Major General John B. Sanborn (1826–1904), who investigated the situation of the freedmen among the old slave-holding tribes of Indian Territory in November 1865, likewise thought they needed federal protection. Not from the whites, however, but from the Indians.[30] Although the Creeks and Seminoles regarded the freedmen "as their equals in right," a significant percentage of the Cherokee wanted the government to move the freedmen away; many of the Choctaw had a "violent prejudice" against their former slaves; and the Chickasaw Nation was "still holding most of their negroes in slavery." Sanborn thought the freedmen the most industrious, economical, and intelligent residents of Indian Territory. It's not hard to see the irony in his recommendation that they get their own "reservation" or tract of land where they could homestead and live under martial law or a territorial government, secure in their rights. Like one of the visions discussed in Nicholas Guyatt's chapter in this volume, this particular reservation for emancipated slaves would keep Indians out, not in.[31]

Gardner's photograph thus reminds us that the Peace Commissioners brought to Fort Laramie ideas about racial hierarchies and the economic and social consolidating project of Reconstruction learned from personal experience with antebellum slavery and with the federal effort to integrate the freedmen into the fabric of the nation. No simple equation linked the racial ideas forged in one situation to those developed in another. But the commissioners could not help but view their mission out West through the lens of personal experience. As Civil War soldiers they had fought to protect federal power and crush slavery. As military leaders during Reconstruction in the South some of them had helped to put in place the programs that would protect the freedmen. Now at Fort Laramie, still as representatives of the federal government, still engaged with those struggles over centralized power and citizenship, they sought to define a new place for the western Indian tribes in the consolidating nation. Experience was an unsteady guide, however. The freedmen may have wanted into the mainstream. Many Indians did not.

If the men in the picture connect us to larger stories about slavery and freedom, what of the girl? Like so many Native American subjects of nineteenth-century photographs, she remained anonymous in the archives. But more than a century after Gardner made the image, a Lakota man identified the girl as his grandmother, Sophie Mousseau.[32] She looks small and vulnerable in the photograph, peripheral to the larger events and ideas embodied in the Peace Commissioners. But to follow her story back into the archives is to discover the international stretch of her life and her own links to larger stories about race, violence, and citizenship, reminding us that a hard-won peace in one part of the country did not create a new peace farther west.

Sophie, named after her paternal grandmother, was born around 1860 to an Oglala Lakota named Yellow Woman and her French Canadian husband, the trader and rancher M. A. Mousseau. In fur trade country, interethnic marriages had long offered advantages to whites and Indians alike, creating a middle ground of cultural and economic possibilities and tangled webs of family ties.[33] Sophie's father worked for the sprawling American Fur Company and later built an early Wyoming ranch. Her uncle, Joseph-Alfred Mousseau, who moved among Canada's political elite, became prime minister of Québec. And young Sophie herself likely spoke French, as well as Lakota and English, making her more multilingual than of any of the Peace Commissioners with whom she posed.[34]

Sophie lived her entire life on the northern Plains, far from the debates about emancipation and black citizenship that occupied so many Americans in other parts of the nation. But she experienced firsthand how race could shape a person's options in the post-Reconstruction West. She grew up in a mixed-race family and she created one herself. As racial boundaries hardened throughout the South in the late nineteenth century, however, they hardened in Indian Country, too. Sophie married an Irish-born Civil War veteran named John "Posey" Ryan around 1878 and had five children with him over the next eight years. In 1886, after he fell in love with a white woman, Ryan took his young children and sent Sophie to Pine Ridge. He "dumped" her on the reservation, a family member recalled.[35] Aware that his part-Indian wife would have slight chance of getting her children back through the territorial courts, Ryan moved them into a white man's world.

In Pine Ridge in 1893, Sophie remarried. John Monroe, a performer in Buffalo Bill's Wild West show, was, like her, the child of a white father and an Indian mother, whose options were largely circumscribed by his mother's race. Sophie had another eleven children with him, and lived the rest of her life in a dug-out in a rural part of the Pine Ridge reservation. The niece of a Canadian politician and the multilingual daughter of a successful French Canadian businessman, Sophie died in 1936 in one of the poorest regions of a Depression-stricken nation, a bear skin flapping across the entrance to her sod home.[36]

The personal stories that run through Gardner's photograph thus take us from 1830s St. Louis to the Great Depression, from the freedmen's world to buffalo country, from the eastern battlefields of the Civil War to the killing fields of the Indian wars. They introduce us to murdered slaves, idealistic socialists, and Cheyenne orphans. But larger political stories run through the photograph as well, connecting us to events unfolding far from this military fort in the far West. The photograph does not illustrate these ideas precisely. It cannot make visible these complex events. But it provides us a way in.

In July 1868, not long after Gardner made his photograph, the last of the twenty-eight states necessary for its passage ratified the Fourteenth Amendment to the Constitution of the United States, extending citizenship to the freedmen. As Joshua Paddison explains in his chapter in this volume, however, it implicitly denied such rights to "Indians not taxed." The Lakota chiefs meeting with the Peace Commissioners at Fort Laramie might not have cared about that. The amendment indirectly reaffirmed their status as members of sovereign nations, with a right to engage in treaty negotiations with the federal government. How, after all, could a government sign a diplomatic treaty with its own citizens?[37]

The first group, the Brulé, signed the Fort Laramie Treaty on April 29, 1868. The Minniconjou, Yankton, and one of the Oglala bands followed. Red Cloud's band of Oglala held out until early November 1868, when Red Cloud—accompanied by 130 chiefs and headmen—finally came into the fort, long after the commissioners had left. He had refused to sign the treaty until the United States honored its commitment to abandon its forts along the Bozeman Trail, long a source of Indian animosity. Now, as an Army officer later reported, he appeared "with a show of reluctance and tremulousness, washed his hands with the dust of the floor . . . signed it, and required all the whites present to touch the pen."[38]

The Treaty promised peace, and sacrosanct borders within which the multiple Lakota bands would be protected from white incursions. The Great Sioux Reservation would stretch west from the Missouri River and include the tribe's sacred Black Hills. The Lakota would get "absolute and undisturbed use and occupation" of some 31 million acres, access to another 50 million acres of "unceded Indian territory," and the right to hunt "on any lands north of the North Platte, and on the Republican Fork of the Smoky Hill, so long as the buffalo may range thereon in such numbers as to justify the chase." In exchange, they would have to abandon all lands beyond those stipulated by the treaty and "withdraw all opposition to the construction of the railroads now being built on the plains." This clause portended just how permeable the boundaries of this new reservation would be. Should rail lines or roads someday cross the reservation, the government would compensate the Lakota, but the tribes could not challenge the incursions.[39]

The treaty also laid out a plan for the "civilization" of the Indians, with the promise of an agent, physician, carpenter, farmer, blacksmith, miller, engineer, and teacher, all intended to help the Lakota give up their nomadic ways. In addition, it called for the mandatory education of all children between the ages of six and sixteen. Like the federal agenda for the freedmen, the plans for the Lakota underscored the value of behavior that would make the recipients of all this government largesse seem more like white men.

In fact, even as the final states were ratifying the constitutional amendment that seemed to ban Indians from citizenship, the treaty held out the possibility of citizenship for those Lakota men who became responsible homesteaders. Male heads of families could claim up to 320 acres for farming. Both men and women over the age of eighteen who were not heads of households could claim up to eighty acres. After three years of residence, and with $200 of improvements, men (and men only) could receive a patent for up to 160 acres of their land and then become citizens of the United States.[40]

This homesteading clause echoed the promises of private land ownership made in the general Homestead Act of 1862, the 1865 bill establishing the Freedmen's Bureau, and the Southern Homestead Act of 1866 created, at least in part, to distribute lands to freedmen. Coupled with the stipulation about education and the services designed to promote a particular kind of settled self-sufficiency, the homestead provision suggests just how much the Peace Commissioners' toolkit of social fixes resembled the strategies being deployed by the Freedmen's Bureau to support the economic self-sufficiency of the ex-slaves. But there was one crucial difference. Other homesteaders, including the freedmen, would get land owned by the federal government. The Sioux would, in effect, get land that was already theirs. Each private homestead would diminish the land held in common by the tribe. The Fort Laramie Treaty thus held the seeds of an idea that would find full and calamitous expression in the Dawes Severalty Act of 1887, which gave the president the power to break up communally held Indian lands for distribution in severalty.

The treaty likewise held the seeds of a movement to exert greater federal power over legal affairs in Indian Country, a plan that again invites comparison to federal programs in the former Confederate states. As Greg Downs notes, in theory federal troops in the Reconstruction South secured and enforced the rights of the freedmen and protected them from violence. The U.S. government's law enforcement role in Indian country, however, seemed less clear. If the freedmen needed federal help to protect their rights against their former masters and the broken legal systems of a slave society, the tribes had their own systems of legal prosecution and punishment that did not, to their minds, need repair.

Nonetheless, the first article of the Fort Laramie Treaty set out a new system of justice. The so-called "bad man" clause specified that if "bad among the whites" harmed an Indian, proof would be given to the agent, then forwarded to the Commissioner of Indian Affairs, and the offender would be punished according to the laws of the United States. "If bad among the Indians" committed a crime, the Indians would have to turn the wrongdoer over to U. S. authorities. If they refused, an appropriate sum would be withheld from their annual annuities. The two sides interpreted this provision differently. The government thought it gained greater jurisdictional oversight on the reservation. But for their part, many Lakota—used to the idea of material compensation for crimes—saw it as a reiteration of the status quo. More than a century later, defendants charged with criminal acts in conjunction with the 1973 occupation of Wounded Knee, on the Pine Ridge reservation, tried unsuccessfully to use the 1868 treaty in their defense. They claimed the federal government had no legal jurisdiction over their internal affairs. In legal affairs, as in matters of private land ownership, the Fort Laramie Treaty laid the groundwork for a troubled century of disputes that would be fought in courtrooms rather than on battlefields.[41]

During the second week of October 1868, the Peace Commissioners reconvened in Chicago to make their final set of recommendations to the president. They disagreed among themselves as to whether Indian affairs should be put back under the control of the War Department, where it had resided from the earliest days of the republic until it was moved to the Department of the Interior in 1849.[42] But they voted unanimously to support a resolution proposed by General Terry that declared the "the Government should cease to recognize the Indian tribes as 'domestic dependent nations.'" From here on out "all Indians should be considered and held to be individually subject to the laws of the United States . . . entitled to the same protection from said laws as other persons owing allegiance to the federal government."[43] In giving up their status as sovereign nations, Indians would receive equal protection under the law, but they would not be citizens. At least not without becoming dutiful homesteaders.

The commissioners had spent more than a year in the field negotiating treaties with different tribes, pushing peoples onto reservations, establishing civilizing programs, and creating a safe corridor for the transcontinental rail lines. Now they proposed that all treaty making end. And it did. With the exception of a treaty that General Augur negotiated a few weeks later at Fort Hall on July 4, 1868, the Fort Laramie Treaty proved the last agreement negotiated between the federal government and Indian tribes recognized as sovereign nations. The House of Representatives, tired of having to vote appropriations in support of treaties executed by the executive branch and ratified by the Senate without having any say of its own, tacked a sentence on to an 1871 appropriations bill declaring that "hereafter, no Indian nation or tribe within the United States shall be recognized or acknowledged as an independent nation, tribe or power with whom the United States may contract by treaty. . . ."[44] With that endorsement of the commission's recommendation, a diplomatic practice stretching back to the earliest days of the republic ended and a new era of federal Indian policy began.

The stories embedded in this photograph continued to evolve long after young Sophie Mousseau went back to her family and the commissioners headed out to negotiate with the Shoshones, the Bannocks, and the Navajos.

General Sherman clung to his old ideas about the inferiority of African Americans and become an outspoken opponent of Radical Reconstruction while he commanded the U.S. Army during the Indian wars of the 1870s.[45] General Terry assumed command of the military district in Atlanta in 1869 to fight against the Ku Klux Klan, and later went back west where, just before the nation's centennial in 1876, he found General Custer and his men dead on the battlefield at Little Big Horn.[46] The antislavery activist Samuel Tappan married Cora Scott, one of the nation's leading spiritualists, and with her help tried to persuade his old abolitionist heroes, William Lloyd Garrison and Wendell Phillips, to join him in creating a new movement to support a "humane policy toward the Indians."[47] As Cora Tappan remarked in 1869, "A government that has for nearly a century enslaved one race (African), that proscribes another (Chinese), proposes to exterminate another (Indians), and persistently refuses to recognize the rights of one-half of its citizens (women), cannot justly be called perfect."[48] After the Tappans' marriage failed, Samuel Tappan became the superintendent of an Indian industrial school in Nebraska.[49]

The Indian characters associated with the photograph moved on, too, though to less secure worlds. Sixteen-year-old Minnie Tappan, who had survived Sand Creek, died in 1873 of an illness acquired at Howard University, the school founded in Washington, D.C., for the education of African American youth. Her adoptive father had sent her there to join a handful of other Indian students so that she could pursue her dream of becoming a teacher. She died in the care of the daughters of freedmen.[50] Sophie Mousseau was on the Pine Ridge Reservation in late December 1890, when the U.S. Army massacred at least 150 of her fellow Lakota there at Wounded Knee. Her brother Louis, who ran the local trading post and worked as a translator, still plied the family's old trade as a cultural intermediary. He tried to work with both sides. "It was a bungle and a botch," Louis Mousseau said later, "no need of anybody being injured if it had been properly managed."[51]

The geographical terrain to which Gardner's picture introduces us stayed put, but the maps of it proved as unsteady as the political designs and commitments of the federal government. Just weeks after Gardner made his picture, Fort Laramie, originally in Dakota Territory, became part of the newly created Wyoming Territory, where Virginia Scharff's chapter about women's suffrage unfolds. Cartographers drew it in and added the boundaries of the Great Sioux Reservation to the nation's maps. But they had to redraw the boundaries in 1877 once again when, ceding to pressure from gold seekers, the federal government abandoned all efforts to protect the boundaries of the Sioux Reservation, seized the Black Hills, and declared the reservation diminished in size.[52] That same year, federal troops withdrew from the South, marking the end of Radical Reconstruction. The Lakota and the freedmen alike found themselves newly vulnerable to assaults on their rights and their property, their separate stories unfolding in tandem.

When he finished his work at Fort Laramie, the photographer Alexander Gardner headed back to Washington, D.C. During the early 1870s, he photographed visiting Indian delegations to the nation's capital, including leaders who sought to resolve differences regarding the interpretation and enforcement of the 1868 Fort Laramie Treaty. But more and more, he found himself attracted to philanthropy and the high-minded principles that had first drawn him to the United States and the failed utopian community in Iowa. In his final years, Gardner devoted himself to the Masonic Mutual Relief Association and the Washington Beneficial Relief Association. As his eulogist wrote, "He was deeply interested in all plans to encourage self-reliance among the poor and lowly and to recognize the common brotherhood of man."[53]

For Gardner, the Fort Laramie photograph was simply a work for hire, the product of his short-term employment by the Peace Commission. For the commissioners, it was a keepsake. For the girl, no more than a memory. The photograph did not circulate back to Indian Country, and she never saw it. For us, the photograph survives as an historical relic, found among the personal papers of the commissioners.[54] It does not yield its stories easily. Indeed, the formality of the quirky line-up of men and the unexplained presence of the girl erase the mechanics of the treaty-making process itself.

Yet if we stop to scrutinize the subjects who came together on that May day at Fort Laramie in 1868 and follow them backward and forward in time, we can recover some of the fluidity and contingency of American life that a still photograph always obscures and denies. This frontier military outpost was not so very remote at all. The people gathered there had intimate connections to more than a century of American history of violence and dislocation, racial tension and ongoing debates about who could be (or become) American. The photograph documents their passing proximity to one another and puts their different stories into dialogue. Through those personal stories, as well as through politics and policy, we can see how the racial concerns of the east flowed west, how the debates about the status of the freedmen inflected conversations about the Indians, and how the federal government tested new methods of bringing Indians under tighter control, even as its agents set up and then abandoned their efforts to protect the newly emancipated slaves. In East and West alike, families found themselves riven by violence, people struggled to define and defend their rights, and the federal government sought new ways to flex its power. In the tangle of stories preserved in the brief encounter among a photographer, six federal agents, and a Lakota child lays a broad history of American life. In small photographs, sometimes, lay traces of big tales.

NOTES

1. Gardner made some two hundred photographs while at Fort Laramie, roughly half large format, and half stereographic views. See, Raymond J. Demallie, "'Scenes in the Indian Country': A Portfolio of Alexander Gardner's Stereographic Views of the 1868 Fort Laramie Treaty Council," *Montana: The Magazine of Western History* 31, no. 3 (Summer 1981): 48.

2. N.G. Taylor, "Report to the President by the Indian Peace Commission, January 7, 1868," in *Annual Report of Commissioner of Indian Affairs 1868*, 1366 H.exdoc.1/7, 40–3 Congress, 486.

3. Abraham Lincoln, "Gettysburg Address," November 19, 1863, www.abrahamlincolnonline.org/lincoln/speeches/gettysburg.htm

4. Thanks to Kathleen Whitaker for identifying the blanket as indigo stroudcloth, a material popular among the Lakota during this time period. Gardner was the first photographer at Fort Laramie save for the ill-fated Ridgeway Glover who photographed there in 1866, shortly before his murder. The Mousseau family lived on a ranch north of the fort then, and it is highly unlikely young Sophie would have been at the fort during Glover's brief visit. The Glover negatives have never been located. See Paula Fleming, "Photographing the Plains Indians: Ridgeway Glover at Forts Laramie and Phil Kearney 1866," in Colin F. Taylor and Hugh A. Dempsey, eds., *The People of the Buffalo: The Plains Indians of North America*, vol. 2 (Wyck auf Foehr, Germany: Tatanka Press, 2005) and Paula Fleming, "Photographing the Plains Indians: Ridgeway Glover at Forts Laramie and Phil Kearney 1866, part II," in Arni Brownstone and Hugh Dempsey, eds. *Generous Man Ahxsi-tapina: Essays in Memory of Colin Taylor Plains Indian Ethnologist* (Wyk, Germany: Tatanka Press, 2008).

5. The National Anthropological Archives at the Smithsonian Institution, formerly known as the Bureau of American Ethnology (BAE), includes both the stereographic variant and the negative. Founded in 1879, the BAE became the repository for materials previously residing in the Department of the Interior. It is not possible to track precisely when Gardner's work entered the collection. A stereographic version of Gardner's group portrait is accessible at http://sirismm.si.edu/naa/90–1/09824100.jpg. The cracked glass negative (possibly a nineteenth-century copy) is at http://sirismm.si.edu/naa/baegn/gn_03687.jpg.

6. William T. Sherman, *Memoirs of General W. T. Sherman* (New York: Library of America, 1990), 903.

7. Vine Deloria and Raymond J. DeMallie, eds., *Documents of American Indian Diplomacy: Treaties, Agreements and Conventions, 1775–1979*, vol. 1 (Norman: University of Oklahoma Press, 1999), 179; "Council of the Indian Peace Commission with the Ogallala Sioux Indians at Fort Laramie, Dak. T. (May 24, 1868)" in *Papers Relating to Talks and Council Held with the Indians in Dakota and Montana Territories in the Years 1866–1869* (Washington, DC: Government Printing Office, 1910), 85.

8. Sherman took credit for the idea of putting military men in charge of the protection of the railroad workers. As he wrote in his memoirs, "The construction of the Union Pacific Railroad was deemed so important that the President, at my suggestion, constituted on the 5th of March, 1866, the new Department of the Platte . . . with orders to give ample protection to the working-parties, and to afford every possible assistance in the construction of the road; and subsequently in like manner the Department of Dakota was constituted . . . to give similar protection and encouragement to the Northern Pacific Railroad." *Memoirs*, 902. For general biographical information on Terry, see John W. Bailey, *Pacifying the Plains: General Alfred Terry and the Decline of the Sioux, 1866–1890* (Westport, CT: Greenwood Press, 1979). On Augur's role in the aftermath of the Lincoln assassination, see George A. Woodward, "The Night of Lincoln's Assassination," *United Services: A Quarterly Review of Military and Naval Affairs* 1, no. 5 (May 1889): 471.

9. Paraphrase of organizational papers for the Clydesdale Colony as found in Realto E. Price, ed., *History of Clayton County, Iowa* (Chicago: Robert O. Law Co., 1916), 321.

10. For general biographical information on Gardner, see D. Mark Katz, *Witness to an Era: The Life and Photographs of Alexander Gardner* (New York: Viking Penguin, 1991), and Josephine Cobb, "Alexander Gardner," *Image* no. 62 (June 1958): 124–36. Unfortunately, both works are undersourced.

11. The most accessible version of the rare Gardner album is the modern Dover reprint: Alexander Gardner, *Alexander Gardner's Photographic Sketchbook of the Civil War* (New York: Dover, 1959).

12. Joseph M. Wilson, *A Eulogy on the Life and Character of Alexander Gardner* (Washington, DC.: R. Beresford, printer, 1883), 9.

13. Colln G. Calloway, *Pen and Ink Witchcraft: Treaties and Treaty Making in American Indian History* (New York: Oxford University Press, 2013), 187. For a biographical overview of Harney, see George Rollie Adams, *General William S. Harney: Prince of Dragoons* (Lincoln: University of Nebraska Press, 2001).

14. Nathan Cole to Arthur Tappan, July 2, 1834, in Theodore Dwight Weld, *American Slavery as It Is: Testimony of a Thousand Witnesses* (New York: American Anti-Slavery Society, 1839), 89.

15. Adams, *General William S. Harney*, 47–51.

16. "Was Pioneer, Soldier and Humanitarian" [obituary], *Boston Daily Globe*, January 12, 1913, 9. Tappan, who gets passing mention in works on Bleeding Kansas, the Sand Creek Massacre, and the Peace Commission, merits further attention.

17. " ... Evidence Taken at Denver and Fort Lyon, Colorado Territory, by a Military Commission, Ordered to Inquire into the Sand Creek Massacre, November 1864," 1277 S. exdoc 26, p. 8.

18. Cited in Ari Kelman, *A Misplaced Massacre: Struggling over the Memory of Sand Creek* (Cambridge, MA: Harvard University Press, 2013), 176.

19. Joint Commission on the Conduct of War, "Massacre of Cheyenne Indians," in *The Reports of the Committees of the Senate of the United States for the Second Session Thirty-Eighth Congress, 1864–65*, 38–2 S.Rep.v.4n. 142pt.3, pp. iii-iv.

20. The Doolittle Report first appeared, with a ten-page report and a 532-page appendix, as *Conditions of the Indian Tribes*, 39th Cong., 2d sess., 1867, Rept. 156, serial 1279, 3. It was later combined and issued as *Condition of the Indian Tribes* (Washington, DC: Government Printing Office, 1867).

21. Ann Braude, "The Baptism of a Cheyenne Girl," in Susan B. Ridgley, ed., *The Study of Children in Religion: A Methods Handbook* (New York: New York University Press, 2011), 236–51.

22. Ibid., 248.

23. "In Memory of Gen. Sherman: Paper Read by His Brother," *New York Tribune*, April 7, 1892, p. 11.

24. William Sherman to John Sherman, November 30, 1854, in Rachel Thorndike Sherman, ed., *The Sherman Letters: Correspondence between General and Senator Sherman from 1837 to 1891* (New York: Charles Scribner's Sons, 1894), 53–54.

25. A. Baird to Gerrit Smith, January 1865, in *Memoirs of General Sherman*, 570.

26. William T. Sherman to General A. Baird, April 8, 1865, in *Memoirs of General Sherman*, 571.

27. William T. Sherman to Samuel F. Tappan, August 13, 1868, Samuel Forster Tappan Collection (MSS #617), Colorado Historical Society (hereafter CHS).

28. Sherman to Tappan, September 6, 1868, Tappan Collection, CHS.

29. "Reconstruction: Testimony of Major General Alfred H. Terry before the Joint Committee on Reconstruction," *Chicago Tribune*, March 29, 1866, p. 1.

30. On Sanborn, see Seelye A. Wilson, "John B. Sanborn," in *Nation: A Monthly Journal of American History* (Cleveland: Magazine of Western History Publishing Co., 1887), vol. VII, pp. 666–75; Greenleaf Clark and Henry W. Childs, "Memorial Addresses in Honor of General John B. Sanborn, at the Monthly Council Meeting of the Minnesota Historical Society, in the State Capitol, St. Paul, Minn., Monday Evening, October 10, 1904," in *Minnesota Historical Society Collections* (1905) X, pt. 2, 833–56.

31. John B. Sanborn to James Harlan, Secretary of the Interior, January 5, 1866, in *Report of the Commissioner of Indian Affairs for the Year 1866* 1284H.exdoc. 1/6, 284–85. Only a few months later, he modified his recommendations in the face of improved conditions. With the old slave codes repealed and employment contracts in place, the freedmen were becoming self-supporting and "the freedom of the black race and the harmony and happiness of both races in that territory was secured." John B. Sanborn to James Harlan, April 13, 1866, in *Report of the Commissioner ... 1866*, p. 287; unidentified Sanborn report excerpted in "John B. Sanborn," 672.

32. Eddie Ryan, grandson of Sophie and her first husband Posey Ryan, provided the identification to staff members at the Fort Laramie National Historic Site in 1978. Sandra Lowry email to author, June 10, 2010.

33. For an excellent survey of the mixed-race world of fur traders across the West during the first half of the nineteenth century, see Anne F. Hyde, *Empires, Nations, and Families: A New History of the North American West, 1800–1860* (Lincoln: University of Nebraska Press, 2011). For a more regional study, see Andrew R. Graybill, *The Red and the White: A Family Saga of the American West* (New York: Liveright, 2013).

34. Eli Seavey Ricker and Richard E. Jensen, eds., *Voices of the American West: The Settler and Soldier Interviews of Eli S. Ricker, 1903–1919* (Lincoln: University of Nebraska Press, 2005), 190–210; Jean-Pierre-Yves Pepin, *Généalogie ascendante de Joseph-Alfred Mousseau, Premier ministre du Québec* (Longueuil, Quebec: Les Éditions historiques et généalogiques Pepin, 2001); various family genealogies posted online, including http://familytreemaker.genealogy.com/users/k/i/l/Brandy—M-Kilby/GENE23-0013.html.

35. Bill Meckfessel email to the author, March 2, 2011.

36. Donald Miller email to the author, March 19, 2011. Sophie Mousseau Ryan Monroe's family can be traced through federal census records.

37. For a discussion of the assembled tribes' ideas about sovereignty, see the testimony by Father Peter John Powell, Raymond Demallie, and Wilbur Jacobs in Roxanne Dunbar Ortiz, ed., *The Great Sioux Nation: Sitting in Judgment on America: An Oral History of the Sioux Nation* (New York: American Indian Treaty Council Information Center, 1977), 105–18.

38. [unid.] to William T. Sherman, "Account of Red Cloud Signing the Treaty," November 20, 1868, in *Proceedings of the Great Peace Commission of 1867–1868* (Washington, DC : Institute for the Development of Indian Law, 1975), 174–75.

39. Jeffrey Ostler, *The Lakotas and the Black Hills: The Struggle for Sacred Ground* (New York: Viking Penguin, 2010), 58–79. The text of the 1868 Fort Laramie Treaty can be accessed at www.ourdocuments.gov/doc.php?flash = true&doc = 42&page = transcript.

40. Fort Laramie Treaty (1868). The Dawes Act (1887) would require a much longer twenty-five-year "waiting" period.

41. Fort Laramie Treaty (1868). On the lingering legal disputes spawned by the treaty, see *The Great Sioux Nation*, 100–109, 141–46, 172–73, 192–98.

42. *Proceedings of the Great Peace Commission*, 159–60. The vote was 5 (Sherman, Harney, Augur, Sanborn, and Terry) to 2 (Tappan and Taylor). Congress never acted on the recommendation and the bureau remained in the Department of the Interior.

43. *Proceedings of the Great Peace Commission*, p. 165.

44. George William Rice, "Indian Rights: 25 U.S.C. § 71: The End of Indian Sovereignty or a Self-Limitation of Contractual Ability?" *American Indian Law Review* 5, no. 1 (1977): 239–53.

45. On Sherman's consistent racial attitudes, see Robert K. Murray, "General Sherman, the Negro, and Slavery: The Story of an Unrecognized Rebel," *Negro History Bulletin* 22, no. 6 (March 1959): 125–30.

46. See *Pacifying the Plains,* 70–159.

47. "Peace with the Indians," *Boston Daily Journal,* May 26, 1870, p. 4.

48. *Standard* (Boston), May 29, 1869, quoted in Elliott West, "Reconstructing Race," *Western Historical Quarterly* 34, no. 1, 26.

49. Mrs. Helen Palmer, [no title] in *Facts* (Facts Publishing Company, 1882), 259–61; "Was Pioneer, Soldier and Humanitarian" [Tappan obituary].

50. Braude, "The Baptism of a Cheyenne Girl."

51. Donald Danker, ed., "The Wounded Knee Interviews of Eli S. Ricker," *Nebraska History* 62 (1981): 231.

52. *Report and Journal of Proceedings of the Commission Appointed to Obtain Certain Concessions from the Sioux Indians,* 44th Cong., 2d sess., 1876077, S.Ex. Doc. 9, serial 1718.

53. Wilson, *A Eulogy,* 9.

54. Send Gardner "and one gallon of whiskey," the commission's secretary telegraphed to the Union Pacific Railroad agent expediting their official photographer's trip west. A. S. H. White at Fort Laramie to L. S. Bent, UPRR agent in Omaha, April 15, 1868, in Robert E. Lester, ed., *Records of the Indian Division, Office of the Secretary of the Interior, Special Files, 1848–1907* (microfilm; Bethesda: LexisNexis, 2006), reel 3. Original copies of the print have been located in the papers of Sherman (Mercantile Library, St. Louis), Augur (Newberry Library, Chicago), and Sanborn (Minnesota Historical Society). Prints from the same series, if not this exact one, are included in the Harney papers at the Missouri Historical Society.

PART THREE

Borders of Citizenship

NINE

Race, Religion, and Naturalization

HOW THE WEST SHAPED CITIZENSHIP DEBATES IN THE RECONSTRUCTION CONGRESS

Joshua Paddison

A PIECE OF BRUTALLY EFFECTIVE POLITICAL PROPAGANDA from 1867 reminds us that Reconstruction looked very different in California than in Mississippi or Massachusetts. "The Reconstruction Policy of Congress, as Illustrated in California" was a lettersheet released by the Democratic Party of California during the gubernatorial race of 1867. Its target was the white man depicted at the bottom of the stack of humans in the cartoon's center: George C. Gorham, Republican candidate for governor and proponent of suffrage for African American men. "*Manhood alone* shall be the test of the right to a voice in the Government," Gorham declares in the cartoon. Holding him to his words, the Democrats portray Gorham not just as carrying an African American man on his shoulders but a Chinese man and Native American man as well.

In looks, dress, and speech, the cartoonist represents each of Gorham's "burdens" in typical mid-nineteenth-century racial caricature: the African American is depicted as a slave, marked by his rolled-up work shirt with open collar, tattered and patched pants, and no shoes. His face is grinning, pop-eyed, and thick-lipped—a stereotypical "coon" straight out of a minstrel show. His speech balloon further racializes him as uneducated and inferior, with its colloquial grammar and regional dialect: "Massa Gorum, I spose we'se bliged to carry dese brudders, kase des'se no stinkshun ob race or culler any more, for kingdom cum."

The Chinese man above him is shown in what the artist imagines as traditional Chinese garb, holding firecrackers and a fan, with his hair in a queue—all suggestive of the foreignness, androgyny, and inassimilability assumed of the Chinese. "John Chinaman" also approves of Gorham, in words again colored by racialized dialect: "Boss Gollam belly good man. He

FIGURE 9.1. The Reconstruction Policy of Congress, as Illustrated in California. Lettersheet, 1867. Courtesy of the Bancroft Library, University of California, Berkeley.

say chinaman vo_tee all same melican man. Ketch_ee all same_ no pay taxee_ belly good." Finally, teetering on top there is a so-called California "Digger" Indian, supposedly the lowest of a low race, whose animalistic ferocity is so strong he cannot even stand up straight. He wears only a loincloth and carries a bow and arrow, a sign not only of violence but technological backwardness. As Stephen Kantrowitz discusses elsewhere in this volume, clothing was an especially important marker of the supposed "civilization" of Indian groups; the Indian man here falls far from the ideal of "citizen's dress" hoped for by missionaries. This man's speech is portrayed as the crudest of the three figures: "Chemuc Walla! Ingen vote! Plenty whisky all time. Gorom big ingin." Meanwhile, in the bottom right, a Republican Party operative named Cuffy declares, "Say Gorham! Put this Brother up," leading an ape to be added to the stack.

In grappling with the questions of belonging, equality, citizenship, and civil rights in Reconstruction, the cartoonist seems to ask, Where exactly is the dividing line between human and animal once you get this far down the racial hierarchy? California's Democrats here implored voters to stick with the tried-and-true American policy of exclusive white male suffrage. On the bottom left, Brother Jonathan—a precursor to Uncle Sam—sternly rebukes Gorham, "This ballot box was dedicated to the white race, alone. The load you are carrying will sink you to perdition, where you belong, or my name is not Jonathan."[1]

The ferocity of this cartoon's racism is not surprising. By 1867, in the United States as in much of the world, scientific and popular notions of racial difference and hierarchy had become culturally entrenched. Despite emancipation, the Democratic Party proudly championed white male supremacy throughout the nation.[2] However, the Democrats' strategy here *is* surprising in that we are used to thinking about Reconstruction as a story of only North and South, black and white.[3] Yet Reconstruction was a national project, and the multiracial demographics of the West complicated the meanings of the core legislature of Reconstruction: the Civil Rights Act of 1866, the Fourteenth and Fifteenth Amendments, and the Naturalization Act of 1870.

The presence of tens of thousands of Chinese immigrants and hundreds of thousands of Native Americans in the West played on the minds of federal lawmakers as they attempted to protect southern freedmen and replace the hazy antebellum definition of citizenship with a new set of uniform federal parameters in the wake of emancipation.[4] Again and again, during the second half of the 1860s, congressional debate over Reconstruction circled back to the multiracial populations of the West. Eastern and western Republicans differed over the desirability of truly colorblind universal manhood suffrage, with those from the West refusing to support legislation that would grant citizenship or suffrage to Native American or Chinese immigrant men.

Ultimately, congressional Republicans restricted the benefits of Reconstruction to only African Americans and immigrants of African descent. Led by western Republicans and compelled by a mix of political necessity, racial logic, and heartfelt religious conviction, congressmen lumped Native Americans and Chinese immigrants into the old but newly politicized category of "heathens" (or, less commonly, "pagans"), banned from the body politic. As in "The Reconstruction Policy of Congress, as Illustrated in California," Democrats exploited the specter of Chinese and Native American voters to battle any erosion of white male suffrage, even going so far as to mockingly champion the virtues of "heathen" peoples to better expose the contradictions of the Republican plan. The politics and demographics of the West profoundly shaped the contours of national identity at a crucial moment of constitutional engineering.

THE CIVIL RIGHTS ACT OF 1866

The first step in the federal government's postwar process of redefining U.S. citizenship was the Civil Rights Act of 1866. Introduced by Lyman Trumbull, a moderate Republican senator from Illinois, the act represented Republicans' efforts to protect the "fundamental rights" of the freedmen. Unthinkable just a few years earlier, federal lawmakers now strove to use congressional power to guarantee African Americans the right to make labor contracts, receive wages for their labor, sue in court, hold personal property, and enjoy "full and equal benefit of all laws and proceedings for the security of person and property, as is enjoyed by white citizens."[5]

To accomplish this, Republican lawmakers recognized that they also needed to confirm African Americans as citizens. The infamous *Dred Scott v. Sandford* case of 1857 had disqualified all members of the "African race" from citizenship, a status left unchanged by the Thirteenth Amendment. In the words of John B. Henderson, senator from Missouri, "in passing this [Thirteenth] amendment we do not confer upon the negro the right to vote. We give him no right except his freedom, and leave the rest to the States."[6] Northerners were enraged at the new "black codes" passed in southern states in 1865 and 1866, which took advantage of African Americans' lack of U.S. citizenship to strip ex-slaves of economic freedoms and legal protections.[7]

Although the situation in the South was the impetus for action, congressional debate over the Civil Rights Act of 1866 swerved quickly to the topic of its effect on Indians and Chinese immigrants in the West. Initially, Trumbull worded the Civil Rights Act of 1866 in order to declare as citizens "all persons of African descent born in the United States."[8] In the face of criticism that such phrasing excluded whites from the protections of the act, Trumbull had to shift to broader language that would extend citizenship to "all persons born in the United States, and not subject to any foreign Power."[9] The second clause was necessary because of his colleagues' worries about inadvertently including "piebald races" of the West, Asian workers (perhaps still loyal to their homelands) among them. Peter Van Winkle, a conservative Unionist senator from West Virginia, reminded his colleagues that the bill affected "not only the negro race, but other inferior races that are now settling on our Pacific coast. . . . If you make these people citizens of the United States, I should feel that they were entitled to the right of suffrage."[10] Rather than open the door to potential Chinese voters, Trumbull excluded all immigrants "subject to any foreign Power."

However, other senators immediately raised the question of whether Trumbull intended to "naturalize all the Indians of the United States."[11] John Conness, Republican from California, shuddered at the prospect. "It would be a great public evil and wrong," he warned, because California's "Diggers" were "perhaps the lowest class known of Indians and utterly and totally unfit to become citizens."[12] Trumbull assured his colleagues that he had no intention of making Indians citizens but he was uncertain how best to exclude them. After extended debate over different possible wordings, Republicans ultimately resorted to a phrase borrowed from the notorious Three-Fifths Clause of the original 1787 Constitution: they excluded "Indians not taxed."[13] The designation referred to the vast majority of Indians who continued to resist federal authority. Taxed Indians were the small number—only about twenty-five thousand in 1870, many of whom were "mixed bloods"—who had explicitly given up sovereignty rights, as in the multitribal Brothertown and Stockbridge communities in Wisconsin.[14] The fact that "Indians not taxed" would be excluded from the benefits of the bill was never in doubt; the question was simply how best to accomplish it.

Enacted over President Andrew Johnson's veto, the final language of the Civil Rights Act of 1866 declared as citizens "all persons born in the United

States and not subject to any foreign power, excluding Indians not taxed." All Chinese immigrants and the vast majority of Indians had been carefully and explicitly excluded from the act's basic civil rights protections.

THE FOURTEENTH AMENDMENT

Even as Congress debated the Civil Rights Act of 1866, its members knew that the act's underlying constitutionality was in question. Only a constitutional amendment would guarantee citizenship and equal protection under the law for the freedmen. Once again, the question of whether or not *everyone* in the United States should be granted citizenship under the Fourteenth Amendment arose almost immediately in congressional debates. Republican senator Jacob Howard from Michigan, who crafted the first section of the amendment, proposed to limit citizenship to "all persons born or naturalized in the United States, and subject to the jurisdiction thereof." The latter clause was necessary, he explained, to exclude "foreigners, aliens."

James Rood Doolittle, Howard's Republican colleague from Wisconsin, objected that unless Howard intended to "include the Indians," a clause explicitly banning "Indians not taxed" should be added, as in the Civil Rights Act of 1866. As written, complained Doolittle, the amendment "would bring in all the Digger Indians of California," as well as other western Indian groups. Howard agreed that "Indians not taxed" should be excluded from citizenship but maintained that his wording already accomplished that goal because they "are not, in the sense of this amendment, born subject to the jurisdiction of the United States." Discussion of how to best word the amendment so as to exclude Indians was protracted, but once again the question was how rather than whether they should be excluded.[15]

However, Edgar Cowan, a Republican from Pennsylvania, saw that the matter was more complicated than just Indians. "What is its length and breadth" of citizenship?," he asked his colleagues. "Is the child of the Chinese immigrant in California a citizen? Is the child of a Gypsy born in Pennsylvania a citizen? If so, what rights have they?" The Chinese, he went on to explain, posed a terrible threat to America's racial and religious purity; they were a "people of a different race, of different religion, of different manners, of different traditions, different tastes and sympathies."[16] Western Republicans, especially those from the Pacific coast, forcefully echoed Cowan's hostility to any extension of political rights to the Chinese. "The Chinese are nothing but a pagan race," protested California's Republican Representative William Higby. "They are an enigma to me, although I have lived among them for fifteen years.... They bring their clay and wooden gods with them to this country, and as we are a free and tolerant people, we permit them to bow down and worship them."[17]

Democrats responded by cynically attacking Republicans on this apparent inconsistency: How could they justify extending suffrage to African Americans and not Indians and the Chinese? At times Democrats went so far as to extol the virtues of "Lo, the poor Indian" to better dramatize the Republican contradiction. "If these negroes are to be made citizens of the United States, I can see no reason in justice or in right why the Indians should not be made citizens," announced Delaware's Willard Saulsbury. "If our citizens are to be increased in this wholesale manner, I cannot turn my back upon that persecuted race, among whom are many intelligent, educated men."[18] Similarly, Democrat William Ellis Niblack from Indiana asked, with mock sincerity, "If a Chinaman is one of the human race, why should he be degraded below the negro? ... Why should he not receive the same right as the negro? I should like to understand it. The negro is of a pagan race, and is a pagan before he came here." The Republican Higby fired back, "But he is not a pagan now. The negro is as much a native of this country as the gentleman or myself."[19]

Out of such exchanges, the Republican strategy emerged. African American men alone deserved full citizenship because they were morally superior to Chinese and Native American men. Republicans pointed to African American men's service to the Union during the Civil War, their English-language skills, their American nativity, their supposed love of country, and—above all—their Protestant Christianity.[20] African Americans' Protestant beliefs elevated them above Native Americans and Chinese immigrants, who were imagined as quintessentially and intractably heathenish, the scattered examples of their conversions notwithstanding.

This Republican strategy of using religion to distance African Americans from other racialized groups had been enacted in California earlier in the 1860s. There, Republicans had in 1862 extended full legal testimony rights to Africans Americans (but not to Indians or the Chinese) by arguing that African Americans "speak the same language and profess the same religion that we do."[21] The state's leading African Americans at times expressed mixed feelings about this strategy but came to embrace it as a bulwark against Democratic attacks linking "Chinese, Niggers, and Diggers."[22] For example, newspaper editor Peter Anderson complained in 1867, "In their speeches they have given us Negro for breakfast, Chinese for dinner, and Digger Indian for supper, until such miserable twaddle have become sickening to all sensible men."[23] For the time being, African American spokesmen acquiesced to gaining rights at the expense of solidarity with other peoples of color.

As historian Helen Heran Jun has shown, African American newspapers throughout the United States used the specter of the Chinese immigrant to generate their own "narratives of black moral, political, and cultural development."[24] However, San Francisco's two black newspapers, the *Elevator* and the *Pacific Appeal*, traded in xenophobic diatribes. Black writers wondered what employer could possibly prefer a "filthy, dishonest, infidel Chinaman" to a "clean, honest female contraband [escaped slave], with her Christian education, limited through it be."[25] In an echo of the ways Irish immigrants used whiteness to claim a shred of advantage, African Americans used religion to protest that they, "native Christian Americans," were lumped in with "foreign heathens" by Democrats.[26] It would not be until after the winning of suffrage in 1870 that Peter Anderson and other African American leaders would begin, at times, to express a measure of cross-racial sympathy for Indians and the Chinese.[27]

In the end, the Fourteenth Amendment went forward to the states with Jacob Howard's original wording intact; it read "and subject to the jurisdiction thereof" without specifying the exclusion of "Indians not taxed." The Republicans decided that such a clause was unnecessary and, furthermore, worried that it might backfire by accidentally granting Indians citizenship if state governments decided to start taxing reservation commerce at some point in the future.[28] In the amendment's second section, still echoing the Three-Fifths clause, Republican sponsors emphasized that "Indians not taxed" were to be disregarded when establishing a state's representation in Congress. However, because of the amendment's somewhat ambiguous wording and the fact that the federal government refused to recognize Indian groups as sovereign nations during the late 1860s, as Martha Sandweiss discusses in this volume, in 1870 the U.S. Senate issued a special report confirming that the Fourteenth Amendment had "no effect whatever" on the status of Indians.[29] In *Elk v. Wilkins* (1884), the U.S. Supreme Court would deny citizenship even to Indians who left their reservations and "fully and completely surrendered" themselves to federal jurisdiction. As for the Chinese, the wording of the Fourteenth Amendment's first section likewise did not mention them, because they remained barred from becoming U.S. citizens under the Naturalization Act of 1790.[30]

THE FIFTEENTH AMENDMENT

Although their exclusion from citizenship under the Fourteenth Amendment should have foreclosed any chance of suffrage for Native Americans or Chinese immigrants, congressional debate of the Fifteenth Amendment nonetheless featured discussion over differences between "the white race and the black race and the yellow race and the red race."[31] Western congressmen called for an explicit clause denying suffrage to unnaturalized aliens, prompting extended debate. Republican Frederick Frelinghuysen of New Jersey found such a clause unnecessary but reassured his western colleagues, "I am not in favor of giving the rights of citizenship or the right of suffrage to either pagans or heathen. I believe that the history of this country, and its laws as well as the spirit of the people, declare just as clearly that this is a Christian as a free country; and I am not in favor of taking steps backward into the slough of ignorance and of vice, even under the cry of progress."[32]

In an echo of the earlier Fourteenth Amendment debates, Thomas A. Hendricks, a Democrat from Indiana, attacked Frelinghuysen's line of reasoning, refusing to accept the notion that African American men deserved better treatment than "heathen" men. "The tendency of the colored race is downward," Hendricks thundered. "I am speaking of a race which in its own country is now enshrouded by the darkness of heathenism, the darkest heathenism that covers any land on earth." Despite these origins, Republicans wanted to give Negroes, and not the Chinese, suffrage? Hendicks was incredulous. "And why? I believe they said they were pagans; but they are not such pagans as we find in Africa. China is the original home of a civilization that the world honors to this day. Why, sir, in China they had many of the rare and useful inventions long before they were known in Europe." Once again, out of political necessity the Democrats cast themselves as unlikely defenders of Indians and the Chinese, championing gunpowder, fireworks, moveable type, and paper—all in an effort to keep out "civilized" Chinese as well as suspect African Americans.[33]

Hendricks concluded his attack by mocking the Republican notion of citizenship based on Christianity: "Is it the business of this Government to proscribe what God or in what form men shall worship? [Frelinghuysen] says that we are a Christian country. Not altogether, sir. We have no such test as that." Hendricks noted that "the Jew, who does not believe in the Savior that the Senator and I believe in," could vote, as could "the infidel, who recognizes no God at all." In response, Frelinghuysen stood to clarify the Republican argument: It was "not that a man must be a Christian to be a voter, but that it was not our duty to extend the rights of naturalization and citizenship to a pagan and heathenish class." Hendricks scoffed and replied, "Sir, I am in favor of men voting in this country who belong to the white race, and conduct themselves properly," with no further extension needed or desired.[34]

In this exchange, Hendricks and Frelinghuysen vocalized the two political parties' competing notions of American citizenship, each of which combined religious and racial thinking but in opposing ways. Republicans insisted that religious rather than racial manhood lay at the core of American identity. Judged inferior in racial stock and religious belief—that is, in body and soul—"heathens" had to be excluded from the body politic. Explaining why "the Chinaman" should never be offered the right to naturalize, Nevada's William Stewart summarized the Republican position: "I should be willing to allow him to become a citizen as much as anybody else if he would renounce his pagan religion, and his attachment to his own Government, which bind him irrevocably, which bind him for all time and in all countries and in all places." The "colored man," on the other hand, Stewart insisted, was "an American and a Christian, as much so as any of the rest of the people of the country. He loved the American flag."[35] In the Republican formulation, religious belief could not be separated from national allegiance and trustworthiness.

From the Civil Rights Act of 1866 to the Fifteenth Amendment, Republican lawmakers' rejection of "heathen" citizens sprang from a mix of political necessity, racial prejudices, and deeply held religious convictions. The Republicans could not risk alienating their western constituency, which threatened to reject the Fourteenth and Fifteenth Amendments if Indians or the Chinese were included. This might even have opened the West to a renewal of Confederate or filibustering visions. "I would not agree to this proposed [Fourteenth] constitutional amendment if I supposed it made Indians not taxed citizens of the United States," Oregon's Republican senator, George Henry Williams, informed his party.[36] Beyond needing to placate western colleagues in Congress, Republicans also faced the task of asking western state legislatures to ratify the amendments. Demonizing "heathens" served concrete political ends.

At this same moment, Republican lawmakers rejected suffrage for white women out of a similar blend of political necessity and deep-seated prejudice. Elsewhere in this volume, Virginia Scharff explains how Wyoming's white women won the right to vote in 1869, consolidating their status as agents of

U.S. imperialism. Wyoming's circumstances were exceptional, however, as Scharff notes. Elsewhere in the West, and at the federal level, Republicans ignored calls from Elizabeth Cady Stanton and other feminists who argued that now was the moment, when the "Constitutional door" was open, for woman suffrage. Republican leadership instead insisted that it was only "the Negro's hour," explicitly reinscribing male supremacy into the Constitution.[37]

However, in the cases of both women and "heathen" men, there was more than *realpolitik* at work. Just as most Republicans considered male supremacy natural and inevitable, they also viewed Indians and the Chinese as racially inferior and below (or at least behind) African Americans in development. The long-standing existence of free black communities in the North—together with Abraham Lincoln's wartime embrace of emancipation and the Republicans' subsequent casting of the Confederacy's defeat in abolitionist rather than simply constitutional or economic terms—had convinced most Republicans that African Americans could be Americanized and "uplifted." Most viewed Indians, by contrast, as a "savage" race on the verge of dying out and at any rate incapable of true self-governance. By the 1860s, most Republicans saw Chinese "aliens" as even more inassimilable, foreign, and culturally stagnant than Indians.[38]

The depth of the violence of the Civil War—at times senseless in its cruelty—had threatened the moral call of defeating the Confederacy. Thus, Republicans were also motivated by a powerful desire to shore up America's status as a uniquely Christian nation.[39] Proposing that "an irreligious government begets an irreligious people," a coalition of Protestant denominations sent a volley of petitions to Congress throughout the 1860s calling for the inclusion of explicit references to Jesus Christ in the Constitution's preamble.[40] Acting from a similar impulse toward restoring national purity, Republican congressmen criminalized the mailing of "vulgar and indecent" materials in 1865 (later expanded into the Comstock Act of 1873) and attacked Mormon polygamy.[41] Republicans' renunciation of "heathen" citizenship was thus a part of the larger postwar movement concerned with reinforcing the nation's holiness and sense of divine approval. If the defeat of the Confederacy had cleansed the United States of the sin of slavery, Republicans hoped to further purify their broken nation by defining and expelling the imagined "heathen" threat to its character.

Democrats, by contrast, tended to be more tolerant of religious nonconformity—to a point—but less tolerant of racial diversity. Democrats drew strong support from Irish Catholic immigrants and championed religious liberty in the face of America's Protestant moral establishment. For example, they generally opposed Republicans' federal antipolygamy efforts aimed at Mormons.[42] However, Democrats joined most Republicans in viewing "heathens" as too far outside America's cultural norms to be granted citizenship—but they differed in viewing African Americans, Christianized or not, as equally dangerous. Democrats clung to what they termed the "old and well-tried" notion of a "white man's Government" that they believed rested on biblical authority as well as ethnological theories that affirmed Africa's supposed backwardness.[43]

For Democrats, racial equality was tantamount to spiritual apocalypse. In a particularly florid vision, California's Democratic representative James A. Johnson warned in 1870 that, should the congressmen grant citizenship to "the Hottentot, the cannibal from the jungles of Africa, the West Indian negro, the wild Indian, and the Chinaman," they might as well "tear down your school-houses, convert your churches into dens and brothels, wherein our young may receive fatal lessons to end in rotting bones, decaying and putrid flesh, poisoned blood, leprous bodies, and leprous souls."[44] In the 1870s, it was Irish Catholic Democrats in the West, eager to shore up their own whiteness, who most loudly opposed Chinese immigration and President Ulysses S. Grant's Peace Policy, which aimed to Christianize, "civilize," and eventually assimilate Indians.[45]

THE NATURALIZATION ACT OF 1870

There were a few genuinely radical Republicans who did not share their party's conception of a United States in need of protection against pagan forces. Led by Massachusetts senator Charles Sumner, these Republicans instead espoused a Christianity of tolerance, egalitarianism, and benevolent uplift. They worked closely with Wendell Phillips and other abolitionists in calling for another, broader constitutional amendment guaranteeing full citizenship for every man, "be he Indian, negro or Chinaman."[46] Such efforts were an extension of reformers' turn toward the "Indian question" after the Civil War, which would crest in the 1870s with the formation of the Boston Indian Citizenship Association, the Women's National Indian Association, the Indian Rights Association, and other organizations dedicated to forging a new path for U.S.–Indian relations.[47]

Sumner and his radical allies went along with the more restrictive versions of the Civil Rights Act and Reconstruction amendments, but they were merely biding their time. In July 1870, Sumner tried to remove the word *white* from federal naturalization requirements, thereby opening both citizenship and suffrage to Asian immigrants. His effort triggered a showdown between Republican Party factions over the limits of Reconstruction, with both sides laying claim to the mantle of true Christianity. Following Lincoln's rhetorical strategy from the Gettysburg Address, Sumner based his campaign on his reading of the Declaration of Independence: "According to this vow *all men* are created equal and endowed with inalienable rights. But the statutes of the land assert the contrary; they declaring that only all white men are created equal.... How can you hesitate? There are the words. Does any one question the text? Will any one move to amend the text?" Sumner went on to read the story of Peter's three denials of Jesus from the Gospel of Matthew, comparing Nevada's William Stewart—who led the Republican opposition to his plan—to Peter. "Thrice has [Stewart] on this floor denied these great principles of the Declaration of Independence. The time may come when he will weep bitterly," as Peter did upon realizing his sins.[48]

Stewart and other western and moderate Republicans countered with indignation. "Because I am opposed to pagan imperialists, Chinese who do not understand the obligation of a Christian oath being incorporated into the body politic, the Senator from Massachusetts reads from a Christian book, from the Bible, to prove that I have denied my faith!" fumed Stewart. "I say that any Christian gentleman, any Christian man who will trust our institutions to the hands of pagans, has denied the faith of his fathers."[49] Oregon's George Henry Williams agreed: "Does the Declaration of Independence mean that Chinese coolies, that the Bushmen of south Africa, that the Hottentots, the Digger Indians, heathen, pagan, and cannibal, shall have equal political rights under this Government with citizens of the United States? Sir, that is the absurd and foolish interpretation."[50]

Even Henry Wilson, Sumner's fellow senator from Massachusetts, opposed the change because he believed it would further encourage coolie labor, violating "the sublime doctrines of the New Testament" upon which the Constitution rested. China, he said, was a "country of paganism, a country with a civilization wholly distinct from our own."[51] As historian Moon-Ho Jung has shown, Republicans had objected to the arrival of so-called coolies from China throughout the 1860s, viewing them as nothing more than slaves under a different name.[52] Wilson's remarks demonstrate how Republican worries about "coolieism" sprang not only from concerns about protecting free white labor but also from self-appointed religious duty.

Sumner and his allies tried to respond with their own, more universalist Christian nationalism. Radical Republican senator Samuel C. Pomeroy of Kansas argued that the "paganism" practiced by Chinese immigrants was more holy than the Christianity practiced by some Americans. "The gospel that is preached and revered here is twisted into a system to protect caste and prejudice and slavery," he announced. "I say, Mr. President, that when the gospel is distorted in that manner, commend me to paganism. Let me be a pagan if I have got to give adherence to a gospel that does not believe in the brotherhood of mankind."[53] Sumner agreed: "Worse than any pagan or heathen abroad are those in our midst who are false to our institutions."[54] Ultimately, however, Sumner's plan lost, thirty votes to fourteen. The dominant Republican vision of a nonheathen male citizenship held.[55]

In a nod to those children born to Underground Railroad fugitives in Canada, the Naturalization Act of 1870 did grant "aliens of African nativity and persons of African descent" the right to naturalize. The status of children born in the United States to Asian parents would remain unclear for three decades until the Supreme Court confirmed their citizenship in *U.S. v. Wong Kim Ark* in 1898. Banned from entering the country after 1882 because of a federal exclusion law, Chinese immigrants would receive the right to naturalize as U.S. citizens only in 1943 after China became an ally to the United States against Japan during World War II.[56]

Despite Republican efforts to carefully restrict the Fourteenth and Fifteenth Amendments to African American men, winning ratification from western states still proved difficult. In California, Democrats used the specter of Indian and Chinese voters to wrest power from Republicans beginning in 1867, part of a larger reversal in which Democrats made stunning gains not just in the far West but also in Missouri, Ohio, Pennsylvania, New York, and elsewhere.[57] Stung by the viciously racist cartoon and unable to beat back the Democrats' attacks, George C. Gorham lost the governor's race that year to Henry Haight, part of a Democratic takeover of both the California governorship and the state assembly (and nearly the state senate). In his message transmitting the Fifteenth Amendment to the state legislature, Governor Haight warned that, if it were to be adopted, "the most degraded Digger Indian within our borders becomes at once an elector and, so far, a ruler. His vote would count for as much as that of the most intelligent white man in the State." Haight also called Chinese male suffrage "inevitable."[58]

In the end, California's legislature refused to vote one way or another on the Fourteenth Amendment—effectively casting a no vote—but rejected the

Fifteenth Amendment outright. Making a similar move, Oregon's legislature initially ratified but soon withdrew its support for the Fourteenth Amendment and refused to vote on the Fifteenth.[59] Nevada legislators narrowly ratified the Fifteenth Amendment only after receiving reassurance from the U.S. Senate that it would not apply to Chinese men.[60]

America's long-standing restriction of full citizenship to white men had been broken at the height of Radical Reconstruction, but it had not been demolished; U.S. citizenship during Reconstruction still did not extend to women or "heathen" men. Not only Democrats but the majority of Republicans—especially in the West—rejected citizenship and suffrage for Native Americans and Chinese immigrants. These Republicans' attitudes toward "heathens," as shown in these early Reconstruction debates, make the party's shift away from racial justice in the mid-1870s more understandable. Mingled white supremacy and religious bigotry had *always* lingered within the Republican vision. After the Liberal Republican challenge, the Panic of 1873, the strong Democratic gains that followed, and then the deaths of key Radical Republicans, the party moved farther and farther away from a commitment to racial egalitarianism, with disastrous results for all ethnic and racial minorities and the nation as a whole.[61]

Congressional debates over citizenship, suffrage, and immipration during Reconstruction show how the multiracial West was integral to how America's leaders redefined national character in a crucial moment of political flux. From these debates emerged a newly federalized definition of citizenship that, due to the now firmly established authority of the U.S. government, would be enforced in the North, South, and West. Debates over the interwoven Negro, Chinese, and Indian "questions" show the truly national scope of America's public sphere after Appomattox, a moment in which actors from all three regions helped shape federal policy.

NOTES

Along with this volume's editors and contributors, I thank David Prior, Sherry L. Smith, and Stephen Aron for their comments.

1. The Reconstruction Policy of Congress, as Illustrated in California," 1867, Bancroft Library, University of California, Berkeley. This lettersheet was so well known in 1867 that Gorham felt he needed to address it, declaring that he "could go through the campaign with the weights they had placed upon me if they wouldn't place a Copperhead upon the top of the whole"; Sacramento *Daily Union,* August

14, 1867, p. 1. Nonetheless, historians have failed to subject the cartoon to much analysis, although it appears in Eric Foner, *Reconstruction: America's Unfinished Revolution, 1863–1877* (New York: Harper & Row, 1988), 312; D. Michael Bottoms, *An Aristocracy of Color: Race and Reconstruction in California and the West, 1850–1890* (Norman: University of Oklahoma Press, 2013), 80; and Stacey L. Smith, *Freedom's Frontier: California and the Struggle over Unfree Labor, Emancipation, and Reconstruction* (Chapel Hill: University of North Carolina Press, 2013), 212.

2. George M. Fredrickson, *White Supremacy: A Comparative Study in American and South African History* (New York: Oxford University Press, 1981); Alexander Saxton, *The Rise and Fall of the White Republic: Class Politics and Mass Culture in Nineteenth-Century America* (London: Verso, 1990); Audrey Smedley, *Race in North America: Origin and Evolution of a Worldview*, 2nd ed. (Boulder, CO: Westview, 1999); George M. Fredrickson, *Racism: A Short History* (Princeton: Princeton University Press, 2002); Najia Aarim-Heriot, *Chinese Immigrants, African Americans, and Racial Anxiety in the United States, 1848–82* (Urbana: University of Illinois Press, 2003); Edward J. Blum, *Reforging the White Republic: Race, Religion, and American Nationalism, 1865–1898* (Baton Rouge: Louisiana State University Press, 2005).

3. Scholars have just begun to consider Reconstruction as a multiregional, multiracial, transnational process of national reimagining and reconstitution; see Elliott West, "Reconstructing Race," *Western Historical Quarterly* 34 (2003): 7–26; Claudio Saunt, "The Paradox of Freedom: Tribal Sovereignty and Emancipation during the Reconstruction of Indian Territory," *Journal of Southern History* 70 (2004): 63–94; Heather Cox Richardson, *West from Appomattox: The Reconstruction of America after the Civil War* (New Haven : Yale University Press, 2007); Elliott West, *The Last Indian War: The Nez Perce Story* (New York: Oxford University Press, 2009); Adam Arenson, *The Great Heart of the Republic: St. Louis and the Cultural Civil War* (Cambridge, MA: Harvard University Press, 2011), 178–216; Alison Clark Efford, *German Immigrants, Race, and Citizenship in the Civil War Era* (New York: Cambridge University Press, 2013); David Prior, "Civilization, Republic, Nation: Contested Keywords, Northern Republicans, and the Forgotten Reconstruction of Mormon Utah," *Civil War History* 56 (2010): 283–310; Bottoms, *An Aristocracy of Color;* Joshua Paddison, *American Heathens: Religion, Race, and Reconstruction in California* (Berkeley and Los Angeles: University of California Press and Huntington Library, 2012); and Smith, *Freedom's Frontier.* An important older work is Eugene H. Berwanger, *The West and Reconstruction* (Urbana: University of Illinois Press, 1981). Two studies of the national anti-Chinese movement that make useful comparisons to the treatment of African Americans are Andrew Gyory, *Closing the Gate: Race, Politics, and the Chinese Exclusion Act* (Chapel Hill: University of North Carolina Press, 1998), 17–59; and Aarim-Heriot, *Chinese Immigrants, African Americans, and Racial Anxiety.* This chapter adapts and expands on *American Heathens,* 22–27.

4. Prior to the 1860s, states rather than the federal government exercised most control in defining citizenship; see William J. Novak, "The Legal Transformation

of Citizenship in Nineteenth-Century America," in Meg Jacobs, William J. Novak, and Julian E. Zelizer, eds., *The Democratic Experiment: New Directions in American Political History* (Princeton: Princeton University Press, 2003), 85–119; and Christian G. Samito, *Becoming American under Fire: Irish Americans, African Americans, and the Politics of Citizenship during the Civil War Era* (Ithaca, NY: Cornell University Press, 2009), 1–4.

5. On the background of the Civil Rights Act of 1866, see Robert J. Kaczorowski, "To Begin the Nation Anew: Congress, Citizenship, and Civil Rights after the Civil War," *American Historical Review* 92 (1987): 45–68; Foner, *Reconstruction*, 243–47; and George Rutherglen, *Civil Rights in the Shadow of Slavery: The Constitution, Common Law, and the Civil Rights Act of 1866* (New York: Oxford University Press, 2013).

6. Cong. Globe, 38th Cong., 1st sess., 1465.

7. On the black codes, see Edward Royce, *The Origins of Southern Sharecropping* (Philadelphia: Temple University Press, 1993), 63–71; Foner, *Reconstruction*, 199–201, 208–9; and Rutherglen, *Civil Rights in the Shadow of Slavery*, 46–49.

8. Cong. Globe, 39th Cong., 1st sess., 474.

9. Ibid., 498.

10. Ibid., 497.

11. Ibid., 498.

12. Ibid., 526.

13. Ibid., 527.

14. James P. Collins, "Native Americans in the Census, 1860–1890," *Prologue* 38 no. 2 (2006); David J. Silverman, *Red Brethren: The Brothertown and Stockbridge Indians and the Problem of Race in Early America* (Ithaca, NY: Cornell University Press, 2010).

15. Cong. Globe, 39th Cong., 1st sess., 2890, 2892.

16. Ibid., 2890–91. On the congressional discussion of "gypsies," see Foner, *Reconstruction*, 257.

17. Cong. Globe, 39th Cong., 1st sess., 1056.

18. Ibid., 2897.

19. Ibid., 1056.

20. On the importance of African American men's military service to their winning of suffrage, see Donald R. Shaffer, *After the Glory: The Struggles of Black Civil War Veterans* (Lawrence: University Press of Kansas, 2004); and Samito, *Becoming American under Fire*.

21. San Francisco *Daily Evening Bulletin*, March 15, 1862, p. 3.

22. San Francisco *Daily Examiner*, August 13, 1867, p. 2.

23. San Francisco *Pacific Appeal*, August 31, 1867, p. 2.

24. Helen Heran Jun, *Race for Citizenship: Black Orientalism and Asian Uplift from Pre-Emancipation to Neoliberal America* (New York: New York University Press, 2011), 15–32.

25. San Francisco *Elevator*, March 16, 1866, p. 2.

26. San Francisco *Elevator*, October 11, 1867, p. 2. On Irish immigrants' use of whiteness, see David R. Roediger, *The Wages of Whiteness: Race and the Making of*

the American Working Class (London: Verso, 1991); Noel Ignatiev, *How the Irish Became White* (New York: Routledge, 1995); and Matthew Frye Jacobson, *Whiteness of a Different Color: European Immigrants and the Alchemy of Race* (Cambridge, MA: Harvard University Press, 1998). On German immigrants, see Efford, *German Immigrants, Race, and Citizenship in the Civil War Era*.

27. Paddison, *American Heathens,* 47–48, 126–27.

28. Cong. Globe, 39th Cong., 1st sess., 2895.

29. *Report . . . on the Effect of the Fourteenth Amendment to the Constitution upon the Indian Tribes of the Country,* December 14, 1870, Congressional Serial Set vol. no. 1443, 41st Cong., 3d sess., report 268 (Washington, DC: Government Printing Office, 1870), 1.

30. At the local level, naturalization regulations would continue to vary even after the passage of the Fourteenth Amendment, and on the East Coast a very small number of Chinese immigrants did manage to gain citizenship. In New York in the late 1870s, for example, fourteen Chinese men—all "converts to Christianity"—became citizens; see John Kuo Wei Tchen, *New York before Chinatown: Orientalism and the Shaping of American Culture, 1776–1882* (Baltimore: Johns Hopkins University Press, 1999), 247. On the flip side, physician Yung Wing, who had managed to secure naturalization in 1852, found his citizenship revoked in 1898; see Roger Daniels, *Asian America: Chinese and Japanese in the United States since 1850* (Seattle: University of Washington Press, 1995), 27.

31. Cong. Globe, 40th Cong., 3rd sess., 996.

32. Ibid., 979.

33. Ibid., 989.

34. Ibid., 989–90.

35. Cong. Globe, 41st Cong., 2nd sess., 5151–52.

36. Cong. Globe, 39th Cong., 1st sess., 2897.

37. Ellen Carol DuBois, *Feminism and Suffrage: The Emergence of an Independent Women's Movement in America, 1848–1869* (Ithaca, NY: Cornell University Press, 1978), 53–78, 262–302; Foner, *Reconstruction,* 255; Suzanne M. Marilley, *Woman Suffrage and the Origins of Liberal Feminism in the United States, 1820–1920* (Cambridge, MA: Harvard University Press, 1996), 66–99; Rebecca Edwards, *Angels in the Machinery: Gender in American Party Politics from the Civil War to the Progressive Era* (New York: Oxford University Press, 1997); Laura F. Edwards, *Gendered Strife and Confusion: The Political Culture of Reconstruction* (Urbana: University of Illinois Press, 1997); LeeAnn Whites, *Gender Matters: Civil War, Reconstruction, and the Making of the New South* (New York: Palgrave Macmillan, 2005).

38. On cultural perceptions of the Chinese, see Stuart Creighton Miller, *Unwelcome Immigrant: The American Image of the Chinese, 1785–1885* (Berkeley: University of California Press, 1969); Ronald T. Takaki, *Iron Cages: Race and Culture in Nineteenth-Century America* (New York: Knopf, 1979); Robert G. Lee, *Orientals: Asian Americans in Popular Culture* (Philadelphia: Temple University Press, 1999); Tchen, *New York before Chinatown;* and Linda Frost, *Never One*

Nation: Freaks, Savages, and Whiteness in U.S. Popular Culture, 1850–1877 (Minneapolis: University of Minnesota Press, 2005). On perceptions of Indians, see Roy Harvey Pearce, *Savagism and Civilization: A Study of the Indian and the American Mind* (Baltimore: Johns Hopkins University Press, 1967); Robert F. Berkhofer, *The White Man's Indian: Images of the American Indian from Columbus to the Present* (New York: Knopf, 1978); Richard Drinnon, *Facing West: The Metaphysics of Indian-Hating and Empire-Building* (Minneapolis: University of Minnesota Press, 1980); Brian W. Dippie, *The Vanishing American: White Attitudes and U.S. Indian Policy* (Middletown, CT: Wesleyan University Press, 1982); Helen Carr, *Inventing the American Primitive: Politics, Gender and the Representation of Native American Literary Traditions, 1789–1936* (New York: New York University Press, 1996); Susan Scheckel, *The Insistence of the Indian: Race and Nationalism in Nineteenth-Century American Culture* (Princeton: Princeton University Press, 1998); Philip J. Deloria, *Playing Indian* (New Haven: Yale University Press, 1998); Sherry L. Smith, *Reimagining Indians: Native Americans through Anglo Eyes, 1880–1940* (New York: Oxford University Press, 2000); and Shari M. Huhndorf, *Going Native: Indians in the American Cultural Imagination* (Ithaca, NY: Cornell University Press, 2001).

39. James H. Moorhead, *American Apocalypse: Yankee Protestants and the Civil War, 1860–1869* (New Haven: Yale University Press, 1978), 173–235; Jon C. Teaford, "Toward a Christian Nation: Religion, Law and Justice Strong," *Journal of Presbyterian History* 54 (1976): 422–37; Daniel W. Stowell, *Rebuilding Zion: The Religious Reconstruction of the South, 1863–1877* (New York: Oxford University Press, 1998).

40. National Association for the Amendment of the Constitution, *The National Association for the Amendment of the Federal Constitution* (Philadelphia: 1864), 6–7.

41. Cong. Globe, 38th Cong., 2d sess., 661; Cong. Globe, 41st Cong., 2d sess., 1373; Mark W. Cannon, "The Mormon Issue in Congress 1872–1882: Drawing on the Experience of Territorial Delegate George Q. Cannon," PhD diss., Harvard University, 1960; Gaines M. Foster, *Moral Reconstruction: Christian Lobbyists and the Federal Legislation of Morality, 1865–1920* (Chapel Hill: University of North Carolina Press, 2002), 27–71; Sarah Barringer Gordon, *The Mormon Question: Polygamy and Constitutional Conflict in Nineteenth-Century America* (Chapel Hill: University of North Carolina Press, 2002); Helen Lefkowitz Horowitz, *Rereading Sex: Battles over Sexual Knowledge and Suppression in Nineteenth-Century America* (New York: Vintage Books, 2003), 359–85; Prior, "Civilization, Republic, Nation."

42. David Buice, "A Stench in the Nostrils of Honest Men: Southern Democrats and the Edmunds Act of 1882," *Dialogue: A Journal of Mormon Thought* 21 (Autumn 1988): 100–113; Jay P. Dolan, *In Search of an American Catholicism: A History of Religion and Culture in Tension* (New York: Oxford University Press, 2002), 47–70; Foster, *Moral Reconstruction,* 60–62; John T. McGreevy, *Catholicism and American Freedom: A History* (New York: Norton, 2003), 91–126; Tracy Fessenden, "The Nineteenth-Century Bible Wars and the Separation of Church and State," *Church History* 74 (2005): 784–811; Matthew J. Grow, *"Liberty to the Downtrodden":*

Thomas L. Kane, Romantic Reformer (New Haven: Yale University Press, 2009); Patrick Q. Mason, *The Mormon Menace: Violence and Anti-Mormonism in the Postbellum South* (New York: Oxford University Press, 2011), 91; David Sehat, *The Myth of American Religious Freedom* (New York: Oxford University Press, 2011), 156–75.

43. Sacramento *Daily Union*, March 3, 1866, p. 1.
44. Cong. Globe, 41st Cong., 1st sess., 756.
45. Paddison, *American Heathens*, 35–102.
46. New York *Times*, January 2, 1869, p. 1.
47. Henry E. Fritz, *The Movement for Indian Assimilation, 1860–1890* (Philadelphia: University of Pennsylvania Press, 1963), 198–221; Robert Winston Mardock, *The Reformers and the American Indian* (Columbia: University of Missouri Press, 1971), 150–59, 168–210; Francis Paul Prucha, *American Indian Policy in Crisis: Christian Reformers and the Indian, 1865–1900* (Norman: University of Oklahoma Press, 1976), 128–43; Robert H. Keller Jr., *American Protestantism and United States Indian Policy, 1869–82* (Lincoln: University of Nebraska Press, 1983), 188–204; Frederick E. Hoxie, *A Final Promise: The Campaign to Assimilate the Indians, 1880–1920* (Lincoln: University of Nebraska Press, 1984), 1–43; Valerie Sherer Mathes and Richard Lowitt, *The Standing Bear Controversy: Prelude to Indian Reform* (Urbana: University of Illinois Press, 2003).
48. Cong. Globe, 41st Cong., 2d sess., 5515.
49. Ibid.
50. Ibid., 5155–56.
51. Ibid., 5162.
52. Moon-Ho Jung, "Outlawing 'Coolies': Race, Nation, and Empire in the Age of Emancipation," *American Quarterly* 57 (2005): 677–701; Moon-Ho Jung, *Coolies and Cane: Race, Labor, and Sugar in the Age of Emancipation* (Baltimore: Johns Hopkins University Press, 2006). On the construction of the "coolie," see also Sucheng Chan, *This Bittersweet Soil: The Chinese in California Agriculture, 1860–1910* (Berkeley: University of California Press, 1986), 31, 38–41; Gyory, *Closing the Gate*, 32–33, 61–63; Lee, *Orientals*, 51–82; and Tchen, *New York before Chinatown*, 172–75.
53. Cong. Globe, 41st Cong., 2d sess., 5168–69.
54. Ibid., 5172.
55. Xi Wang, *The Trial of Democracy: Black Suffrage and Northern Republicans, 1860–1910* (Athens: University of George Press, 1997), 76–77.
56. Charles J. McClain, *In Search of Equality: The Chinese Struggle against Discrimination in Nineteenth-Century America* (Berkeley: University of California Press, 1994); Rogers M. Smith, *Civic Ideals: Conflicting Visions of Citizenship in U.S. History* (New Haven: Yale University Press, 1997); Yong Chen, *Chinese San Francisco, 1850–1943: A Trans-Pacific Community* (Stanford: Stanford University Press, 2000); Madeline Hsu, *Dreaming of Gold, Dreaming of Home: Transnationalism and the Migration between the United States and South China, 1882–1943* (Stanford: Stanford University Press, 2000); Aarim-Heriot, *Chinese Immigrants, African*

Americans, and Racial Anxiety, 149–50; Erika Lee, *At America's Gates: Chinese Immigration during the Exclusion Era, 1882–1943* (Chapel Hill: University of North Carolina Press, 2003).

57. Michael Les Benedict, *A Compromise of Principle: Congressional Republicans and Reconstruction, 1863–1869* (New York: Norton, 1974), 272–73; Arenson, *The Great Heart of the Republic,* 186–88.

58. H. H. Haight, *Message of H. H. Haight, Governor of the State of California, Transmitting the Proposed Fifteenth Amendment to the Federal Constitution* (Sacramento: D. W. Gelwicks, State Printer, 1870), 10; H. H. Haight, *Speech of Governor Haight, at the Democratic State Convention at Sacramento, June 29, 1869* (San Francisco: 1869), 4.

59. Both states did, for symbolic purposes, eventually ratify both amendments in the wake of the modern civil rights movement.

60. Don W. Driggs and Leonard E. Goodall, *Nevada Politics and Government: Conservatism in an Open Society* (Lincoln: University of Nebraska Press, 1996), 10.

61. Foner, *Reconstruction,* 449–53, 475–524; Aarim-Heriot, *Chinese Immigrants, African Americans, and Racial Anxiety,* 152–54.

TEN

Broadening the Battlefield

CONFLICT, CONTINGENCY, AND THE MYSTERY OF
WOMAN SUFFRAGE IN WYOMING, 1869

Virginia Scharff

OF ALL THE PLACES AND TIMES in the history of the United States that you might expect woman suffrage to have achieved its first triumph, Wyoming Territory, which enfranchised women in December 1869, likely ranks right down at the bottom. Surely, you'd think that women first won the right to vote in someplace seemingly more civilized and progressive, a Massachusetts or a New York, say, where women had access to education early and broadly, where the movement for the abolition of slavery and African American citizenship had been strongest, and where women had exercised a measure of power in social and political reform movements.

Or, failing that, one might imagine that, in the years after the Civil War, in the rush to revolutionize the states of the former Confederacy, the Radical Republicans who oversaw Reconstruction in the South might have added the enfranchisement of women to the effort for civil rights for freedpeople. Women had, after all, been instrumental in the abolitionist movement, and men like Frederick Douglass and William Lloyd Garrison had been vocal advocates of female suffrage. And surely, a government that could pass three constitutional amendments and two civil rights acts might, in theory, have included votes for women in the package of privileges and immunities of citizenship they sought to enforce, in the South, at the point of a bayonet?[1]

But no. Women first got the vote way out West, in 1869, on the high plains and in the mountain reaches of the federal Territory of Wyoming. Wyoming? It makes no sense. And what was "Wyoming Territory" anyway? In 1869, it was more a projection or expectation or wish than a statement of fact. At the moment that women won the vote, this frontier backwater was barely under U.S. control. Along the southern edge of the territory, a succession of

FIGURE 10.1. *Janet Sherlock Smith and H. G. Nickerson at South Pass City.* Photograph by Grace Raymond Hebard, 1915. Wyoming State Archives.

construction camp towns busted nearly as fast as they boomed, as the Union Pacific Railroad crews moved through.

Indigenous people far outnumbered emigrants. Lakota, Shoshone, Arapaho, Crow, Cheyenne, and Bannock people held most of the land inside and adjacent to the territory's borders, by right of the recently concluded treaties of Fort Laramie and Fort Bridger, and by virtue of residence. North of the railroad, the United States had established forts along the Bozeman Trail. But in the face of fierce indigenous resistance the Army had agreed to abandon those forts, leaving the Powder River country and most of the putative federal territory under the control of Indian peoples. Only along the railroad corridor could the United States claim real authority, and not always even there.

Most of the U.S. citizens who lived in Wyoming in the late 1860s were thus confined to slices and pockets of the terrain. They were transient rough-and-ready men (emigrant males outnumbered females by at least five to one), many of them hardened veterans of the Civil War. They brawled readily with one another, but they were hardly interested in fighting for the cause of women's rights. By 1868, some five thousand American voters claimed residency, enough that Wyoming could be organized as a territory of the United States. But when the victory for women's enfranchisement came, some denounced it as criminal folly, some considered it a non-event, a coincidence, or a joke, and only a few marked the occasion as the opening fanfare for an epoch of peace, justice, and progress.

And who among the newcomers could claim citizenship? The question was certainly up for grabs. Anglo and African Americans, Chinese and Irish and German and French immigrants, and ethnic Mexicans from both inside and outside the United States had made the trek to Wyoming Territory, but which of them were entitled to the privileges and immunities of citizenship? Even among Anglo men, many had served in the Confederate Army, and the U.S. Congress had explicitly excluded them from exercising the full rights of citizenship (unless granted amnesty), by virtue of the Fourteenth Amendment to the U.S. Constitution, adopted in May 1868. Women, too, had been excluded from full citizenship in that landmark provision. What a motley rabble and shaky foundation upon which to erect Thomas Jefferson's empire for liberty!

All of this makes the triumph of woman suffrage in Wyoming all the more mysterious. Most American citizens in Wyoming were males of the unruly sort, and most women in Wyoming were inhabitants of indigenous communities. Who, really, was even there to advocate for the reform, and why did they succeed, at a time when, in the most forward-looking precincts of the American nation, the possibility of enfranchising women seemed too radical even to those who styled themselves Radicals in word and deed?

Suppose we shift our point of view, widening the lens of historical inquiry to encompass a longer time scale and a larger geographical field. Let us frame this question not in local terms, or in a matter of months or years, but instead, along continental lines, and on a timeline of decades. Envision the Territory of Wyoming as a work-in-progress and a product of the politics of both slavery and national expansion, of war and settlement, of white supremacy and increasing demographic diversity, of struggles over who counted as an American and a citizen, and of who had the right to call their bodies or their homelands their own? Then, I argue, we can begin to understand how it came to pass that in this remote (not to say godforsaken) place on the wind-seared high plains, straddling the Continental Divide, a moment of justice walked side by side with dispossession and incorporation. If we view the Civil War and the conquest of the West as a single historical phenomenon, a war on behalf of the United States of America for control as well as emancipation; a continental war over white supremacy and a war over the rights of people excluded from the rights of white men; and sometimes even a war for progress and justice, we begin to see how such things could happen.[2]

Historical conflicts occur in moments of contingency that spawn unintended consequences. Imagine the continental span of the United States in the nineteenth century as a broad battlefield, where various combatants struggled for self-determination and for preeminence, especially volatile and unpredictable at the edges. We can begin to understand how woman suffrage in America would have been born on the ground of conquest and race war, in the inconceivably remote hamlet of South Pass City, Wyoming Territory.

Just as Americans had carried the politics of slavery into western territory, sparking violent incidents that led to the larger Civil War, so, too, they brought the tensions of Reconstruction to places they sought to conquer on behalf of the nation, far removed from the recently reconquered South. Military conquest and genocide were only the two most horrible means of domination. If the United States was to gain permanent control of places far from Washington, D.C., they needed other, less bloody instruments. Federal officials began with the grid, a land survey system perfected for expansion, designed to locate, allocate, and market parcels of land anywhere the empire might reach, anywhere, indeed, on planet Earth. The grid ignored topography, geology, previous survey and property practices, and the very fact that places gridded were already occupied. It precipitated disappointment and confusion and furious conflict, despite its seeming simplicity and logical elegance. But it worked brilliantly as an instrument of conquest. "By the

1860s," wrote landscape historian John Stilgoe, "the grid objectified national, not regional order."[3]

Land thus surveyed had then to be governed. Once those five thousand U.S. voters claimed to live someplace, they could organize a territorial government, elect an assembly, and send a nonvoting delegate to the U.S. Congress. Most officeholders, however, including the territorial governor and judges, would be federal appointees. The system worked well on occasion, but at great distance from the nation's capital it sometimes broke under the strain.[4]

Capital and technology also undergirded conquest, and never more powerfully than in the case of the transcontinental railroad. Corrupt and inefficient as the railroads certainly were, they were no less crucial to the project of occupying the continent in the name of the United States. Beginning in 1862 when Congress chartered the Union Pacific and Central Pacific Railroads and charged the corporations with building a rail line that would link east and west, the government embarked on a massive program to subsidize a network of rail lines that would, in time, create a transportation network for a continental nation. Just as goods and people moved along the rails and wagon trails, so ideas also moved along newly strung telegraph wires, in newspapers carried from place to place, and in the mails.[5]

As important as these mathematical, geographical, technological, institutional, military, financial, and material resources were to nation building, nothing mattered more than people. No quantity of land offices and armies and railroads and government bureaus could do the job of unsettling the original inhabitants of the lands the United States claimed, and domesticating those lands as American places, unless Americans and would-be Americans agreed to go and live in those places. Some of those places were unpromising, to say the least. Thus the prospects of the expanding nation were in the hands of fractious people with myriad motives and means, facing novel and unpredictable challenges.

Wyoming was surely such a place. Americans of the mid-nineteenth century called the effort to install loyal American farm families on indigenous lands "progress." We call it "settler colonialism."

On July 25, 1868, the federal act organizing the U.S. Territory of Wyoming became law, anticipating the arrival of the Union Pacific Railroad, then making its way along the southern edge of the territory toward a meeting with its transcontinental partner, the Central Pacific. As John A. Campbell, the first territorial governor, explained in his cheerfully imperialist inaugural message, "For the first time in the history of our country, the organization of a territorial government was made necessary by the building of a railroad. Heretofore the railroad had been the follower instead of the pioneer of civilization."[6]

The people who came to Wyoming carried cultural as well as physical baggage, including ideas about race and gender. Such ideas were both unstable and important in such a place, which presented all too many opportunities for newcomers to wonder who they were, and what in the world they were doing. Eternally quarrelling among themselves, emigrants knew that the distant government hardly had the power to enforce order in the territory. Even as the Fort Laramie Treaty ceded most of the northern span of the territory to Native control, white prospecting parties—protected by federal troops—repeatedly entered Lakota country, particularly in the Big Horn basin and the Black Hills. Gold had been discovered along the Sweetwater River in the western part of Wyoming, and miners flocked to camps at South Pass City, Atlantic City, and Miner's Delight. Those hamlets bordered the Shoshones' Wind River Reservation, established by the Fort Bridger Treaty of July 3, 1868, and when they were looking for gold, fortune hunters seldom respected the reservation boundary. Emigrant prospectors clamored for the government to send troops to protect them, but they rebelled at attempts to restrain them from encroaching on Indian lands.

Coincidence, bad luck, and rumor combined with fear, misunderstanding and malevolence to spark violence. Indians and whites attacked one another, whites (and a few African Americans) shot and stabbed each other, and it was all too easy to point the finger at almost anybody else. Long after and far from the places where the Civil War had been fought, Confederate die-hards, "Galvanized Yankees," and Union stalwarts nursed raging grudges.

Most emigrants were transient "white" men, working the mines or toiling for the railroad, unmarried or at least living as if they were single. They had no intention of staying in Wyoming after the work moved on. They had little interest in fostering harmony with indigenous residents, or with each other for that matter. They took for granted their rights to property and political participation as prerogatives of white manhood, expected the U.S. government to provide them with armed protection, and could be mobilized as militia in emergencies, but they weren't much interested in empire building. Many, in fact, were actively fleeing the forces of law and order. Policymakers thus viewed them as necessary but unreliable tools of conquest.

A far smaller contingent of white male emigrants counted themselves the real bearers of "civilization," a state of affairs in which they stood as heads of white families, destined to supplant indigenous villages, establish farms, institute self-government, and permanently join the American republic. They were, according to the editors of the *Sweetwater Mines* newspaper, a "class of men ... who possessed sufficient energy and stamina to overcome the many obstacles found in their path. Upon men of this kind do we depend for the future development of this country."[7] Feckless single men might move on or join their ranks by marrying and fathering children, but these more rooted men believed that families were the key to domesticating occupied territory, to shaping a continuously American landscape of farms and towns and cities.

At least in public, such men embraced a simple, sentimental, hierarchical, and highly idealized image of what, who, and how those families would operate. They would embody a particular dynamic of power and affection, within the household and in the larger world. Wyoming's middle-class Victorians (like those elsewhere in the country) avowed that men and women were fitted by nature for different but complementary "spheres" in life, with men restraining their base instincts in order to build civil society in a savage place, using their superior intellect and strength. In terms of the ideology of "true womanhood," those women who accompanied such men to the mines were charged with serving and pleasing their husbands and fathers, nurturing and educating their children, and maintaining moral order in the household, the infant territory, and more grandly, in the nation.[8]

When they went to school and to church, when they read magazines, novels, and advice books, middle-class Americans absorbed lessons about how proper men and women ought to behave. The problem with lessons, of course, is that they are not always easy or useful to learn. However much a person might strive to embody the ideal type of American man or women (and many, of course, were excluded by virtue of race or class or culture, or had little interest in aspiring to upright behavior), pretty much everybody fell short in one way or another. Pillars of the community got in fights and gambled away the rent money. Model mothers lost their tempers and screamed at their husbands and children. People who vowed to do better every day found themselves gossiping with neighbors, stopping off at the saloon, drowning their sorrows and angers with laudanum or rotgut whiskey. Drunken men, and even occasionally, women, were a common sight in the streets of South Pass City, and of course, the settlements attracted their share of prostitutes, women who made a living on men's deviations from the path of righteous Victorian manliness. In such a dusty, cold, wind-scoured place, it was hard to be good, even for those who wanted to do so.[9]

In the summer of 1868, thousands of people of variable virtue found their way to Wyoming, carting along their talents, hopes, and enterprise, as well as their foibles, fears, and shortcomings. Within two years, many had passed on through, but some remained, in hope of finding their fortunes. According to the 1870 census, South Pass City, the largest of the three isolated settlements of the Sweetwater mining district, was home to a population of 460 souls, with men outnumbering women four to one.[10] Along with the streets and the mines, places that traded in alcohol (seven retail liquor dealers, three breweries, and one liquor wholesaler in South Pass City alone) dominated social life. Chicago journalist James Chisholm, who spent a summer in the settlement, observed that "a vast amount of gold dust is ground in the whiskey mill," and judging from the dozens of advertisements in the territory's newspapers, happy hour began at dawn. One bar owner insisted that "there is no better appetizer than one of [this establishment's] cocktails taken before breakfast in the morning," and newspaper editors gleefully recommended their favorite watering holes in the editorial columns of their papers.[11]

In such circumstances, what was a "true woman" to do? The few white, middle-class women who had landed in South Pass City did their best to "elevate" the tone of local society, but they had their work cut out for them. Fourteen of them, who had hung on through the howling winter of 1868–69, threw a Christmas party in the Sholes Exchange saloon, featuring a lavish spread of "pies, cakes, and confectionary ... turkeys, game, salads, and jellies," not to mention plenty of champagne. The *Sweetwater Mines* reported that though the party went into the early morning hours, no one was drunk. Referring to the women by their marital status and initials (Mrs. S., Miss T.) to preserve feminine modesty, the *Mines* used the presence of genteel ladies to advertise the arrival of civilization in the Wild West. "We have formed a nucleus of female society in our midst," the editors wrote, "that may give an assurance to some families who expect to visit us next spring and summer, that the hardy pioneers of the Rocky Mountains still hold dear the principles and examples inculcated I their minds by their mothers and sisters in their far off eastern and western homes."[12]

Some women, of course, rejected the conventions of true womanhood. Martha Jane Cannary, otherwise known as Calamity Jane, claimed to have scouted for the Army, worked as a bullwhacker, and driven stage coaches, though we know for certain only that she did do some freighting, drank to excess, sometimes made a living selling sex and often found it expedient to wear men's clothes. Somewhere along her picaresque trails, she made an appearance in South Pass City, and may have provoked a comment in the *Frontier Index,* the press on wheels operated by brothers Fred and Legh Freeman, who rode west with the Union Pacific. Faced with the rising call for votes for women, the *Index* observed that "you just as well set a woman upon a stage driver's box, with a whip in hand, as to allow her at the ballot box with whisky in her head and oaths upon her lips."[13]

Other women were disqualified from true womanhood on racial grounds. Judging from local newspapers, vicious sexism and ugly racism went hand in hand, or perhaps fist in palm. The *Mines* and *Index* focused on indigenous women, declaring that "the depraved nature of [Indian] women is manifest. We are taught to associate the sex with everything that is lovely, and gentle, and amiable, and kind, but the squaw becomes an instrument in the hands of the buck for torture." Going the *Mines* one better, the *Index* printed dispatches, jokes, and anecdotes that portrayed indigenous women as more violent and carnal than even Native men. In a story on a "tragic affair" in a Ute camp near Tierra Amarilla, New Mexico, the *Index* reported that a man named Chino had been shot by another Indian man, adding that "the sister of Chino then killed his wife by cutting her head open with a hatchet, to prevent her from marrying anyone else." For the *Index,* Indian women who were not crazy were at best creatures of their sexuality, subject to ridicule at their most dignified. "Riding along," the editors wrote, "a companion remarked of a squaw that 'she walks like a soldier.' I responded, 'Yes, she looks like she's been drilled.'"[14]

In fact, the *Frontier Index* made racist and sexist invective its specialty. The *Index* reprinted stories from eastern newspapers, vilifying blacks and white Radical Republicans, and often reported on anti-Chinese activity in the West, while missing no chance to malign indigenous people, or for that matter, government officials who favored any Indian policy short of extermination. All these purported enemies were, in the eyes of the *Index,* co-conspirators against white men's liberty, with the Republicans using racially inferior pawns to serve their own tyrannical ends. The *Index* embraced a role as mouthpiece for the extension of a white man's empire across the continent, revealing both continuity with the race politics of the Civil War era, and the expansion of the geography of conflict over those politics. "As the emblem of American Liberty," the editors trumpeted from Green River, Wyoming,

"*THE FRONTIER INDEX* is now perched upon the summit of the Rocky Mountains, flaps its wings over the Great West, and screams forth in thunder and lightning tones, the principles of an unterrified anti-Nigger, anti-Chinese, anti-Indian party—Masonic Democracy!!!!!!!"[15]

For many white Wyomingites, ideas about race and gender worked together. But upholding the privileges of race on the Sweetwater proved trying. Visiting the tiny hamlet of Miner's Delight, journalist James Chisholm found twenty-four-year-old Frances Gallagher, wife of an Army major, whom he greatly admired. "Apart from woman in the abstract, for whom I retain an unspeakable veneration, she must be a brave soul who, accustomed to the refinements of life, can voluntarily front the hardships and perils of a mining camp like this," Chisholm observed. Frances Gallagher did her best, keeping house and teaching school, but according to James Chisholm, her confidante, "She sometimes pines for home so pinefully that I get quite sympathetic on the subject."[16]

The *Frontier Index* had some advice for the likes of Frances Gallagher: "A modest woman must often neither see nor hear." Neither, according to white commentators, should good women be seen or heard. But women had plenty to say, both privately and publicly, especially when the men in their lives failed to fulfill the measure of manliness. "None but the brave deserve the fair," said the *Frontier* Index. "And none but the brave can live with some of them." In South Pass City, a housewife named Carr sent her children to a local saloon to fetch their inebriated father, who replied that "he was too drunk to com home and if she wanted him to return home, they would have to come after him with a wheelbarrow. This they did."[17]

Other women found the need to take their moral authority to the streets. Janet Sherlock Smith, whose descendants persisted in the South Pass area into the middle of the twentieth century, was the most successful of the town's handful of businesswomen, keeping a lodging house and partnering with her husband in the mercantile store. She had already demonstrated remarkable hardiness, as the daughter of a Scottish Mormon family who had immigrated to the United States and walked most of the way to Utah, where she married her first husband, a Mormon man named Richard Sherlock. She would prove brave and adaptable, when, widowed with three young children, she married a second husband, James Smith, nominally converting to Catholicism. When a man named Al Tompkins shot and killed Janet's brother, George McOmie, a mob gathered in the town's main street to hang Tompkins without benefit of a trial. According to her grandson, James

Sherlock, Janet interceded "in her devout Christian and characteristically kind and sensible manner." She told the crowd that she had already lost enough, without having Tompkins's blood on her hands, "and she knew that in living with his own conscience and Divine judgment, the man would receive his just punishment."[18]

Empire builders celebrated women like Janet Sherlock Smith as shining examples of moral white womanhood, a kind of cultural property that made it possible to turn Indian country into U.S. territory. There was more than cloying sentiment involved when the *Sweetwater Mines* rehearsed the bromide, "The wife makes the home, and the home makes the man." In Wyoming, erecting the domicile in question required the dispossession of Native peoples, the suppression or elimination of anyone who made bold to contest the claims of the white republic. But it also implied that women would be content to confine themselves to the household and defer to their husbands at moments of friction. Homilies barely masked the fear that women might go too far in exerting their influence, might, like an angry wife with a wheelbarrow, turn on their supposed protectors and providers. The true white woman was, in short, both a necessary partner and a somewhat unreliable ally in the enterprise of conquest. When so many of the inhabitants of Wyoming had survived war and lived lives on the move, tranquility and stability were dreams, not realities. The *Mines* observed that "a cynical journalist says the reason so many marriages occur immediately after a war, is that bachelors become so accustomed to strife that they learn to like it, and after the return of peace, they enlist in matrimony as the next thing to war."[19]

But why should we expect stability at the edge of a nation recently ripped apart, and only tensely and tenuously beginning to piece itself together? In 1868, the South was governed under the Military Reconstruction Act, which divided the terrain of the former Confederacy into districts that collapsed the boundaries of states that had so recently insisted on their sovereign rights. Uniformed officers governed those districts, and they ruled by right of appointment from Washington, D.C., exactly as did the governing officials of Wyoming Territory. The president of the United States, Ulysses S. Grant, embodied both kinds of authority, and it was he who appointed Wyoming's first governor, John A. Campbell of Ohio, along with its secretary, Edward M. Lee of Connecticut, senior territorial judge John W. Kingman of New Hampshire, and U.S. marshal Church Howe of Massachusetts, Republicans all. All four men embraced the Radical Republican agenda, and both Campbell and Lee had risen to the rank of brigadier general in the Union

Army. These battle-hardened idealists meant to put Wyoming in the vanguard of the march toward equality and justice, by honoring treaty obligations, enforcing African American male suffrage, and yes, when the astonishing time came, supporting woman suffrage.

Unabashed progressives were by no means in the majority among white men in Wyoming. After all, who had better reason to head west than those who had lost most in the war, northern "Copperheads," and residents of the border states and the former Confederacy? In May 1868, as the presidential election approached, Wyoming politics got truly ugly. The *Frontier Index* predicted that a Grant victory would mean race war, with Grant and his supporters thwarting "conservative white men" and planning to "Africanise and Indianise our whole mongrel region." Aware as the *Index* editors were of the Chinese immigrants who comprised such a substantial part of the labor force for the Central Pacific Railroad, then making its way across the West, they added a local note: "Four hundred millions of Chinamen [will be] 'knocking at our national door.' . . . Our white laborers and their wives and children will suffer for bread. Americans you will have to subsist (not live) on rats, and rice and drink tea made from the grounds emptied from Chinamen's teapots. . . . The war of races will have commenced." And just to underline the point, the *Index* offered a battle cry: "Our watchword will be Revolution or Death! Up with white men, down with the devil!"[20]

The Freemans echoed southern secessionists in the editorial columns of their *Frontier Index*, declaring that "the clouds of revolution are lowering. On with it! Off with the crown of the military dictator—Grant!" But they put a local spin on their rage. For them, the chief threat to white supremacy came not from a potentially revolutionary enslaved labor force, but from the original inhabitants of the territory. They predicted that Grant would send federal appointees who would be soft on the Indian "problem," would give the Indians "full rations as long as they carry on a vigorous and successful war upon the whites. . . . Go in, Lo: Thad. Stevens and Ben Butler will back you!"[21]

A group of seventeen men in South Pass City, including a Virginian and Union veteran named William H. Bright, took a similar position, in terms slightly less unhinged. They signed a circular announcing a mass meeting of Democrats, "all good and true men, who repudiate the Reconstruction policy of congress, negro suffrage, and the principles espoused by the Radical Republican Party, and who are in favor of equal and exact justice to all sections of the union."[22]

Since they resided in a territory rather than a state, Wyoming voters could not cast ballots in the presidential election. But on September 2, 1869, they had their chance to vote for territorial legislators and a nonvoting delegate to the U.S. Congress. As some fifteen or twenty African American voters went to the polls in South Pass City, a white mob determined to keep them from exercising their rights. Justice John Kingman described the scene:

> At South Pass City some drunken fellows with large knives and loaded revolvers swaggered around the polls, and swore that no Negro should vote.... When one man remarked quietly that he thought the Negroes had as good a right to vote as any of them had, he was immediately knocked down, jumped on, kicked, and pounded without mercy and would have been killed had not his friends rushed into the brutal crowd and dragged him out, bloody and insensible. There were quite a number of colored men who wanted to vote, but did not dare approach the polls until the United States Marshal, himself at their head and with a revolver in hand, escorted them through the crowd, saying he would shoot the first man that interfered with them. There was much quarreling and tumult, but the Negroes voted.[23]

That year, the Democratic Party, which stood for white supremacy and against recognition of the rights of nonwhite people, swept the territorial elections. In South Pass City, William Bright was elected to the territorial council. Even so, federal officials determined to do their duty in a tense political and geographic landscape. Governor John Campbell had to mediate between white emigrants who believed Indians had no claim to liberty, land, or life, and desperate indigenous people who regarded the Americans with distrust and disillusionment, if not rage and hatred. Individuals of every origin sought to exploit confusion to their own ends. Though he and his allies acted in the name of federal authority, Campbell could hardly rely on the power of the government, remote and corrupt, to carry out its promises. Ever pleading with Washington for support, he knew he was in a fix. "I believe it to be unwise and wrong to insist of a faithful obeissance of the Treaty stipulations on the part of the Indians without a corresponding faithfulness on our part," Campbell wrote to Commissioner of Indian Affairs Ely S. Parker, after a disheartening visit to the Shoshone agency at Wind River shortly after he arrived in the territory.

Clearly, the stage was set for a clash between the Republican governor and the Democratic legislature when lawmakers convened in November, 1869. As T. A. Larson pointed out, Campbell vetoed a number of bills sent to him by the legislature, which in turn overrode his vetoes.[24] One such bill was a measure prohibiting "intermarriage between white persons and those of Negro or Mongolian blood," a measure in line with the Democrats' determination to prevent "mongrelization" by any means necessary. Campbell, however, declared that he was not sure "how far it may be expedient or well to attempt to govern social life and taste by legislative prohibitions." But, he reasoned, if it actually was desirable to prevent persons of different races from marrying, the bill as passed did not go far enough. It did not prohibit intermarriage between different kinds of nonwhite people. Indeed, the bill made no provision "to restrict the intermingling of the white race or any other race with the American race," by which last he meant indigenous people. Given the skewed sex ratio among emigrants and the presence of Indian communities in the territory, Campbell reasoned that "there have been and probably will be more marriages in this territory between Indians and whites, than between person of all other races combined."[25]

Although Democrats and Republicans might differ on the details, virtually all European and African American emigrants agreed on one thing: the right and duty of emigrants to settle the territory (or in other words, to displace indigenous occupants and replace them with Americans, preferably in family groups). By 1870, Wyoming Republicans adopted a platform repudiating the practice of making treaties with Indians as sovereign nations. Governor Campbell, knowing how little assistance would come from the government, asked the first legislature to pass a militia law so that citizens could organize in their own defense, but lawmakers adjourned without attending to that piece of business.

Samuel A. Bristol, editor of the *Wyoming Tribune,* was a Union veteran who had been captured at Chancellorsville and spent weeks in a Confederate prison. He was a staunch Republican and the brother-in-law of Secretary Edward M. Lee. He deplored the legislature's "leaving the people to the red men's tender mercies, except where U.S. troops happen to be stationed," and insisted that the people of Wyoming "desired to prepare themselves for future emergencies, and place themselves on a defensive *quasi* war footing."[26] For his part, the harried governor did what he could to honor treaty provisions, and when that failed, worked to get Indians to cede more land to prospectors, miners, and settlers who were already encroaching upon, fighting for, and squatting on lands legally in the hands of the Shoshones and Lakotas.[27]

In a landscape of constant conflict, it seems, then, that emigrants found some common ground. Whatever side they had taken during the war, and whatever views they held toward the Republican-controlled federal government, most everyone agreed that by right and by might, the territory belonged to the United States, that the permanent presence of American families signified destiny fulfilled and progress on the way, and that Indian peoples ought to be defeated, displaced, confined or eliminated. This slice of consensus led, in 1869, to a moment of paradoxical and unlikely agreement between antagonists, between most of the Democrats in the legislature and the Republican governor. And at that moment, women won the right to vote.

Just as the politics of black citizenship spanned the Civil War, so did the struggle for women's rights. Indeed, before Reconstruction, the histories of the organized movements for the abolition of slavery and emancipation of women twined together, though only a fraction of male abolitionists went so far as to embrace the struggle of their female comrades for full citizenship. But by the time Wyoming Territory was established, the two movements had parted company. Onetime allies of veteran abolitionist crusaders Elizabeth Cady Stanton and Susan B. Anthony had urged the women to postpone their own agenda, assuring them that their time would come, eventually. Abolitionists-cum-Radical Republicans did not want to jeopardize the party's program of pursuing full rights for African American men; woman suffrage struck some as a marginal matter, others as too extreme, and still others as a bad idea altogether.[28]

Thus Anthony and Stanton, feeling betrayed, sought backing for their efforts wherever they could find it. They turned to the eccentric Bostonian Democrat and shipping magnate George Francis Train to back their newspaper, the *Revolution,* and took to the lecture circuit to make the case for woman suffrage on the basis of race. Before the war, Stanton and Anthony—as well as most advocates of women's enfranchisement—had rested their arguments on justice, insisting that as human beings and as citizens women deserved equal rights with men. But now they changed tactics, leaning more heavily on the supposed special qualities of women embodied in the moral authority of true womanhood. They insisted that white women were at least as entitled to the vote as black men, because they were generally better educated and purportedly morally superior not only to African American men, but to all males, for that matter.[29]

The mails on the rails brought such ideas (including copies of the *Revolution*) to Wyoming Territory, and local newspapers devoted lots of ink to the national movement in 1868 and 1869. They noted meetings and speakers' appearances and excerpted and publicized suffragist publications around the nation. The *Frontier Index,* in an about-face from its earlier opposition to woman suffrage, avowed its approval of the *Revolution*'s campaign against "the smelliferous skullduggery being played by the niggeropolists" in Washington, and cheered: "Hip! hip! hip! hurrah for the telling efforts of the *Revolution.* God bless the ladies, may their noble, patriotic, honest influence bring our poor distracted country back to peace and *white* prosperity, and crown their own adorable sex with all the rights, immunities, privileges and marked honors the earth can bestow upon merit, purity, and shining Christianity.".[30]

The movement also reached Cheyenne in 1869 in the persons of two members of Anthony and Stanton's National Woman Suffrage Association. Missourian Redelia Bates, and the far better known Anna Dickinson, had taken up the taxing but increasingly common career for women as itinerant lecturers, braving the rigors of the road in the effort to make a living and to reach new audiences in seemingly unpromising places like Wyoming Territory.[31]

Some Wyomingites were receptive to the message, including a newly elected member of the territorial council, William H. Bright. Bright was a Democrat and a Mason, a popular man with his fellows. He had come to South Pass City with his wife and infant son, and though he represented the kind of family man who might hold the terrain for empire and civilization, he still struggled to make a living as a miner and saloonkeeper. When he announced, on November 12, 1869, that he intended to introduce a bill for woman suffrage, many of his fellow legislators were sure he was joking.[32]

Others assumed that his wife had put him up to the task. This Victorian couple seemed to take their manliness and womanliness seriously, and if they sometimes fell short of the ideal, it was not for lack of trying. A woman like Julia Bright, in favor of both suffrage and feminine deference, would not have dreamed of going public with her views, though she might well have pressed her ideas on her husband in private. The Republican justice John Kingman recalled later that Bright "did his wife's bidding," and that Bright's "character was not above reproach, but he had an excellent, well-informed wife and he was a kind, indulgent husband. In fact, he venerated his wife and submitted to her judgment and influence more willingly than one could have supposed, and she was in favor of woman suffrage."[33]

Kingman was a supporter of the measure, but even the leader of the legislative opposition, South Pass City representative Ben Sheeks, agreed that Julia Bright had, in the seemly way of deferential true women, manipulated her husband into introducing the measure. "Mrs. Bright," Sheeks wrote to historian Grace Raymond Hebard, "was a very womanly suffragist, and I always understood and still believe that it was through her influence that the bill was introduced. I know that I supposed at the time that she was the author of the bill. What reason, if any, I had for thinking so, I do not remember. Possibly it was only that she seemed intellectually and in education superior to Mr. Bright."[34]

Whatever Bright's motives, his fellow Democrats may have had any number of reasons to vote for the measure. Some may well have thought he was joking. Some may have wanted to embarrass Governor Campbell, whom they thought would surely be compelled to veto the measure. Some may have thought that passing such an unconventional law would be good publicity for the territory, and possibly inspire some white women to move west. And some may have believed that white women would vote their racial interests and thus support the Democratic Party. "Womanly" suffragists like Julia Bright, content to raise her baby and leave public business to her husband, gave lie to the argument that the vote would turn all women into Calamity Janes or, as Horace Walpole famously called Mary Wollstonecraft, "hyenas in petticoats" (and it seems that at least the newsmen of Wyoming were of the opinion that confinement to domesticity did not inhibit women from exhibiting combative behavior). And who is to know whether some of those legislators, on the morning of the vote, had done as they were bid in so many newspaper advertisements, and stopped off for a refreshing cocktail or two on the way to work?

Whatever their inclinations, territorial legislators evidently agreed on the benefits of attracting more white women to Wyoming, who would demonstrate with their very presence the permanence of American empire. Consequently and without much debate, Wyoming's first legislature passed a slate of women's rights measures, including laws giving married women control over their property and earnings, and mandating equal pay for women teachers. Of course, by 1869, teaching school had become a female-dominated profession, so the latter law was clearly a bid to recruit workers in the face of a labor scarcity. But advocates touted the former measure as particularly important to the enterprise of empire building. Recognizing women's right to acquire, hold, and use property on their own behalf was "eminently just," according to the *Cheyenne Leader,* and "is one of those rights which should be vouchsafed to women as protection from shiftless and improvident husbands. It is perhaps more necessary in this Territory than in a more settled state of society in the East. Men risk oftener their means in venturesome speculation than elsewhere."[35]

Not all Democrats were persuaded that woman suffrage implied white supremacy. In the legislative debate, Ben Sheeks mocked advocates by offering an amendment adding the phrase "all colored women and squaws" to the ranks of those to be enfranchised.[36] But Sheeks's amendment failed, and Bright's bill passed both houses, 7–4 with one abstention in the House, and 6–2, with one absent, in the council. Now it was up to Governor Campbell, who signed the bill on December 10, 1869. By the consent of a mere fourteen men, woman suffrage was established in Wyoming. Territorial Secretary Edward M. Lee predicted that women would now exercise the same "civilizing influence" on politics as they had at home. Wyoming had been "placed far in advance of every other political community on the subject of human rights," he wrote in the *Wyoming Tribune:* "That the policy of suffrage without regard to race or sex will ultimately be adopted by the entire nation may be regarded as no longer a matter of doubt, and to Wyoming belongs the proud privilege of pioneership in this grand modern reform.... Let fogyism, prejudice and caste find refuge among the *ghouls* of darkness and the dead past. Among the Rocky Mountains, seeking to establish an empire, we have inaugurated for the first time in history complete civil and political equality."[37]

What happened after the law was passed is a story for another time, though a few events underline the significance of empire to this excursion in liberty. The fragile coalition that had enfranchised Wyoming women began almost immediately to fall apart, in a hail of invective and dire predictions. As the railroad crews left the territory, and the mining boom busted, those who never meant to stay in Wyoming moved on. In 1871, when the legislature met again, the only man to return was Ben Sheeks. He led a successful campaign for a bill to repeal woman suffrage in Wyoming Territory, but Governor Campbell understood the historical significance of what Wyoming had done, however mixed the motives or motley the circumstances. Campbell vetoed the repeal. In his veto message, Campbell cited "certain universally admitted principles... which through the whole course of our national history have been powerfully and beneficially operative in making our institutions more and more popular, in framing laws more and more just." Campbell insisted that all citizens had a right to be represented in government and to be equal before the law, and he appealed to the guiding hand of experience in such matters. Echoing but going far beyond Locke and Jefferson, Campbell reasoned that woman suffrage was further fulfillment of the American ideal of "a government which 'derives all its just powers from the consent of the governed.'" And in phrases frankly borrowed from Jefferson's *Declaration of Independence,* Campbell insisted that "a regard for the genius of our institutions—for the fundamental principles of American autonomy—and for the immutable principles of right and justice, will not permit me to sanction this change."[38]

But in Campbell's stirring invocation of the long battle for ever-expanding liberty, there was also a strong nod to empire. Those who wanted to take the vote from women would "remand woman to that condition of tutelage and dependence which is her lot in all barbarous and uncivilized countries, and out of which she has been for eighteen centuries gradually but slowly emerging in all nations that have been blessed by the benign rays of a christian civilization."[39]

By the light of such stirring, disturbing folktales are families and communities dispossessed, territories expropriated and settled, liberties secured and smashed, rights won through wrongs.

NOTES

This chapter draws extensively from the chapter, "Empire, Liberty, and Legend: Woman Suffrage in Wyoming," in Virginia Scharff, *Twenty Thousand Roads: Women, Movement, and the West* (Berkeley: University of California Press, 2003).

1. The best analysis of the politics of woman suffrage in the period is still Ellen Carol Dubois, *Feminism and Suffrage: The Emergence of an Independent Women's Movement in America, 1848–1869* (Ithaca, NY: Cornell University Press, 1978).

2. See Elliott West, "Reconstructing Race," *Western Historical Quarterly* 34, no. 1 (Spring 2003): 6–26; and Heather Cox Richardson, *West from Appomattox: The Reconstruction of America after the Civil War* (New Haven: Yale University Press, 2007). Feminist scholars have explored the gendered, racial, and imperial politics of empire. See, for example, Ann Laura Stoler, "Making Empire Respectable: The Politics of Race and Sexual Morality in Twentieth-Century Colonial Cultures," *American Ethnologist* 16, no. 4 (1989): 634–60; Ann Laura Stoler, "Carnal Knowledge and Imperial Power: Gender, Race, and Morality in Colonial Asia," in *Gender at the Crossroads of Knowledge: Feminist Anthropology in the Postmodern Era,* ed. Micaela di Leonardo (Berkeley: University of California Press, 1991); Chandra Talpade Mohanty et al., eds., *Third World Women and the Politics of Feminism* (Bloomington: Indiana University Press, 1991); and Antoinette Burton, *Burdens of History: British Feminists, Indian Women, and Imperial Culture, 1865– 1915* (Chapel Hill: University of North Carolina Press, 1995). Scholars of race also

help us see Wyoming in a new light. See Peggy Pascoe, *Relations of Rescue: The Search for Female Moral Authority in the American West, 1874–1939* (New York: Oxford University Press, 1990); Alexander Saxton, *The Rise and Fall of the White Republic: Class, Politics, and Mass Culture in Nineteenth-Century America* (New York: Verso, 1990).

For diverse views of the story of woman suffrage in Wyoming, see Grace Raymond Hebard, "How Woman Suffrage Came to Wyoming" (1920), Box 6, Grace Raymond Hebard Collection, Acc. 8, American Heritage Center, University of Wyoming (hereafter cited as Hebard Papers); T. A. Larson, "Petticoats at the Polls: Woman Suffrage in Territorial Wyoming," *Pacific Northwest Quarterly* 44, no. 2 (April 1953): 74–78; T. A. Larson, "Dolls, Vassals, and Drudges: Pioneer Women of the West," *Western Historical Quarterly* 3, no. 1 (January 1972); T. A. Larson, *History of Wyoming* (Lincoln: University of Nebraska Press, 1978); Miriam Ganz Chapman, "The Story of Woman Suffrage in Wyoming, 1869–1890," MA thesis, University of Wyoming, 1952; Virginia Scharff, "The Case for Domestic Feminism: Woman Suffrage in Wyoming," *Annals of Wyoming* 56, no. 2 (Fall 1984): 29–37; Michael A. Massie, "Reform Is Where You Find It: The Roots of Woman Suffrage in Wyoming," *Annals of Wyoming* 62, no. 1 (Spring 1990): 2–21.

3. John R. Stilgoe, *Common Landscapes of America, 1580–1845* (New Haven: Yale University Press, 1982), 106–7. See also Peter S. Onuf, *Statehood and Union: A History of the Northwest Ordinance* (Bloomington: University of Indiana Press, 1987).

4. Richard White, *"It's Your Misfortune and None of My Own": A New History of the American West* (Norman: University of Oklahoma Press, 1991), 155–78.

5. Richard White, *Railroaded: The Transcontinentals and the Making of Modern America* (New York: Norton, 2011).

6. Larson, *History of Wyoming*, 36.

7. *Sweetwater Mines*, May 27, 1868. Microfilm in Coe Library, University of Wyoming, Laramie, Wyoming.

8. Barbara Welter, "The Cult of True Womanhood, 1820–1860," *American Quarterly* 18 (2):151–74.

9. Linda Kerber, in "Separate Spheres, Female Worlds, Woman's Place: The Rhetoric of Women's History," *Journal of American History* 75, no. 1 (June 1988): 9–39, demonstrated the problems with assuming that Victorians practiced what the preached. On prostitution in the West, see Anne M. Butler, *Daughters of Joy, Sisters of Misery: Prostitutes in the American West* (Urbana: University of Illinois Press, 1991); Marion Goldman, *Gold Diggers and Silver Miners: Prostitution and Social Life on the Comstock Lode* (Ann Arbor: University of Michigan Press, 1981); Paula M. Petrik, "Capitalists with Rooms: Prostitution in Helena, Montana, 1865–1900," *Montana: The Magazine of Western History* 31, no. 2 (Spring 1981): 28–41.

10. U.S. Department of the Interior, *Compendium of the Ninth Census (June 1, 1870)*, 372, 592. See also Wyoming Territory Manuscript Census 1870, American Heritage Center, University of Wyoming, Laramie.

11. Lola M. Homsher, ed., *South Pass, 1868* (Lincoln: University of Nebraska Press, 1978), 204; *Sweetwater Mines*, June 3, 1868.

12. *Sweetwater Mines,* December 30, 1868; January 9, 1869.
13. *Frontier Index,* June 5, 1868. On Calamity Jane, see James D. McLaird, *Calamity Jane: The Woman and the Legend* (Norman: University of Oklahoma Press, 2005), and a forthcoming biography by Richard W. Etulain.
14. *Sweetwater Mines,* March 28, 1868; *Frontier Index,* March 6, 1868, June 2, 1868. Microfilm in Coe Library, University of Wyoming, Laramie, Wyoming.
15. *Frontier Index,* June 5, 1868.
16. Homsher, ed., *South Pass,* 80–81, 104. See also Marjorie C. Trevor, "History of Carter-Sweetwater County, Wyoming, to 1875," MA thesis, University of Wyoming, 1954, 111–12.
17. *Frontier Index,* March 24, 1868; James Sherlock, *South Pass and Its Tales* (New York: Vantage Press, 1978), 44.
18. Sherlock, *South Pass and Its Tales,* 68–69.
19. *Sweetwater Mines,* April 4, 1868.
20. *Frontier Index,* August 18, 1868.
21. Ibid., April 21, 1868.
22. Ibid., May 30, 1868.
23. Carrie Chapman Catt and Nettie Rogers Shuler, *Woman Suffrage and Politics* (New York: Charles Scribner, 1923), 76.
24. Larson, *History of Wyoming,* 75–76.
25. *House Journal of the Legislative Assembly of the Territory of Wyoming,* 1st Sess., 1869 (Cheyenne: Tribune Office, 1870), 210, 262; *Council Journal of the Legislative Assembly of the Territory of Wyoming,* 1st Sess. (Cheyenne: Tribune Office, 1870), 79, 167. See also Roger D. Hardaway, "Prohibiting Interracial Marriage: Miscegenation Law in Wyoming," *Annals of Wyoming* 52, no. 1 (Spring 1980): 55–60. On miscegenation law more generally, see Peggy Pascoe, *What Comes Naturally: Miscegenation Law and the Making of America* (New York: Oxford University Press, 2010).
26. *Wyoming Tribune,* December 18, 1869. On S. A. Bristol, see *Wyoming Tribune,* April 9, 1920.
27. Campbell to Ely S. Parker, February 21, 1870, Records of the Office of Indian Affairs; *Wyoming Tribune,* January 29, 1871.
28. Again, see Dubois, *Feminism and Suffrage.*
29. This is not the place to rehash the historiography of the black freedom struggle, but for a fine recent study of the former see Stephen Kantrowitz, *More than Freedom: Fighting for Black Citizenship in a White Republic, 1829–1889* (New York: Penguin, 2012). The latter has an equally huge historiography, beginning with the multivolume narrative by Susan B. Anthony, Elizabeth Cady Stanton, and Matilda Joslyn Gage, *History of Woman Suffrage* (Rochester, NY: Charles Mann, 1887). Still unsurpassed, though usefully critiqued and revised, is Eleanor Flexner's pioneering, *Century of Struggle: The Woman's Rights Movement in the United States* (Cambridge, MA: Harvard University Press, 1959). Dubois, *Feminism and Suffrage,* detailed the connections between race and gender politics in the women's rights movement. The most recent major survey of the topic is Nancy F. Cott, *The Grounding of Modern*

Feminism (New Haven: Yale University Press, 1989). For the Wyoming case, see Scharff, "The Case for Domestic Feminism."

30. *Frontier Index,* March 6, 1868. Dubois, *Feminism and Suffrage,* chaps. 3 and 4, offers a detailed analysis of Stanton and Anthony's racist argument for white woman suffrage.

31. Larson, *History of Wyoming,* 81; Larson, "Dolls, Vassals, and Drudges"; Larson, "Petticoats at the Polls." See also G. Thomas Edwards, *Sowing Good Seeds: The Northwest Suffrage Campaigns of Susan B. Anthony* (Portland: Oregon Historical Society Press, 1990) and Dubois, *Feminism and Suffrage.* On Wyoming newspapers, see *Frontier Index,* March 6, March 24, June 5, November 13, 1868; *Sweetwater Mines,* December 2, December 5, December 23, 1868; *Cheyenne Leader,* November 22, November 24, December 2, December 10, 1869; *Wyoming Tribune,* December 4, 1869. See also Larson, *History of Wyoming,* 78–83.

32. Stanton, Anthony, and Gage, *History of Woman Suffrage,* vol. 3, 730.

33. Ibid.

34. Ben Sheeks to Grace Raymond Hebard, n.d. (1920?), Grace Raymond Hebard Papers, American Heritage Center, University of Wyoming, Laramie, Wyoming.

35. *Council Journal,* 1st Sess., 54, 66, 110, 121–23, 141, 155, 158, 188; *Cheyenne Leader,* November 10, 1869.

36. Larson, *History of Wyoming,* 78–83; Scharff, "Case for Domestic Feminism," 34; Massie, "Reform Is Where You Find It," 8–10.

37. Larson, *History of* Wyoming, 78–83; Wyoming *Tribune,* December 18, 1869.

38. *House Journal of the Legislative Assembly of the Territory of Wyoming,* 2nd Sess. (Cheyenne: Tribune Office, 1872), 112–18.

39. Ibid., 115.

ELEVEN

"Dis Land Which Jines Dat of Ole Master's"

THE MEANING OF CITIZENSHIP FOR THE CHOCTAW FREEDPEOPLE

Fay A. Yarbrough

"AFTER DE WAR I WAS WHAT YOU CALL a freedman. De Indians had to give all dey slaves forty acres of land. I'se allus lived on dis land which jines dat of Ole master's and I'se never stayed away from it long at a time." Thus did Frances Banks describe herself and the situation facing former slaves in Indian Territory when interviewed by a Works Progress Administration (WPA) field worker in 1938. Banks was born on a farm near Doaksville in the southeastern corner of the Choctaw Nation (in present-day Oklahoma) before the Civil War. Her parents had been held by the Wright family, whose prominent members included Allen Wright, principal chief of the Choctaws from 1866 to 1870.[1] Banks's short interview, barely a page, offers a provocative glimpse at slavery, emancipation, the Civil War era, and Reconstruction from a less familiar vantage point: Indian Territory.

The indigenous peoples living in Indian Territory did not consider themselves a part of the United States. Rather, they functioned as individual sovereign nations with constitutions and governments.[2] These Indian nations threatened American national sovereignty in the antebellum period in ways that were similar to those discussed by Gregory P. Downs in his chapter in this volume. Several of these nations did adopt the institution of enslaving people of African descent, and some individual Indians practiced large-scale plantation agriculture. Questions about the legitimacy of slavery in the United States, then, had consequences for the Indian nations west of the Mississippi River. In the end, U.S. officials negotiated a treaty with the Choctaws in 1866 that included provisions for granting the Choctaw freedpeople citizenship in the Choctaw Nation, civil rights, including the vote as well as access to land, something that the federal government neglected to do for its own ex-slave population in the South. But the Choctaw Nation evaded these measures, creating regulations only for its enactment in their tribal Freedman's Bill of 1883. Thus, it was not only federal and state authorities who struggled to determine the place of formerly enslaved people in U.S. society; the Civil War forced Native nations to address this question as well.

This chapter considers how slavery was structured in the Choctaw Nation and how former slaves of Choctaw Indians, and in the Indian Territory more generally, experienced emancipation and Reconstruction, utilizing the memories of these events recorded in the WPA slave narratives.[3] These former slaves often described owners and overseers and the announcement of emancipation in language very similar to that of those familiar with the accounts of ex-slaves from the Confederate states. Where their accounts differ markedly, however, is in their access to land once the Civil War ended and the process of Reconstruction began: the former slaves of Native peoples in Indian Territory gained rights to land, while those from the southern states did not.

Property ownership, however, did not necessarily improve the political or legal status of the freedmen in Indian Territory. In part, this story reveals Choctaw lawmakers' attempts to determine the status of people of African descent in the nation through legislative activity during the larger nineteenth century, a time in which the Choctaw Nation struggled with dramatic internal and external upheaval. As it turns out, Choctaw officials opposed the extension of full citizenship rights to their former slaves almost as fiercely as many white southerners did.

During the 1830s, the Choctaw Nation experienced the trauma of forced relocation from their territory in the southeastern United States (which had included a large diagonal swath of central Mississippi territory extending from the northwest to the southeast and including a small portion of the present-day state of Alabama) to the Indian Territory, some 550 miles away.[4] Choctaw slaveholders brought their human property on this journey. There, the Choctaws established a government "not inconsistent with the constitution, Treaties and laws of the United States."[5] Within that bureaucracy, four branches shared power: the legislative, executive, judiciary, and military. The General Council, composed of forty annually elected representatives, formed the legislative branch, whose members debated and passed legislation. All voters and representatives were male Choctaw citizens. Four district chiefs made up the executive branch, which was responsible for approving or rejecting proposed legislation, notifying the council about the affairs in each district, and enforcing the laws. The judiciary included both supreme and district courts that oversaw civil and criminal matters. And finally, an elected general from each district served in the military department. In the event of an invasion or the outbreak of war (for instance, the Choctaws had battled against the Chickasaws and Creeks in the past), the district general commanded the district military force.[6] The constitution also included a Declaration of Rights very similar to the American Bill of Rights.[7] It was within this larger legal apparatus and with the constitution as a foundation that the Choctaw Nation produced legislation regarding people of African descent.

European traders and settlers introduced the Choctaws to African slaves as early as the 1720s, and census materials demonstrate that some Choctaws adopted the peculiar institution by the nineteenth century.[8] A census conducted by the U.S. government in 1831 in preparation for removing the Choctaws to Indian Territory listed 17,963 Indians, 151 white persons, and 521 slaves.[9] Just eight years later in 1839, there were approximately 600 slaves of African descent living among the Choctaws.[10] And by 1860, black slaves made up 14 percent of the population of the Choctaw Nation.[11] Slaves in the nation performed agricultural labor and, when fluent in both English and Choctaw, served as interpreters for their Choctaw slaveholders.[12] Like their counterparts elsewhere in the American South, Choctaw slaveholders carefully circumscribed the behavior of their human property by enacting legislation that prevented slaves from owning property or carrying guns without permission from their owners and that prohibited the education of bondspeople.[13]

These Choctaw statutes were indicative of a larger unwillingness to include people of African descent in the polity and prescribed the place of people of African descent in the Choctaw Nation. For instance, Choctaws did not want people of African descent who were not slaves to reside in the nation unless they were also of Choctaw or Chickasaw descent. As their constitution stated, "No free negro, or any part negro, unconnected with Choctaw and Chickasaw blood, shall be permitted to come and settle in the Choctaw Nation."[14] Although the General Council had the authority to "naturalize and adopt as citizens of this Nation any Indian or descendant of other Indian tribes," people of African descent could not access Choctaw citizenship in this manner.[15] Thus, the people of African descent who remained in the Choctaw Nation after the passage of this constitution were slaves by default unless they also had a "blood" connection to the tribe. Free people of mixed Choctaw and African ancestry who resided in the nation could be recognized as citizens and, if male, could vote in elections after age sixteen and serve on juries; however, "No person who is any part negro shall ever be allowed to hold any office under this government."[16] Restrictions on office holding for people of African descent and on their residence in the nation would persist throughout the nineteenth century in the Choctaw Nation.

Choctaw officials also prohibited relationships between peoples of African descent and Choctaw citizens at the same moment that authorities were crafting increasingly complicated legislation to regulate marriages between Choctaw women and white men. In 1838, just two years after the General Council began outlining the proper procedure for white men to marry Choctaw women, the council also stated that "if any person or persons, citizens of this Nation, shall publicly take up with a negro slave, he or she so offending shall be liable to pay a fine not less than ten dollars nor exceeding twenty five dollars—and shall be separated."[17] A second offense warranted a penalty of between five and thirty-nine lashes on the bare back as well as forced separation.

The council did not stipulate a punishment for the "negro slave" partner who violated this act. Perhaps the authorities thought that the Choctaw partner was more culpable or assumed that slaveholders would punish the slave for violating this statute. The council also did not assume the gender of the Choctaw offender. The target of this statute was not fornication or cohabitation; the statute punished only the Choctaw participant in the relationship, not both parties, as one generally finds in a fornication or cohabitation statute.[18] Furthermore, in practice the law banned marriage between Choctaw citizens and slaves of African descent because of the presumption that married couples cohabitate.

As historian Peggy Pascoe points out in her larger study of miscegenation in the United States, "Laws against interracial marriage didn't prevent masters from having sex with slave women or having mixed race children, both of which were common occurrences. Rather, they prevented masters from turning slaves they slept with into respectable wives who might claim freedom, demand citizenship rights, or inherit property, and so undermine the foundations of racialized slavery."[19] This proved to be true in Indian Territory as well. WPA field worker Bradley Bolinger interviewed Peggy McKinney

Brown, who claimed to be a young woman at the time of the Civil War: "Her appearance told me that she is a mixed breed. She told me personally herself that her master, Jesse McKinney, was her father and also her master." Brown described Jesse McKinney as one-half Choctaw, and related that her master "had no regard for himself or any of the negro slave women, especially if they were of pleasant looks. He did not hesitate to bring half-breed children into the world."[20] The Choctaw legal statute, then, did not prevent Jesse McKinney from having sex with Brown's mother or with other enslaved women, but it did mean Brown was illegitimate and her mother would remain enslaved.

On the surface, the 1838 statute simply banned a particular type of relationship; however, the law revealed a great deal about nascent ideas regarding "race" in the Choctaw Nation. At the heart of this prohibition on relationships between "negro" slaves and Choctaw citizens was the question of whether it was the "negro" slave's African ancestry or slave status that was so objectionable. Combined with the earlier constitutional provisions that excluded people of African descent from public office and prevented free people of African descent from settling in the nation, the logical conclusion is that it was their African ancestry that made slaves unacceptable as sexual partners.

The constitution's refusal to permit free people of African descent to settle in the nation also meant the vast majority of people of African descent in the nation were slaves; in effect, then, the statute outlawed cohabitation between the African-descended and citizen population in the nation. As written, the law would permit the few Choctaw citizens of mixed African and Indian ancestry who did remain in the Choctaw Nation to live with Choctaw Indians as man and wife, an exemption suggesting that the importance of the connection to Choctaw identity retained some strength and that ideas about "race" had not fully hardened. This law demonstrates that Choctaw Indians had ideas about what it meant to be of African descent in the United States, and that Choctaws wanted to distance themselves from that identity and its ramifications.

As debate over the expansion of slavery came to dominate American politics in the antebellum era, indigenous groups such as the Choctaws refused at first to side with the southern states or tried to maintain neutrality. As late as April 1861, prominent Choctaw statesman Peter Pitchlynn remained convinced that the Choctaws should continue to ally with the federal government. At the very least, Pitchlynn and other Choctaws feared that the Lincoln administration would refuse to pay net proceeds funds due to the

Choctaws because of previous land cession treaties should the nation side with the Confederacy. Principal Chief George Hudson was poised to recommend neutrality in the war at a special session of the council that spring, but not everyone within the Choctaw Nation agreed. In anticipation of Hudson's remarks, Robert M. Jones, a wealthy Choctaw slaveholder, declared that those who opposed the Confederate secession should be hanged. White southerners in nearby states also weighed in and made ominous threats against those who did not support the Confederate cause. In the face of this opposition, Chief Hudson changed course and urged the council to side squarely with the South.[21]

Thus committed to the Confederacy, the Choctaw Nation allocated money and troops to the war effort.[22] Choctaw legislative documents from the era reveal that lawmakers spent a great deal of time talking about their alliance with the Confederate States of America. Choctaw legal authorities even passed a measure demanding that all whites living within the Choctaw Nation swear allegiance to the Confederate cause. They then deemed any criticism of the Confederacy or its Army to be a form of treason against the Choctaw Nation and punishable by death. Lawmakers raised an infantry force, and later a cavalry, to fight with the Confederate forces.[23]

Given that Indian removal had occurred just a few decades prior to the war, and at the urging of southern governments, one might find Choctaw support of the Confederacy puzzling. Three points help explain the Choctaw decision: first, removal policy fell under the purview of the federal government, so Native groups did not solely blame southern states for their relocation; second, groups such as the Choctaw also held a vested interest in the preservation of the institution of slavery; and third, and perhaps most important, some Native groups found room within the rhetoric about states' rights for claims to Native sovereignty.

Though indigenous groups such as the Choctaws as well as others in the Indian Territory offered support for the Confederacy, President Lincoln did not mention the territory or its indigenous populations when he penned the Emancipation Proclamation. As historian Claudio Saunt noted, it was unclear even among federal officials if the Thirteenth Amendment applied to the Indian Territory.[24] And slave owners in the territory were not always forthcoming with news about emancipation. For instance, Mollie Barber's mother was a slave in the Creek Nation and learned about freedom from a serendipitous conversation with a passerby. She had been cooking dinner for her mistress, but upon learning of her freedom, "she run back in de house, grab up what little clothes she had, made a bundle and leave dat place wid de dinner 'most ready. Bless her old black heart! She was glad to be free!"[25] At the same time, other masters did inform their slaves of emancipation and held true to their obligation to release these people from bondage. Mary Lindsay's Chickasaw mistress informed Lindsay and another household slave of their freedom: "She say, 'You and Vici jest as free as I am. . . .'"[26] She then offered the women room, board, and several dresses if the freedwomen continued to work for her.

Former slaves from Indian Territory and southern states repeated similar stories of former slaveholders using this kind of phrasing, "as free as I am." For instance, Phyllis Petite, Sina Banks, L. B. Barner, and Doc Daniel Dowdy each recalled owners using similar language when the owners gathered slaves together to inform them of emancipation.[27] This language underscores the very personal terms in which masters saw freedom and how they understood its meanings in juxtaposition to slavery. That is, freedom took on a very specific meaning (freedom to move, freedom to control one's family, freedom to choose one's labor) in a landscape that included chattel slavery.

Sarah Wilson's Cherokee owner Ben Johnson also told his slaves of emancipation, but reluctantly. Johnson received word of emancipation from Fort Smith, Arkansas, but because of his illiteracy he asked his daughter to read the letter aloud: "He went wild and jumped on her and beat the devil out of her. Said she was lying to him. It near about killed him to let us loose, but he cooled down after awhile and said he would help us all get back home if we wanted to come."[28] Wilson described her former master as a hellion; however, despite his resentment for this change in status for his human property, he honored it all the same. Wilson's account also reveals the attachment many slave owners, even those in Indian Territory, had to the institution of slavery: Johnson beat his own daughter when she relayed the news of emancipation. Johnson was convinced that his daughter must be lying; a world without slaves must have seemed inconceivable to him.

Some former slaves in Indian Territory were quite specific about the date of their freedom. Sally Henderson Moss remembered that Choctaw freedmen celebrated emancipation on August 4, the date that the Choctaws freed their slaves, according to Moss.[29] Similarly, Cherokee freedman R. C. Smith also linked emancipation to August 4, 1866.[30] Curiously, Smith did not invoke February 1863, the date when the Cherokee General Council abolished slavery in the Cherokee Nation, as the moment of his emancipation. This likely reflects the division among the Cherokees: the nation officially sided with the Confederacy in 1861, but many nation members then fought with the Union Army, and Confederate Cherokees refused to recognize legislation passed by Union sympathizers within Cherokee officialdom.[31] Moss and Smith might have been referencing the August date rather than the issuance of the Emancipation Proclamation or the ratification of the Thirteenth Amendment because the summer of 1866 coincided with the ratification of the Treaty of 1866 for the various Native groups in Indian Territory who sided with the Confederacy during the Civil War. The stipulations of the treaties included the abolition of slavery among Confederate Indians.

Former slaves differed in their descriptions of what emancipation meant to them individually, and this variation was similar both among the former slaves of Indian Territory and those from nearby southern states. Such former slaves as the father of Paul Garnett Roebuck, who had been a slave among the Choctaw and Chickasaw Indians, told their children that emancipation did not mean a change in their treatment: they had been treated well under slavery and continued to receive fair treatment from their former owners' families after the Civil War.[32] Matilda Poe experienced better material conditions as a slave in the Chickasaw Nation than as a freedwoman: "I never did know I was a slave, 'cause I couldn't tell I wasn't free. I always had a good time, didn't have to work much, and allus had something to eat and wear and that was better than it is with me now."[33] Eliza Evans went so far as to assert that John Mixon's slaves did not want to be freed and they hated Yankee soldiers.[34]

These descriptions of slavery in the Indian Territory as less harsh and exploitative have contributed to the notion that Indian slaveholders were kinder than their southern brethren. And again, particularly in the narratives collected by the WPA in the era of the Great Depression, one must take into consideration the contemporary circumstances of the ex-slave informants.[35] William Walters, who had been a slave in Tennessee, did not have much patience for such talk: "Those were awful times. Yet I have heard many of the older Negroes say the old days were better. Such talk always seemed to be but an expression of sentiment for some good old master, or else the older Negroes were just too handicapped with ignorance to recognize the benefits of liberty or the opportunities of freedom."[36]

Kiziah Love described her Choctaw owner Frank Colbert as fairly kind, yet she reveled in news of her freedom nonetheless: "I was glad to be free. What did I do and say. Well I jest clapped my hands together and said, 'Thank God Almighty, I'se free at last!'"[37] Henry Bibb, author of the famous autobiography that poignantly depicts the impact of slavery on family relationships, described his Cherokee master as humane and stated that Indian masters offered adequate food and clothing and better treatment to their slaves than did their white counterparts.[38] Yet even Bibb, after his owner's passing, could only pretend "to be taking on at a great rate about his death," while Bibb was actually more excited about planning his escape.[39] Lizzie Jackson, formerly a slave in the Creek Nation, offered a succinct assessment: "I'm glad that slave days is gone. Even if the master was good the slaves was bad off."[40] As scholars such as Claudio Saunt, Rudi Halliburton, Celia Naylor, and Barbara Krauthamer have argued convincingly, indigenous slaveholders and white slaveholders had much in common, and their treatment of their human property could range from cruel to kind, which is reflected in the comments of former slaves about the meanings of emancipation.[41]

In the wake of the Confederacy's defeat, Choctaw authorities strained against federal demands during Reconstruction just as their white southern brethren did. In treaty discussions in 1866, the federal government, as it did with the South, required the Choctaw Nation to accept its newly emancipated slaves as citizens with political and civil rights in the nation.[42] The Choctaw Nation balked at this condition and requested that the federal government remove the freedmen from their territory.[43] Indeed, as Martha A. Sandweiss discusses in her chapter in this volume, U.S. General John B. Sanborn described many Choctaws as having a "violent prejudice" against their former slaves. The federal government did not comply with the Choctaw request, and for nearly twenty years, the freedmen in the Choctaw Nation existed in a kind of legal limbo. During this time, Choctaw authorities treated the freedmen as white American citizens, and as such, the freedmen generally fell under the legal jurisdiction of federal courts.

Likewise, the Choctaw Nation did not provide any schools for the children of freedpeople, which induced federal authorities to do so. However, by common assent Choctaws permitted the freedmen to cultivate as much land as they desired in the nation, in spite of the fact that the 1866 treaty required only that freedmen receive forty acres.[44] This figure resonated with the idea of "forty acres and a mule" and subsequent misunderstandings about General William Tecumseh Sherman's Special Field Order #15 of January 1865, but it is unclear if either the federal authorities or Choctaw officials had been referencing Sherman's order during treaty negotiations. The time lag between the 1866 Treaty and the formal adoption of the freedmen into the Choctaw

Nation was due, in part, to the reluctance of the Choctaws to accept their former chattel as citizens.

The Choctaws' Freedmen Bill of 1883 finally clarified the status of the roughly 3,500 Choctaw freedmen and enumerated their rights in the nation.[45] The freedmen gained citizenship rights, including suffrage; the right to equal process in civil and criminal matters in the Choctaw courts; forty acres of land to be held in the manner of other Choctaws (though other Choctaws held land communally and could improve as much land as they wished); equal educational opportunities; and the right to hold political offices in the nation, other than principal or district chief.[46] The freedmen were not entitled, however, to any annuity monies from previous treaty agreements or access to the public domain of the nation, which would have meant they could receive payments for future land cessions.[47] Nor could freedmen confer Choctaw citizenship on others through marriage.[48] Those freedmen who chose to leave the nation were entitled to $100.[49] Before the end of 1883, the law was tightened: the General Council voted to revoke the freedmen's right to hold any political offices whatsoever.[50]

Although Choctaw freedmen lacked the full legal and political rights of Choctaw citizens by blood, their access to land was a concrete and significant benefit of citizenship, one that the former slaves in southern states lacked and desperately wanted.[51] Sally Henderson Moss recalled that her stepfather Robert Wright had a right to land in the Choctaw Nation as a freedman.[52] Squire Hall and his wife both received freedmen allotments "partly in the rich land of the Arkansas River bottom and the remainder on the high ground which skirts the valley land."[53] Robert Lewis stated, "I had a lot of relatives there who owned quite a bit of land that they had been allotted; they were freedmen."[54] While the Choctaw Freedman's Bill confirmed the forty acres specified in the 1866 treaty, once again the source of the amount of land stipulated is uncertain. Perhaps more pertinent is that this number was only one-quarter of the territory allotted to heads of households by the Homestead Act of 1862 and that Choctaw Indians did not have any restrictions placed on the amount of land they could improve in the nation at that time.

Land ownership by freedpeople had implications for their offspring as well: children could inherit the property or the land right. Lula Neighbors lived on land she accessed through her mother, a Choctaw freedwoman: "This forty acres where I live now was given to me after statehood; it is my claim. I have a 'right' from Mother's being a freedwoman."[55] Similarly, Thomas Franklin described his mother as "slave-Choctaw" and stated,

"When I was born in 1873, I became a member of the tribe and years later I received an allotment of forty acres in Garvin County."[56] And there were greater consequences for this distribution of land to freedpeople in Indian Territory: some of these allotments would become the basis of the creation of all-black towns such as Boley in Oklahoma in the early twentieth century.[57] Alas, the colored population did not always manage to maintain title: Matthew Maytubbie was born in 1889, not long after the passage of the Freedmen Bill. In the WPA interviews he noted with chagrin: "We all had land given us by the government but fiddled it away drinking and gambling. My pappy didn't drink and I wish I didn't."[58] The inability to retain possession of allotments was part of a larger pattern of American Indian land loss because of federal policy. Tribal groups controlled 138 million acres of land in the nineteenth century prior to allotment, but by the time of the Indian Reorganization Act in 1934, shortly before many of the WPA interviews were recorded, Native people held just 55 million acres.[59]

White Americans had long recognized the possibility of improving one's economic standing by marrying Native women to gain access to land, and some commented on how the former slaves of Indian masters also had a right to land.[60] For some African Americans from southern states, the ability of the freedmen to access land suggested that there was more opportunity for people of color in general in Indian Territory.[61] Lula Neighbors' African American father was a "state man" who moved to Choctaw Nation from Georgia: "When he saw that the Civil War was over he decided to come west where colored people were given a better chance to make a living. He came to the Choctaw Nation and married my mother, a freedwoman."[62] This marriage enabled Neighbors's father to access landownership more readily than would have been possible in Georgia. Lucy Cherry's mother moved to Indian Territory from Alabama after emancipation and married William Crush, a Choctaw Indian.[63] One cannot help but wonder if the attraction of this move for Cherry's mother, just as it was for Neighbors's father, was the perception that conditions for freedpeople might be better in Indian Territory.

Alice Alexander had been a slave in Louisiana and walked to Oklahoma with her husband and other freedmen "in search of education.... We come to Oklahoma looking for de same thing then that darkies go North looking fer now. But we got disappointed."[64] Alexander and her fellow freedmen were likely unaware of the resistance Native groups displayed toward incorporating their former slaves into society and their unwillingness to provide schools for the colored population immediately after the war, whether newly arrived or long established. Upon passage of the Freedmen Bill, Choctaw authorities created neighborhood schools and later a boarding school for their former slaves; however, colored citizens would later complain to American officials about the inadequacy of such institutions.[65]

The rights articulated in the Freedmen Bill were an obvious improvement in the condition of the former slaves of the Choctaw Nation, but they also exposed the continuing resistance of the Choctaw Nation to fully incorporate their ex-slaves into Choctaw society. Choctaw authorities simultaneously declared that the freedmen possessed "all the rights, priviliges *[sic]* and immunities" of Choctaw citizens, but then carefully circumscribed those rights.[66] And freedmen citizenship rights did not extend to their spouses, who were obligated, in the case of men, to obtain permits to reside in the nation "and allowed to remain during good behavior only."[67] The language of this limit on freedmen's ability to bestow Choctaw citizenship on their spouses assumed that such spouses would not be Choctaw, further ensuring that a larger population of people of African descent would not be incorporated into the Choctaw Nation. This lengthy process of granting incomplete rights to the freedpeople of the Choctaw Nation, coupled with its continuous renegotiation of terms, demonstrates the lack of enthusiasm with which the Choctaws approached the project of reconstruction foisted upon them by the federal government.

In 1885, not long after the Choctaw freedmen had received civil as well as some political rights in the nation, the Choctaw legislature passed a marriage act to further clarify the freedmen's new rights. The legislation declared simply, "It shall not be lawful for a Choctaw and a negro to marry." Choctaw men or women who violated this statute faced felony charges in Choctaw circuit court and, if found guilty, received fifty lashes on the bare back.[68] Although the freedmen might have obtained Choctaw citizenship, participated in the Choctaw courts as legal actors, and voted in Choctaw elections, they could not legally marry Choctaw Indians. In the language of the day, civil and political equality might be permissible, but social equality was not. Perhaps Choctaw lawmakers limited the rights they extended to the freedmen because they were all too aware that "debates about the status of the freedmen inflected conversations about the Indians" in the federal context, as both Martha Sandweiss and Joshua Paddison suggest in their chapters in this volume. The Choctaw wanted to sharpen the distinction between themselves and formerly enslaved peoples.

By 1886, the General Council passed an act to define "the quantity of blood necessary for citizenship." Quite tellingly, the act stipulated that "all applicants for rights in this Nation shall prove their mixture of blood to be white and Indian."[69] Though the act did not apply to those who were already citizens in the Choctaw Nation, it did mean that in the future people of Choctaw and African ancestry could not claim Choctaw citizenship, a departure from older practice that would have permitted such individuals with blood ties to Choctaw Nation members to access citizenship. So though emancipation led to a limited form of citizenship for freedpeople in both the Choctaw Nation and the American South, in Indian Territory this citizenship came with land, something for which most former slaves in the United States could only wish. And yet this land did not come with equality.[70] Former South Carolina slave "Uncle" George G. King's words proved true both for freedpeople in Indian Territory and the American South, whether they owned land or not: "The Master says we are all free, but it don't mean we is white. And it don't mean we is equal."[71]

The Civil War and Reconstruction raised fundamental questions about the meaning of citizenship in both the United States and for Indian nations. The era's attempted legal resolutions continue to reverberate today, as descendants of Choctaw freedpeople currently cannot obtain citizenship in the Choctaw Nation unless they can demonstrate descent from an individual enrolled by the Dawes Commission as a "by blood" member of the Choctaw Nation.[72] Similar requirements have led some descendants of people enslaved by indigenous masters in the larger Indian Territory—specifically in the Cherokee and Seminole Nations—to pursue legal action to gain full citizenship rights in their respective nations.[73] Just as in the nineteenth century, the question of who should determine the citizenship status of former slaves and their descendants in indigenous nations continues to raise uncomfortable questions about governmental authority, native sovereignty, and race.

NOTES

I thank Adam Arenson in particular for his careful reading of my work and the other contributors to this volume for the stimulating and helpful conversations about this chapter.

1. T. Lindsay Baker and Julie P. Baker, eds., *The WPA Oklahoma Slave Narratives* (Norman: University of Oklahoma Press, 1996), 28–29.

2. Many contemporary members of indigenous groups continue to argue for Native rights as separate, sovereign entities. For example, see Susan A. Miller, *Coacoochee's Bones: A Seminole Saga* (Lawrence: University Press of Kansas, 2003), xii.

3. I draw particularly on the WPA narratives collected from informants living in the state of Oklahoma, which capture the experiences both of enslaved people owned by members of Indian nations and those former slaves owned by American citizens. I supplement these narratives with Indian Pioneer History (IPH) interviews of residents of Indian Territory also conducted during the 1930s in an initiative similar to the collection of the slave narratives. To be sure, the WPA slave narratives have their problems, as do all sources, but they remain one of the few connections to an otherwise almost silent mass of people, a population legally prohibited from accessing literacy to record their own experiences. For more on the controversy surrounding the use of the narratives, see C. Vann Woodward, "History from Slave Sources," *American Historical Review* 79 (April 1974): 472; Elizabeth Fox-Genovese, *Within the Plantation Household: Black and White Women of the Old South* (Chapel Hill: University of North Carolina Press, 1988), 32–34; James Mellon, *Bullwhip Days: The Slaves Remember* (New York: Weidenfeld & Nicolson, 1988), xvi-xviii; Marion Wilson Starling, *The Slave Narrative: Its Place in American History*, 2nd ed. (Washington, DC: Howard University Press, 1988), especially chap. 4; David Thomas Bailey, "A Divided Prism: Two Sources of Black Testimony on Slavery," *Journal of Southern History* 46 (August 1980): 381–404; Donna J. Spindel, "Assessing Memory: Twentieth-Century Slave Narratives Reconsidered," *Journal of Interdisciplinary History* 27 (Autumn 1996): 247–61; Paul D. Escott, *Slavery Remembered: A Record of Twentieth-Century Slave Narratives* (Chapel Hill: University of North Carolina Press, 1979), 7–13; Frances Smith Foster, *Witnessing Slavery: The Development of Antebellum Slave Narratives*, 2nd ed. (Madison: University of Wisconsin Press, 1994), especially chaps. 4 and 7; and John Sekora and Darwin T. Turner's edited volume of essays, *The Art of the Slave Narrative: Original Essays in Criticism and Theory* (Macomb: Western Illinois University Press, 1982).

4. Muriel H. Wright, "The Removal of the Choctaws to the Indian Territory 1830–1833," *Chronicles of Oklahoma* 6 (1928): 110.

5. *The Constitution and Laws of the Choctaw Nation*, vol. XIII of *The Constitution and Laws of the American Indian Tribes Series* (1840; reprint, Wilmington: Scholarly Resources, 1975), 3. Hereafter referred to as CLCN XIII.

6. CLCN XIII: 5–10, articles II-VI. These articles stipulate the distribution of powers as well as the duties of each branch of the government. For a discussion of warfare between Choctaws and various groups, see Angie Debo, *The Rise and Fall of the Choctaw Republic* (Norman: University of Oklahoma Press, 1934), 27–31, or Patricia Galloway, *Choctaw Genesis, 1500–1700* (Lincoln: University of Nebraska Press, 1995).

7. CLCN XIII: 4–5, art. I.

8. Michelene E. Pesantubbee, *Choctaw Women in a Chaotic World: The Clash of Cultures in the Colonial Southeast* (Albuquerque: University of New Mexico Press, 2005), 97. Jesse O. McKee and Jon A. Schlenker find that most Choctaw were aware of enslaved Africans by 1750, *The Choctaws: Cultural Evolution of a Native American Tribe* (Jackson: University Press of Mississippi, 1980), 39.

9. Arthur H. DeRosier Jr., *The Removal of the Choctaw Indians* (Knoxville: University of Tennessee Press, 1970), 137.
10. McKee and Schlenker, *The Choctaws*, 120–21.
11. William Loren Katz, *Black Indians: A Hidden Heritage* (New York: Athenaeum, 1986), 135.
12. Mary Cole claimed to have learned the Choctaw language before she learned to speak English, Indian Pioneer History Collection, Roll 33, vol. 100, 56–59. Paul Garnett Roebuck's grandfather, a slave, acted as an interpreter for Choctaw and Chickasaw Indians in federal court at Paris, Texas, Roll 27, vol. 81, 438–41. The Indian Pioneer History Collection is available at the Oklahoma Historical Society and hereafter is referred to as IPH.
13. CLCN XIII: 19 and 20–21.
14. CLCN XIII: 11, sec. 6. The Choctaw and Chickasaw Indians have a shared history, sometimes contentious, that includes an origin story that accounts for their separation into two nations. The Chickasaws also formed a district in the Choctaw Nation from 1837 to 1855 through treaty agreements that accounts for this exception in the provision. See DeRosier, *The Removal of the Choctaw Indians*, 6–7; Tom Mould, *Choctaw Tales* (Jackson: University of Mississippi, 2004), 71–72; H. B. Cushman, *History of the Choctaw, Chickasaw and Natchez Indians*, ed. Angie Debo (Norman, University of Oklahoma Press, 1999), 18–21; Clara Sue Kidwell's *Choctaws and Missionaries in Mississippi, 1818–1918* (Norman: University of Oklahoma Press, 1995), 10; Debo, *The Rise and Fall of the Choctaw Republic*, 71; and McKee and Schlenker, *The Choctaws*, 84–87. The Treaty of 1855 more clearly defined the relationship between the Choctaw and Chickasaw Nations so that each could establish a separate government, see Debo, *The Rise and Fall of the Choctaw Republic*, 71–73; Kidwell, *Choctaws and Missionaries*, 173–74; and Grant Foreman, *The Five Civilized Tribes* (Norman: University of Oklahoma Press, 1934), 130–32.
15. CLCN XIII: 12, sec. 15.
16. CLCN XIII: 6, sec. 7 and 12, sec. 14. See p. 9, sec. 6, regarding jury service. The language about jury service is a little less clear about the age and gender of jury members; however sec. 5 refers to the district court judges' ability to call "jury men," and it seems unlikely those citizens who could not yet vote would be permitted to serve on juries.
17. CLCN XIII, 27–28.
18. Kirsten Fischer, *Suspect Relations: Sex, Race, and Resistance in Colonial North Carolina* (Ithaca, NY: Cornell University Press, 2002), 102–3. See also Peter Wallenstein, *Tell the Court I Love My Wife: Race, Marriage, and Law—an American History* (New York: Palgrave MacMillan, 2002), 116.
19. Peggy Pascoe, *What Comes Naturally: Miscegenation Law and the Making of Race in America* (New York: Oxford University Press, 2009), 27.
20. IPH Roll 6, vol. 16: 476–81. Bradley Bolinger interviewed Charley Moore Brown and his mother Peggy McKinney Brown.
21. W. David Baird, *Peter Pitchlynn: Chief of the Choctaws* (Norman: University of Oklahoma Press, 1972), 126–27.

22. Debo, *The Rise and Fall of the Choctaw Republic*, chap. 4, esp. 80–83; Kidwell, *Choctaws and Missionaries*, 170 and 174; and Choctaw Nation Records Roll CTN 8, vol. 295: 32 and 229 and Roll CTN 8, vol. 297: 279. The Choctaw Nation Records are available at the Oklahoma Historical Society and hereafter are referred to as CNR.

23. CNR Roll CTN 16, Document 18302: 238, 251–52, 254–56, 289, 301–2, and 322.

24. Claudio Saunt, *Black, White, and Indian: Race and the Unmaking of an American Family* (New York: Oxford University Press, 2005), 114.

25. Baker and Baker, *Oklahoma Slave Narratives*, 44.

26. Ibid., 251.

27. Ibid., 319, 40, 61, and 130. Petite had been a slave in the Cherokee Nation. Banks was enslaved in Missouri. Barner was born in Texas nine years before the Civil War. And Dowdy was a slave from Georgia.

28. Ibid., 497–98.

29. IPH Roll 36, vol. 108: 465–73.

30. Baker and Baker, *Oklahoma Slave Narratives*, 401.

31. Annie Heloise Abel, *The American Indian as Slaveholder and Secessionist* (Lincoln: University of Nebraska Press, 1992), see chap. 4 for an extensive discussion of the alliances made between the Confederacy and various tribes in Indian Territory.

32. IPH Roll 27, vol. 81: 438–48, see 442–43.

33. Baker and Baker, *Oklahoma Slave Narratives*, 325–26.

34. Ibid., 146.

35. Stephanie J. Shaw, "Using the WPA Ex-Slave Narratives to Study the Impact of the Great Depression," *Journal of Southern History* 69 (August 2003): 623–58, esp. 624–26.

36. Baker and Baker, *Oklahoma Slave Narratives*, 444.

37. Ibid., 262.

38. Henry Bibb, *Narrative of the Life and Adventures of Henry Bibb, An American Slave, Written by Himself* (New York, 1850), 152–53. Uncle Tom's Cabin & American Culture: A Multi-media Archive, http:utc.iath.virginia.edu.

39. Ibid., 155.

40. Baker and Baker, *Oklahoma Slave Narratives*, 219.

41. See Claudio Saunt, "The Paradox of Freedom: Tribal Sovereignty and Emancipation during the Reconstruction of Indian Territory," *Journal of Southern History* 70 (February 2004): 63–94; R. Halliburton, *Red over Black: Black Slavery among the Cherokee Indians* (Westport, CT: Greenwood, 1977); Celia Naylor, *African Cherokees in Indian Territory: From Chattel to Citizens* (Chapel Hill: University of North Carolina Press, 2008); and Barbara Krauthamer, *Black Slaves, Indian Masters: Slavery, Emancipation, and Citizenship in the Native American South* (Chapel Hill: University of North Carolina Press, 2013).

42. *Treaty with the Choctaw and Chickasaw, 1866*, Institute for the Development of Indian Law, *Treaties and Agreements of the Five Civilized Tribes*, American Indian

Treaties Series (Washington, DC: Institute for the Development of Indian Law, 1974), 131–32, art. 3 and 4.

43. Debo, *Rise and Fall of the Choctaw Republic*, 101.

44. Ibid., 102–4. *Treaty with the Choctaw and Chickasaw, 1866*, art. 3.

45. CNR Roll CTN 5, 1872–1908 Documents, Document 13631. The citizenship commission reported 14,476 Choctaws in Choctaw Nation with an additional 1,777 Choctaws residing in Chickasaw Nation. The total number of Choctaw freedmen was 3,985, which included 468 Choctaw freedmen residing in Chickasaw Nation.

46. *The Freedmen and Registration Bills*, vol. XVIII of *The Constitution and Laws of the American Indian Tribes Series* (1883; reprint, 1975), 1–4. Hereafter referred to as FRB XVIII.

47. FRB XVIII, 2 (sec. 1).

48. FRB XVIII, 3 (sec. 7).

49. FRB XVIII, 3 (sec. 6).

50. *Laws of the Choctaw Nation*, vol. XVIII of *The Constitution and Laws of the American Indian Tribes Series* (1883; reprint, 1975), 23.

51. See Murray R. Wickett, *Contested Territory: Whites, Native American and African Americans in Oklahoma, 1865–1907* (Baton Rouge: Louisiana State University Press, 2000), 53, and Leon F. Litwack, *Been in the Storm So Long: The Aftermath of Slavery* (New York: Vintage Books, 1979), 399–408.

52. IPH Roll 36, vol. 108: 465–73, see 466.

53. IPH Roll 31, vol. 92: 77–84, see 84. Given the surrounding records, Hall was likely a Choctaw freedman.

54. IPH Roll 35, vol. 106: 342–49, see 345.

55. IPH Roll 13, vol. 37: 473–81, see 479.

56. IPH Roll 30, vol. 91: 455–56.

57. Sarah Deutsch, "Being American in Boley, Oklahoma," in *Beyond Black and White*, eds. Stephanie Cole and Allison Parker (Arlington: University of Texas, 2004), 102–3. Creek freedmen land claims were at the center of the founding of Boley. See also David A. Chang, *The Color of the Land: Race, Nation, and the Politics of Landownership in Oklahoma, 1832–1929* (Chapel Hill: University of North Carolina Press, 2010), 158–59 and 163. For a more popular perspective, see also Chad Previch, "Diversity: Oklahoma once had 40 all-black towns, formed because their citizens weren't welcome elsewhere—Longtime resident fears worst for Boley—He says lure of cities, stagnant economies are leading to town's death," *Oklahoman*, April 22, 2007, p. 25.

58. IPH Roll 12, vol. 34: 326–35, see 335. Maytubbie's status as a Choctaw freedman or Choctaw citizen by blood is unclear. He described his grandmother as a native of Africa who was purchased by a member of the Choctaw Nation and then freed so that she could marry her master's son.

59. Rose Stremlau, *Sustaining the Cherokee Family: Kinship and the Allotment of an Indigenous Nation* (Chapel Hill: University of North Carolina Press, 2011), 5.

60. See Wickett, *Contested Territory*, 36–37 and Fay A. Yarbrough, *Race and the Cherokee Nation: Sovereignty in the Nineteenth Century* (Philadelphia: University

of Pennsylvania Press, 2008), 30–31 and 58–59. See IPH Roll 3, vol. 7: 296–305, see 302 and IPH Roll 31, vol. 92: 264–68, see 265. The descendants of John Guest, a slave owned by Zadoc John Harrison's grandfather, continued to live in the vicinity of the family farm: "Those of the descendants of that old darkey who survived at the time of the allotment of land were each given their lawful share, as freemen."

61. See Naylor, *African Cherokees in Indian Territory*, 187–190, and Wickett, *Contested Territory*, 54–59. Both authors also reference this migration of African Americans to Indian Territory as a part of the larger "Black Exodus" of former slaves to western states.

62. IPH Roll 13, vol. 37: 473–81, see 473. Chang discusses the tensions that sometimes arose in the Creek Nation between Creek freedpeople who received allotments and "State Negroes," as black Creeks referred to African American migrants to Indian Territory, *The Color of the Land*, 159.

63. IPH Roll 26, vol. 79: 155–73, see 155–56.

64. Baker and Baker, *Oklahoma Slave Narratives*, 24.

65. Debo, *The Rise and Fall of the Choctaw Republic*, 109 and 249.

66. FRB XVIII, 1.

67. FRB XVIII, 3 (sec. 7).

68. *Constitution, Treaties and Laws of the Choctaw Nation, Made and Enacted by the Choctaw Legislature, 1887*, vol. XIX of *The Constitution and Laws of the American Indian Tribes Series* (1887; reprint 1975), 156–57.

69. *Laws of the Choctaw Nation Made and Enacted by the General Council, from 1886–1890 Inclusive*, vol. XXI of *The Constitution and Laws of the American Indian Tribes Series* (1891; reprint 1975), 8–9.

70. Nor did this land guarantee economic success for former slaves. As Eric Foner asserts for Africa and the Caribbean, "ownership of land was not necessarily a panacea for the economic plight of postemancipation blacks," *Nothing but Freedom: Emancipation and Its Legacy* (1983; reprint, Baton Rouge: Louisiana State University Press, 2007), 34.

71. Baker and Baker, *Oklahoma Slave Narratives*, 238.

72. Emphasis from the original Certificate of Degree of Indian Blood application available on the Choctaw Nation of Oklahoma website, choctawnation.com.

73. For more on the freedmen controversy, see Krauthamer, *Black Slaves, Indian Masters*, 154; Yarbrough, *Race and the Cherokee Nation*, chap. 7; Naylor, *African Cherokees in Indian Territory*, 206–19; Tiya Miles, *Ties That Bind: the Story of an Afro-Cherokee Family in Slavery and Freedom* (Berkeley: University of California Press), preface; and Miller, *Coacoochee's Bones*, 183–88. Saunt's work *Black, White, and Indian* focuses on a Creek family and also addresses contemporary discussions about race, particularly people of African descent.

TWELVE

"Citizen's Clothing"

RECONSTRUCTION, HO-CHUNK PERSISTENCE, AND
THE POLITICS OF DRESS

Stephen Kantrowitz

DID CLOTHES MAKE THE CITIZEN? In the early post–Civil War years, there was little reason to think so. President Ulysses S. Grant's 1869 inaugural address seemed to aim at something much grander, declaring support for any Indian policy "which tends to their civilization and ultimate citizenship." Indeed, this handful of words outlined a project of staggering ambition: the transformation of fundamental aspects of Native people's behavior, self-conception, and community; the dissolution of the tribes and the appropriation of their lands; and the incorporation of individual Indians into the citizenry. During the 1870s, that was precisely what the new Christian agents of the reformed Indian Office sought to achieve as they took aim at Indian patterns of property ownership, residence, labor, speech, and worship.[1] How Indians clothed themselves was, at the outset, just one in a long list of conversions to be encouraged and measured.

But clothing soon came to mean much more. By the mid-1870s, these same Indian agents became preoccupied with the adoption of what official reports dubbed "citizen's dress," offering it as a key measure of Native peoples' readiness for incorporation into the body politic.[2] This was more than a footnote to the unfolding story of Indian "civilization," which settlers and officials had pursued for centuries before the United States entered the era of Reconstruction. In fact, the agents' preoccupation with clothing helps explain a great deal about their broader vision of what "civilization" should mean, and its relationship to mid-nineteenth-century conceptions of freedom, individuality, and political fitness.[3]

As Grant's inaugural words implied, both Indian policy and the implications of Indian civilization were powerfully affected by Reconstruction's remaking of national authority and national citizenship. After emancipation, only the stubborn resistance of Native Americans and former slaveholders seemed to stand in the way of the wholesale transformation of the nation. If recalcitrant Indians were to avoid a worse fate than defeat and occupation, if they were to avoid extinction, they would have to be remade into people who understood and embraced the new order. In other words, they would have to become liberal citizens.[4] Indians must take on the rights and responsibilities of "self-owning" individuals, normatively men, arranging their affairs around private property ownership, market exchange, and well-ordered households. Such individuals would embody the triumph of industry over indolence, of foresight over fecklessness, of contract freedom over chattel slavery—and of conquest led by homesteading, ranching, mining, and lumbering over Native modes of life and subsistence.

In this context, the adoption of "citizen's dress" seemed to offer a compact and efficient marker of Native people's willingness to dissolve their tribal ties and become liberal individuals who could take up the mantle of citizen. Both U.S. officials and Native Americans understood citizen's clothing in these terms. But, crucially, they did not attach the same values to it or have the same endpoints in mind. Although whites used clothing as an index of the tractability, progress, or worthiness of the people they hoped to reconstruct and "civilize," that was not always what it meant. Some Indians embraced the broader project, often as a means of avoiding dispossession and removal; others more expediently took on "citizen's clothing," wholly or in part, as a means of improving their position relative to settlers, employers, agents, missionaries, and lawmakers. Through the experience of the Ho-Chunk and Winnebago people, in their Wisconsin homeland and in their nineteenth-century diaspora across the eastern Great Plains, this chapter explores how Native people could turn citizen's clothing from a metric of civilization into a strategy of persistence.[5] They might sometimes wear civilization's clothing, but not always as a sign of their incorporation into the American order.[6] Indeed, almost as soon as "citizen's clothing" became a part of Indian policy, the Ho-Chunk redeployed the concept to subvert the twin projects of removal and cultural transformation. Understanding both its power and its limitations, they quietly seized that tool of the conquerors for purposes of their own.

. . .

For centuries, colonists and settlers in the Americas had understood the adoption of European clothing by indigenous peoples to mark an important step on the road from "savagery" to "civilization." Early French and British settlers in North America believed that as Indians adopted material culture imported from Europe, they would themselves be transformed. In the eighteenth-century Illinois country, for example, authorities hoped to produce "Frenchified Indians"—people whose material and cultural "manner of living" indicated that they had become "'true' French men and women."[7] But Native Americans did not adopt European material culture in precisely the ways colonial thinkers expected. New sartorial options allowed some Indians to "reinvent themselves," putting new forms of clothing to work in their own ways and for their own purposes. They incorporated into their dress elements of European material culture—cloth of various kinds, hunting shirts, medallions, pieces of metal—"in a distinctive way that contemporaries recognized as the 'Indian fashion.'" Particularly for those serving as negotiators, the artful presentation of self through dress became a means of self-expression and communication across cultural and experiential divides.[8]

Under the U.S. order, men of all backgrounds who wanted to be treated as political citizens were expected to dress in certain ways. By the middle of the nineteenth century, especially in the northeastern cities of the United States, the model male political and economic actor wore a "suit." This newly composed ensemble of ready-made articles, renouncing conspicuous adornment, represented the standardization not only of garment production and exchange but also the creation of "a male business persona." The man wearing it, whether comfortably bourgeois or merely aspiring to that status, represented the ideal liberal subject; his respectable self-presentation and engagement in commercial exchange marked him as a self-disciplined contract actor, the formal equal of other white men.[9] It became "a legitimate form of disguise," as historian Karen Halttunen has put it, the adoption of which signaled that one was willing to behave properly.[10] At the same time, as historian Michael Zakim argues, wearing "the simple dress of an American citizen" distinguished "civilized man" from tyrants and aristocrats above and from potentially dangerous folk below.[11] The material culture represented by particular forms of clothing became political culture.[12]

The same was true in the West. As the United States gained hegemony over the upper Mississippi Valley during the first half of the nineteenth century, clothing frequently marked the boundary between cultural and political worlds. In reality, upper Mississippi Valley society included many people of mixed descent and culture, and women and men who functioned as cultural intermediaries often alternated between styles of clothing or adopted elements of both.¹³ Many observers nevertheless used contrasting styles of dress to suggest a rigid binary, with the derogatory term "blanket Indian" standing in opposition to the "civilization" of the mostly white newcomers—never mind that the blanket was itself a comparatively recent replacement for or supplement to animal skins.¹⁴ Some Native American visitors to Washington, D.C., wore elaborate regalia, designed to make a forceful impression on eastern whites, while also receiving gifts of quite different "American" clothing from their hosts.¹⁵ George Catlin's antebellum portrait of an Indian diplomat in "Native" regalia headed to Washington and his similarly elaborate "American" costume on the way home argued that Indian dress was as worthy of note in Washington as an Indian in American costume was on the Plains.

The boundary between Indian and white could only be appropriately breached if Indians accepted what settler constitutions dubbed the "habits and customs of civilization."¹⁶ Few men on the western frontier thought it sensible to wear suits, but settlers and Indians both sometimes acted as though Indians could achieve political inclusion by adopting "American" patterns of property ownership, land use, exchange, and clothing. Some Native Americans concluded that only this adoption could protect them from utter destruction. In 1857, for example, one group of Dakota asked to be recognized as citizens of Minnesota on the basis of their adoption of a wide range of American practices and customs: republican government, education, labor, literacy in English, and what they called "the dress and habits of civilized men."¹⁷ Other groups, in Wisconsin and elsewhere, pursued similar strategies, with some becoming U.S. citizens by act of Congress in exchange for surrendering claims to tribal land and adopting appropriate "habits and customs."¹⁸

Yet clothing was as unreliable a marker of political fitness as it was of civilization. One white delegate to Minnesota's state constitutional convention complained about the "grand frauds" perpetrated under the standard of civilization—of "putting a coat upon one Indian, and when he has voted, stripping it off and putting it on another, and thus running them up to the poll by hundreds."¹⁹ A half-century later, a commentator claimed that, in the first statewide election, "half-breed" men in the northern districts had provided the margin of victory for the victorious candidate. In his tale, the men arrived in a "swarm," with a single pair of pants among them: "One would don the trousers and go out and vote, and, soon coming back, passed the garment to the next man, while he resumed the breech clout [sic] and blanket."²⁰

FIGURE 12.1. George Catlin, "Wi-jún-jon, Pigeon's Egg Head (The Light) Going To and Returning From Washington," oil on canvas, 1837–1839, 1985.66.474; Smithsonian American Art Museum, Gift of Mrs. Joseph Harrison Jr.

Whatever fractional truth the story conveyed about the events themselves, it accurately represented the perplexities of determining whether people were genuinely adopting "habits and customs" or, instead, deploying them expediently. The story pointed to clothing's ability to open a gaping breach in the wall between savagery and civilization: attire might be a sign of a person's inner self, but it could just as easily be a disguise.[21]

The Ho-Chunk spent the nineteenth century opening and navigating that breach. They lost their title to what is now northern Illinois and southern Wisconsin during the 1820s and 1830s, in coerced treaties that offered a substantial tribal fund but demanded removal across the Mississippi. Further removals over the next decades left a majority of the tribe on a reservation in southern Minnesota. But throughout this period, nearly half of the Ho-Chunk population either refused to leave Wisconsin or left only to quickly return. These so-called stray bands of Ho-Chunk—sometimes mingled with Potawatomi, Sauk and Fox, and other groups—remained a persistent presence within a number of U.S. territories and states, pursuing a mixed subsistence on the margins of white settlement, largely beyond the inspection or control of Indian agents.[22]

The "stray bands" vexed policymakers by refusing to abandon Wisconsin at all. But even those Ho-Chunk who accepted reservation life often seemed only superficially committed to "civilization." In 1860, for example, the white director of the manual labor school on the Ho-Chunks' Minnesota reservation spoke proudly of the effort his female charges put into making "garments." But in the next breath, he admitted that this was only true during part of the year: in most seasons, enrollments plummeted as the Ho-Chunk made camp in various locations to take up hunting, gathering, or planting—what the agent fretfully called their "continual migration."[23] Persuading them to take up civilized dress was an inherently impermanent—perhaps even an illusory—achievement.

During the fight against the Confederacy, the Union government largely suspended efforts to inculcate civilization. For the Ho-Chunks' Minnesota neighbors, the Dakota, the consequences were dire. Restricted to lands on which they could not subsist, they had relied on federal annuity payments; when those payments did not arrive on time in 1862, local merchants refused to offer credit, officials provided no aid, and the Dakota began to starve. In August, Dakota warriors rebelled, killing hundreds of Minnesota settlers and sending thousands more fleeing for their lives. When U.S. forces regained control of the territory that fall, they hanged thirty-eight Dakota men, in the largest mass execution in U.S. history.[24] The Ho-Chunk played no significant role in the uprising, but the government acceded to anti-Indian sentiment, exiling both the Dakota and the Ho-Chunk to a remote and barren tract in the federal territory that bore the Dakotas' name. Many of the Ho-Chunk quickly fled, with some returning to Wisconsin and Iowa and many others sheltering with friends in Nebraska. In 1865, the federal government allowed the refugees to trade their lands in the Dakota Territory for more than 100,000 acres of eastern Nebraska, some of which today remains the home of the Winnebago Nation.

Reconstruction debates over U.S. citizenship, as discussed throughout part 3 of this volume, also reshaped Ho-Chunk life. As Joshua Paddison explains, the Fourteenth Amendment made citizens of "all persons born or naturalized" who were "subject to the jurisdiction" of the United States. Under this standard, Indians would not be so "subject"—nor therefore citizens—until the tribes to which they held allegiance (and as members of which they collectively held land) were dissolved.[25] It was in this context that President Ulysses S. Grant offered his formula for Indian political incorporation—"civilization and ultimate citizenship"—and promised peace to those Indians who respected reservation boundaries and military action against those who did not. At the same time, he moved to reform the administration of those reservations, putting Quakers, Catholics, and an array of Protestant denominations in charge of the agencies. Supervised by religious reformers, reservation Indians would gain a true understanding of civilization and ultimately become fit for citizenship.

Reconstruction thus proceeded in the West and South and incorporated military, political, and cultural efforts at national incorporation that overlapped in a variety of ways.[26] They reflected the common commitment of the victorious Republican Union to a classically liberal vision of social and economic relations, contracts, and formal equality before the law. This was easily articulated in principle, but achieving it on the ground was another matter. To imagine that Native Americans could achieve the degree of "civilization" necessary to merit citizenship, agents and missionaries needed tangible evidence: significant numbers of people taking up land in severalty; farming; worshiping in Christian churches; attending school. They needed data that would demonstrate that Indians were abandoning the collective and illiberal past for the liberal future. Hence they started counting, and discovered the utility of "citizen's clothing."

Until the late 1860s, the term "citizen's clothing" was employed primarily to describe the clothes worn by soldiers or policemen when out of uniform, or to the garments given convicts upon their release. That is to say, citizen's clothing was the garb of people who, though at other times part of an illiberal collective, were currently self-determining and self-owning—in a word, free. In the 1870s, as Indian agents and missionaries sought to turn Indians into liberal individuals worthy of U.S. citizenship, the term seemed to perfectly capture the necessary transformation of tribal members. Citizen's clothing, which already distinguished the idealized liberal individual from the soldier, inmate, or noble, now distinguished him from the "savage" as well.

Like other Reconstruction-era federal Indian agents, the Quakers who oversaw the Winnebago Reservation in Nebraska wrote as though the adoption of citizen's dress, or citizen's clothing, signaled Indians' evolution into "industrious and sober people" who would soon be ready for political incorporation.[27] In 1871, less than two years after Quakers took charge, children at the reservation school were said to have "discarded" moccasins and Native modes of dress in favor of shoes, stockings, and clothes fashioned from "an excellent fabric of plain construction."[28] By 1873, the tribe as a whole were "on the high road to civilization": Winnebago "farmers own their wagons, horses, harness, and furniture of their houses, dress in civilized costume, raise crops and take them to market for sale."[29] And in 1874 the agent flatly declared success: "All these Indians wear citizen's clothing," he wrote, accompanying this indisputable proof of progress with approving descriptions of the tribe's agricultural production, wooden houses, elected government, police force, and acceptance of the bedrock liberal principle that they would have to work for their subsistence.[30] Even the Ho-Chunk stray bands in Wisconsin seemed to be moving in the right direction: the agent appointed to them reported optimistically that the younger Ho-Chunk were learning to speak English and that "many of them are also adopting a civilized dress." If this were to continue, he wrote, "I see no reason why they cannot become ... good and useful citizens."[31]

In the Indian Office's tabulations, Native people's adoption of citizen's clothing came to stand for their embrace of civilization generally. At first, in the early 1870s, the chief metrics of Indian civilization were numbers of schools and pupils, churches and church members, acres cultivated and bushels produced. But federal officials also began to track the "number of Indians brought immediately under the civilizing influence of the agency," and soon after, in 1874, began to offer compiled statistics of the number who "wear citizens' dress." That first year, the number reported was just under 44,000 out of a total Native population of about 275,000—about one in seven.[32] Though small, this fraction was comparatively impressive: it was twice the proportion of Indians who were church members and four times the proportion attending school.[33] And unlike the others, it quickly grew. The number of Indians reported to be wearing citizen's dress more than doubled by 1875 and reached 138,000 by the end of the decade—more than half the reported total Indian population, with roughly even numbers of men and women.³⁴ And as the numbers swelled, the category gained ever-greater prominence in the Indian Office's statistical summary of its achievements. For colonial officials hoping to demonstrate the success of their policies, it made sense to emphasize the most encouraging numbers.

Yet dress was not a simple matter of one style or another. As they had for centuries, Native people continued to blend the flood of newly available clothing with older styles. In 1881, the Indian Office acknowledged this reality by dividing its category of "Indians who wear citizens' dress" into two subcategories: "Wholly" and "In part," providing gradations in their sartorial and civilizational measurements.³⁵ In 1877, the agent to the Dakota found that "the men have adopted citizens' dress in full, the women partially. They still cling to their shawls, which they use for bonnet and shawl." As the historian Colette Hyman has noted, even in the late nineteenth century Dakota women who wore Euro-American clothing "continued to complete their attire with blankets" and beadwork.³⁶ Still, agents across the West saw even the partial adoption of "citizen's clothing" as a sign of "progress."³⁷

The agents on the Winnebago Reservation understood citizen's dress to mean different things for men and for women. Men were supposed to adopt citizen's dress as a sign of appropriate economic engagement as farmers or laborers—what the statistical tables called "civilized pursuits"—but they were not expected to produce the clothing itself. Women, by contrast, were not supposed to enter the wage-labor market but were expected to learn how to produce citizen's clothing, embracing their own proper role in the modern economic order. So as the Quakers began their work, the agent "ordered a suit of clothes for each man" but bought or requested donations of cloth and patterns, "so that the agents' wives could let the women come to their houses and cut for themselves, which they would do, and soon be able to take them home and cut without assistance, as they are very apt to imitate any work they see others do."³⁸ The adoption of citizen's dress by these means would signal a gendered, "civilized" division of labor.

But things did not play out as the agents hoped. Although in the aggregate Indian men and women were reported to be taking on citizen's clothing in roughly equal numbers during the 1870s, the nature and meaning of this adoption varied enormously across space and gender. Citizen's dress does seem to have helped men be hired for agricultural work, an increasingly common dimension of subsistence as the territory around Plains reservations filled up with white settlers. This was the economic reality behind the Indian

Office's statistical category "male Indians engaged in manual labor in civilized pursuits." An 1869 Quaker delegation to the Winnebago's Nebraska reservation professed to be dazzled by the exotic "ancient caravans" arriving at the agency to receive annuities, but the Friends also noted more soberly that "these Indians are mostly willing to work for wages, and when they ask for work, they come, 'dressed like white men,' knowing the Agent will not employ them when 'dressed in blankets.'"[39] Elsewhere, some agents were said to treat "farmer Indians" wearing "citizen's clothes" better than other Indians.[40]

These examples suggest how citizen's dress was a matter of expediency. As the 1869 Quaker delegation noted, men put on the clothing to gain employment; certainly those men took it off again, resuming the male "Indian dress" that the same delegation carefully described—breech cloth, blanket, leggings, and moccasins, the latter two often "finely worked and beaded."[41] Similarly, Dakota men (also under the Quakers' charge) changed their hair and clothes in order to receive annuities, agents reported, but resumed their traditional ways at other times and in other places.[42] In these contexts, dressing as a "citizen" was a self-conscious performance for the benefit of agents, missionaries, and prospective employers.

Although citizen's clothing might provide Winnebago men access to wage work, it conferred no similar benefits on women. So perhaps it is not surprising that by 1872 the agent saw a pattern emerging: "The men have nearly all adopted the dress of the whites." But he could only "anticipat[e] . . . that the women will do the same so soon as they shall come to live in houses."[43] The one official enumeration that broke down citizen's dress by gender revealed a stark division: in 1878 the Winnebago agent reported that while 694 men had adopted citizen's dress, only one woman had done so.[44] Perhaps here, as in other modern colonial contexts, women's exclusion from the world of wage work and its requirements left them the primary (though not sole) bearers of "indigenous" forms of dress.[45] Perhaps it is equally predictable that the efforts of agents' wives to instruct Indian women in the production of clothing did not come off as planned. Reconsidering their call for fabric and patterns, the report's authors urged that "when new cloth is sent it would be well that it first be cut into garments," as agents' wives "devote much time in this way without any reward from man."[46] Winnebago women, it seemed, were not as eager to "imitate" as could be hoped.

The sartorial stream flowing from "savagery" to "civilization" may have seemed difficult to control on the Nebraska plains, but its course through the

Wisconsin woodlands left Indian agents frankly baffled. The Ho-Chunk bands who refused to leave the state showed few signs of embracing the Reconstruction project of civilization. For the most part, they pursued a seasonal migration around the state that included farming, hunting, berrying, and various forms of market engagement. Yet in the midst of a renewed removal effort urged by their white neighbors, the expedient adoption of citizen's clothing helped the Wisconsin Ho-Chunk win a stunning victory in 1874. Learning from the experiences of other parts of their diaspora, taking advantage of cracks, breaches, and vacillations in federal policy, they parlayed a nominal adoption of the forms of civilization into a right to remain in Wisconsin, on terms substantially their own.

The Wisconsin Ho-Chunk do not appear to have interested themselves in what citizenship could offer until it bore fruit for some of their kin in Minnesota. Despite the removal of most of the Minnesota Ho-Chunk from the state following the Dakota War, a few Ho-Chunk had remained on lands they had earlier taken in allotment. In 1870, as Congress debated wholesale changes in its naturalization law, and in a fit of bad conscience over the 1863 removal,[47] the federal government created a naturalization policy for Minnesota's Ho-Chunk. Under this special enactment, heads of household could formally abandon their tribal ties, become U.S. citizens, and secure lands to which they were previously entitled. Within less than two years, more than 150 Minnesota Ho-Chunk made the required attestation and received certificates of naturalization. Critically, they retained their rights to the tribal funds—in both absolute and per capita terms, one of the largest held in trust by the federal government—which up to that point had only been available to their compatriots on the Nebraska reservation.[48] They could retain the financial benefits of tribal status while gaining immunity from removal. In the midst of the Reconstruction citizenship restrictions explored by Paddison and Sandweiss in their chapters in this volume, the Minnesota Ho-Chunk were able to garner citizenship for themselves, and with it the right to remain where they wished.

The Ho-Chunk in Wisconsin quickly learned of these developments, and they seem to have taken the lesson that if they purchased land, as the Minnesota Ho-Chunk had done, they could claim to be "citizens" rather than "vagabonds" or "strays." They began buying up small parcels, sometimes as little as a few acres, in the western part of Wisconsin. For many these homesteads were mere bases of operations for a continued seasonal pattern of residence and subsistence that included some farming, but not "farms" in the sense understood by congressmen and Indian agents; others may never have occupied their lands at all. Nevertheless, by the time Congress appropriated funds to remove the "stray bands" from Wisconsin and the federal machinery began to creak into action in 1873, the Ho-Chunk were already pointing to their acquisition of land and petitioning the federal government to make them citizens like their Minnesota brethren.[49]

When federal troops began rounding up Ho-Chunk families and bands in December 1873, landownership and clothing quickly emerged as intertwined means of distinguishing "strays" who were to be removed from "citizen" Indians whose rights the government was bound to respect. The small Army units assigned the task of removal proceeded rapidly against no physical resistance. But as some Indians began to make claims to be citizens, immune to removal, policymakers found it surprisingly difficult to determine which claims were legitimate. For example, the deportation of the family of a man named Ah-ha-Cho-Ker (known to many whites as "Artichokes"), who owned forty acres, put the officer in charge at a disadvantage. "Said Artichokes does own 40 acres of land in Monroe Co. and has lived upon it some time," he explained to his superior.

Although land ownership appeared to establish Ah-ha-Cho-Ker's personal right to remain in the state, other members of his family seemed to fall outside that narrow exception. Justifying their deportation, the officer explained that they had been "found in Sauk Co. 50 miles away from [Ah-ha-Cho-Ker's] land encamped with [a party of] Indians.... The family was dressed the same as others of the tribe and lived the same with no way to distinguish them from the others. Consequently they were secured and marched to depot with the others." But questions had then been raised about the deportation of a landowner's family. "Now I wish for instructions," the officer complained, "as to who is and who is not a Winnebago Indian of Wisconsin." In the absence of such instructions, he fell back on what he considered the most telling marker: how people lived, and in particular how they dressed.[50] Another federal officer, Captain Thomas, similarly determined "that the law was opposed to fraud, and looked at the intent." In cases where the landowner "was a wandering, blanket, Indian, living in a tepe [sic], hunting for a subsistence, ... the mere fact of a 'deed' conveying a few acres of worthless unimproved land, on which it was evident, that no one could get a living, would not convert him into a 'bona fide' citizen." By contrast, those Indians living in houses and working land—whether they owned it or not—should be given the benefit of the doubt when they "carried the evidence of civilization."[51] And no "evidence" was more obviously "carried" than that worn on the body.

The Ho-Chunk quickly perceived the breach opened by this regime of "evidence." The nearly one thousand people removed to Nebraska during the winter of 1873–74 quickly began migrating back to Wisconsin, and as they did so they paid close attention to the criterion of dress that removal officers had inadvertently established. The pro-removal editor of the *Prairie Du Chien Courier* complained venomously about the "filthy, idle set of vagrants" taking advantage of this "new dodge" to return from Nebraska. They "now rig up with any whitemen clothing they can buy, beg, or steal," he complained.[52] By the time Ho-Chunk families returning from the west reached Black River Falls, Wisconsin, later in 1874, a less vitriolic editor noted that "[s]ome sport[ed] full suits of civilized apparel while others adhere to the aboriginal garb."[53] A reporter in Winona, Minnesota, noted the "picturesque appearance" of a caravan of forty or fifty who moved through his town in summer 1874. But he also reported that one of the leaders of the party "shrewdly said that he [w]as going to have them all dress like white folks and then the Government could not take them back." That man had learned the lesson well.[54]

Indeed, the federal program of civilization through clothing may have helped the returning Ho-Chunk achieve their goals. Taylor Bradley, the Nebraska Winnebago agent, fumed to his superiors that the Wisconsin Ho-Chunk recently removed to his jurisdiction had been a terrible influence on the Winnebago—they had "unsettled and demoralized" a number of young men, even inducing some to return to Wisconsin with them. Against his better judgment, Bradley had allowed himself to be persuaded to issue clothing to the new arrivals, on that theory that this would "make them the better contented" with their new circumstances. But the plan backfired: "many who received the goods have left the reservation" for Wisconsin. In other words, it seems to have been the donations of the New York Friends and the payments of the U.S. government itself that provided the returning Ho-Chunk with the citizen's clothing—the camouflage—they required to meet the requirements that removal officials had, in frustration, established.[55]

In the end, the Ho-Chunks' long-term persistence in Wisconsin hinged on their ability to acquire land, which the federal government—frustrated by a half-century of failed removals—quietly granted in 1875.[56] But the role played by clothing sheds light on the nature of the intertwined projects of civilization and citizenship as they took shape on the ground. Those projects had begun in the war's heady aftermath, rich with progressive hopes of broad cultural transformation and incorporation. The Ho-Chunk experience tells us that, by the mid-1870s, it was enough to give symbolic honor to these principles. Many Wisconsin Ho-Chunk remained seasonally mobile, pursuing a range of activities and donning citizen's clothing as seemed appropriate. Native Americans, that is, might understand Indian agents' project without internalizing it.

The Indian agents and federal officers overseeing the 1873–74 removal must have had some inkling of what was going on. They still hoped that their reconstruction plan, of citizen's clothing, land ownership, the English language, formal instruction, and Christian worship, would create transformations that extended well beyond the reach of the naked eye. But they also knew that any of the tangible markers of civilization, calculated as signs of fitness for citizenship, might be a ruse, a decoy. The dogmas of Christianity could be mouthed insincerely. People who learned that land ownership would protect them from expulsion would pretend to be homesteaders. And citizen's dress, instead of marking Native Americans' emergence from a state of illiberal dependency, might be an expedient disguise. So the agents counted what could be counted, put a hopeful gloss on the numbers in their reports, and went about their business.

The Ho-Chunks' path through the late nineteenth and early twentieth centuries suggest that whatever transformations did take place did not align well with U.S. official expectations. Those who remained in Wisconsin integrated themselves into the midwestern economy on the bottom rung of the economic ladder, while simultaneously pursuing many aspects of their lives in ways wholly foreign to the project of civilization. In fact, Ho-Chunk engagement with the capitalist economy sometimes pressed them in directions that made a mockery of citizen's clothing: by the late nineteenth century, many Ho-Chunk people were participating in the emergent tourist economy of the Wisconsin Dells, dressing up for photographs and pageants in white entrepreneur H. H. Bennett's version of "Indian" costumes.[57] Here, "civilization" was not a goal to be attained, but a hierarchy in which the colonized indigenous would be forever found wanting.

But the continuing history of dress contained other elements as well. At the turn of the nineteenth century, Ho-Chunk families from Wisconsin and beyond streamed through the doors of Charles Van Schaick's photo studio in Black River Falls, commissioning portraits that reflected their own choices and desires more than those of the photographer. The complex patterns of

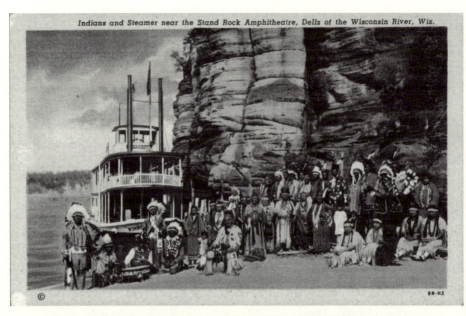

FIGURE 12.2. H.H. Bennett, "Indians and Steamer near the Stand Rock Amphitheatre," postcard, n.d. (WHi-34535; Wisconsin Historical Society, photo by Milwaukee Journal Sentinel).

self-representation revealed in these photographs cannot be reduced to simple expressions of nostalgia or colonial power.[58] When able to exert control over their own images, Ho-Chunk men and women depicted themselves in a range of styles, sometimes partly or entirely in citizen's dress, but in many cases displaying beadwork, appliqué, and other distinctive cultural styles.[59] Photographs of young women such as Annie Blowsnake Thundercloud were circulated across the dispersed world of the Ho-Chunk to indicate her wealth and availability for marriage; in these matters, her traditional skills and substantial dowry, both represented by Ho-Chunk material culture, were important.[60] Other photographs might have less directly instrumental purposes, commemorating favorite possessions, friendships, family relationships, or milestones of various kinds. Ho-Chunk studio portraits suggest a mixed and varied palette of needs, desires, and expressions. They do not suggest that men simply adopted (or that women simply shunned) "citizen's dress," accepting or resisting the progressive, unidirectional course of "civilization" promoted by the agents. Their purposes were various, but that is precisely the point.

For the Ho-Chunk, then, citizen's clothing remained less a path to civilization than part of a cultural repertoire of self-expression, resistance, and

FIGURE 12.3. Studio portrait of three unidentified Ho-Chunk men, ca. 1880, photograph by Charles Van Schaick (WHi-63697, Wisconsin Historical Society).

play. In a twentieth-century narrative, Mountain Wolf Woman recalled her Ho-Chunk girlhood in turn-of-the-century Wisconsin, a period during which she both attended an English-language boarding school and spent time among more traditionally oriented friends and family. She described one memorable moment of collision between these worlds, when the Oneida matron of her boarding school brought her to a Native ceremonial dance. Mountain Wolf Woman took part, despite the fact that she was wearing what she called "citizen's clothing." It was her own translation of a Ho-Chunk phrase—one which her Ho-Chunk-speaking interviewer rendered more

FIGURE 12.4. Studio Portrait of Annie Blowsnake Thundercloud, ca. 1882, photograph by Charles Van Schaick (WHi-65692, Wisconsin Historical Society).

literally as "I made myself into a white person." In important ways, it is clear, Mountain Wolf Woman had not.[61]

Mountain Wolf Woman's experience, like the story of citizen's clothing itself, reverberates into the present. On Christmas Day 2012, Julian Boucher stood in a Marriott dining room on the outskirts of Mankato. He described his childhood on a Dakota Reservation, and his anger at the churches that would only offer food and clothing to needy boys and girls if they became worshipers. He wanted his people to know where they came from, and he wanted the world to know their story. That was why he had made a hard journey of many weeks on horseback from his South Dakota home, retracing in reverse the migrations forced upon the Dakota a century and a half before. The next morning he and dozens of others would mount their horses for the short, final leg of their trip, arriving in Mankato's small downtown at the precise moment that, 150 years before, thirty-eight Dakota men were hanged by the U.S. government.

The coming ceremony of remembrance and forgiveness was foremost in everyone's mind that night, but Boucher's mention of clothing made me take another look at his weathered western hat and pearl-buttoned shirt. I asked, Have you heard the term "citizen's clothing"? Boucher looked at me gravely for a moment, then broke into a wide grin and nodded vigorously, pinching the fabric of his shirt with both hands and shaking it at me for emphasis. Older people call it that sometimes, he explained. "If you wanted to be a citizen, you had to look and play the part."

Was it playing a part, then, I asked? Something you could put on and take off?

He nodded again.[62]

NOTES

Thanks to those who helped me navigate this new field: Larry Nesper, Aaron Bird Bear, Patty Loew, Janice Rice, John Hall, Susan Johnson, Ari Kelman, Miranda Johnson, Richard Monette, Andrew Fisher, Damon Akins, Kate Masur, Greg Downs, Joe Genetin-Pilawa, Steve Aron, Virginia Scharff, Sherry Smith, and the editors and authors of this volume.

1. It was in this decade that an official consensus emerged "that tribes should be dissolved and Indians incorporated into the citizenry." Cathleen Cahill, *Federal Mothers and Fathers: A Social History of the United States Indian Service, 1869–1933* (Chapel Hill: University of North Carolina Press, 2011), 20.

2. See, e.g., U.S. Office of Indian Affairs, *Annual Report of the Commissioner of Indian Affairs*... (Washington: Government Printing Office., 1826–1932) [hereafter cited as *Annual Report*], 1874, 408ff. For a penetrating analysis of the role of clothing in a parallel project of "civilization," see John L. Comaroff and Jean Comaroff, *Of Revelation and Revolution: The Dialectics of Modernity on a South African Frontier*, 2 vols. (Chicago: University of Chicago Press, 1991–97), vol. 2, 218–73.

3. On postbellum ideas about Indians and "civilization," see David Wallace Adams, *Education for Extinction: American Indians and the Boarding School Experience, 1875–1928* (Lawrence: University Press of Kansas, 1995), esp. 12–21. The contours of postbellum liberal ideology are explored in Amy Dru Stanley, *From Bondage to Contract: Wage Labor, Marriage, and the Market in the Age of Slave Emancipation* (Chicago: University of Chicago Press, 1998).

4. The definitive synthesis of the period is Eric Foner, *Reconstruction: America's Unfinished Revolution, 1863–1877* New York: Harper & Row, 1988. For a focus on

the Trans-Mississippi West see Heather Cox Richardson, *West from Appomattox* (New Haven: Yale University Press, 2007). On the complexities of Native American U.S. citizenship, see Earl Maltz, "The Fourteenth Amendment and Native American Citizenship, 17 *Const. Comment* 555 (2000). For the ideology and background of the postwar Indian service, see Cahill, *Federal Mothers and Fathers,* and Francis Paul Prucha, *American Indian Policy in Crisis: Christian Reformers and the Indian, 1865–1900* (Norman: University of Oklahoma Press, 1976).

5. During the period of European colonization, the group known to outsiders as the Winnebago made their homes in southern Wisconsin and northern Illinois. The tumultuous era of removals covered in this essay (ca. 1825–75) partially dispersed this linguistic and cultural community, producing political and terminological separations and, today, both the Winnebago Nation of Nebraska and the Ho-Chunk Nation of Wisconsin. For purposes of clarity, *Ho-Chunk* ("People of the Big Voice") is used in this essay to denote people who claimed nonreservation homes in Wisconsin, while *Winnebago* refers to those primarily resident on the Nebraska reservation established in 1865.

6. In this sense, the Ho-Chunk took part in creating what Kevin Bruyneel calls a "third space of sovereignty," a political location "neither simply inside nor outside the American political system." Bruyneel, *The Third Space of Sovereignty: The Postcolonial Politics of U.S.-Indigenous Relations* (Minneapolis: University of Minnesota Press, 2007), xvii.

7. Sophie White, *Wild Frenchmen and Frenchified Indians: Material Culture and Race in Colonial Louisiana* (Philadelphia: University of Pennsylvania Press, 2012), quote 232.

8. Quotations from Timothy Shannon, "Dressing for Success on the Mohawk Frontier: Hendrick, William Johnson, and the Indian Fashion," *William and Mary Quarterly* 53, no. 1 (January 1996): 20–22. See also Blanca Tovías, *Colonialism on the Prairies: Blackfoot Settlement and Cultural Transformation, 1870–1920* (Eastbourne, UK: Sussex Academic Press, 2011), 63–65, 84–93; Laura E. Johnson, "'Goods to Clothe Themselves': Native Consumers and Native Images on the Pennsylvania Trading Frontier, 1712–1760," *Winterthur Portfolio* 43, no 1 (Spring 2009): 115–40; Jane Simonsen, "Descendants of Black Hawk: Generations of Identity in Sauk Portraits," *American Quarterly* 63, no. 2 (June 2011): 301–35.

9. Michael Zakim, *Ready-Made Democracy: A History of Men's Dress in the American Republic, 1760–1860* (Chicago: University of Chicago Press, 2003), 3–10.

10. Karen Halttunen, *Confidence Men and Painted Women: A Study of Middle-Class Culture in America, 1830–1870* (New Haven: Yale University Press, 1982), 196.

11. Zakim, *Ready-Made Democracy,* 193. The phrase was used by the secretary of state in an order forbidding ambassadors to European countries from adopting "court dress."

12. Ibid., 213, 7. For the analogous relationship of the man's suit to the political culture of the "self-made man" in mid-nineteenth-century English society, see David Kuchta, *The Three-Piece Suit and Modern Masculinity: England, 1550–1850* (Berkeley: University of California Press, 2002), 133–72.

13. E.g., Tovías, *Colonialism on the Prairies*, 96–99. More generally, see Anne F. Hyde, *Empires, Nations, and Families: A History of the North American West, 1800–1860* (Lincoln: University of Nebraska Press, 2011).

14. Sandra Lee Evenson and David J. Trayte, "Dress and Interaction in Contending Cultures: Eastern Dakota and Euroamericans in Nineteenth Century Minnesota," in Linda B. Arthur, ed., *Religion, Dress and the Body* (New York: Berg/Oxford, 1999), 102.

15. Herman J. Viola, *Diplomats in Buckskin: A History of Indian Delegations in Washington City* (Washington, DC: Smithsonian Institution Press, 1981), 117–20; Tovías, *Colonialism on the Prairies*, 92–3.

16. Deborah A. Rosen, *American Indians and State Law: Sovereignty, Race, and Citizenship, 1790–1880* (Lincoln: University of Nebraska Press, 2007).

17. *Debates and Proceedings of the [Democratic] Minnesota Constitutional Convention including the Organic Act of the Territory* (St. Paul: Earle S. Goodrich, 1857), 430–31; White, "Whiteness," 190–92.

18. James W. Oberly, *A Nation of Statesmen: The Political Culture of the Stockbridge-Munsee Mohicans, 1815–1972* (Norman: Univ. of Oklahoma Press, 2005), 64–77. For the similar experience of the Wyandot in Kansas, who took up allotments and (in theory) U.S. citizenship during the 1850s and early 1860s, see John P. Bowes, *Exiles and Pioneers: Eastern Indians in the Trans-Mississippi West* (New York: Cambridge Univ. Press, 2007), 201, 210, 217. On allotment, see Paul W. Gates, "Indian Allotments Preceding the Dawes Act," in ed. John G. Clark, *The Frontier Challenge: Responses to the Trans-Mississippi West* (Lawrence: University of Kansas Press, 1971) and C. Joseph Genetin-Pilawa, *Crooked Paths to Allotment: The Fight over Federal Indian Policy after the Civil War* (Chapel Hill: University of North Carolina Press, 2012).

19. T. F. Andrews, comp., *Debates and proceedings of the [Republican] Constitutional Convention for the Territory of Minnesota: To Form a state Constitution Preparatory to Its Admission into the Union as a State* (St. Paul: George W. Moore, 1858) (Google eBook), 34[7]; Rosen, *American Indians and State Law*, 138.

20. Harland Page Hall, *H. P. Hall's Observations, Being More or Less a History of Political Contests in Minnesota from 1849 to 1904* (St. Paul, 1904), 51.

21. On this anxiety generally in antebellum American culture, see Halttunen, *Confidence Men*, 56–91.

22. Key works in the historiography on the Ho-Chunk include Nancy O. Lurie, "Winnebago," in ed. Bruce G. Trigger, *Handbook of North American Indians, vol. 15, Northeast* (Washington, DC: Smithsonian Institution Press, 1978), 690–707; Lucy Eldersveld Murphy, *A Gathering of Rivers: Indians, Métis, and Mining in the Western Great Lakes, 1737–1832* (Lincoln: University of Nebraska Press, 2000); Kathleen Neils Conzen, "The Winnebago Urban System: Indian Policy and Townsite Promotion on the Upper Mississippi," in Rondo Cameron and Leo F. Schnore, eds., *Cities and Markets: Studies in the Organization of Human Space* (Lanham, MD, 1997), 269–310; Lawrence W. Onsager, "The Removal of the Winnebago Indians from Wisconsin in 1873–1874," MA thesis, Loma Linda

University, 1985; Steven D. Hoelscher, *Picturing Indians: Photographic Encounters and Tourist Fantasies in H. H. Bennett's Wisconsin Dells* (Madison: University of Wisconsin Press, 2008); and Tom Jones et al., *People of the Big Voice: Photographs of Ho-Chunk Families by Charles Van Schaick, 1879–1942* (Madison: Wisconsin Historical Society Press, 2011).

23. *Annual Report* 1860, 79.

24. Gary Clayton Anderson, *Kinsmen of Another Kind: Dakota-White Relations in the Upper Mississippi Valley, 1650–1862* (1984; St. Paul: Minnesota Historical Society, 1997); Scott Berg, *Thirty-Eight Nooses: Lincoln, Little Crow, and the Beginning of the Frontier's End* (New York: Pantheon, 2012).

25. Maltz, "Fourteenth Amendment."

26. Steven Hahn, "Slave Emancipation, Indian Peoples, and the Projects of a New American State," *Journal of the Civil War Era* 3:3 (September 2013), 307–30.

27. 1869 *Annual Report*, 777, 783. "Soon" here signals a complicating element of this vision: the indefinite deferral of colonized peoples' "readiness" on the grounds of cultural or racial incapacity—their relegation to "an imaginary waiting room of history." Dipesh Chakrabarty, *Provincializing Europe: Postcolonial Thought and Historical Difference* (rev. ed., Princeton: Princeton University Press, 2009), 8. Native Americans' relegation to this liminal zone, which became unmistakable by the 1880s, was less clear in the 1870s; many Indian agents and bureaucrats, buoyed by the apparent revolutionary triumph of slave emancipation and African American political incorporation, seemed to believe that Native Americans could similarly break the shackles of "savagery" and join the body politic on equal terms. See Cahill, *Federal Mothers and Fathers*, 17–31.

28. 1871 *Annual Report*, 865–67.

29. 1873 *Annual Report*, 185.

30. 1874 *Annual Report*, 347. Elsewhere, the same report offered a less sweeping conclusion, finding 1,785 of 2,262 Winnebagos in "citizens' dress." Ibid., 408–9.

31. 1870 *Annual Report*, Sept. 20, 1870, 788.

32. 1873 *Annual Report*, 332–46; 1874 *Annual Report*, 408–22. These numbers excluded the Native population of Alaska, which had recently been brought under U.S. rule.

33. 1874 *Annual Report*, 408–9.

34. 1875 *Annual Report*, 622–23; 1878 *Annual Report*, 776–93; 1879 *Annual Report*, 350–51.

35. 1881 *Annual Report*, 330–49.

36. Quotations from Colette A. Hyman, *Dakota Women's Work: Creativity, Culture, and Exile* (St. Paul: Minnesota Historical Society, 2012), 130–33.

37. See, e.g., *Annual Report* 1871, 857; *Annual Report* 1872, 673; *Annual Report* 1873, 201–2. Cf. Comaroff and Comaroff, *Of Revelation and Revolution*, II: 242–43.

38. *Second Annual Report of the Joint Delegation*, 45–47; see also, e.g., 1875 *Annual Report*, 715.

39. *Report of the Joint Delegation Appointed by the Committees on the Indian Concern of the Yearly Meetings of Baltimore, Philadelphia, and New York . . . To Visit*

the *Indians Under the Care of Friends in the Northern Superintendency, State of Nebraska, 7th & 8th Mos., 1869* (Baltimore: J. Jones, 1869), 29.

40. Evenson and Trayte, "Dress and Interaction in Contending Cultures," 110.

41. *Report of the Joint Delegation*, 36.

42. Rosen, *American Indians and State Law*, 138–39.

43. 1872 *Annual Report*, 415, 602.

44. 1878 *Annual Report*, 786.

45. See, for comparison, Comaroff and Comaroff, *Of Revelation and Revolution*, II: 256–62. On Lakota women as the late-nineteenth-century bearers of "traditional" culture, particularly clothing, see Marsha Clift Bol, "Lakota Beaded Costumes of the Early Reservation Era, in eds. Janet Catherine Berlo and Lee Anne Wilson, *Arts of Africa, Oceania, and the Americas: Selected Readings* (Englewood Cliffs, NJ: Prentice Hall, 1993), 365.

46. *Second Annual Report of the Joint Delegation*, 45–47.

47. Cong. Record, U.S. Senate, 41st Cong., June 3, 1870.

48. Senate, 42nd Cong., April 5, 1872. On the fund's size, see Gates, "Indian Allotments."

49. See Petition of "Indians of the Winnebago Tribe, and more particularly described as the descendants of what was known in the year 1837, and subsequent, as Dandy's Band," [May], 1873, Letters Received by the Office of Indian Affairs, 1824–1881, Microcopy No. 234, (Washington, 1956), Roll 944: Winnebago Agency, 1873 (hereafter cited as Roll 944). For more on this story, see the author's "'Not Quite Constitutionalized': The Meanings of 'Civilization' and the Limits of Native American Citizenship" in Kate Masur and Gregory P. Downs, eds., *The World the Civil War Made* (Chapel Hill: University of North Carolina Press, forthcoming).

50. Hunt to Smith, Dec. 29, 1873, Cash to Hunt, Dec. 27, 1873, Letters Received by Office of Indian Affairs, 1824–81, Winnebago agency, 1826–1875—Roll 945, 1874 (Microcopy No. 234, Washington, 1956).

51. Thomas to AAG, Dept. of Dakota, Jan. 2, 1874, Roll 945.

52. *Prairie du Chien Courier*, May 12, 1874, p. 3.

53. *Janesville Gazette*, August 21, 1874, p. 1.

54. Winona (Minn.) *Daily Republican*, August 3, 1874, p. 3.

55. 1874 *Annual Report*, 519.

56. This was the so-called Indian Homestead Act, 18 Stat. 420. The provision, added to a long Indian appropriation bill at the very end of the 1875 session, does not appear to have been debated in Congress. The records of the Senate Committee on Indian Affairs shed no light on any debate over its contents or merits. For more on this legislation, including its apparent origins in efforts to allow the Ho-Chunk remain in Wisconsin, see Kantrowitz, "'Not Quite Constitutionalized.'"

57. Hoelscher, *Picturing Indians*.

58. On the history of such representations, see Martha A. Sandweiss, *Print the Legend: Photography and the American West* (New Haven: Yale University Press, 2002), esp. 207–73.

59. Jones et al., *People of the Big Voice*.

60. Ibid., 26, 44.

61. *Mountain Wolf Woman, Sister of Crashing Thunder: The Autobiography of a Winnebago Indian*, ed. Nancy Oestreich Lurie (1961; rpt. Ann Arbor: University of Michigan Press, 1966), 121, n. 22.

62. Julian Boucher, personal communication with the author, Mankato, MN, Dec. 25, 2012.

EPILOGUE

The Widest Implications of Disorienting the Civil War Era

Steven Hahn

ONE OF THE GREAT IRONIES, AND ODDITIES, of American historical writing is the scant attention that has been paid to the Civil War and Reconstruction in the Trans-Mississippi West. Ever since the 1890s—when the historical profession was in its infancy and Frederick Jackson Turner suggested that the frontier was the crucible of American development—its challenge, mystique, environment, conquest, settlement, exploitation, forms of political conflict, and ethnic diversity have been at the center of a great many debates about the country's past and how to understand it. None of these debates has been more significant than the coming of the Civil War. Whatever else they may disagree about, scholars of the nineteenth century almost universally acknowledge that the sectional conflict between North and South, and then the war between the Union and the Confederacy, was over the future of the West on the North American continent, and especially over the place of slaveholders and their slaves there. Yet, once hostilities commence, the West all but drops out of the main narrative of warfare, emancipation, state building, and reunification.[1]

Scholars might well respond that, however much the Trans-Mississippi West drew the attention and concern of political leaders from 1800 to 1860, most of the action that consumed the country during the Civil War era, and most of the immediate consequences of the war's signal events, occurred east of the Mississippi River. To the east, after all, was to be found most of the country's population, most of the troops deployed, most of the battles fought, and of course most of the slaves. And there is nothing in this volume to suggest that these numerical balances are incorrect or are in need of revision. But what the chapters do, in very striking ways, is remind us that the Civil War and Reconstruction were truly continental and international in their dynamics. And, perhaps more important, this volume demonstrates how our conceptualization of the Civil War and Reconstruction could well be enlarged and transformed.

Students of the Civil War era will surely have found in the volume's chapters a new geography and cast of actors than those with which they are familiar. They will have moved, not from Virginia to the lower Mississippi Valley, but from the borderlands of the desert Southwest to California, from northern Mexico to southern British Columbia, from Wyoming to Missouri. They will have seen a Confederate invasion of the West from Texas as something of a counterpoint to the Union invasion of the South from Washington, D.C. They will have discovered an effort to thwart secessionism in the Pacific Northwest and not simply in the deep and border South. They will have encountered struggles over the future civic standing and political belonging of Native Americans and immigrants from China as well as former slaves and free people of African descent. They will have confronted the meaning of the Civil War from the perspectives of Apaches, Comanches, Navajos, Choctaws, and Ho-Chunks together with Mexican Liberals battling against a French invasion of their own country. They will have glimpsed how ideas about the colonization of emancipated African American slaves in Mexico could be tied to visions of U.S. hegemony in the hemisphere. They will have found their way through a very different physical landscape of warfare than anything they have known in what are considered the Civil War's main theaters. And they will have been convinced that Appomattox—that iconic place and surrender—did not mark the true end of hostilities. In many ways, that is, the chapters in this volume provide a new and rather breathtaking panorama of the Civil War era's reach and compass.

But there are potential dangers here as well. Like many new approaches to familiar if not timeworn subjects, they can be—and usually are—assimilated to the prevailing frameworks of analysis. They can become add-ons or sidebars to the standard narratives and interpretations, brief excursions into less traversed territory that do not really disrupt or reroute what have long been the main thoroughfares of study and writing. Truth is that we as historians generally become invested—subtly and not so subtly—in ways of thinking about the past that discourage us from taking the full measure of new episodes, new evidence, and new historiographical challenges. Through our training in graduate school and our reading of historical literatures, we come to accept certain periodizations, vectors of conflict and change, political cartographies, and ideas about who are the legitimate participants, even if new findings raise doubts about some or all of these.

Disorienting a subject area as vast, trod over, and synthesized as the Civil War and Reconstruction is difficult enough; reorienting understanding of it may be well-nigh impossible. It is, therefore, probably wise to avoid grand claims for what the chapters in this volume add up to, fascinating as they are individually and intriguing as they may become collectively. It makes more sense to see them as part of an intellectual and scholarly project, already underway, that is beginning to expand the map, the problems, the characters, and the potential comparisons: one that is simultaneously disorienting and reorienting, though for the most part still in modest respects.

Nonetheless, taking account of what the authors provide, I suggest what a larger reorientation might look like, and what difference these studies and others like them may make in how we view the era specifically and the history of the nineteenth-century United States more generally. For one thing, we may come to recognize that while the slaveholders' rebellion was the direct—and surely the most massive—precipitant of the Civil War, it was only one of several rebellions against the presumed authority of the federal government that rattled the country during the first six decades of the nineteenth century, and threatened to pull the Union apart from a number of different directions, not just along the Mason-Dixon Line. Think, for example, of the Nullification Crisis in South Carolina (1831–32), the Second Seminole War in Florida (1835–42: the longest American war until Vietnam), and white settler rejections of Supreme Court decisions having to do with Indian land claims in the 1830s. Think of filibustering operations in Texas, Canada, Cuba, northern Mexico, and Central America (especially Nicaragua) in clear violation of the federal government's Neutrality Law, and of the Mormon War of 1857 out in what the federal government called the Utah Territory and what Mormon residents hoped to make the state of Deseret (an insurrection that required the dispatch of twenty-five hundred U.S. troops).[2]

Think, too, in closer proximity, of secessionist sentiments and projects up and down the Pacific coast, in the Midwest, and in the New York City, where the renegade mayor Fernando Wood hoped to turn it into a port of free entry. Think of Copperheadism and working-class insurrections against conscription and other federal policies (including the enlistment of African American soldiers into the Union Army); of slave rebellions not only against the authority of their masters but also against the early policies of the Lincoln administration meant to keep the slavery question at the margins of state warfare; and of Native American uprisings, especially on the northern Plains, against federal expropriations of homelands and subsistence.[3]

In all of these we can see powerful centrifugal forces and counter-sovereignties at work against the United States, struggles having much in common with those of the West and South discussed here. These conflicts, too, were ready to take states, regions, and constituencies out of the Union. It may well be the case that what we are looking at is better termed a collection of civil wars, of wars of the rebellions rather than a War of the Rebellion. The geographical scope of these centrifugal forces raises serious questions about the axis of North/South sectionalism that has organized historical writing on the Civil War and Reconstruction—indeed, the vast majority of nineteenth-century U.S. history—since the time of the Civil War itself, and has a great deal to do with why the Trans-Mississippi West tends to drop out or at best, assumes limited importance in the ensuing narrative.

Indeed, for quite some time there has been good reason to interrogate long-held assumptions about the bases of sectionalism, owing to the work of historians who have complicated the divide between slavery and freedom in the United States. They have demonstrated that slavery unraveled slowly in the Northeast and Midwest and often gave way to forms of servitude rather than freedom; that slave hiring took place in states like Pennsylvania, Illinois, and Ohio; and that the Fugitive Slave Law, together with rulings of the Supreme Court in the 1840s and 1850s, made slavery national and freedom local (the inverse of what the fledgling Republican party claimed). Small wonder that the historian Don Fehrenbacher called the United States in this period "the Slaveholding Republic." [4]

Once we take the measure of these findings—that sectionalism may have been more of a powerful political construction than a social reality, much as Frederick Jackson Turner (of all people) once claimed—it may be possible for us to take a new look at developmental issues that have as much of an East/West as a North/South dynamic, as suggested by the recent spate of scholarship that focuses on the Mississippi Valley as an alternative political center to the eastern seaboard.[5]

Though the traditional North/South sectionalism turns us to the Atlantic and to the attendant Euro-American connections and entanglements, the Mississippi Valley turns us to the Caribbean basin and the Western Hemisphere, with imagined links between Chicago, New Orleans, and Havana. It was from here, with the aid of shipping channels and rail lines, that Stephen Douglas and his allies in the South hoped to propel the expansion of a massive commercial empire. It was here, too, and especially on the western side of the Mississippi, that early test cases over the future of slavery took place (St. Louis), that armed struggle over popular sovereignty erupted (Missouri and Kansas), that initial wartime forays toward emancipation—catalyzed by German refugees from the Revolutions of 1848—occurred (Missouri), that contract leasing and black landholding experiments gained footing (Louisiana, Mississippi, Arkansas, and Tennessee), and that the military balances began to tip decisively to the Union side. The results of the Civil War thereby undermined the Mississippi Valley's quest for hegemony over American development and secured the power of the Northeast.[6]

Historians might, of course, have an easy time minimizing the significance of the Trans-Mississippi West as a specific theater of Civil Warfare. But here again there is much more than immediately meets the eye. As Megan Kate Nelson describes in her chapter, Jefferson Davis as secretary of war under Franklin Pierce had been vitally interested in securing a southern route for a transcontinental railroad and to that end pressed forward with what became the Gadsden Purchase while arranging for the importation of forty-one camels from North Africa as a transportation and labor experiment. Once the Confederate rebellion became organized, Davis moved to establish friendly relations with the Juárez government in Mexico (he failed) and made overtures to the governors of the northern Mexican states while at the same time sending an emissary to Indian Territory to establish alliances with the tribes there (which included representation in the Confederate Congress and participation in the Confederate Army), as Nicholas Guyatt and Fay Yarbrough show.[7]

The invasion of New Mexico in early 1862 thus had far-reaching ambitions. New Mexico already had a slave code as well as Confederate supporters, and, as Megan Kate Nelson demonstrates in this volume, Davis imagined it as a potential gateway both to Southern California (with many Confederate sympathizers) and to the mineral wealth of the gold and silver regions of the desert and mountain West, riches that the rebels desperately needed to fill a virtually empty treasury. As one Union Army officer put it, the objective of the New Mexico invasion was no less than the conquest of California, Sonora, Chihuahua, New Mexico, Arizona, and Utah—and, above all, the possession of the entire gold supply on the Pacific Coast. The defeat of Confederate forces just east of Santa Fe at Glorieta Pass in late March 1862 was therefore a decisive moment in the War of the Rebellion, but it also helps us to recognize that the battle for control of the Trans-Mississippi West was ongoing, before, during, and after the customary chronological boundaries of the Civil War.

The examples are many. As Lance Blyth reveals in his chapter, Kit Carson in the Southwest and John Pope in the upper Plains were ordered that year to turn their attention from Confederate rebels to Native American rebels in what became a lengthy, and federally directed, effort to subdue Indian peoples, place them under federal jurisdiction, and confine them to prescribed reservations. At the same time, Congress passed the Homestead Act, created six new territories (Dakota, Colorado, Nevada, Arizona, Idaho, and Montana), abolished slavery, and authorized the construction of a transcontinental railroad, the context for the chapters by Martha Sandweiss, Virginia Scharff, and Stephen Kantrowitz. For the next three decades, much of the West was effectively occupied by the federal Army, which performed a number of developmental functions: hunting down Indian rebels, protecting railroad lines and surveying parties, supplying manpower, suppressing labor strikes, and responding to the calls of territorial governors—who had no militias at their disposal—for assistance. Indeed, as Gregory Downs suggests, the Trans-Mississippi West, perhaps even more than the rebellious South, became a testing ground for the principles and authority of the nation-state that the War of the Rebellion brought into being.

By fully integrating the West into the story we can, in fact, gain a much better sense of what the Civil War and Reconstruction, which were coincidental rather than sequential, meant on an international stage in the mid-nineteenth century: an immensely important example of nation-state building with imperial dimensions. The federal government territorialized much of the South and interior West, especially those areas where rebellious populations had their strongest bases. It moved forcefully against alternative sovereignties by rejecting the treaty process in dealings with Native Americans, confining Indians to small reservations, and of course by changing the character of the nation by abolishing slavery first as a military strategy, then by executive order, and finally in a constitutional amendment whose acceptance by ex-Confederate states was a requirement for readmission to the Union under the Radical Republicans' plans. (Until the Civil War, slavery had only been abolished by individual states.) As a result of these conflicts, the federal government established a national citizenship tied to cultural notions of belonging, which, as Joshua Paddison and the chapters of part 3 illustrate, encouraged missionary activities among subject populations and set certain limits to who could belong. This played out nowhere more compellingly than with Native Americans, Chinese, and peoples of Mexican descent in the Trans-Mississippi West.[8]

No wonder then that the language of colonialism was widely invoked in reference to the governance and economic organization of both the South and West, that regionalism became a metaphor for capturing the new power relations between center peripheries, and that the character of and policies toward the South and West were seen as harbingers for subsequent endeavors in the global tropics. Massachusetts senator Henry Dawes, sponsor of the Dawes Severalty Act of 1887, argued that efforts to manage Indians should guide encounters with other alien races whose future "has been put in our keeping," and his sensibility was widely shared in national political circles. Thus, when the United States occupied the Philippines during and after the Spanish–American War in 1898, the experience of the South and especially the West hovered, supplying the racialist discourses and images of struggle between the forces of savagery and civilization. When the new Bureau of Insular Affairs was established, its directors already had important experience in the West. For instance, the military governors of the Philippines between 1898 and 1902 had all been in Indian service. Almost all of the top U.S. military officers had previously battled and negotiated with western Indians. And most of the federal troops came from the western states and territories.[9]

Finally, a history of the Civil War era that seriously encompasses the Trans-Mississippi West will serve to emphasize the significance of the Pacific to virtually all of American history. Americanists who are attentive to transnational approaches to history writing have been deeply concerned with what they call the Atlantic World, which, at its best, reaches from North America across to Europe, West Africa, Brazil, and the Caribbean basin. This has been to good effect. But lest we forget, from the middle of the eighteenth century, North American merchants, shippers, and whalers—many based in the Northeast—were out in the Pacific and Indian oceans involving themselves in the lucrative trade with South Asia and China, and they were an active presence on the islands we now know as Hawai'i. Surely from the time of Thomas Jefferson, the Pacific was regarded by most political leaders as crucial to America's destiny and prosperity. The purchase of Louisiana, the annexation of Texas, the invasion of Mexico, and indeed the entire frenzy for Manifest Destiny were driven in large part by eyes on the Pacific, a country spread sea to shining sea. Consider that antislavery senator William Seward was so concerned about bringing California into the Union as a state, and thereby securing its ports, that he would have held his nose and agreed, if necessary, to the legality of slavery there. The Civil War and the defeat of rebellions in the South and West completed the continentalism that Seward so desperately sought, and he emerged as an architect of U.S. relations with Asia made possible by that control over the Pacific Coast.[10]

In short, the outcome of the intellectual project envisioned here is a new set of vantage points from which to explore the history of the United States and its peoples. Ever since the late nineteenth century, when the American history profession was born, the story of the United States has been told chiefly from the perspective of the Northeast. This was, to be sure, the result of the empowerment of that section of the country at the expense of the others, a pattern marked by the ascendancy of the Republican Party, intensified by the Civil War, and then completed through the consolidation of centers of finance and intellectual life there. The result is that the Northeast has too often stood in for the nation (center) while the South and West have come to be regarded as regions (peripheries), described as different and distinctive, and posing an assortment of problems. For its part, the historical literature has long reflected this hierarchy of power and significance: until the civil rights movement made African Americans subjects of national concern, southern history developed as a field apart, very much obsessed with the elements of its own special character. Western history, for all its vitality and its challenges to the categories of the national story, still is a field apart, so much so that historians of our greatest conflict and turning point have been able to ignore their connection to it.

The incorporation of the Trans-Mississippi West into the history of the Civil War era thus gives us the opportunity not only to add to our knowledge and examine the North/South issues in deeper and more expansive ways, but also to reposition ourselves in relation to the course of American development. We may, that is, be able to look at the unfolding of U.S. history as much from West to East and South to North as from East to West and North to South, interrogating centers and peripheries as well as nations and regions. In so doing, we can connect the experience of the United States much more firmly to the rest of the hemisphere, and, by extension, to much of the globe. It is a rich and tantalizing prospect.

NOTES

1. See, for example, some of the classic treatments of the Civil War and Reconstruction: Allan Nevins, *The War for the Union*, 4 vols. (New York: Scribner, 1959–71); James M. McPherson, *Battle Cry of Freedom: The Civil War Era* (New York:

Oxford University Press, 1987); Richard E. Beringer et al., *Why the South Lost the Civil War* (Athens: University of Georgia Press, 1986); David Blight, *Race and Reunion: The Civil War in American Memory* (Cambridge, MA: Harvard University Press, 2011); William A. Dunning, *Reconstruction, Political and Economic, 1865–1877* (New York: Harper, 1907); Eric L. McKitrick, *Andrew Johnson and Reconstruction* (Chicago: University of Chicago Press, 1960); James M. McPherson, *The Struggle for Equality: The Abolitionists and the Negro in the Civil War and Reconstruction* (Princeton: Princeton University Press, 1964); and Kenneth M. Stampp, *The Era of Reconstruction, 1865–1877* (New York: Knopf, 1965). Eric Foner in *Reconstruction: America's Unfinished Revolution, 1863–1877* (New York: Harper & Row, 1988) does a better job of looking at Reconstruction nationally and of integrating the West, but it does not figure very importantly. William McFeely's outstanding treatment of General O. O. Howard ends with his service as commissioner of the Freedmen s Bureau and does not look at his subsequent role in the trans-Mississippi West. See his *Yankee Stepfather: General O. O. Howard and the Freedmen* (New York: Norton, 1968).

2. For good treatments, see William W. Freehling, *Prelude to Civil War: The Nullification Crisis in South Carolina, 1816–1836* (New York: Oxford University Press, 1964); John K. Mahon, *History of the Second Seminole War, 1835–1842* (Gainesville: University of Florida Press, 1967); Robert E. May, *Manifest Destiny's Underworld: Filibustering in Antebellum America* (Chapel Hill: University of North Carolina Press, 2002); and Will Bagley and David L. Bigler, *The Mormon Rebellion: America's First Civil War, 1857–1858* (Norman: University of Oklahoma Press, 2011).

3. Jennifer L. Weber, *The Copperheads: The Rise and Fall of Lincoln's Opponents in the North* (New York: Oxford University Press, 2008); Iver Bernstein, *The New York City Draft Riots: Their Significance in American Society and Politics in the Age of the Civil War* (New York: Oxford University Press, 1990); D. W. Meinig, *Shaping of America, Vol. 2: Continental America, 1800–1867* (New Haven: Yale University Press, 1993), 489–502; Steven Hahn, *The Political Worlds of Slavery and Freedom* (Cambridge, MA: Harvard University Press, 2009), 55–114; and Alvin M. Josephy, *The Civil War in the American West* (New York: Knopf, 1991), 94–154. In his chapter in this volume, Lance Blyth also suggests thinking of conflicts erupting during and after the period we usually mark for the Civil War.

4. Don E. *The Slaveholding Republic: An Account of the United States Government's Relation to Slavery* (New York: Oxford University Press, 2001). See also Arthur Zilversmit, *The First Emancipation: The Abolition of Slavery in the North* (Chicago: University of Chicago Press, 1967); Gary B. Nash and Jean R. Soderlund, *Freedom by Degrees: Emancipation in Pennsylvania and Its Aftermath* (New York: Oxford University Press, 1991); Joan Pope Melish, *Disowning Slavery: Gradual Emancipation and "Race" in New England, 1780–1860* (Ithaca: Cornell University Press, 1998); Leon F. Litwack, *North of Slavery: The Negro in the Free States* (Chicago: University of Chicago Press, 1961), 3–29; Don E. Fehrenbacher, *The Dred Scott Case: Its Significance in American Law and Politics* (New York: Oxford University Press, 1979); and Hahn, *The Political Worlds of Slavery and Freedom*.

5. On the Mississippi Valley and slavery during the antebellum decades see especially Walter Johnson, *River of Dark Dreams: Slavery and Empire in the Cotton Kingdom* (Cambridge, MA: Harvard University Press, 2013). Johnson does not pursue the idea of the Mississippi Valley as a developmental alternative, although he does explore its imperial reach.

6. See, for example, Adam Arenson, *The Great Heart of the Republic: St. Louis and the Cultural Civil War* (Cambridge, MA: Harvard University Press, 2011); Nicole Etcheson, *Bleeding Kansas: Contested Liberty in the Civil War Era* (Lawrence: University Press of Kansas, 2004); Robert W. Johannsen, *Stephen A. Douglas* (New York: Oxford University Press, 1973), 158–65; Robert E. May, *Slavery, Race, and Conquest in the Tropics: Lincoln, Douglas, and the Future of Latin America* (New York: Cambridge University Press, 2013); Andrew Zimmerman, "From the Rhine to the Mississippi: Property, Democracy, and Socialism in the American Civil War" (unpublished paper, University of Pennsylvania, 2013); and Ira Berlin et al, *Freedom: A Documentary History of Emancipation, 1861–1867*, series I, vol. III: *The Wartime Genesis of Free Labor: The Lower South* (New York: Cambridge University Press, 1990).

7. See, for instance, Robert M. Utley, *The Indian Frontier of the American West, 1846–1890* (Albuquerque: University of New Mexico Press, 1984), 65–98; Clarissa W. Confer, *The Cherokee Nation in the Civil War* (Norman: University of Oklahoma Press, 2007); Donald S. Frazier, *Blood and Treasure: Confederate Empire in the Southwest* (College Station: Texas A&M University Press, 1995); and Josephy, *The Civil War in the American West*, 3–92.

8. Joshua Paddison, *American Heathens: Religion, Race, and Reconstruction in California* (Berkeley: University of California Press, 2012).

9. See Natalie Ring, *The Problem South: Region, Empire, and the Liberal State, 1880–1930* (Athens: University of Georgia Press, 2012), and Walter L. Williams, "U.S. Indian Policy and the Debate over Philippine Annexation: Implications for the Origins of American Imperialism," *Journal of American History* 66, no. 4 (March 1980): 810–31.

10. James R. Fichter, *So Great a Proffit: How the East Indies Trade Transformed Anglo-American Capitalism* (Cambridge, MA: Harvard University Press, 2010); Alan Taylor, *American Colonies: The Settling of North America* (New York: Penguin, 2001), 444–77; and Ernest N. Paolino, *The Foundations of the American Empire: William Henry Seward and United States Foreign Policy* (Ithaca: Cornell University Press, 1973).

ACKNOWLEDGMENTS

This book was created to solve a problem.
In 2009, when Adam was halfway through revising the manuscript of his first book, *The Great Heart of the Republic: St. Louis and the Cultural Civil War* (2011), he realized that the ways he had framed the history of the city and the Civil War era were all wrong. The fate of St. Louis was shaped not only by the politics of slavery or westward expansion, nor simply by the growing conflict between North and South. On the streets of St. Louis, supporters of northern free-labor ideology jostled with southern proslavery advocates, both of whom had their eyes set on the West but with vastly different ideas about how to manage the twin problems of slavery and Manifest Destiny.
The West, Adam argued in that book, provided its advocates with new answers to the pressing questions of national unity and the proper relationship to land and labor, turning often on plans for the proposed transcontinental railroad. Political, economic, and cultural questions arising in the West were different, and they were crucial to the history of St. Louis he had written.
But then there was this dilemma: there was no scholarship that considered the whole of the American West in the Civil War era while conceptualizing the challenges to the nation that emerged there. Though Adam would research, analyze, and describe these conflicts and challenges in St. Louis, what about the rest of the story? He thus asked historians working on similar topics to join him in panel proposals for various academic conferences serving either the Civil War crowd or Western history types, but most of these submissions were rejected.
Along the way, he fell into a conversation venting these frustrations outside of his office at the University of Texas at El Paso (UTEP), on a day that

Sherry Smith, the associate director of the William P. Clements Center for Southwest Studies at Southern Methodist University, was back visiting her former UTEP colleagues. From that first discussion, Sherry was confident that such efforts to bring western and Civil War history into a shared conversation would create a provocative Clements Center symposium. The next slot available was the 2013–14 academic year—far off, to be sure, but providing ample time to find a suitable partner institution.

The next piece fell into place when Erik Greenberg, the director of education at the Autry National Center in Los Angeles, invited Adam to speak about his book. Dan Finley, then the president of the Autry, mentioned in his introduction that the museum had considered a Civil War and the West exhibition but that nothing had come of it yet. With that opening, Adam contacted Steve Aron, executive director of the Institute for the Study of the American West at the Autry and a professor of history at UCLA. The pair then huddled with Carolyn Brucken (curator of western women's history at the Autry), Virginia Scharff (professor of history at the University of New Mexico and the Autry's Chair of Western Women's History), and Brenda Stevenson (professor of history at UCLA) to imagine what might be possible. Their subsequent call for contributors resulted in sixty applications from around the world, demonstrating the depth of this supposedly nonexistent field as well as substantial enthusiasm for the possibilities such a project would offer. Andy Graybill, appointed as director of the Clements Center in the summer of 2011, joined the group that fall.

Even given those expansive first conversations, it is amazing to consider what has emerged: a museum exhibition curated by Carolyn Brucken and Virginia Scharff, designed by Patrick Fredrickson and his staff, and supported throughout the divisions of the Autry; this edited volume; and a companion volume edited by Gingy which considers the signature artifacts from the exhibition. This collaborative work, including university professors, museum professionals, and many more, aim to address a broad public, including scholars. For the conceptual work of framing this volume, Adam received particular help from Andy, Carolyn, Gingy, and Steve, but all of the contributors to this collection have been willing to pitch in whenever needed, and they seem to have enjoyed the challenge, even when asked for complete rewrites or pressed to meet rigid deadlines.

For the Clements Center's half of the two-part symposium, the scholars in this volume were able to gather at SMU's satellite campus in Taos, New Mexico, on a gorgeous weekend in fall 2013 to grapple with the conceptual challenges of unifying Civil War and western history . . . while getting in a hike, exploring the re-creation of Fort Burgwin, and taking a tour through the excavations of Pot Creek Pueblo. For this (as with so much else), the editors are enormously grateful to Ruth Ann Elmore, assistant director of the Clements Center. Mike Adler and his staff at SMU-in-Taos—especially Cyndy Gimble and Ginny Greeno—treated the group with the warmth and hospitality for which they are known and beloved.

The spring 2014 gathering at the Autry included a conversation in front of the exhibition storyboard with both artists and scholars, as well as a lightning-round presentation of the volume's contents—just three minutes allowed for each presenter, followed by an engaged Q&A session—that convinced the group that this should be the format of conference presentations everywhere. At the lightning round, Bill Deverell was inspired to propose *Civil War Wests* as the volume title, which ended a months-long quest. The Los Angeles weekend was delightful and all expertly coordinated by the Autry staff, including David Burton, Ben Fitzsimmons, and Belinda Nakasato-Suarez.

Niels Hooper of the University of California Press has been an enthusiastic supporter of this volume from the beginning, participating in both symposium gatherings and guiding the book through the publication process on its tight timeline. Kim Hogeland has provided wonderful and expert assistance. Copyeditor Pam Suwinsky helped perfect the volume's final form, and—as ever—the maps by Ezra Zeitler sparkle.

Finally, the editors thank their families for their support and forbearance, none more than Adam's wife Rebecca Rosenthal and their sons Simon and Leo, who have endured Adam's five semesters spent commuting weekly from Los Angeles to El Paso. The publication of this book marks their own chance to be united in the West and then across the nation in New York City.

SECONDARY BIBLIOGRAPHY

Aarim-Heriot, Najia. *Chinese Immigrants, African Americans, and Racial Anxiety in the United States, 1848–82.* Urbana: University of Illinois Press, 2003.
Abel, Annie Heloise. *The American Indian as Participant in the Civil War.* Cleveland: Arthur H. Clark Co., 1919.
———. *The American Indian as Slaveholder and Secessionist.* 1915; Lincoln: University of Nebraska Press, 1992.
Adams, David Wallace. *Education for Extinction: American Indians and the Boarding School Experience, 1875–1928.* Lawrence: University Press of Kansas, 1995.
Adams, George Rollie. *General William S. Harney: Prince of Dragoons.* Lincoln: University of Nebraska Press, 2001.
Adams, John. *Old Square Toes and His Lady: the Life of James and Amelia Douglas.* Victoria, BC: Horsdal and Schubert, 2001.
Adams, Rachel. "Blackness Goes South: Race and Mestizaje in Our America." In *Imagining Our Americas: Towards a Transnational Frame,* edited by Sandhya Shukla and Heidi Tinsman, 214–48. Durham, NC: Duke University Press, 2007.
Adelman, Jeremy and Stephen Aron. "From Borderlands to Borders: Empires, Nation-States, and the Peoples in Between in North American History." *American Historical Review* 104, no. 3 (June 1999): 814–41.
Anderson, Gary Clayton. *Kinsmen of Another Kind: Dakota-White Relations in the Upper Mississippi Valley, 1650–1862.* 1984; St. Paul: Minnesota Historical Society Press, 1997.
———. *The Conquest of Texas: Ethnic Cleansing in the Promised Land, 1820–1875.* Norman: University of Oklahoma Press, 2005.
Anderson, Mabel Washbourne. *Life of General Stand Watie: The Only Indian Brigadier General of the Confederate Army and the Last General to Surrender.* Pryor, OK: Mayes County Republican, 1915.
Anthony, Susan B., Elizabeth Cady Stanton, and Matilda Joslyn Gage. *History of Woman Suffrage.* Rochester, NY: Charles Mann, 1887.
Arenson, Adam. *The Great Heart of the Republic: St. Louis and the Cultural Civil War.* Cambridge, MA: Harvard University Press, 2011.

Armstrong, William Howard. *Warrior in Two Camps: Ely S. Parker, Union General and Seneca Chief.* Syracuse, NY: Syracuse University Press, 1978.
Aron, Stephen. *American Confluence: The Missouri Frontier from Borderland to Border State.* Bloomington: Indiana University Press, 2006.
Arthur, Anthony. *General Jo Shelby's March.* New York: Random House, 2010.
Astor, Aaron. *Rebels on the Border: Civil War, Emancipation, and the Reconstruction of Kentucky and Missouri.* Baton Rouge: Louisiana State University Press, 2012.
Bagley, Will and David L. Bigler. *The Mormon Rebellion: America's First Civil War, 1857–1858.* Norman: University of Oklahoma Press, 2011.
Bailey, David Thomas. "A Divided Prism: Two Sources of Black Testimony on Slavery." *Journal of Southern History* 46, no. 3 (August 1980): 381–404.
Bailey, John W. *Pacifying the Plains: General Alfred Terry and the Decline of the Sioux, 1866–1890.* Westport, CT: Greenwood, 1979.
Bailey, Lynn R. *If You Take My Sheep: The Evolution and Conflicts of Navajo Pastoralism.* Pasadena, CA: Westernlore, 1980.
Baird, W. David. *Peter Pitchlynn: Chief of the Choctaws.* Norman: University of Oklahoma Press, 1972.
Baker, T. Lindsay and Julie P. Baker, eds. *The WPA Oklahoma Slave Narratives.* Norman: University of Oklahoma Press, 1996.
Basehart, Harry W. "The Resource Holding Corporation among the Mescalero Apache." *Southwestern Journal of Anthropology* 23, no. 3 (Autumn 1967): 277–91.
Baum, Dale. "Slaves Taken to Texas for Safekeeping during the Civil War." In *The Fate of Texas,* edited by Charles D. Grear, 83–103. Fayetteville: University of Arkansas Press, 2008.
Bayly, C. A. *The Birth of the Modern World, 1780–1914: Global Connections and Comparisons.* Malden, MA: Blackwell, 2004.
Beckham, Stephen Dow. *Requiem for a People: The Rogue Indians and the Frontiersmen.* Norman: University of Oklahoma Press, 1971.
Beilein, Joseph M. Jr. "Household War: Guerrilla Men, Rebel Women, and Guerrilla Warfare in Civil War Missouri." PhD diss., University of Missouri, 2012.
Benedict, Bryce. *Jayhawkers: The Civil War Brigade of James Henry Lane.* Norman: University of Oklahoma Press, 2009.
Benedict, Michael Les. *A Compromise of Principle: Congressional Republicans and Reconstruction, 1863–1869.* New York: Norton, 1974.
Benton, Lauren A. *A Search for Sovereignty: Law and Geography in European Empires, 1400—1900.* New York: Cambridge University Press, 2010.
Berg, Scott. *Thirty-Eight Nooses: Lincoln, Little Crow, and the Beginning of the Frontier's End.* New York: Pantheon, 2012.
Bergeron, Paul H. *The Presidency of James K. Polk.* Lawrence: University Press of Kansas, 1987.
Beringer, Richard E., et al. *Why the South Lost the Civil War.* Athens: University of Georgia Press, 1986.

Berkhofer, Robert F. *The White Man's Indian: Images of the American Indian from Columbus to the Present.* New York: Knopf, 1978.

Berlin, Ira, et al., eds. *The Black Military Experience.* Cambridge: Cambridge University Press, 1983.

———*Freedom: A Documentary History of Emancipation, 1861–1867, series I, vol. I: The Destruction of Slavery.* Cambridge: Cambridge University Press, 1985.

———. *The Wartime Genesis of Free Labor: The Upper South.* Cambridge: Cambridge University Press, 1985.

———. *Freedom: A Documentary History of Emancipation, 1861–1867, series I, vol. III: The Wartime Genesis of Free Labor: The Lower South.* New York: Cambridge University Press, 1990.

———. *The Destruction of Slavery.* Cambridge: Cambridge University Press, 1993.

Bernstein, Iver. *The New York City Draft Riots: Their Significance in American Society and Politics in the Age of the Civil War.* New York: Oxford University Press, 1990.

Berwanger, Eugene H. *The West and Reconstruction.* Urbana: University of Illinois Press, 1981.

Bierce, Lucius. *Travels in the Southland, 1822–1823: The Journal of Lucius Verus Bierce.* Edited by George W. Knepper. Columbus: Ohio State University Press, 1966.

Blackhawk, Ned. *Violence over the Land: Indians and Empires in the Early American West.* Cambridge, MA: Harvard University Press, 2006.

Blair, William A. and Karen Fisher Younger. *Lincoln's Proclamation: Emancipation Reconsidered.* Chapel Hill: University of North Carolina Press, 2009.

Blassingame, John. "The Recruitment of Negro Troops in Missouri during the Civil War." *Missouri Historical Review* 58, no. 3 (April 1964): 326–38.

Blight, David. *Race and Reunion: The Civil War in American Memory.* Cambridge, MA: Harvard University Press, 2001.

Blum, Edward J. *Reforging the White Republic: Race, Religion, and American Nationalism, 1865–1898.* Baton Rouge: Louisiana State University Press, 2005.

Blume, Donald T. *Ambrose Bierce's Civilians and Soldiers in Context: A Critical Study.* Kent, OH: Kent State University Press, 2004.

Bol, Marsha Clift. "Lakota Beaded Costumes of the Early Reservation Era." In *Arts of Africa, Oceania, and the Americas: Selected Readings,* edited by Janet Catherine Berlo and Lee Anne Wilson, 363–70. Englewood Cliffs, NJ: Prentice Hall, 1993.

Boman, Dennis K. *Lincoln and Citizens' Rights in Civil War Missouri: Balancing Freedom and Security.* Baton Rouge: Louisiana State University Press, 2011.

Boritt, Gabor. *The Gettysburg Gospel: The Lincoln Speech That Nobody Knows.* New York: Simon and Schuster, 2008.

Bottoms, D. Michael. *An Aristocracy of Color: Race and Reconstruction in California and the West, 1850–1890.* Norman: University of Oklahoma Press, 2013.

Bowes, John P. *Exiles and Pioneers: Eastern Indians in the Trans-Mississippi West.* Cambridge: Cambridge University Press, 2009.

Bradbury, John F. Jr. "'Buckwheat Cake Philanthropy': Refugees and the Union Army in the Ozarks." *Arkansas Historical Quarterly* 57, no. 3 (Autumn 1998): 233–54.

Braude, Ann. "The Baptism of a Cheyenne Girl." In *The Study of Children in Religion: A Methods Handbook,* edited by Susan B. Ridgley, 236–51. New York: New York University Press, 2011.

Britton, Wiley. *The Union Indian Brigade in the Civil War.* Kansas City: F. Hudson, 1922.

Brooks, James F. "Violence, Justice, and State Power in the New Mexican Borderlands, 1780–1880." In *Power and Place in the North American West,* edited by Richard White and John M. Findlay, 23–60. Seattle: University of Washington Press, 1999.

———. *Captives and Cousins: Slavery, Kinship, and Community in the Southwest Borderlands.* Chapel Hill: University of North Carolina Press, 2002.

Brown, Charles Henry. *Agents of Manifest Destiny: The Lives and Times of the Filibusters.* Chapel Hill: University of North Carolina Press, 1980.

Brown, Richard Maxwell. *Strain of Violence: Historical Studies of American Violence and Vigilantism.* New York: Oxford University Press, 1975.

———. *No Duty to Retreat: Violence and Values in American History and Society.* New York: Oxford University Press, 1991.

———. "Western Violence: Structure, Values, Myth." *Western Historical Quarterly* 24, no. 1 (February 1993): 4–20.

———. "Violence." In *Oxford History of the American West,* edited by Clyde A. Milner, Carol A. O'Connor, and Martha A. Sandweiss, 393–425. New York: Oxford University Press, 1994.

Brownlee, Richard S. *Gray Ghosts of the Confederacy.* Baton Rouge: Louisiana State University Press, 1984.

Bruyneel, Kevin. *The Third Space of Sovereignty: The Postcolonial Politics of U.S.-Indigenous Relations.* Minneapolis: University of Minnesota Press, 2007.

Buice, David. "A Stench in the Nostrils of Honest Men: Southern Democrats and the Edmunds Act of 1882." *Dialogue: A Journal of Mormon Thought* 21, no. 3 (Autumn 1988): 100–113.

Burke, Diane Mutti. *On Slavery's Border: Missouri's Small Slaveholding Households, 1815–1865.* Athens: University of Georgia, 2010.

———. "'Slavery Dies Hard': Enslaved Missourians' Struggle for Freedom." In *Bleeding Kansas, Bleeding Missouri: The Long Civil War on the Border,* edited by Jonathan Earle and Diane Mutti Burke, 151–68. Lawrence: University Press of Kansas, 2013.

Burke, Diane Mutti and John P. Herron, eds. *Kansas City, America's Crossroads: Essays from the Missouri Historical Review, 1906–2006.* Columbia: State Historical Society of Missouri, 2007.

Burton, Antoinette. *Burdens of History: British Feminists, Indian Women, and Imperial Culture, 1865–1915.* Chapel Hill: University of North Carolina Press, 1995.

Butler, Anne M. *Daughters of Joy, Sisters of Misery: Prostitutes in the American West.* Urbana: University of Illinois Press, 1991.
Butler, Clayton. "Understanding our Past: An Interview with Historian Gary Gallagher," Civil War Trust, 2013. www.civilwar.org/education/history/civil-war-history-and-scholarship/gary-gallagher-interview.html
Cahill, Cathleen. *Federal Mothers and Fathers: A Social History of the United States Indian Service, 1869–1933.* Chapel Hill: University of North Carolina Press, 2011.
Calloway, Colin G. *Pen and Ink Witchcraft: Treaties and Treaty Making in American Indian History.* New York: Oxford University Press, 2013.
Campbell, Randolph B. *Grass-Roots Reconstruction in Texas, 1865–1880.* Baton Rouge: Louisiana State University Press, 1997.
———. *Empire for Slavery: The Peculiar Institution in Texas, 1821–65.* Baton Rouge: Louisiana State University Press, 1991,
Cannon, Mark W. "The Mormon Issue in Congress 1872–1882: Drawing on the Experience of Territorial Delegate George Q. Cannon." PhD diss. Harvard University, 1960.
Cantrell, Gregg. *Stephen F. Austin: Empresario of Texas.* New Haven: Yale University Press, 2001.
Carr, Helen. *Inventing the American Primitive: Politics, Gender and the Representation of Native American Literary Traditions, 1789–1936.* New York: New York University Press, 1996.
Castel, Albert. "Orders No. 11 and the Civil War on the Border." *Missouri Historical Review* 57, no. 4 (1963): 357–68.
Castel, Albert and Thomas Goodrich. *Bloody Bill Anderson: The Short, Savage Life of a Civil War Guerrilla.* Mechanicsburg, PA: Stackpole, 1998.
Catt, Carrie Chapman and Nettie Rogers Shuler. *Woman Suffrage and Politics.* New York: Charles Scribner, 1923.
Chan, Sucheng. *This Bittersweet Soil: The Chinese in California Agriculture, 1860–1910.* Berkeley: University of California Press, 1986.
Chang, David A. *The Color of the Land: Race, Nation, and the Politics of Landownership in Oklahoma, 1832–1929.* Chapel Hill: University of North Carolina Press, 2010.
Chakrabarty, Dipesh. *Provincializing Europe: Postcolonial Thought and Historical Difference.* Rev. ed. Princeton: Princeton University Press, 2009.
Chapman, Miriam Ganz. "The Story of Woman Suffrage in Wyoming, 1869–1890." MA thesis, University of Wyoming, 1952.
Chávez, Ernesto. *The U.S. War with Mexico: A Brief History with Documents.* Boston: Bedford/St. Martin's, 2008.
Cheek, William and Aimee Lee Cheek. *John Mercer Langston and the Fight for Black Freedom, 1829–65.* Champaign: University of Illinois Press, 1989.
Chen, Yong. *Chinese San Francisco, 1850–1943: A Trans-Pacific Community* Stanford: Stanford University Press, 2000.
Cobb, Josephine. "Alexander Gardner." *Image* no. 62 (June 1958): 124–36.
Collins, James P. "Native Americans in the Census, 1860–1890." *Prologue* 38, no. 2 (Summer 2006): 54–58.

Collins, Robert. *Jim Lane: Scoundrel, Statesman, Kansan.* New Orleans: Pelican, 2007.
Colton, Ray Charles. *The Civil War in the Western Territories: Arizona, Colorado, New Mexico, and Utah.* Norman: University of Oklahoma Press, 1959.
Comaroff, John L. and Jean Comaroff. *Of Revelation and Revolution: The Dialectics of Modernity on a South African Frontier.* 2 vols. Chicago: University of Chicago Press, 1991–97.
Confer, Clarissa W. *The Cherokee Nation in the Civil War.* Norman: University of Oklahoma Press, 2007.
Connelly, Thomas L. "The American Camel Experiment: A Reappraisal." *Southwestern Historical Quarterly* 69, no. 4 (April 1966): 442–62.
Conzen, Kathleen Neils. "The Winnebago Urban System: Indian Policy and Townsite Promotion on the Upper Mississippi." In *Cities and Markets: Studies in the Organization of Human Space,* edited by Rondo Cameron and Leo F. Schnore, 269–310. Lanham, MD: University Press of America, 1997.
Cooper, William J. Jr. *Jefferson Davis, American.* New York: Vintage, 2001.
Cornell, Sarah E., "Citizens of Nowhere: Fugitive Slaves and Free African Americans in Mexico, 1833–1857," *Journal of American History* 100, no. 2 (September 2013): 351–74.
Cott, Nancy F. *The Grounding of Modern Feminism.* New Haven: Yale University Press, 1989.
Crouch, Barry A. *The Freedmen's Bureau and Black Texans.* Austin: University of Texas Press, 1992.
———, ed. *The Dance of Freedom: Texas African Americans during Reconstruction.* Austin: University of Texas Press, 2007.
Dando-Collins, Stephen. *Tycoon's War: How Cornelius Vanderbilt Invaded a Country to Overthrow America's Most Famous Military Adventurer.* Boston: Da Capo Press, 2007.
Daniels, Roger. *Asian America: Chinese and Japanese in the United States since 1850.* Seattle: University of Washington Press, 1995.
Danker, Donald, ed. "The Wounded Knee Interviews of Eli S. Ricker." *Nebraska History* 62, no. 2 (Summer 1981): 151–243.
Debo, Angie. *The Rise and Fall of the Choctaw Republic.* Norman: University of Oklahoma Press, 1934.
DeLay, Brian. *War of a Thousand Deserts: Indian Raids and the U.S.-Mexican War.* New Haven: Yale University Press, 2008.
———, ed. *North American Borderlands.* New York: Routledge, 2013.
Deloria, Philip J. *Playing Indian.* New Haven: Yale University Press, 1998.
Deloria, Vine and Raymond J. DeMallie, eds. *Documents of American Indian Diplomacy: Treaties, Agreements, and Conventions, 1775–1979,* vol. 1. Norman: University of Oklahoma Press, 1999.
Demallie, Raymond J. "'Scenes in the Indian Country': A Portfolio of Alexander Gardner's Stereographic Views of the 1868 Fort Laramie Treaty Council." *Montana: The Magazine of Western History* 31, no. 3 (Summer 1981): 42–59.

Denny, James and John Bradbury. *The Civil War's First Blood, Missouri, 1854–1861.* Boonville: Missouri Life, 2007.

DeRosier, Arthur H. Jr. *The Removal of the Choctaw Indians.* Knoxville: University of Tennessee Press, 1970.

Deutsch, Sarah. "Being American in Boley, Oklahoma." In *Beyond Black and White: Race, Ethnicity, and Gender in the U.S. South and Southwest,* edited by Stephanie Cole and Allison Parker, 97–122. College Station: Texas A&M University Press, 2004.

Diné College. *Navajo Stories of the Long Walk Period.* Tsaile, AZ: Diné College Bookstore Press, 1983.

Dippie, Brian W. *The Vanishing American: White Attitudes and U.S. Indian Policy.* Middletown, CT: Wesleyan University Press, 1982.

Dobak, William A. *Freedom by the Sword: The U.S. Colored Troops, 1862–1867.* Washington, DC: U.S. Army Center of Military History, 2011.

Dolan, Jay P. *In Search of an American Catholicism: A History of Religion and Culture in Tension.* New York: Oxford University Press, 2002.

Downs, Gregory P. "The Mexicanization of American Politics: The United States' Transnational Path from Civil War to Stabilization." *American Historical Review* 117, no. 2 (April 2012): 387–409.

Downs, James. *Sick from Freedom: African-American Illness and Suffering during the Civil War and Reconstruction.* New York: Oxford University Press, 2012.

Drake, Frederick C. *The Empire of the Seas: A Biography of Rear Admiral Robert Wilson Shufeldt, USN.* Honolulu: University of Hawaii Press, 1984.

Driggs, Don W. and Leonard E. Goodall. *Nevada Politics and Government: Conservatism in an Open Society.* Lincoln: University of Nebraska Press, 1996.

Drinnon, Richard. *Facing West: The Metaphysics of Indian-Hating and Empire-Building.* Minneapolis: University of Minnesota Press, 1980.

DuBois, Ellen Carol. *Feminism and Suffrage: The Emergence of an Independent Women's Movement in America, 1848–1869.* Ithaca, NY: Cornell University Press, 1978.

Dunn, Jacob Piatt and William Harris Kemper. *Indiana and Indians: A History of Aboriginal and Territorial Indiana and the Century of Statehood.* Chicago and New York: American Historical Society, 1919.

Dunning, William A. *Reconstruction, Political and Economic, 1865–1877.* New York: Harper, 1907.

Edwards, G. Thomas. *Sowing Good Seeds: The Northwest Suffrage Campaigns of Susan B. Anthony.* Portland: Oregon Historical Society Press, 1990.

Edwards, Laura F. *Gendered Strife and Confusion: The Political Culture of Reconstruction.* Urbana: University of Illinois Press, 1997.

Edwards, Rebecca. *Angels in the Machinery: Gender in American Party Politics from the Civil War to the Progressive Era.* New York: Oxford University Press, 1997.

Efford, Alison Clark. *German Immigrants, Race, and Citizenship in the Civil War Era.* New York: Cambridge University Press, 2013.

Eggan, Fred. "Pueblos: Introduction." In *Handbook of North American Indians, Vol. 9: Southwest,* edited by Alfonso Ortiz, 224–35. Washington DC: Smithsonian Institution Press, 1979.

Egnal, Marc. *Clash of Extremes: The Economic Origins of the Civil War.* New York: Hill and Wang, 2009.

Eiselt, Sunday. *Becoming White Clay: A History and Archaeology of Jicarilla Apache Enclavement.* Salt Lake City: University of Utah Press, 2012.

Ely, Glen Sample. "What to Do about Texas? Texas and the Department of New Mexico in the Civil War." *New Mexico Historical Review* 85, no. 4 (Fall 2010): 375–408.

Escott, Paul D. *Slavery Remembered: A Record of Twentieth-Century Slave Narratives.* Chapel Hill: University of North Carolina Press, 1979.

Etcheson, Nicole. *Bleeding Kansas: Contested Liberty in the Civil War Era.* Lawrence: University Press of Kansas, 2004.

———. "The Goose Question: The Proslavery Party in Territorial Kansas and the Crisis of 'Law and Order.'" In *Bleeding Kansas, Bleeding Missouri: The Long Civil War on the Border,* edited by Jonathan Earle and Diane Mutti Burke, 47–63. Lawrence: University Press of Kansas, 2013.

Etulain, Richard. *Lincoln and Oregon Country Politics in the Civil War Era.* Corvallis: Oregon State University Press, 2013.

Evans, Sterling, ed. *The Borderlands of the American and Canadian Wests: Essays on Regional History of the Forty-ninth Parallel.* Lincoln: University of Nebraska Press, 2006.

Evenson, Sandra Lee and David J. Trayte. "Dress and Interaction in Contending Cultures: Eastern Dakota and Euroamericans in Nineteenth-Century Minnesota." In *Religion, Dress and the Body,* edited by Linda B. Arthur, 95–116. New York: Berg/Oxford, 1999.

Fatout, Paul. *Ambrose Bierce: The Devil's Lexicographer.* Norman: University of Oklahoma Press, 1951.

Faust, Drew Gilpin. *The Creation of Confederate Nationalism: Ideology and Identity in the Civil War South.* Baton Rouge: Louisiana State University Press, 1988.

Fausz, J. Frederick. "Becoming 'A Nation of Quakers': The Removal of the Osage Indians from Missouri." *Gateway Heritage* 21, no. 1 (Summer 2000): 28–39.

Fehrenbacher, Don E. *The Dred Scott Case: Its Significance in American Law and Politics.* New York: Oxford University Press, 1979.

———. *The Slaveholding Republic: An Account of the United States Government's Relation to Slavery.* New York: Oxford University Press, 2001.

Fellman, Michael. *Inside War: The Guerrilla Conflict in Missouri during the American Civil War.* New York: Oxford University Press, 1989.

Ferguson, Niall. *The House of Rothschild: The World's Banker, 1849–1999.* New York: Viking, 1999.

Fessenden, Tracy. "The Nineteenth-Century Bible Wars and the Separation of Church and State." *Church History* 74, no. 4 (December 2005): 784–811.

Fichter, James R. *So Great a Proffit: How the East Indies Trade Transformed Anglo-American Capitalism*. Cambridge, MA: Harvard University Press, 2010.
Fischer, Kirsten. *Suspect Relations: Sex, Race, and Resistance in Colonial North Carolina*. Ithaca, NY: Cornell University Press, 2002.
Fleming, Paula. "Photographing the Plains Indians: Ridgeway Glover at Forts Laramie and Phil Kearney 1866." In *The People of the Buffalo: The Plains Indians of North America*, edited by Colin F. Taylor and Hugh A. Dempsey, vol. 2. Wyck auf Foehr, Germany: Tatanka Press, 2005.
———. "Photographing the Plains Indians: Ridgeway Glover at Forts Laramie and Phil Kearney 1866, Part II." In *Generous Man Ahxsi-tapina: Essays in Memory of Colin Taylor, Plains Indian Ethnologist*, edited by Arni Brownstone and Hugh Dempsey. Wyck auf Foehr, Germany: Tatanka Press, 2008.
Flexner, Eleanor. *Century of Struggle: The Woman's Rights Movement in the United States*. Cambridge, MA: Harvard University Press, 1959.
Foner, Eric. *Reconstruction: America's Unfinished Revolution, 1863–1877*. New York: Harper & Row, 1988.
———. *Nothing but Freedom: Emancipation and Its Legacy*. 1983; Baton Rouge: Louisiana State University Press, 2007.
———. *The Fiery Trial: Abraham Lincoln and American Slavery*. New York: Norton, 2010.
Foreman, Grant. *The Five Civilized Tribes*. Norman: University of Oklahoma Press, 1934.
Foster, Frances Smith. *Witnessing Slavery: The Development of Antebellum Slave Narratives*. 2nd ed. Madison: University of Wisconsin Press, 1994.
Foster, Gaines M. *Moral Reconstruction: Christian Lobbyists and the Federal Legislation of Morality, 1865–1920*. Chapel Hill: University of North Carolina Press, 2002.
Fox-Genovese, Elizabeth. *Within the Plantation Household: Black and White Women of the Old South*. Chapel Hill: University of North Carolina Press, 1988.
Frazier, Donald S. *Blood and Treasure: Confederate Empire in the Southwest*. College Station: Texas A&M University Press, 1995.
Fredrickson, George M. *White Supremacy: A Comparative Study in American and South African History*. New York: Oxford University Press, 1981.
———. *Racism: A Short History*. Princeton: Princeton University Press, 2002.
Freehling, William W. *Prelude to Civil War: The Nullification Crisis in South Carolina, 1816–1836*. New York: Oxford University Press, 1964.
Frehner, Brian. *Finding Oil: The Nature of Petroleum Geology, 1859–1920*. Lincoln: University of Nebraska Press, 2011.
Fritz, Henry E. *The Movement for Indian Assimilation, 1860–1890*. Philadelphia: University of Pennsylvania Press, 1963.
Frost, Linda. *Never One Nation: Freaks, Savages, and Whiteness in U.S. Popular Culture, 1850–1877*. Minneapolis: University of Minnesota Press, 2005.
Gallagher, Gary W. *The Confederate War*. Cambridge, MA: Harvard University Press, 1997.

———. *The Union War*. Cambridge, MA: Harvard University Press, 2011.
Galloway, Patricia. *Choctaw Genesis, 1500–1700*. Lincoln: University of Nebraska Press, 1995.
Gardner, Alexander. *Alexander Gardner's Photographic Sketchbook of the Civil War*. New York: Dover, 1959.
Gates, Paul W. "Indian Allotments Preceding the Dawes Act." In *The Frontier Challenge: Responses to the Trans-Mississippi West*, edited by John G. Clark, 147–58. Lawrence: University Press of Kansas, 1971.
Geiger, Mark W. *Financial Fraud and Guerrilla Violence in Missouri's Civil War, 1861–1865*. New Haven: Yale University Press, 2010.
Genetin-Pilawa, C. Joseph. *Crooked Paths to Allotment: The Fight over Federal Indian Policy after the Civil War*. Chapel Hill: University of North Carolina Press 2012.
Gerteis, Louis S. *The Civil War in Missouri: A Military History*. Columbia: University of Missouri Press, 2012.
Geyer, Michael and Charles Bright. "Global Violence and Nationalizing Wars in Eurasia and America: The Geopolitics of War in the Mid-Nineteenth Century." *Comparative Studies in Society and History: An International Quarterly* 38, no. 4 (October 1996): 619–57.
Gilbert, Benjamin F. "Rumors of Confederate Privateers Operating in Victoria, Vancouver Island." *British Columbia Historical Quarterly* 18, nos. 3–4. July-October 1954): 239–55.
Gillett, Mary C. *The Army Medical Department, 1818–1865*. Washington, DC: Government Printing Office, 1987.
Gilmore, Donald. *Civil War on the Missouri/Kansas Border*. Gretna, LA: Pelican Press, 2006.
Gitlin, Jay, Barbara Berglund, and Adam Arenson, eds. *Frontier Cities: Encounters at the Crossroads of Empire*. Philadelphia: University of Pennsylvania Press, 2013.
Goetzmann, William H. *When the Eagle Screamed*. New York: Wiley, 1966.
Goldfield, David. *America Aflame: How the Civil War Created a Nation*. New York: Bloomsbury, 2011.
Goldman, Marion. *Gold Diggers and Silver Miners: Prostitution and Social Life on the Comstock Lode*. Ann Arbor: University of Michigan Press, 1981.
Goodrich, Thomas. *Black Flag: Guerrilla Warfare on the Western Border, 1861–1865*. Bloomington: Indiana University Press, 1995.
Gordon, Leslie J. *General George E. Pickett in Life and Legend*. Chapel Hill: University of North Carolina Press, 2001.
Gordon, Sarah Barringer. *The Mormon Question: Polygamy and Constitutional Conflict in Nineteenth-Century America*. Chapel Hill: University of North Carolina Press, 2002.
Graybill, Andrew R. *Policing the Great Plains: Rangers, Mounties, and the North American Frontier, 1875–1910*. Lincoln: University of Nebraska Press, 2007.
———. *The Red and the White: A Family Saga of the American West*. New York: Liveright, 2013.

Greenberg, Amy. "A Gray-Eyed Man: Character, Appearance, and Filibustering." *Journal of the Early Republic* 20, no. 4 (Winter 2000): 673–99.

———. *A Wicked War: Polk, Clay, Lincoln, and the 1846 U.S. Invasion of Mexico.* New York: Knopf, 2012.

Griffin, Martin. *Ashes of the Mind: War and Memory in Northern Literature, 1865–1900.* Amherst: University of Massachusetts Press, 2009.

Grow, Matthew J. *"Liberty to the Downtrodden": Thomas L. Kane, Romantic Reformer.* New Haven: Yale University Press, 2009.

Guterl, Matthew Pratt. *American Mediterranean: Southern Slaveholders in the Age of Emancipation.* Cambridge, MA: Harvard University Press, 2008.

Guyatt, Nicholas. "America's Conservatory: Race, Reconstruction, and the Santo Domingo Debate." *Journal of American History*, 97, no. 4 (March 2011): 974–1000.

———. "'An Impossible Idea?' The Curious Career of Internal Colonization," *Journal of the Civil War Era* 4, no. 2 (June 2014): 234–63.

Gyory, Andrew. *Closing the Gate: Race, Politics, and the Chinese Exclusion Act.* Chapel Hill: University of North Carolina Press, 1998.

Hahn, Steven. *The Political Worlds of Slavery and Freedom.* Cambridge, MA: Harvard University Press, 2009.

———. "Slave Emancipation, Indian Peoples, and the Projects of a New American State." *Journal of the Civil War Era* 3, no. 3 (September 2013): 307–330.

Haley, J. Evetts. "The Comanchero Trade." *Southwestern Historical Quarterly* 38, no. 3 (January 1935): 157–76.

Hall, Martin Hardwick. *Sibley's New Mexico Campaign.* 1960; Albuquerque: University of New Mexico Press, 2000.

Hall, Thomas D. *Social Change in the Southwest, 1350–1880.* Lawrence: University Press of Kansas, 1989.

Haller, Granville O. *San Juan and Secession.* 1896; Seattle: Shorey Book Store, 1967.

Halliburton, R. *Red over Black: Black Slavery among the Cherokee Indians.* Westport, CT: Greenwood, 1977.

Halttunen, Karen. *Confidence Men and Painted Women: A Study of Middle-Class Culture in America, 1830–1870.* New Haven: Yale University Press, 1982.

Hämäläinen, Pekka. *The Comanche Empire.* New Haven: Yale University Press, 2008.

Hämäläinen, Pekka and Benjamin H. Johnson, eds. *Major Problems in the History of North American Borderlands.* Boston: Wadsworth Cengage Learning, 2011.

Hanna, Alfred Jackson and Kathryn Abbey Hanna. *Napoleon III and Mexico: American Triumph over Monarchy.* Chapel Hill: University of North Carolina Press, 1971.

Hardaway, Roger D. "Prohibiting Interracial Marriage: Miscegenation Law in Wyoming." *Annals of Wyoming* 52, no. 1 (Spring 1980): 55–60.

Hardy, William E. "South of the Border: Ulysses S. Grant and the French Intervention," *Civil War History* 54, no. 1 (2008): 63–86.

Harris, Charles. "Catalyst for Terror: The Collapse of the Women's Prison in Kansas City." *Missouri Historical Review* 89, no. 3 (April 1995): 290–305.

Harris, William C. *Lincoln and the Border States: Preserving the Union.* Lawrence: University Press of Kansas, 2011.

———. "The Hampton Roads Peace Conference: A Final Test of Lincoln's Presidential Leadership," *Journal of the Abraham Lincoln Association* 21, no. 1 (Winter 2000): 30–61.

Harrold, Stanley. *Border Wars: Fighting over Slavery before the Civil War.* Chapel Hill: University of North Carolina Press, 2010.

Harter, Eugene C. *The Lost Colony of the Confederacy.* College Station: Texas A&M University Press, 2000.

Hauptman, Laurence M. *Between Two Fires: American Indians in the Civil War.* New York: Free Press, 1995.

Henderson, Timothy J. *A Glorious Defeat: Mexico and Its War with the United States.* New York: Hill and Wang, 2007.

Hietala, Thomas R. *Manifest Design: American Exceptionalism and Empire.* Rev. ed. Ithaca, NY: Cornell University Press, 2003.

Hill, W.W. *Navaho Warfare.* Yale University Publications in Anthropology 5. New Haven: Yale University Press, 1936.

Hoelscher, Steven D. *Picturing Indians: Photographic Encounters and Tourist Fantasies in H. H. Bennett's Wisconsin Dells.* Madison: University of Wisconsin Press, 2008.

Homsher, Lola M., ed. *South Pass, 1868.* Lincoln: University of Nebraska Press, 1978.

Horowitz, Helen Lefkowitz. *Rereading Sex: Battles over Sexual Knowledge and Suppression in Nineteenth-Century America.* New York: Vintage Books, 2003.

Hoxie, Frederick E. *A Final Promise: The Campaign to Assimilate the Indians, 1880–1920.* Lincoln: University of Nebraska Press, 1984.

Hsu, Madeline. *Dreaming of Gold, Dreaming of Home: Transnationalism and the Migration between the United States and South China, 1882–1943.* Stanford: Stanford University Press, 2000.

Huhndorf, Shari M. *Going Native: Indians in the American Cultural Imagination.* Ithaca, NY: Cornell University Press, 2001.

Hunt, Aurora. *The Army of the Pacific: Its Operations in California, Texas, Arizona, New Mexico, Utah, Nevada, Oregon, Washington, Plains Region, Mexico, etc., 1860–1866.* Glendale, CA: Arthur H. Clark, 1951.

Hunt, Jeffrey W. *The Last Battle of the Civil War: Palmetto Ranch.* Austin: University of Texas Press, 2002.

Hutchinson, Bruce. *The Struggle for the Border.* Toronto: Longmans, Green, and Co., 1955.

Hutchinson, William H. *Oil, Land, and Politics: The California Career of Thomas Robert Bard,* vol. 1. Norman: University of Oklahoma Press, 1965.

Hyde, Anne F. *Empires, Nations, and Families: A History of the North American West, 1800–1860.* Lincoln: University of Nebraska Press, 2011.

Hyman, Colette A. *Dakota Women's Work: Creativity, Culture, and Exile.* St. Paul: Minnesota Historical Society Press, 2012.
Ignatiev, Noel. *How the Irish Became White.* New York: Routledge, 1995.
Jacobson. Matthew Frye. *Whiteness of a Different Color: European Immigrants and the Alchemy of Race.* Cambridge, MA: Harvard University Press, 1998.
Jacoby, Karl. "Between North and South: The Alternative Borderlands of William H. Ellis and the African American Colony of 1895." In *Continental Crossroads: Remapping U.S.-Mexico Borderlands History,* ed. Samuel Truett and Elliot Young, 209–40. Durham, NC: Duke University Press, 2004.
Johannsen, Robert W. *Stephen A. Douglas.* New York: Oxford University Press, 1973.
Johnson, Benjamin H. and Andrew R. Graybill, eds. *Bridging National Borders in North America: Transnational and Comparative Histories.* Durham, NC: Duke University Press, 2010.
Johnson, Laura E. "'Goods to Clothe Themselves': Native Consumers and Native Images on the Pennsylvania Trading Frontier, 1712–1760." *Winterthur Portfolio* 43, no. 1 (Spring 2009): 115–40.
Johnson, Patricia M. "McCreight and the Law." *British Columbia Historical Quarterly* 12, no. 2 (1948): 127–49.
Johnson, Susan Lee. *Roaring Camp: The Social World of the California Gold Rush.* New York: Norton, 2000.
Johnson, Walter. *River of Dark Dreams: Slavery and Empire in the Cotton Kingdom.* Cambridge, MA: Harvard University Press, 2013.
Jones, Howard. *Abraham Lincoln and a New Birth of Freedom: The Union and Slavery in the Diplomacy of the Civil War.* Lincoln: University of Nebraska Press, 1999.
Jones, Tom, et al. *People of the Big Voice: Photographs of Ho-Chunk Families by Charles Van Schaick, 1879–1942.* Madison: Wisconsin Historical Society Press, 2011.
Josephy, Alvin M. *The Civil War in the American West.* New York: Knopf, 1991.
Jun, Helen Heran. *Race for Citizenship: Black Orientalism and Asian Uplift from Pre-Emancipation to Neoliberal America.* New York: New York University Press, 2011.
Jung, Moon-Ho. "Outlawing 'Coolies': Race, Nation, and Empire in the Age of Emancipation." *American Quarterly* 57, no. 3 (September 2005): 677–701.
———. *Coolies and Cane: Race, Labor, and Sugar in the Age of Emancipation.* Baltimore: Johns Hopkins University Press, 2006.
Kaczorowski, Robert J. "To Begin the Nation Anew: Congress, Citizenship, and Civil Rights After the Civil War." *American Historical Review* 92, no. 1 (February 1987): 45–68.
Kantrowitz, Stephen. *More Than Freedom: Fighting for Black Citizenship in a White Republic, 1829–1889.* New York: Penguin, 2012.
———. "'Their Civilization and Ultimate Citizenship': Land-ownership, Written and Unwritten Laws, and a Native American Path through Reconstruction." In

The World the Civil War Made, edited by Kate Masur and Gregory P. Downs. Chapel Hill: University of North Carolina Press, forthcoming.

Katz, D. Mark. *Witness to an Era: The Life and Photographs of Alexander Gardner*. New York: Viking, 1991.

Katz, William Loren. *Black Indians: A Hidden Heritage*. New York: Atheneum, 1986.

Keehn, David C. *Knights of the Golden Circle: Secret Empire, Southern Secession, Civil War*. Baton Rouge: Louisiana State University Press, 2013.

Keller, Robert H. Jr. *American Protestantism and United States Indian Policy, 1869–82*. Lincoln: University of Nebraska Press, 1983.

Kelly, Lawrence C. *Navajo Roundup: Selected Correspondence of Kit Carson's Expedition against the Navajo, 1863–1865*. Boulder, CO: Pruett, 1970.

Kelly, Patrick J. "The North American Crisis of the 1860s." *Journal of the Civil War Era* 2, no. 3 (September 2012): 337–68.

Kelley, Sean. "'Mexico in His Head': Slavery and the Texas-Mexico Border, 1810–1860," *Journal of Social History* 37, no. 3 (2004): 709–23.

Kelman, Ari. *A Misplaced Massacre: Struggling over the Memory of Sand Creek*. Cambridge, MA: Harvard University Press, 2013.

Kenner, Charles L. *The Comanchero Frontier: A History of New Mexican-Plains Indian Relations*. Norman: University of Oklahoma Press, 1994.

Kerber, Linda. "Separate Spheres, Female Worlds, Woman's Place: The Rhetoric of Women's History." *Journal of American History* 75, no. 1 (June 1988): 9–39.

Kessell, John L. "General Sherman and the Navajo Treaty of 1868: A Basic and Expedient Misunderstanding." *Western Historical Quarterly* 12, no. 3 (July 1981): 251–72.

Kidwell, Clara Sue. *Choctaws and Missionaries in Mississippi, 1818–1918*. Norman: University of Oklahoma Press, 1995.

Krauthamer, Barbara. *Black Slaves, Indian Masters: Slavery, Emancipation, and Citizenship in the Native American South*. Chapel Hill: University of North Carolina Press, 2013.

Kuchta, David. *The Three-Piece Suit and Modern Masculinity: England, 1550–1850*. Berkeley: University of California Press, 2002.

Laing, F. W. "Some Pioneers of the Cattle Industry." *British Columbia Historical Quarterly* 6, no. 4 (October 1942): 257–75.

Lamar, Howard R. *Dakota Territory, 1861–1889: A Study of Frontier Politics*. New Haven: Yale University Press, 1956

———. *The Far Southwest, 1846–1912: A Territorial History*. 1966; Albuquerque: University of New Mexico Press, 2000.

Larson, T. A. "Petticoats at the Polls: Woman Suffrage in Territorial Wyoming." *Pacific Northwest Quarterly* 44, no. 2 (April 1953): 74–78.

———. "Dolls, Vassals, and Drudges: Pioneer Women of the West." *Western Historical Quarterly* 3, no. 1 (January 1972): 4–16.

———. *History of Wyoming*. Lincoln: University of Nebraska Press, 1978.

Lee, Erika. *At America's Gates: Chinese Immigration during the Exclusion Era, 1882–1943*. Chapel Hill: University of North Carolina Press, 2003.

Lee, Robert G. *Orientals: Asian Americans in Popular Culture.* Philadelphia: Temple University Press, 1999.
Leiker, James N. *Racial Borders: Black Soldiers along the Rio Grande.* College Station: Texas A&M University Press, 2002.
LeSueur, Stephen C. *The 1838 Mormon War in Missouri.* Columbia: University of Missouri Press, 1987.
Limerick, Patricia Nelson. *Desert Passages: Encounters with the American Deserts.* Albuquerque: University of New Mexico Press, 1985.
———. *The Legacy of Conquest: The Unbroken Past of the American West.* New York: Norton, 1987.
Litwack, Leon F. *North of Slavery: The Negro in the Free States.* Chicago: University of Chicago Press, 1961.
———. *Been in the Storm So Long: The Aftermath of Slavery.* New York: Vintage Books, 1979.
Lurie, Nancy Oestreich, ed. *Mountain Wolf Woman, Sister of Crashing Thunder: The Autobiography of a Winnebago Indian.* 1961; Ann Arbor: University of Michigan Press, 1966.
———. "Winnebago." In *Handbook of North American Indians, Vol. 15: Northeast,* edited by Bruce G. Trigger, 690–707. Washington, DC: Smithsonian Institution Press, 1978.
Lutz, Stuart. "Terror in St. Albans." *Civil War Times Illustrated* 40, no. 3 (June 2001): 42–48.
Madley, Benjamin Logan. "American Genocide: The California Indian Catastrophe, 1846–1873." PhD diss. Yale University, 2009.
Magness, Phillip W. and Sebastian N. Page. *Colonization after Emancipation: Lincoln and the Movement for Black Resettlement.* Columbia: University of Missouri Press, 2011.
Mahin, Dean B. *One War at a Time.* Washington, DC: Brassey's, 2000.
Mahon, John K. *History of the Second Seminole War, 1835–1842.* Gainesville: University of Florida Press, 1967.
Maier, Charles S. "Consigning the Twentieth Century to History: Alternative Narratives for the Modern Era." *American Historical Review* 105, no. 3 (June 2000): 807–31.
Malm, Norman R. "Climate Guide, Las Cruces, 1892–2000." Las Cruces: New Mexico State University. Agricultural Experiment Station, 2003.
Maltz, Earl. "The Fourteenth Amendment and Native American Citizenship." 17 *Const. Comment* 555. 2000.
Mardock, Robert Winston. *The Reformers and the American Indian.* Columbia: University of Missouri Press, 1971.
Marino, C. C. "The Seboyetanos and the Navahos." *New Mexico Historical Review* 29, no. 1 (January 1954): 8–27.
Marilley, Suzanne M. *Woman Suffrage and the Origins of Liberal Feminism in the United States, 1820–1920.* Cambridge, MA: Harvard University Press, 1996.

Marquis, Greg. *In Armageddon's Shadow*. Montreal: McGill-Queen's University Press, 1998.
Masur, Kate. "The African American Delegation to Abraham Lincoln: A Reappraisal," *Civil War History* 56, no. 2 (June 2010): 117–44.
Mason, Patrick Q. *The Mormon Menace: Violence and Anti-Mormonism in the Postbellum South*. New York: Oxford University Press, 2011.
Massie, Michael A. "Reform Is Where You Find It: The Roots of Woman Suffrage in Wyoming." *Annals of Wyoming* 62, no. 1 (Spring 1990): 2–21.
Mather, Ken. *Buckaroos and Mud Pups: The Early Days of Ranching in British Columbia*. Surrey, BC: Heritage House, 2006.
Mathes, Valerie Sherer and Richard Lowitt. *The Standing Bear Controversy: Prelude to Indian Reform*. Urbana: University of Illinois Press, 2003.
May, Robert E., ed. *The Union, the Confederacy, and the Atlantic Rim*. West Lafayette, IN: Purdue University Press, 1995.
——. *Manifest Destiny's Underworld: Filibustering in Antebellum America*. Chapel Hill: University of North Carolina Press, 2002.
——. *The Southern Dream of a Caribbean Empire, 1854–1861*. 1973; Gainesville: University Press of Florida, 2002.
——. *Slavery, Race, and Conquest in the Tropics: Lincoln, Douglas, and the Future of Latin America*. New York: Cambridge University Press, 2013.
McCann, William. "Introduction," in *Ambrose Bierce, Ambrose Bierce's Civil War*. Chicago: Gateway Editions, 1956.
McFeely, William S. *Yankee Stepfather: General O. O. Howard and the Freedmen*. New York: Norton, 1968.
McGaugh, Scott. *Surgeon in Blue: Jonathan Letterman, the Civil War Doctor Who Pioneered Battlefield Care*. New York: Arcade, 2013.
McGreevy, John T. *Catholicism and American Freedom: A History*. New York: Norton, 2003.
McKee, Jesse O. and Jon A. Schlenker. *The Choctaws: Cultural Evolution of a Native American Tribe*. Jackson: University Press of Mississippi, 1980.
McKitrick, Eric L. *Andrew Johnson and Reconstruction*. Chicago: University of Chicago Press, 1960.
McClain, Charles J. *In Search of Equality: The Chinese Struggle against Discrimination in Nineteenth-Century America*. Berkeley: University of California Press, 1994.
McLaird, James D. *Calamity Jane: The Woman and the Legend*. Norman: University of Oklahoma Press, 2005.
McLarney, Donald F. "The American Civil War in Victoria, Vancouver Island Colony." Unpublished paper, Highline, Washington, Community College.
McManus, Sheila. *The Line Which Separates: Race, Gender, and the Making of the Alberta-Montana Borderlands*. Lincoln: University of Nebraska Press, 2005.
McNitt, Frank. "The Long March: 1863–1867. In Albert Schroeder, ed., *The Changing Ways of Southwestern Indians*, 145–69. Glorieta, NM: Rio Grande Press, 1973.

McPherson, James M. *The Struggle for Equality: The Abolitionists and the Negro in the Civil War and Reconstruction*. Princeton: Princeton University Press, 1964.
———. *Battle Cry of Freedom: The Civil War Era*. New York: Oxford University Press, 1988.
McWilliams, Carey. *Ambrose Bierce: A Biography*. 1929; Hamden, CT: Archon Books, 1967.
Meinig, D. W. *Shaping of America, Vol. 2: Continental America, 1800–1867*. New Haven: Yale University Press, 1993.
Melish, Joan Pope. *Disowning Slavery: Gradual Emancipation and "Race" in New England, 1780–1860*. Ithaca, NY: Cornell University Press, 1998.
Mellon, James. *Bullwhip Days: The Slaves Remember*. New York: Weidenfeld & Nicolson, 1988.
Merk, Frederick. *The Monroe Doctrine and American Expansion*. New York: Vintage Books, 1966.
Miles, Tiya. *Ties That Bind: the Story of an Afro-Cherokee Family in Slavery and Freedom*. Berkeley: University of California Press, 2005.
Miller, Floyd J. *The Search for a Black Nationality: Black Emigration and Colonization, 1787–1863*. Urbana-Champaign: University of Illinois Press, 1975.
Miller, George. *Missouri's Memorable Decade: 1860–1870*. Columbia, MO: E.W. Stephens, 1898.
Miller, Stuart Creighton. *Unwelcome Immigrant: The American Image of the Chinese, 1785–1885*. Berkeley: University of California Press, 1969.
Miller, Susan A. *Coacoochee's Bones: A Seminole Saga*. Lawrence: University Press of Kansas, 2003.
Mohanty, Chandra Talpade, et al., eds. *Third World Women and the Politics of Feminism*. Bloomington: Indiana University Press, 1991.
Monaghan, Jay. *Civil War on the Western Border, 1854–1865*. Boston: Little Brown, 1955.
Moneyhon, Carl H. *Texas after the Civil War: The Struggle of Reconstruction*. College Station: Texas A&M University Press, 2004.
Montgomery, Charles. *The Spanish Redemption: Heritage, Power, and Loss on New Mexico's Upper Rio Grande*. Berkeley: University of California Press, 2002.
Moorhead, James H. *American Apocalypse: Yankee Protestants and the Civil War, 1860–1869*. New Haven: Yale University Press, 1978.
Morrison, Michael A. *Slavery and the American West: The Eclipse of Manifest Destiny and the Coming of the American Civil War*. Chapel Hill: University of North Carolina Press, 1997.
Moses, Wilson Jeremiah. *The Golden Age of Black Nationalism, 1850–1925*. New York: Oxford University Press, 1988.
Mould, Tom. *Choctaw Tales*. Jackson: University of Mississippi, 2004.
Mullis, Tony R. *Peacekeeping on the Plains: Army Operations in Bleeding Kansas*. Columbia: University of Missouri Press, 2004.
———. "The Illusion of Security: The Government's Response to the Jayhawker Threat of Late 1860." In *Bleeding Kansas, Bleeding Missouri: The Long Civil War*

on the Border, edited by Jonathan Earle and Diane Mutti Burke, 99–117. Lawrence: University Press of Kansas, 2013.

Murphy, Lawrence R. "Reconstruction in New Mexico." *New Mexico Historical Review* 43, no. 2 (April 1968): 99–115.

Murphy, Lucy Eldersveld. *A Gathering of Rivers: Indians, Métis, and Mining in the Western Great Lakes, 1737–1832.* Lincoln: University of Nebraska Press, 2000.

Murray, Keith A. *The Pig War.* Tacoma: Washington State Historical Society Press, 1968.

Murray, Robert A. "The Hazen Inspections." *Montana: The Magazine of Western History* 18, no. 1 (Winter 1968): 24–33.

Murray, Robert K. "General Sherman, the Negro, and Slavery: The Story of an Unrecognized Rebel." *Negro History Bulletin* 22, no. 6 (March 1959): 125–30.

Myers, Lee. "New Mexico Volunteers, 1862–1866." *Smoke Signal* 37 (1979): 138–51.

Nash, Gary B. and Jean R. Soderlund. *Freedom by Degrees: Emancipation in Pennsylvania and its Aftermath.* New York: Oxford University Press, 1991.

Naylor, Celia. *African Cherokees in Indian Territory: From Chattel to Citizens.* Chapel Hill: University of North Carolina Press, 2008.

Neely, Jeremy. *The Border Between Them: Violence and Reconciliation on the Kansas-Missouri Line.* Columbia: University of Missouri Press, 2007.

Neely, Mark E. Jr. *The Fate of Liberty: Abraham Lincoln and Civil Liberties.* New York: Oxford University Press, 1991.

———. "Colonization and the Myth That Lincoln Prepared the People for Emancipation." In William A. Blair and Karen Fisher Younger, *Lincoln's Proclamation: Emancipation Reconsidered.* Chapel Hill: University of North Carolina Press, 2009.

Nelson, Megan Kate. "Dying in the Desert." *Civil War Monitor* 2, no. 1 (Spring 2012): 48–53, 71–73.

———. "Indians Make the Best Guerrillas: Native Americans in the War for the Desert Southwest, 1861–1862." In *The Civil War Guerrilla: Unfolding the Black Flag in History, Memory, and Myth,* edited by Joseph M. Beilein Jr. and Matthew C. Hulbert, 45–74. Lexington: University of Kentucky Press, forthcoming, 2015.

Nevins, Allan. *The War for the Union,* 4 vols. New York: Scribner, 1959–71.

Nichols, David A. *Lincoln and the Indians: Civil War Policy and Politics.* Columbia: University of Missouri Press, 1978.

Niepman, Ann Davis. "General Orders No. 11 and Border Warfare during the Civil War." In *Kansas City, America's Crossroads: Essays from the Missouri Historical Review, 1906–2006,* edited by Diane Mutti Burke and John P. Herron, 96–121. Columbia: State Historical Society of Missouri, 2007.

Novak, William J. "The Legal Transformation of Citizenship in Nineteenth-Century America." In *The Democratic Experiment: New Directions in American Political History,* edited by Meg Jacobs, William J. Novak, and Julian E. Zelizer, 85–119. Princeton: Princeton University Press, 2003.

Oakes, James. *Freedom National: The Destruction of Slavery in the United States, 1861–1865.* New York: Norton, 2013.

Oberly, James W. *A Nation of Statesmen: The Political Culture of the Stockbridge-Munsee Mohicans, 1815–1972.* Norman: University of Oklahoma Press, 2005.

Oertel, Kristen Tegtmeier. *Bleeding Borders: Race, Gender, and Violence in Pre-Civil War Kansas.* Baton Rouge: Louisiana State University Press, 2009.

———. "'Nigger-Worshipping Fanatics' and 'Villain[s] of the Blackest Dye': Racialized Manhoods and the Sectional Debates." In *Bleeding Kansas, Bleeding Missouri: The Long Civil War on the Border,* edited by Jonathan Earle and Diane Mutti Burke, 65–80. Lawrence: University Press of Kansas, 2013.

Onsager, Lawrence W. "The Removal of the Winnebago Indians from Wisconsin in 1873–1874." MA thesis, Loma Linda University, 1985.

Onuf, Peter S. *Statehood and Union: A History of the Northwest Ordinance.* Bloomington: Indiana University Press, 1987.

Ortiz, Roxanne Dunbar, ed. *The Great Sioux Nation: Sitting in Judgment on America: An Oral History of the Sioux Nation and Its Struggle for Sovereignty.* New York: American Indian Treaty Council Information Center, 1977.

Ostler, Jeffrey. *The Lakotas and the Black Hills: The Struggle for Sacred Ground.* New York: Viking, 2010.

Owens, David M. *The Devil's Topographer: Ambrose Bierce and the American War Story.* Knoxville: University of Tennessee Press, 2006.

Paddison, Joshua. *American Heathens: Religion, Race, and Reconstruction in California.* Berkeley: University of California Press, 2012.

Page, S. N. "Lincoln and Chiriquí Colonization Revisited." *American Nineteenth Century History* 12, no. 3 (2011): 289–325.

Pani, Erika. "Dreaming of a Mexican Empire: The Political Projects of the 'Imperialistas.'" *Hispanic American Historical Review,* 82, no. 1 (2002): 1–31.

Paolino, Ernest N. *The Foundations of the American Empire: William Henry Seward and United States Foreign Policy.* Ithaca, NY: Cornell University Press, 1973.

Parker, Arthur Caswell. *The Life of General Ely S. Parker: Last Grand Sachem of the Iroquois and General Grant's Military Secretary.* Buffalo, NY: Buffalo Historical Society, 1919.

Parrish, William. *David Rice Atchison of Missouri: Border Politician.* Columbia: University of Missouri Press, 1961.

———. *Turbulent Partnership: Missouri and the Union, 1861–65.* Columbia: University of Missouri Press, 1963.

Pascoe, Peggy. *Relations of Rescue: The Search for Female Moral Authority in the American West, 1874–1939.* New York: Oxford University Press, 1990.

———. *What Comes Naturally: Miscegenation Law and the Making of Race in America.* New York: Oxford University Press, 2009.

Pearce, Roy Harvey. *Savagism and Civilization: A Study of the Indian and the American Mind.* Baltimore: Johns Hopkins University Press, 1967.

Pepin, Jean-Pierre-Yves. *Généalogie ascendante de Joseph-Alfred Mousseau, Premier ministre du Québec.* Longueuil, Quebec: Les Éditions historiques et généalogiques Pepin, 2001.

Perrine, Fred S. "Uncle Sam's Camel Corps." *New Mexico Historical Review* 1, no. 4 (October 1926): 434–44.

Pesantubbee, Michelene E. *Choctaw Women in a Chaotic World: The Clash of Cultures in the Colonial Southeast.* Albuquerque: University of New Mexico Press, 2005.

Petrik, Paula M. "Capitalists with Rooms: Prostitution in Helena, Montana, 1865–1900." *Montana: The Magazine of Western History* 31, no. 2 (Spring 1981): 28–41.

Pettis, George H. *Kit Carson's Fight with the Comanche and Kiowa Indians.* Santa Fe: Historical Society of New Mexico, 1908.

Phillips, Christopher. *Missouri's Confederate: Claiborne Fox Jackson and the Creation of Southern Identity in the Border West.* Columbia: University of Missouri Press, 2000.

———. "'A Question of Power Not One of Law': Federal Occupation and the Politics of Loyalty in the Western Border Slave States during the American Civil War." In *Bleeding Kansas, Bleeding Missouri: The Long Civil War on the Border,* edited by Jonathan Earle and Diane Mutti Burke, 131–50. Lawrence: University Press of Kansas, 2013.

Piston, William Garrett and Richard W. Hatcher III. *Wilson's Creek: The Second Battle of the Civil War and the Men Who Fought It.* Chapel Hill: University of North Carolina Press, 2000.

Poll, Richard D. and Ralph W. Hansen. "'Buchanan's Blunder': The Utah War, 1857–1858." *Military Affairs* 25, no. 3 (Fall 1961): 121–31.

Poll, Richard D. and William P. MacKinnon. "Causes of the Utah War Reconsidered." *Journal of Mormon History* 20, no. 2 (Fall 1994): 16–44.

Ponce, Pearl T. "'The Noise of Democracy': The Lecompton Constitution in Congress and Kansas." In *Bleeding Kansas, Bleeding Missouri: The Long Civil War on the Border,* edited by Jonathan Earle and Diane Mutti Burke, 81–96. Lawrence: University Press of Kansas, 2013.

Potts, Louis, and Ann Siglar. *Watkins Mill: Factory on the Farm.* Kirksville, MO: Truman State University Press, 2004.

Price, Realto E., ed. *History of Clayton County, Iowa.* Chicago: Robert O. Law, 1916.

Prior, David. "Civilization, Republic, Nation: Contested Keywords, Northern Republicans, and the Forgotten Reconstruction of Mormon Utah." *Civil War History* 56, no. 3 (September 2010): 283–310.

Prucha, Francis Paul. *American Indian Policy in Crisis: Christian Reformers and the Indian, 1865–1900.* Norman: University of Oklahoma Press, 1976.

Raab, Ann. "Warfare as an Agent of Culture Change: The Archaeology of Guerrilla Warfare on the Nineteenth-Century Missouri/Kansas Border." PhD diss. University of Kansas, 2012.

Rafiner, Tom A. *Caught between Three Fires: Cass County, MO., Chaos & Order No. 11, 1860–1865.* Xlibris Corporation, 2010.

Ramsdell, Charles W. *Reconstruction in Texas.* New York: Columbia University Press, 1910.

Redpath, James and Chris Dixon. *African America and Haiti*. Greenwood, CT: Westport, 2000.
Rice, George William. "Indian Rights: 25 U.S.C. § 71: The End of Indian Sovereignty or a Self-Limitation of Contractual Ability?" *American Indian Law Review* 5, no. 1 (1977): 239–53.
Richardson, Heather Cox. *West from Appomattox: The Reconstruction of America after the Civil War*. New Haven: Yale University Press, 2007.
Richter, William L. *The Army in Texas during Reconstruction, 1865–1870*. College Station: Texas A&M University Press, 1987.
Ricker, Eli Seavey and Richard E. Jensen, eds. *Voices of the American West: The Settler and Soldier Interviews of Eli S. Ricker, 1903–1919*. Lincoln: University of Nebraska Press, 2005.
Ring, Natalie. *The Problem South: Region, Empire, and the Liberal State, 1880–1930*. Athens: University of Georgia Press, 2012.
Roediger, David R. *The Wages of Whiteness: Race and the Making of the American Working Class*. London: Verso, 1991.
Rolle, Andrew. *The Lost Cause: The Confederate Exodus to Mexico*. Norman: University of Oklahoma Press, 1965.
Rollings, Willard H. *The Osage: An Ethnohistorical Study of Hegemony on the Prairie-Plains*. Columbia: University of Missouri Press, 1992.
Rosen, Deborah A. *American Indians and State Law: Sovereignty, Race, and Citizenship, 1790–1880*. Lincoln: University of Nebraska Press, 2007.
Royce, Edward. *The Origins of Southern Sharecropping*. Philadelphia: Temple University Press, 1993.
Rutherglen, George. *Civil Rights in the Shadow of Slavery: The Constitution, Common Law, and the Civil Rights Act of 1866*. New York: Oxford University Press, 2013.
Sabin, Edward L. *Kit Carson Days, 1809–1868*. Rev. ed., 2 vols. Lincoln: University of Nebraska Press, 1995.
Samito, Christian G. *Becoming American under Fire: Irish Americans, African Americans, and the Politics of Citizenship during the Civil War Era*. Ithaca, NY: Cornell University Press, 2009.
Sandweiss, Martha A. *Print the Legend: Photography and the American West*. New Haven: Yale University Press, 2002.
Saunt, Claudio. "The Paradox of Freedom: Tribal Sovereignty and Emancipation during the Reconstruction of Indian Territory." *Journal of Southern History* 70, no. 1 (January 2004): 63–94.
———. *Black, White, and Indian: Race and the Unmaking of an American Family*. New York: Oxford University Press, 2005.
Saxton, Alexander. *The Rise and Fall of the White Republic: Class Politics and Mass Culture in Nineteenth-Century America*. London: Verso, 1990.
Schaefer, Michael. *Just What War Is: The Civil War Writings of De Forest and Bierce*. Knoxville: University of Tennessee Press, 1997.
Scharff, Virginia. "The Case for Domestic Feminism: Woman Suffrage in Wyoming." *Annals of Wyoming* 56, no. 2 (Fall 1984): 29–37.

———. *Twenty Thousand Roads: Women, Movement, and the West.* Berkeley: University of California Press, 2003.

———, ed. *Liberty and Empire: The Civil War and the American West.* Berkeley: University of California Press, forthcoming 2015.

Scheckel, Susan. *The Insistence of the Indian: Race and Nationalism in Nineteenth-Century American Culture.* Princeton: Princeton University Press, 1998.

Schoonover, Thomas D. *Dollars over Dominion: The Triumph of Liberalism in Mexican-United States Relations, 1861–1867.* Baton Rouge: Louisiana State University Press, 1978.

———. "Misconstrued Mission: Expansionism and Black Colonization in Mexico and Central America during the Civil War." *Pacific Historical Review* 49, no. 4 (November 1980): 607–20.

———. *Mexican Lobby: Matías Romero in Washington, 1861–1867.* Lexington: University Press of Kentucky, 1986.

———. "Napoleon Is Coming! Maximilian Is Coming? The International History of the Civil War in the Caribbean Basin." In *The Union, the Confederacy, and the Atlantic Rim*, edited by Robert E. May, 101–30. West Lafayette, IN: Purdue University Press, 1995.

Schulten, Susan. "The Civil War and the Origins of the Colorado Territory," *Western Historical Quarterly* 44, no. 1 (Spring 2013): 21–46.

Schwartz, E. A. *The Rogue River Indian War and its Aftermath, 1850–1980.* Norman: University of Oklahoma Press, 1997.

Schwartz, Rosalie. *Across the Rio to Freedom: U.S. Negroes in Mexico.* El Paso: Texas Western Press, 1975.

Sehat, David. *The Myth of American Religious Freedom.* New York: Oxford University Press, 2011.

Sekora, John and Darwin T. Turner, eds. *The Art of the Slave Narrative: Original Essays in Criticism and Theory.* Macomb, IL: Western Illinois University Press, 1982.

Shaffer, Donald R. *After the Glory: The Struggles of Black Civil War Veterans.* Lawrence: University Press of Kansas, 2004.

Shannon, Timothy. "Dressing for Success on the Mohawk Frontier: Hendrick, William Johnson, and the Indian Fashion." *William and Mary Quarterly* 53, no. 1 (January 1996): 20–22.

Shaw, Stephanie J. "Using the WPA Ex-Slave Narratives to Study the Impact of the Great Depression." *Journal of Southern History* 69, no. 3 (August 2003): 623–58.

Sherlock, James. *South Pass and Its Tales.* New York: Vantage Press, 1978.

Shukla, Sandhya and Heidi Tinsman, eds., *Imagining Our Americas: Towards a Transnational Frame.* Durham, NC: Duke University Press, 2007.

Silbey, Joel H. *Storm over Texas: The Annexation Controversy and the Road to Civil War.* New York: Oxford University Press, 2005.

Silverman, David J. *Red Brethren: The Brothertown and Stockbridge Indians and the Problem of Race in Early America.* Ithaca, NY: Cornell University Press, 2010.

Simmons, Marc. "History of the Pueblos since 1821." In *Handbook of North Ameri-*

can Indians, Vol. 9: Southwest, edited by Alfonso Ortiz, 206–23. Washington DC: Smithsonian Institution Press, 1979.
———. *Kit Carson and His Three Wives: A Family History*. Albuquerque: University of New Mexico Press, 2003.
Simonsen, Jane. "Descendants of Black Hawk: Generations of Identity in Sauk Portraits." *American Quarterly* 63, no. 2 (June 2011): 301–35.
Smallwood, James M., Barry A. Crouch, and Larry Peacock. *Murder and Mayhem: The War of Reconstruction in Texas*. College Station: Texas A&M University Press, 2003.
Smedley, Audrey. *Race in North America: Origin and Evolution of a Worldview*. 2nd ed. Boulder, CO: Westview, 1999.
Smith, Rogers M. *Civic Ideals: Conflicting Visions of Citizenship in U.S. History*. New Haven: Yale University Press, 1997.
Smith, Sherry L. *Reimagining Indians: Native Americans through Anglo Eyes, 1880–1940*. New York: Oxford University Press, 2000.
Smith, Stacey L. *Freedom's Frontier: California and the Struggle over Unfree Labor, Emancipation, and Reconstruction*. Chapel Hill: University of North Carolina Press, 2013.
Sonnichsen, C. L. *The Mescalero Apaches*. 2nd ed. Norman: University of Oklahoma Press, 1973.
Spencer, Thomas M., ed., *The Missouri Mormon Experience*. Columbia: University of Missouri Press, 2010.
Spindel, Donna J. "Assessing Memory: Twentieth-Century Slave Narratives Reconsidered." *Journal of Interdisciplinary History* 27, no. 2 (Autumn 1996): 247–61.
Spurgeon, Ian Michael. *Man of Douglas, Man of Lincoln: The Political Odyssey of James Henry Lane*. Columbia: University of Missouri Press, 2008.
Stack, Joan. "Toward an Emancipationist Interpretation of George Caleb Bingham's Order Number 11." *Missouri Historical Review* 107, no. 4 (Summer 2013): 203–11.
Stampp, Kenneth M. *The Era of Reconstruction, 1865–1877*. New York: Knopf, 1965.
Stanley, Amy Dru. *From Bondage to Contract: Wage Labor, Marriage, and the Market in the Age of Slave Emancipation*. Chicago: University of Chicago Press, 1998.
Stannard, David E. *American Holocaust: Columbus and the Conquest of the New World*. New York: Oxford University Press, 1992.
Stark, Peter. *Last Breath: The Limits of Adventure*. 2001. Rpt. ed. New York: Ballantine Books, 2002.
Starling, Marion Wilson. *The Slave Narrative: Its Place in American History*. 2nd ed. Washington, DC: Howard University Press, 1988.
Sternhell, Yael A. *Routes of War: The World of Movement in the Confederate South*. Cambridge, MA: Harvard University Press, 2012.
Stiles, T. J. *The First Tycoon: The Epic Life of Cornelius Vanderbilt*. New York: Knopf, 2009.
Stilgoe, John R. *Common Landscapes of America, 1580–1845*. New Haven: Yale University Press, 1982.
Stoler, Ann Laura. "Making Empire Respectable: The Politics of Race and Sexual

Morality in Twentieth-Century Colonial Cultures." *American Ethnologist* 16, no. 4 (November 1989): 634–60.

———. "Carnal Knowledge and Imperial Power: Gender, Race, and Morality in Colonial Asia." In *Gender at the Crossroads of Knowledge: Feminist Anthropology in the Postmodern Era*, edited by Micaela di Leonardo, 55–101. Berkeley: University of California Press, 1991.

Stowell, Daniel W. *Rebuilding Zion: The Religious Reconstruction of the South, 1863–1877.* New York: Oxford University Press, 1998.

Stremlau, Rose. *Sustaining the Cherokee Family: Kinship and the Allotment of an Indigenous Nation.* Chapel Hill: University of North Carolina Press, 2011.

Sutherland, Daniel E. *A Savage Conflict: The Decisive Role of Guerrillas in the American Civil War.* Chapel Hill: University of North Carolina Press, 2009.

Tabor, Chris. "The Skirmish at Island Mound." Butler, MO: Bates County Historical Society, 2001.

Takaki, Ronald T. *Iron Cages: Race and Culture in Nineteenth-Century America.* New York: Knopf, 1979.

Talley, Sharon. *Ambrose Bierce and the Dance of Death.* Knoxville: University of Tennessee Press, 2009.

Taylor, Alan. *American Colonies: The Settling of North America.* New York: Penguin, 2001.

Taylor, Amy Murrell. "How a Cold Snap in Kentucky Led to Freedom for Thousands: An Environmental Story of Emancipation." In *Weirding the War: Stories from the Civil War's Ragged Edges,* edited by Stephen Berry, 191–214. Athens: University of Georgia Press, 2011.

Taylor, Morris F. "Ka-ni-ache." *Colorado* 43, no. 4 (Fall 1966): 275–302.

Tchen, John Kuo Wei. *New York before Chinatown: Orientalism and the Shaping of American Culture, 1776–1882.* Baltimore: Johns Hopkins University Press, 1999.

Teaford, Jon C. "Toward a Christian Nation: Religion, Law and Justice Strong." *Journal of Presbyterian History* 54, no. 4 (Winter 1976): 422–37.

Terrazas Basante, Marcela. *Los Intereses Norteamericanos en el Noroeste de México.* Mexico City: Universidad Nacional Autónoma de México, 1990.

Thompson, Gerald. *The Army and the Navajo: The Bosque Redondo Reservation Experiment, 1863–1868.* Tucson: University of Arizona Press, 1976.

Thompson, Jerry D. *Desert Tiger: Captain Paddy Graydon and the Civil War in the Far Southwest.* El Paso: Texas Western Press, 1992.

———, ed. *Civil War in the Southwest: Recollections of the Sibley Brigade.* College Station: Texas A&M University Press, 2001.

———. *Cortina: Defending the Mexican Name in Texas.* College Station: Texas A&M University Press, 2007.

Thomsen, Brian. *Shadows of Blue and Gray: The Civil War Writings of Ambrose Bierce.* New York: Tom Doherty Associates, 2002.

Tiller, Veronica E. "Jicarilla Apache." In *Handbook of North American Indians, Vol. 10: Southwest,* edited by Alfonso Ortiz, 440–62. Washington DC: Smithsonian Institution Press, 1983.

Tovías, Blanca. *Colonialism on the Prairies: Blackfoot Settlement and Cultural Transformation, 1870–1920.* Eastbourne, UK: Sussex Academic Press, 2011.

Townsend, Stephen A. *The Yankee Invasion of Texas.* College Station: Texas A&M University Press, 2006.

Trevor, Marjorie C. "History of Carter-Sweetwater County, Wyoming, to 1875." MA thesis, University of Wyoming, 1954.

Trudeau, Noah Andre. *Gettysburg: A Testing of Courage.* New York: Harper Collins, 2003.

Truett, Samuel. *Fugitive Landscapes: The Forgotten History of the U.S.–Mexico Borderlands.* New Haven: Yale University Press, 2006.

Truett, Samuel and Elliott Young, eds. *Continental Crossroads: Remapping U.S.–Mexico Borderlands History.* Durham, NC: Duke University Press, 2004.

Tyler, Ronnie C. "Fugitive Slaves in Mexico," *Journal of Negro History* 57, no. 1 (January 1970): 1–12.

Utley, Robert M. "Kit Carson and the Adobe Walls Campaign." *American West* 2, no. 1 (Winter 1965): 4–11, 73–75.

———. *The Indian Frontier of the American West, 1846–1890.* Albuquerque: University of New Mexico Press, 1984.

Varon, Elizabeth R. *Disunion!: The Coming of the American Civil War, 1789–1859.* Chapel Hill: University of North Carolina Press, 2008.

Viola, Herman J. *Diplomats in Buckskin: A History of Indian Delegations in Washington City.* Washington, DC: Smithsonian Institution Press, 1981.

Waldrip, William I. "New Mexico during the Civil War (continued)." *New Mexico Historical Review* 28, vols. 3–4 (July-October 1953): 251–90.

Wallenstein, Peter. *Tell the Court I Love My Wife: Race, Marriage, and Law—An American History.* New York: Palgrave MacMillan, 2002.

Wang, Xi. *The Trial of Democracy: Black Suffrage and Northern Republicans, 1860–1910.* Athens: University of George Press, 1997.

Weber, Jennifer L. *The Copperheads: The Rise and Fall of Lincoln's Opponents in the North.* New York: Oxford University Press, 2008.

Weeks, Jim. *Gettysburg: Memory, Market, and an American Shrine.* Princeton: Princeton University Press, 2009.

Weisiger, Marsha. *Dreaming of Sheep in Navajo Country.* Seattle: University of Washington Press, 2011.

Welter, Barbara. "The Cult of True Womanhood, 1820–1860," *American Quarterly* 18, no. 2 (Summer 1966):151–74.

West, Elliott. "Reconstructing Race." *Western Historical Quarterly* 34, no. 1 (Spring 2003): 7–26.

———. *The Last Indian War: The Nez Perce Story.* New York: Oxford University Press, 2009.

White, Gerald. *Baptism in Oil: Stephen F. Peckham in Southern California, 1865–66.* San Francisco: Book Club of California, 1984.

White, Richard. *"It's Your Misfortune and None of My Own": A New History of the American West.* Norman: University of Oklahoma, 1991.

———. *Railroaded: The Transcontinentals and the Making of Modern America.* New York: Norton, 2011.
White, Sophie. *Wild Frenchmen and Frenchified Indians: Material Culture and Race in Colonial Louisiana.* Philadelphia: University of Pennsylvania Press, 2012.
Whites, LeeAnn. *Gender Matters: Civil War, Reconstruction, and the Making of the New South.* New York: Palgrave Macmillan, 2005.
———. "Forty Shirts and a Wagonload of Wheat: Women, the Domestic Supply Line, and the Civil War on the Western Border." *Journal of the Civil War Era* 1, no. 1 (March 2011): 56–78.
Whites, LeeAnn and Alecia P. Long, eds. *Occupied Women: Gender, Military Occupation, and the American Civil War.* Baton Rouge: Louisiana State University Press, 2009.
Whitlock, Flint. *Distant Bugles, Distant Drums: The Union Response to the Confederate Invasion of New Mexico.* Boulder: University Press of Colorado, 2006.
"Why You Can't Teach U.S. History without American Indians." A symposium commemorating the fortieth year of the D'Arcy McNickle Center for American Indian Studies Seminar Series at the Newberry Library in Chicago, May 3–4, 2013, www.newberry.org/why-you-cant-teach.
Wickett, Murray R. *Contested Territory: Whites, Native Americans and African Americans in Oklahoma, 1865–1907.* Baton Rouge: Louisiana State University Press, 2000.
Williams, Patrick G. *Beyond Redemption Texas Democrats after Reconstruction.* College Station: Texas A&M University Press, 2007.
Williams, Walter L. "U.S. Indian Policy and the Debate over Philippine Annexation: Implications for the Origins of American Imperialism." *Journal of American History* 66, no. 4 (March 1980): 810–31.
Wilson, Edmund. *Patriotic Gore: Studies in the Literature of the American Civil War.* New York: Norton, 1994.
Wilson, John P. *When the Texans Came: Missing Records for the Civil War in the Southwest.* Albuquerque: University of New Mexico Press, 2001.
Winks, Robin W. *Canada and the United States: The Civil War Years.* Baltimore: Johns Hopkins University Press, 1960.
Winn, Kenneth. "The Missouri Context of Antebellum Mormonism and its Legacy of Violence." In *The Missouri Mormon Experience,* edited by Thomas M. Spencer, 19–26. Columbia: University of Missouri Press, 2010.
Woodward, C. Vann. "History from Slave Sources." *American Historical Review* 79, no. 2 (April 1974): 470–81.
Wooster, Robert. *The American Military Frontiers: The United States Army in the West, 1783–1900.* Albuquerque: University of New Mexico Press, 2009.
Wright, Muriel H. "The Removal of the Choctaws to the Indian Territory, 1830–1833." *Chronicles of Oklahoma* 6, no. 2 (June 1928): 103–28.
Yarbrough, Fay A. *Race and the Cherokee Nation: Sovereignty in the Nineteenth Century.* Philadelphia: University of Pennsylvania Press, 2008.

Younger, Coleman. *The Story of Cole Younger.* 1903; St. Paul: Minnesota Historical Society Press, 2000.

Zakim, Michael. *Ready-Made Democracy: A History of Men's Dress in the American Republic, 1760–1860.* Chicago: University of Chicago Press, 2003.

Zilversmit, Arthur. *The First Emancipation: The Abolition of Slavery in the North.* Chicago: University of Chicago Press, 1967.

Zimmerman, Andrew. "From the Rhine to the Mississippi: Property, Democracy, and Socialism in the American Civil War." Unpublished paper, University of Pennsylvania, 2013.

CONTRIBUTOR AFFILIATIONS

ADAM ARENSON is Associate Professor of History and director of the Urban Studies program at Manhattan College.

LANCE BLYTH is the Command Historian for NORAD and U.S. Northern Command.

DIANE MUTTI BURKE is Associate Professor of History and director of the Center for Midwestern Studies at the University of Missouri, Kansas City.

WILLIAM DEVERELL is Professor and Chair of the Department of History at the University of Southern California, and directs the Huntington–USC Institute on California and the West.

GREGORY DOWNS is Associate Professor of History at City College of New York and the Graduate Center, CUNY.

ANDREW R. GRAYBILL is Professor and Chair of the Department of History and codirector of the Clements Center for Southwest Studies at Southern Methodist University.

NICHOLAS GUYATT is University Lecturer in American History at the University of Cambridge.

STEVEN HAHN is Roy F. and Jeannette P. Nichols Professor in American History at the University of Pennsylvania.

JAMES JEWELL is chair of the history program at North Idaho College.

STEPHEN KANTROWITZ is Professor of History at the University of Wisconsin–Madison.

MEGAN KATE NELSON is a writer, historian, and cultural critic.

JOSHUA PADDISON is Visiting Assistant Professor of History at Wittenberg University.

MARTHA A. SANDWEISS is Professor of History at Princeton University.

VIRGINIA SCHARFF is Associate Provost for Faculty Development and Distinguished Professor of History and Director of the Center for the Southwest at the University of New Mexico, as well as Chair of Western Women's History at the Autry National Center and cocurator (with Carolyn Brucken) of the exhibition and editor of the companion volume Empire and Liberty: The Civil War and the West (University of California Press, 2015).

FAY YARBROUGH is Associate Professor of History at Rice University.

INDEX

Page numbers in *italics* indicate pages with illustrations.

Abel, Annie Heloise, 5
abolitionists, 74, 79, 98, 139–40, 172, 202; American Indians and, 165, 167; colonization advocated by, 97, 102, 114n17; on Peace Commission, 162–64; views on women's rights of, 192, 216
Adobe Walls, 65, *66*
African Americans, 7, 9n3, 80, 162, 171, 191, 262n27, 272; Christianized, 192; citizenship of, 96, 100, 110, 158, 167, 168, 184–87, 202, 204, 216, 225, 233, 235, 236; colonization schemes for, 95–110, 117n31, 266; education of, 172; enslavement of. *See* slavery; free, before emanipation. *See* free blacks; fundamental rights for, 183–86, 233; male suffrage for, 7, 96, 129, 181, 184, 187–89, 194, 213, 214, 233; postwar violence against, 127; in Union Army, 86, 92n34, 96, 97, 101, 105, 108, 114n14, 118, 187, 267; in Wyoming Territory, 207, 210, 211, 215
African Civilization Society, 104
African descent, people of, 21; immigrants, 184, 194
Ah-ha-Cho-Ker, 253
Alabama, 132, 141, 225, 234
Alaska, 262n32
Albuquerque, 41, 53
Alexander, Alice, 234
Allen, A. C., 113n11
Alvord, General Benjamin, 22, 27, 32n63

American Colonization Society (ACS), 97, 98
American Ethnology, Bureau of (BAE), 174n5
American Fur Company, 167
American Indian as Participant in the Civil War, The (Abel), 5
American Indians, 4, 8–9n3, 102, 114n14, 146, 262n27, 263n56, 266, 271. *See also specific tribes;* African Americans enslaved by, 224–36, 237n3, 238n12, n13, 239n27, 240n45, n53, n57, n58, 241n60, n61; Alaskan, 262n32; clothing of, 242–51, 253–59, *256–58;* desert warfare tactics of, 38, 47; of Kansas-Missouri borderlands, 6, 71, 73, 85, 87n5; massacres of, 3, 5; in Pacific Northwest, 19; raids on Texas settlements by, 119, 131–34; during Reconstruction, 7, 158–74, 181, 183, 185–95; on reservations, 66–67, 119–20, 161; Supreme Court decisions on land claims of, 267; in Wyoming Territory, 203–4, 207, 210–16
Anderson, Mabel Washbourne, 4–5
Anderson, Peter, 188
Andrews, General Christopher, 127
Anglos, 35, 36, 38, 54–58, 60, 61, 64–67, 97, 204
Anthony, Susan B., 216, 217
Antietam, Battle of, 149, 162
Apaches, 36, 39, 46, 266; Mescalero, 58

309

Appomattox Court House, Confederate surrender at, 23, 109, 195, 266; aftermath of, 3, 7, 65, 158, 161; continuation of war in Texas following, 118, 122
Arapaho, 5, 163, 203
Arizona Territory, 2, 8n1, 35, 36, 45, 61, 269
Arkansas, 2, 75, 79, 269
Army & Navy Journal, 118–19, 124
Army of the Pacific, 1860–1866, The (Hunt), 5
Ash Hollow, Battle of, 163
Atchison, David Rice, 74, 76
Atlanta (Georgia), 171
Auger, General Christopher C., *159*, 160, 161, 171
Austin, Stephen F., 97
Austin (Texas), 126, 128, 132

Bachelder, John Badger, *151*, 151–53, 157n40
Bagdad (Texas), 108–9, 123
Banks, Frances, 224
Banks, Sina, 230, 239n27
Bannock, 171, 203
Barber, Mollie, 229
Barboncito, 60, 62
Bard, Cephas, 149–50
Bard, Thomas A., 149–50
Barner, L. B., 230, 239n27
Bates, Redelia, 217
Baylor, John, 41
Baynes, Admiral Lambert, 19
Bell, Admiral Charles, 32n63
Benjamin, Judah, 26
Bennett, H. H., 254, *255*
Berwanger, Eugene, 5
Between Two Fires (Hauptman), 5
Bibb, Henry, 231–32
Bible, 193
Bierce, Ambrose, 139–47, 150, 154, 155n16
Bierce, Lucius Verus, 139–40
Bingham, George Caleb, 83, *84*, 90n27
black codes, 36, 184
blacks. *See* African Americans
Blair, Francis, Sr., 121
Blair, Frank P., 98–100, 103
Blair, Montgomery, 99–100, 106, 109
Blair, Preston, 103, 106, 109–10
Bleeding Kansas, 74, 175n16

Boggs, Lilburn, 73–74
Boley (Oklahoma), 234, 240n57
Bolinger, Bradley, 227–28, 238n20
Border, District of the, 71, 82
Bosque Redondo (New Mexico), 60–65
Boston, 8, 103, 163–65, 216
Boston Indian Citizenship Association, 192
Boucher, Julian, 258–59
Bozeman Trail, 168, 204
Bradley, John, 103
Bradley, Taylor, 254
Brannock, Lizzie, 78
Brenham (Texas), 127, 129, 132
Bright, Julia, 217–18
Bright, William H., 213, 214, 217–19
Bristol, Samuel A., 215
Britain, 3, 4, 15–26, 28, 30, 30n23, 95, 104, 134; early settlers from, 244
British Columbia, 6, 19–22, 25, 28, 29n1, 31n36, 277
Brooks, James, 55
Brothertown community, 185
Brown, Charley Moore, 238n20
Brown, John, 15, 74, 139–40
Brown, Peggy McKinney, 227–28, 238n20
Brown, Richard Maxwell, 6
Brown College, 150
Brownlow, Andrew, 78
Brownsville (Texas), 122, 129
Brulés, 168
Bruyneel, Kevin, 260n6
Buena Ventura (California), 149, 150
Buffalo Bill's Wild West show, 168
Bull Run, Battle of, 22, 162
bushwhackers, 6, 76–79, 81, 82
Butler, Ben, 213

Cadete, 59–60
California, 7, 16, 95, 105, 146, 266. *See also* San Francisco; admission to the Union of, 145, 271; antebellum, 8; and Confederate invasion of New Mexico, 26, 35–37, 45, 48, 58, 269; gold in, 1, 21, 149; oil in, 149–51; and Reconstruction, 9n3, 181–96, *182*; slaughter of Pomo Indians in, 3
Californios, 4
Campbell, Commissioner, 18
Campbell, John A., 207, 212, 214, 218–20

310 · INDEX

Canada, 4, 98, 167, 194, 267. *See also specific cities, provinces, regions*
Canby, General Edward R. S., 42, 45, 46, 53, 57, 58
Cannary, Martha Jane "Calamity Jane," 209–10, 218
Canyon de Chelly, 55, 62–63
Carey, Captain Asa B., 63
Carleton, General James H., 45, 58, 60–61, 64
Carson, Kit, 6, 46, 53, 54, 57–66, 270
Catholics, 54, 191, 192, 211, 248
Catlin, George, 245, *246*
Central Pacific Railroad, 206, 213
Chaco, 59–60
Chancellorsville, Battle of, 215
Chapman (ship), 25, 26
Charleston, 8
Chase, Salmon P., 98, 109
Chattanooga, Battle of, 140
Chavez, Colonel José Francisco, 58, 61
Cherokees, 166, 230–32, 236, 239n27
Cherry, Lucy, 234
Chesapeake (ship), 15
Cheyenne (Wyoming), 217
Cheyenne Leader, 218–19
Cheyennes, 5, 163, 164, 168, 203
Chicago, 102, 170–71, 268
Chickamauga, Battle of, 140
Chickasaws, 166, 226, 230, 231, 238n12, n14, 240n45
Child, David and Lydia Maria, 97
China, 26, 271
Chinese immigrants, 111, 181, 183, 198n30, 210–11, 266; citizenship and suffrage denied to, 7, 185–95, 204, 270; colonization proposal for, 107; on transcontinental railroad construction crews, 172, 213
Chisholm, James, 209, 211
Chittenden, Lucius, 103
Chivington, Colonel John M. 41, 163–64
Choctaws, 7, 166, 224–37, 238n12, 240n45, n53, n58, 266; Freedman's Bill enacted by (1883), 225, 233–35
Christianity, 187–90, 193–94, 198n30, 212, 217, 220, 242, 248, 255
Christian Recorder, 103, 105
citizenship, 1, 2, 4, 7, 160, 162, 165–69, 183–201; advocates for elimination of limitations on, 192–94; of African Americans, 96, 100, 110, 158, 167, 168, 184–87, 202, 204, 216, 224–25, 233, 235, 236; in Choctaw nation, 224–26, 233–36; clothing associated with, 242–59; exclusions from rights of, 165–69, 184, 186–92, 195, 202, 204, 216, 226–27
Civil Rights Act (1866), 183–86, 190, 192
Civil War in the Western Territories, The (Colton), 5
Clark, William, 1, 16
Cole, Mary, 238n12
Collins, J.L., 57
colonization, 95–117; of African Americans, 95–110, 117n31, 266; of American Indians. *See* reservations; European, 260n5
Colorado Territory, 6, 8n1, 37, 41, 42, 61, 66, 163–64, 270
Colton, Ray, 5
Comanches, 3, 8, 36, 39, 46, 55–56, 64–66, 119, 131–34, 266
Comstock Act (1873), 191
Confederate Army, 5, 24, 26, 79, 128, 143–44, 147, 158; American Indians in, 229, 269; at Bull Run, 22; in Canada, 15; Fort Sumter fired on by, 1, 19, 33, 37, 71, 99, 140; and French in Mexico, 105, 107, 109; at Gettysburg, 3, 18, 153, 157n37; in Kansas-Missouri borderlands conflicts, 79, 80; at Kennesaw Mountain, 140; in Missouri, 80, 87–88n8; New Mexico campaign of, 6, 33–48, *34*, 53, 57, 58, 163; surrenders of, 121, 125, 128, 131, 133. *See also* Appomattox Courthouse, Confederate surrender at; in Texas, 118, 120–22, 127; veterans of, 144, 154, 204; at Wilson's Creek, 22
Confederate Navy, 24
Congress, U.S., 163, 166, 177n42, 188, 214, 252, 253, 270. *See also* House of Representatives, U.S.; Senate, U.S.; Bureau of Refugees, Freedmen, and Abandoned Lands created by, 86; Civil Rights Act debated in, 185; colonization proposals in, 96, 109–10; Constitutional amendments in, 106, 186, 189, 190, 204; former Confederate states restored by, 133; Joint

Congress *(continued)*
　Committee on Reconstruction, 126; mailing of "vulgar and indecent" materials criminalized by, 191; nonvoting territorial delegates to, 206, 214; Peace Commission created by. *See* Peace Commission; Reconstruction policies of, 131, 183–84, 213
Connelly, Henry, 42, 45
Conness, John, 185
Constitution, U.S., 3, 121, 130, 193; Thirteenth Amendment, 106, 110, 165, 183, 184, 229, 231; Fourteenth Amendment, 165, 168, 183, 186–90, 194–95, 198n30, 204, 248; Fifteenth Amendment, 189–92, 194, 195; preamble, 191; Three-Fifths Clause, 185, 188
contrabands. *See* Slavery, escape from
Cooper, Arvazena "Nan," 79
Cooper, William, 35
Coopwood, Bethel, 43
Copperheads, 213, 267
Corinth, siege of, 140
Corwin, Thomas, 95, 96, 100–101, 108, 113n11
Cowan, Edgar, 186
Creeks, 166, 226, 229, 232, 240n47
Crees, 21
Crows, 203
Crush, William, 234
Cuba, 98–100, 107, 267
Custer, General George Armstrong, 123, 128–29, 172
Cutler, Lyman, 18
Cyane (ship), 25

Dakota, Department of, 161, 175n8
Dakotas, 5, 247, 250, 252, 258–59
Dakota Territory, 158, 172, 247–48, 270
Dakota Territory, 1861–1899 (Lamar), 5
Dallas, 8
David, Jules, 26–27
Davidson, Nathaniel, 107
Davidson, William (Bill), 35, 38, 40–45, 47
Davis, Jefferson, 2, 26, 35–37, 74, 105, 106, 269
Dawes Commission, 236
Dawes Severalty Act (1887), 170, 177n40, 271
Declaration of Independence, 193, 220
Delany, Martin, 98

Delawares, 73
Delgadito, 60, 62, 63
Demerara, 30n28
Democrats, 101, 109, 125, 181, 183, 187–89, 191, 194, 213–19
Denver, 42, 79, 163–64
Deseret, 267
Devil's Dictionary, The (Bierce), 155n16
Digger Indians, 183, 185–88, 193, 194
Dignowity, Anthony, 105
Doblado, Manuel, 100, 101, 113n11
Dohasan (Little Mountain), 65
Dominican Republic, 110
Doolittle, James Rood, 98–100, 109, 113n11, 164, 186
Douglas, James, 15, 19–21, 23, 26, 28, 29n1, 30–31n28
Douglas, Stephen, 268
Douglass, Frederick, 102–3, 202
Dowdy, Doc Daniel, 230, 239n27
Dred Scott v. Sanford (1857), 184
Duncan, Russell, 143
Durham (North Carolina), Confederate surrender at, 118

Easter, Esther, 80
Elk v. Wilkins (1884), 188
El Paso, 38–42, 57, 60
emancipation, 1, 86, 160, 165, 191, 205, 262n27, 265; advocacy for, 260. *See also* abolitionists; citizenship and, 167, 242; imminent, bushwhackers and, 81; in Indian Territory, 224–25, 229–32, 234, 236; proposals for racial separation after. *See* colonization; in Texas, 120, 128–29, 134; white supremacy after, 183; of women, 216
Emancipation Proclamation, 2, 96, 229, 231
enfranchisement. *See* suffrage
Estella, 59–60
Etulain, Richard, 6
Evans, Eliza, 231
Ewing, General Thomas, Jr., 71, 82–83, 85
expansionism, 4, 28, 100, 104, 205. *See also* Manifest Destiny; American Indians impacted by, 55, 163; Confederate, 37, 40, 47; of Polk, 17, 29n5; proslavery, 35, 36, 98, 228

Far Southwest, 1846–1912, The (Lamar), 5
Fehrenbacher, Don, 268
filibusters, 4, 35, 99, 190, 267
Florida, 37, 102, 104, 267
Foner, Eric, 241n70
Fort Bascom, 65
Fort Benton, 141
Fort Bliss, 40, 46, 48
Fort Bridger Treaty, 203, 207
Fort Burgwin, 37
Fort Canby, 61, 63, 64
Fort Clatsop, 16
Fort Craig, 41–43, 53
Fort Davis, 47
Fort Hall, 171
Fort Kearney, 141
Fort Lancaster, 47
Fort Laramie, 177n32; Peace Commission at. *See* Peace Commission, U.S.
Fort Laramie Treaty (1868), 7
Fort Quitman, 46
Fort Scott, 82
Fort Smith, 141, 230
Fort Stanton, 57, 58, 60
Fort Stockton, 47
Fort Sumner, 60
Fort Sumter, 1, 19, 33, 37, 71, 99, 140
Fort Tejon, 146
Fort Union, 42, 53
Fort Vancouver, 27
Fort Wingate, 62–64
France, 30n23, 73, 95, 101, 104–5, 107, 108, 124; early settlers from, 244; immigrants from, 204; Mexican imperial government backed by, 101, 104–9, 119–22, 266
France, Charles, 79
Francis, Allen, 21–27, 29, 31n34
Francis, Simeon, 21–22, 27
Franklin, Thomas, 233–34
Frazier, Donald, 36
Freedmen's Bureau, 109, 127, 131, 163, 169, 273n1
free blacks, 36, 97–98, 102–104, 191
freedpeople. *See* African Americans
Freeman, Fred and Legh, 210, 213
Free Soilers, 6, 71, 74–75
Free Staters, 4, 101, 163

Frelinghuysen, Frederick, 189–90
Frontier Index, 210–11, 213, 217
Fugitive Slave Act (1851), 98, 268

Gadsden Purchase, 269
Gallagher, Cary, 8n3
Gallagher, Frances, 211
Galveston (Texas), 122, 123, 126, 132
Gamble, Hamilton R., 78
Gardner, Alexander, 158–62, 166–68, 172–74, 174n1, n4, n5, 176n54
Garnet, Henry Highland, 104
Garrison, William Lloyd, 97, 172, 202
Genius of Universal Emancipation, 97
Georgia, 109, 131, 132, 234, 239n27
German immigrants, 77, 204, 269
Gettysburg, Battle of, 1–3, 7, 18, 150–52, *151*, 157n37, 162, 193
Gettysburg Address, 158, 193
Gillett, Mary C., 156–57n35
Glorieta Pass, Battle of, 41, 65, 269
Glover, Ridgeway, 174n4
Goicouria, Domingo de, 100, 113n10
gold, 1, 20–22, 34, 37, 79, 209, 269; on American Indian lands, 60, 172, 207; Confederate targeting of shipments of, 20, 24, 28
Goodnight, Charles, 55
Gorham, George C., 181, 194, 195n1
Gould, LaFayette, 154, 156n25
Grande, Herrera, 63
Grant, Ulysses S., 108, 110, 115n25, 129, 133; Blair's colonization proposal to, 109–10; Juárez supported in Mexican civil war by, 121–24; presidency of, 192, 212, 213, 242, 248
Graydon, James "Paddy," 33, 43, 45, 58, 59
Great Basin Indians, 54
Great Depression, 168, 231
Grimes, Lucy, 127
guerrilla warfare, 71, 74–79, 81, 82, 85, 119, 125
Guest, John, 241n60, n61

Haidas, 3, 18
Haight, Henry, 194
Haiti, 98, 114n17
Halliburton, Rudi, 232

Hall, Colonel H. S., 127
Hall, Squire, 233, 204n240
Haller, Granville, 18–19
Halttunen, Karen, 244
Hamilton, Andrew Jackson, 104–5, 125–26, 133
Hampton Roads conference, 106
Harney, General William S., 18, *159*, 160, 162, 164
Harpers Ferry, 15
Harrison, Zadoc John, 241n60, n61
Harte, Bret, 145–47, 150
Hauptman, Laurence, 5
Havana, 95, 268
Hawai'i, 8
Hazen, General William B., 139–42
Hebard, Grace Raymond, 218
Henderson, John B., 184
Hendricks, Thomas A., 189–90
Hiawatha (Longfellow), 164
Higgins, David W., 23, 31n34
Hispanos, 53–59, 63–67
Ho-Chunks, 7, 243, 247–49, 252–57, *257–59*, 260n5, n6, 266
Hollister, Ovando, 42
Holmes, Oliver Wendell, Jr., 155n16
Homestead Act (1862), 79, 169, 233, 270
homesteaders, 169–71, 255
Hopis, 61
Horn, Partheny, 80
House of Representatives, U.S., 17, 29n7, 100, 113n12, 165, 171
Houston (Texas), 126
Howard, Jacob, 186, 188
Howard, Oliver O., 109, 273n1
Howard University, 172
Howe, Church, 212
Hudson, George, 229
Hudson's Bay Company (HBC), 17–18
Hunt, Aurora, 5
Hunt, General Henry Jackson, 153
Hunt, Captain L. C., 18, 19
Hunter, Priscilla, 79–80

Idaho Territory, 6, 270
Illinois, 76, 244, 260n5, 268
immigrants, 99, 105, 195; of African descent, 184; Chinese, 183–89, 192–95; 198n30, 204, 213, 266; German, 77, 204, 269; Irish, 191, 204; to Mexico, 107; Scottish, 161, 211
Indian Affairs, Commissioner of, 170, 214
Indiana, 141
Indian Commission, U.S., 66
Indian Office, U.S., 241, 249–51
Indian Pioneer History (IPH), 237n3
Indian Reorganization Act (1934), 234
Indian Rights Association, 192
Indians. *See* American Indians
Indian Territory, 2, 7, 120, 166, 269. *See also* Oklahoma; military surveying expedition of, 141; Missouri-Kansas borderlands and, 72–74; Southern plains tribes confined to, 161
Insular Affairs, Bureau of, 271
Interior, U.S. Department of, 171, 174n5, 177n42
intermarriage, 215, 227, 233, 235
Iowa, 73, 173, 247
Irish immigrants, 191, 192, 204

Jackson, Andrew, 18
Jackson, Claiborne Fox, 75
Jackson, Lizzie, 232
James brothers, 71
Japan, 26
Jayhawkers, 74, 76–78, 80
Jefferson, Thomas, 98, 204, 219, 220, 271
Jefferson Medical College, 146, 154, 156n25
Jeffreys brothers, 22–24, 31n36
Jennison, Charles "Doc," 74, 77
Jicarillas, 54, 55, 66
Johnson, Andrew, 126, 128, 163, 175n8, 185; colonization plans proposed to, 109, 110; end of Texas insurrection proclaimed by, 119, 130, 133; impeachment of, 125; informed of danger of French-backed monarchy in Mexico, 121–22
Johnson, Ben, 230
Johnson, Charles, 123
Johnson, James A., 192
Jones, Robert M., 229
Josephy, Alvin, 5
Juárez, Benito, 95, 99, 100, 106, 109, 121–24, 269
Jun, Helen Heran, 188

Ka-ni-ache, 60, 61, 64–65
Kansas, 71–78, 102, 114n14, 139, 161; Bleeding, 74, 175n16; entry into Union of, 75; Free State movement in, 101, 163; refuge for former slaves in, 80, 82; violence along Missouri border with, 71–78, 82–83, 269
Kansas-Nebraska Act (1854), 163, 165
Kansas Pacific Railroad, 162
Kelley, William, 106, 115n22
Kennedy, Arthur, 28
Kennesaw Mountain, Battle of, 140
Kentucky, 2, 79, 80
Kerber, Linda, 221n9
Kimmons, Richard, 80
King, "Uncle" George G., 236
Kingman, John W., 212, 214, 217
Kiowas, 3, 55–56, 64–66, 134
Klooster, David, 143
Krauthamer, Barbara, 232
Ku Klux Klan, 171

Lakotas, 158, 163, 167–70, 172–74, 174n4, 203, 207, 215; Oglala, 161, 167, 168
Lamar, Howard, 5
Lane, General James, 77, 81–82, 101–3, 105, 114n14
Langston, Charles, 98
Langston, John Mercer, 98
Largo, Manuelito and José, 59
Larson, T. A., 214
Lawrence (Kansas), 71, 82
Lee, Edward M., 212, 215, 219
Lee, Robert E., 23, 153, 157n37
Leonard, Pat, 157n37
Letterman, Jonathan, 146–54, *148*, 156nn25–27, n29, n30, 157n36, n37
Letterman, Mary, 154
Lewis, Meriwether, 1, 16
Lewis, Robert, 233
Liberals, Mexican, 95, 101, 104, 106, 108, 109, 121, 123–25, 266
Liberator, 106
Liberia, 97, 98
Life of General Stand Watie, The (Anderson), 4–5
Lincoln, Abraham, 2, 6, 30n23, 140, 147, 228–29, 267; assassination of, 1, 151, 161,
162, 164; colonization proposals considered by, 99–107, 110, 113nn10–12; election of, 15, 75; emancipation policy of, 96, 191, 229; Francis brothers and, 21–22; Gettysburg Address, 158, 193
Lincoln, Mary Todd, 22
Lindsay, Mary, 230
Little Big Horn, Battle of, 172
Llaneros, 54
Loan, General Benjamin F., 88n10
Locke, John, 219
Longfellow, Henry Wadsworth, 164
López, Narciso, 100
Los Angeles, 8, 146
Louisiana, 106, 109, 123, 234, 269
Louisiana Purchase, 73, 271
Love, Kiziah, 231
Lovell, Dick, 31n34
Lundy, Benjamin, 97
Lyon, General Nathaniel, 3, 28
Lyons, Lord, 25–26

Manifest destiny, 17, 33–37, 48, 271
Mare Island, 24, 26, 27, 32n63
Martial Law (Bingham), 83, *84*
Masonic Mutual Relief Association, 173
Massachusetts, 6, 181, 202
Matamoros (Mexico), 8, 122–24
Mather, Ken, 31n34
Matthew, Gospel of, 193
Maury, Matthew, 109
Maximilian, Emperor of Mexico, 104–9, 120–21, 124
Maytubbie, Matthew, 234, 240n58
McCann, William, 140
McClellan, General George B., 105
McCown, Jerome B., 47
McFeely, William, 273n1
McGaugh, Scott, 147, 156n30, 157n36
McKinney, Jessy, 228
McOmie, George, 211
McPherson, James M., 8n1
McWilliams, Carey, 139–42, 155n16
Meade, General George Gordon, 152–53
Medical Recollections of the Army of the Potomac (Letterman), 154
Merk, Frederick, 29n7
Mescaleros, 55, 57–60, *59*, 64–66

Mesilla (New Mexico), 43, 45
Mexican Cession, 2
Mexicans, ethnic, 163, 204, 270
Mexico, 4, 55, 118, 134, 158, 269; civil war in, 2, 95, 119, 122; colonization plans for, 7, 109, 115n25; filibustering in, 267; French-backed imperial government in, 101, 104–9, 119–25, 266; independence of Texas from, 35; schemes for African American colonization in,, 95–101, 103–11, 113n12; U.S. War with, 3, 17, 54, 105, 271
Michigan (ship), 15
Miles, General Nelson, 133
Military Reconstruction Act (1867), 212
Miller, Lieutenant Wilson, 127
Minnesota, 247, 252, 253
miscegenation, 227
Missionary Ridge, Battle of, 140
Mississippi, 2, 132, 181, 269
Missouri, 1, 7, 36, 71–85, 194, 239n27, 266. *See also* St. Louis; armed conflict in, 2, 71, 74–79, 81, 82, 85, 92n34, 119, 269; depopulation of western counties of, 6, 71, 74, 78–85; eviction of American Indians from, 73; Mormon War in, 73–74; Platte Purchases in, 86n3; secessionists in, 18, 85, 87–88n87
Mitchell, James, 104
Mixon, John, 231
Monroe, John, 168
Monroe Doctrine, 104, 106
Montana Territory, 8, 79, 141, 270
Montgomery, James, 74, 75
Montgomery (Alabama), 37
Moon-Ho Jung, 193
Morales Montenegro, Abdón, 107
Mormons, 4, 6, 37, 71, 85, 191–92, 211; Wars, 73–74, 267
Morning Mist, 18
Moss, Sally Henderson, 230, 231, 233
Mountain Wolf Woman, 257, 258
Mousseau, Louis, 172
Mousseau, Sophie, 167–68, 171, 172, 174n4, 177n32, n36

Napoleon III, Emperor of France, 101, 104–9, 120, 124

Narragansett (ship), 27
National Anthropological Archives, 174n5
National Woman Suffrage Association, 217
Native Americans. *See* American Indians
naturalization. *See* citizenship
Naturalization Act (1790), 188
Naturalization Act (1870), 183, 192–95
Navajos, 37, 55–58, 60–65, *62*, 171, 266
Naylor, Celia, 232
Nebraska, 141, 161, 163, 172, 247–49, 251, 254, 260n5
Neighbors, Lula, 233, 234
Neutrality Act (1794), 267
Nevada Territory, 8n1, 22, 141, 195, 270
New Mexico, 2, 6, 8n1, 36, 53–67, 129, 131; Carson's campaigns against Indians in, 58–65; Confederate invasion of, 6, 33–48, *34*, 53, 57, 58, 163
New Orleans, 95, 125, 268; Battle of, 18
New York, 194, 198n30, 202
New York City, 267
Newcastle, Duke of, 19
Newgent, Andrew G., 87n7
Niblack, William Ellis, 187
Nicaragua, 100, 267
Nichols, David, 5
Nickerson, H. G., *203*
Noel, Theophilus, 38, 41, 44, 46, 47
Northern Pacific Railroad, 161, 175n8
North West Fur Company, 31n28
Nova Scotia, 15
Nullification Crisis, 267

Oberlin College, 98
Oglala Lakota, 161, 167, 168
Ohio, 139–40, 194, 268
Oklahoma, 1, 66, 224, 234, 240n53. *See also* Indian Territory
Olleros, 54
Oregon, 6, 8n1, 16, 30n18, 31n36, 79, 195
Oregon Trail, 141
Orth, Godlove S., 121
Osages, 73
Osceola (Missouri), 77

Pacific, Department of the, 19, 23, 34, 28
Pacific Squadron, 28, 29, 42
Palmito Ranch, Battle of, 118, 119

Palouse War, 30n18
Panama, isthmus of, 99
Panic of 1873, 195
Parker, Ely S., 214
Pascoe, Peggy, 227
Peace Commission, U.S., 158, *159*, 161–71, 175n16, 178n54; treaties negotiated by, 7, 168–73, 203, 207
Pease, Elisha, 130
Peckham, Stephen, 150–53
Pennsylvania, 194, 268
Pennsylvania Railroad, 149
Peralta (New Mexico), 42
Peticolas, Alfred, 38, 43
Petite, Phyllis, 230, 239n27
Philippines, 271
Pettis, George, 42
Pfeiffer, Captain Albert, 63
Philadelphia, 146–50
Philadelphia & California Petroleum Company, 150, 152
Phillips, Wendell, 165, 172, 192
Photographic Sketch Book of the War (Gardner), 162
Pickett, George, 3, 18–19, 152, 153
Pickett's Mill, Battle of, 140
Pierce, Franklin, 35, 269
Pig War, 18, 19, 28
Pike's Peakers, 163
Pine Ridge Reservation, 167–68, 170, 172
Pitcher, Nancy, 77
Pitchlynn, Peter, 228
Plains Indians, 56, 66, 128, 161, 166. *See also specific tribes*
Platte, Department of the, 161, 175n8
Platte County Self-Defense Association, 74
Platte Purchase, 73, 86n3
Poe, Matilda, 231
Polk, James K., 17, 29n5
Pomeroy, Samuel C., 194
Pomos, 3
Pope, John, 270
post-traumatic stress disorder, 144
Potawatomis, 73, 247
Pottawatomie massacre, 139
Prairie Du Chien Courier, 254
Price, Sterling, 18
Protestants, 187, 191–92, 248

Pueblos, 35, 53–56, 61, 63, 64, 66, 67
Puget Sound War, 30n18

Quakers, 150, 248–51, 254
Quantrill, William, 82
Québec, 15, 167

Raab, Ann, 89n15
Radical Reconstruction, 171, 172, 195
Radical Republicans, 99, 194, 195, 202, 210, 212, 213, 216, 270
Rafiner, Tom, 89n15
railroads, 107, 123, 149, 158, 161. *See also* transcontinental railroad; in Mexico, 113n10; wartime importance of, 75, 156n30
Reconstruction, 1–4, 7, 8–9n3, 135n4, 196n3, 216, 265–68, 270; American Indians and, 133–34, 158–71, 224–36, 242–43, 248, 249, 252; California and, 181–96, *182*; colonization plans during, 110; legislation on governing of South during, 212; Radical, 171, 172, 195, 202; resistance in Texas to federal authority during, 125, 126, 128, 131; in Wyoming Territory, 205, 213, 266
Red Cloud, 168
Red Legs. *See* Jayhawkers
Redpath, James, 114n17
Refugees, Freedmen, and Abandoned Lands, U.S. Bureau of, 86
Reid, Whitelaw, 109
Republicans, 7, 125, 248, 268, 271; colonization schemes of, 95–108; in debates on citizenship and suffrage for non-white males, 181, 183, 185–95; Mexican Liberals and, 121, 124; Radical. *See* Radical Republicans; in Wyoming Territory, 202, 210–17
reservations, 5, 65–67, 120, 164, 188, 270; Apache, 57; Comanche, 66; Dakota, 258; for emancipated slaves, American Indian demands for, 166; Ho-Chunk, 247–48, 254, 260n5; Kiowa, 66; Lakota, 161, 167–73; Navajo, 57, 60, 64, 66; Shoshone, 207; Ute, 57, 66; Winnebago, 249–52, 260n5
resettlement. *See* colonization

INDEX · 317

Revolution, 216–17
Revolutions of 1848, 269
Richardson, Heather Cox, 6
Roebuck, Paul Garnett, 231, 238n12
Rogue River War, 30n18
Romero, Matías, 99–100, 104, 106, 113n10, n11
Ross, Major J. T., 85
Rothschild's bank, 107
Rowe, James, 123
runaway slaves. *See* slavery, escapees from
Ryan, Eddie, 177n32
Ryan, John "Posey," 167, 177n32

Sac and Fox, 73, 163, 247
Sacramento, 141
Saginaw (ship), 26, 27
St. Joseph (Missouri), 79
St. Louis, 6, 8, 73, 75, 76, 163, 168, 269
Salt Lake City, 141
San Antonio, 38–39, 42, 44, 47, 48, 126, 132
San Antonio-El Paso Road, 38–39, 45, 46, 48
Sanborn, General John B., *159,* 160, 161, 166, 176n31, 232
Sand Creek Massacre, 5, 163–65, 172, 175n16
San Francisco, 2, 8, 27, 188; Bierce in, 141–42, 145; Confederate threat to shipping from, 20, 22, 24–26; Letterman in, 149, 153–54
San Jacinto (ship), 30n23
San Juan Island, 17–19, 28, 30
Santa Barbara (California), 149, 150
Santa Fe, 35, 41, 46, 58, 61
Santa Fe Trail, 36, 64
Sauk. *See* Sac and Fox
Saulsbury, Willard, 187
Saunt, Claudio, 229, 232
Sauvage, Enrique, 107, 108
Schofield, General John, 123
Schulten, Susan, 6
Scott, Thomas A., 149–51, 156n30
Scurry, William R., 41
Seattle, 19
secession, 1, 3, 229, 266, 267; Confederate imperialism and, 36; Missourian supporters of, 75–76, 78–79, 81, 83–85, 87n8; of Texas, 33, 102
sectionalism, 35, 161, 265, 268
Selden, Lieutenant, 25
Selfridge, Thomas, 24–25, 32n63
Seminoles, 37, 163, 166, 236, 267
Senate, U.S., 17, 29n7, 100, 101, 105, 113n11, 171, 195; Committee on Indian Affairs, 263n56
Seward, William Henry, 2, 95, 121, 124, 271–72; and Confederate threat in Pacific Northwest, 22, 23, 25–26; and Republican colonization schemes, 95, 100, 101, 108
Shapard, J. S., 23, 28
Shawnees, 73
Sheeks, Ben, 217–19
Shelby, Joseph, 123
Sheridan, General Philip, 3, 108, 115n25, 122–25, 129, 132, 133
Sherlock, James, 211–12
Sherlock, Richard, 211
Sherman, John, 165
Sherman, General William Tecumseh, 126, 132, *159,* 160, 165–66, 171, 175n8, 232
Shiloh, Battle of, 140, 143
Shoshones, 171, 203, 207, 214, 215
Shropshire, John, 39, 40
Shubrick (ship), 24, 31n34
Shufeldt, Robert Wilson, 95–96, 100, 101, 110–11
Sibley, Henry H., 36–40; New Mexico campaign led by, *34,* 42–48
Sioux, 158, 161, 163, 167–70, 172–74
slave rebellions, 267
slavery, 1–4, 167, 194, 267, 268; American Indian involvement in, 67, 224–36, 237n3, 238n12, n13, 239n27, 240n45, n53, n57, n58, 241n60, n61; antebellum debates about, 159; brutality of, 163, 168; end of, 1, 102, 119, 191, 270. *See also* emancipation; escape from, 74–76, 80–82, 98, 102, 104, 139, 188, 232; expansion of, 2, 35–36, 205, 271; Kansas-Missouri borderlands conflicts over, 6, 71–77, 81, 85, 139; opponents of, 73, 77, 97, 139. *See also* abolitionists; Peace

Commissioners' views on, 160–66; in Texas, 97–99, 119, 125, 129, 133, 134
Smith, Caleb, 113n10
Smith, Edmund Kirby, 118, 120
Smith, James, 211
Smith, Janet Sherlock, *203*, 211–12
Smith, R. C., 230, 231
Smithsonian Institution, 174n5
Sordo, 62
Soule, Captain Silas, 164
South Carolina, 6, 121, 126; Nullification Crisis in, 267
Southern Association, 23, 26–28
Southern Homestead Act (1866), 169
South Pass City (Wyoming Territory), *203*, 205, 208–9, 211, 213–14, 217
Spain, 95, 100, 104
Spanish, 8
Spanish-American War, 271
Springfield (Illinois), 21
Stanley, General David, 126
Stanton, Edwin, 103, 129
Stanton, Elizabeth Cady, 191, 216, 217
Sternhell, Yael, 40
Stevens, Thaddeus, 213
Stewart, William, 190
Stilgoe, John, 205–6
Stockbridge community, 185
Stone River, Battle of, 140
Strong, General W. E., 126
Stuart, J.E.B., 3
suffrage, 7, 183–95; for African American men, 96, 181, 184, 185, 187–89, 194, 195, 213, 214, 233; denied to Chinese immigrants and Native Americans, 185–95, 204, 270; universal, 184, 219; white male, 183, 184; for women, 172, 190–91, 195, 202, 204, 205, 210, 213, 216–20
Sumner, Charles, 192
Supreme Court, U.S., 188, 267, 268
Surdo, Soldado, 63
Susquehanna, Department of the, 147
Sweetwater mining district (Wyoming Territory), 207–12

Taladrid, Damaso, 58
Taos (New Mexico), 60, 65
Tappan, Arthur, 163

Tappan, Cora Scott, 172
Tappan, Lewis, 163
Tappan, Minnie, 164, 172
Tappan, Colonel Samuel F., *159*, 160, 163–65, 172, 175n16
Tehuantepec, isthmus of, 95, 96, 101, 110
Tennessee, 2, 109, 126, 132, 269
Terry, General Alfred Howe, *159*, 160, 161, 166, 171–72
Texas, 1, 2, 7, 8, 36, 65, 79, 80, 114n15, 239n37; annexation of, 17, 98, 99, 119, 271; Confederate invasion of west from, 34, 35, 37–48, 53, 58, 266; Confederate surrender in, 118; expansion of slavery into, 97–98; filibustering in, 267; Indian raids in, 55; postwar threats to federal authority in, 118–34, 135n4; schemes for African American colonization in, 97, 102–5, 109; secession of, 33
Thames (ship), 25
Thayer, Eli, 102
Thompson, Ambrose, 99
Thomas, Captain, 253
Thoreau, Henry David, 139
Thundercloud, Annie Blowsnake, 256, *258*
Tompkins, Al, 211–12
Train, George Francis, 216
transcontinental railroad, 1, 2, 36, 171, 269, 275; construction of, 161, 162, 169, 175n8, 206–7, 213, 219, 270
Trans-Mississippi, Department of, 1, 2
Treasury Department, U.S., 103, 141
Trent (ship), 20, 30n23
Truett, Sam, 45
true womanhood, ideology of, 208–10, 216
Trumbull, Lyman, 184, 185
Turner, Frederick Jackson, 265, 268
Turner, Henry McNeal, 105
Tyler, John, 29n7

U.S. Army, 142, 168, 211, 253, 267; campaigns against American Indians by, 3, 5, 36, 37, 171–72; during Civil War. *See* Union Army; Corps of Engineers, 6; First Dragoons, 33; medical corps, 146; in Mexican War, 3, 37; in Pacific Northwest, 18; in postwar Texas 120, 123, 125, 127, 128, 132, 133

Underground Railroad, 194
Union Army, 5, 149, 158, 160–63, 165, 266, 269; African Americans in, 86, 92n34, 96, 97, 101, 105, 106, 108, 114n14, 118, 187, 267; at Antietam, 149; Army of the Potomac, 147–50, 154; Bierce in, 140, 142; campaigns against American Indians of, 46; at Chancellorsville, 215; Cherokees in, 231; Confederate New Mexico campaign defeated by, 33, 34, 37, 38, 41–43, 45, 48, 53, 163, 269; conscription into, 79, 267; at Gettysburg, 152–53; in Kansas-Missouri borderlands conflicts, 71, 75–81, 83–84, 92n34; at Kennesaw Mountain, 140; medical care of soldiers in, 146–47, 149, 156n30, 157n37; proposal for Mexican expedition of, 102, 107; in Texas, 7, 105, 108, 114n15; veterans of, 9, 154, 213, 215; victory of. *See* Appomattox Courthouse, Confederate surrender at; in Washington Territory, 6, 22; at Wilson's Creek, 3
Union Navy, ships of, 15, 24–27, 30
Union Oil Company, 149
Union Pacific Railroad, 161, 175n8, 178n54, 203, 206, 210
Utah Territory, 4, 8, 141, 211, 267, 269
Utes, 53–55, 57, 60–61, 63–66, 210

Valverde, Battle of, 41, 53
"Valverde Guns," 43
Vancouver Island, 6, 15, 17, 19–22, 25–26, 28–29, 29n1
Van Schaick, Charles, 255
Van Winkle, Peter, 185
Veracruz (Mexico), 95, 108, 113n10, 120
Vermont, 15
Victoria (British Columbia), 15, 20–25, 27–28, 31n36
Victorians, 208, 209, 217, 221n9
Vietnam War, 267
Virginia, 119, 126, 131; Department of, 166
voting rights. *See* suffrage

Walker, Robert J., 98
Walker, William, 100
Walpole, Horace, 218

Walters, William, 231
War Department, U.S., 35, 171
Washington Beneficial Relief Association, 173
Washington Territory, 3, 6, 8n1, 15, 22, 23, 27, 30n18
Washita, Battle of, 128
Watkins, George, 79
Watkins, John, 79
Weeks, Jim, 157n40
Weidemeyer, Lelia Crutchfield, 77
Welles, Gideon, 130–31
West, Department of the, 18, 163
West, Elliott, 4, 6
West Point, U.S. Military Academy at, 17
West and Reconstruction, The (Berwanger), 5
White, Richard, 6
white supremacy, 195, 205, 213, 214, 219
Wilderness, Battle of the, 150
Williams, George Henry, 190, 193
Wilson, Edmund, 155n16
Wilson, Henry, 193
Wilson, Sarah, 230
Wilson's Creek, Battle of, 3, 22
Wind River Reservation, 207, 214
Winnebagos, 243, 248–51, 253, 254, 260n5
Wisconsin, 185, 247, 249, 252, 253, 255, 257, 260n5
Wollstonecraft, Mary, 218
women, 78, 211; African American, 82, 160, 227, 228, 230; American Indian, 55–56, 65, 163, 169, 192, 210, 227, 234, 244, 250–51, 256; citizenship and suffrage for, 7, 172, 190–91, 195, 202, 204, 205, 210, 213, 216–20; moral authority of, 211–12, 216; as refugees from wartime violence, 78–82; secessionist, 76, 82, 84, 85, 90n27; unconventional, 209–10; Victorian middle-class, 208–9
Women's National Indian Association, 192
Wood, Fernando, 267
Works Progress Administration (WPA), 224, 225, 227, 231, 234, 237n3
Wounded Knee, 170, 172
Wright, Allen, 224

Wright, General George, 19, 23, 25–27, 32n63
Wright, Henry, 39–40
Wright, Robert, 233
Wyoming Territory, 7, 167, 172, 190–91, 202–20
Wyoming Tribune, 215, 219

Yakima War, 3, 30n18
Younger, Cole, 71
Yung Wing, 198n30

Zakim, Michael, 244
Zuñis, 61